THE LANDSCAPE OF PASTORAL CARE IN THIRTEENTH-CENTURY ENGLAND

The thirteenth century was a crucial period of reform in the English church, during which the church's renewal initiatives transformed the laity. The vibrant lay religious culture of late medieval England cannot be understood without considering the reinvigorated pastoral care that developed between 1200 and 1300. Even before Innocent III called the Fourth Lateran Council of 1215, reform-minded bishops and scholars were focusing attention on the local church, emphasising better preaching and more frequent confession. This study examines the processes by which these clerical reforms moulded the lay religiosity of the thirteenth century, integrating the different aspects of church life, so often studied separately, and combining a broad investigation of the subject with a series of comparative case studies. William Campbell also demonstrates how differences abounded from diocese to diocese, town to country and parish to parish, shaping the landscape of pastoral care as a complex mosaic of lived religion.

WILLIAM H. CAMPBELL graduated with a BA in History from the University of Pittsburgh before completing his PhD in Medieval History at the University of St Andrews. He has written two volumes for the Fasti Ecclesiae Anglicanae series and earned the postdoctoral Licentiate in Mediaeval Studies degree from the Pontifical Institute of Mediaeval Studies in Toronto. He has since returned to the University of Pittsburgh to teach.

D1593218

Cambridge Studies in Medieval Life and Thought
Fourth Series

General Editor:
ROSAMOND McKITTERICK
Emeritus Professor of Medieval History, University of Cambridge, and Fellow of Sidney Sussex College

Advisory Editors:
CHRISTINE CARPENTER
Emeritus Professor of Medieval English History, University of Cambridge
MAGNUS RYAN
University Lecturer in History, University of Cambridge, and Fellow of Peterhouse

The series *Cambridge Studies in Medieval Life and Thought* was inaugurated by G.G. Coulton in 1921; Professor Rosamond McKitterick now acts as General Editor of the Fourth Series, with Professor Christine Carpenter and Dr Magnus Ryan as Advisory Editors. The series brings together outstanding work by medieval scholars over a wide range of human endeavour extending from political economy to the history of ideas.

This is book 106 in the series, and a full list of titles in the series can be found at:
www.cambridge.org/medievallifeandthought

THE LANDSCAPE OF PASTORAL CARE IN THIRTEENTH-CENTURY ENGLAND

WILLIAM H. CAMPBELL

University of Pittsburgh

CAMBRIDGE
UNIVERSITY PRESS

CAMBRIDGE
UNIVERSITY PRESS

University Printing House, Cambridge CB2 8BS, United Kingdom

One Liberty Plaza, 20th Floor, New York, NY 10006, USA

477 Williamstown Road, Port Melbourne, VIC 3207, Australia

314-321, 3rd Floor, Plot 3, Splendor Forum, Jasola District Centre, New Delhi - 110025, India

79 Anson Road, #06-04/06, Singapore 079906

Cambridge University Press is part of the University of Cambridge.

It furthers the University's mission by disseminating knowledge in the pursuit of
education, learning and research at the highest international levels of excellence.

www.cambridge.org
Information on this title: www.cambridge.org/9781316649862
DOI: 10.1017/9781108226837

© William H. Campbell 2018

First published 2018
First paperback edition 2019

A catalogue record for this publication is available from the British Library

Library of Congress Cataloging in Publication data
Names: Campbell, William H. (William Hopkins), 1978– author.
Title: The landscape of pastoral care in 13th-century England / William Campbell.
Description: New York : Cambridge University Press, 2017. |
Includes bibliographical references and index.
Identifiers: LCCN 2017026194 | ISBN 9781316510384 (hardback)
Subjects: LCSH: Pastoral theology – England – History – To 1500. |
Pastoral care – England – History – To 1500. | Church history – 13th century. |
England–Church history.
Classification: LCC BV4006.C36 2017 | DDC 253.0942/09022 – dc23
LC record available at https://lccn.loc.gov/2017026194

ISBN 978-1-316-51038-4 Hardback
ISBN 978-1-316-64986-2 Paperback

CONTENTS

MAPS

ACKNOWLEDGEMENTS

In the sixteen years in which I have been at work on this book, I have contracted many scholarly debts, which I hope its publication will help to repay. Chris Given-Wilson and Robert Bartlett capably shepherded me through the earlier stages of research, while Michèle Mulchahey, Janet Burton and Carol Davidson Cragoe asked helpful and pertinent questions. Joe Goering generously provided me with a copy of his annotated typescript of the Dominican *Speculum iuniorum*, on which he has been patiently working for much of his career. David d'Avray redirected me when my initial questions about preaching turned out to be a wild goose chase. Christine Carpenter and the anonymous reader for Cambridge University Press offered straightforward solutions to problems that had long vexed me and pushed me to go further in my research in specific areas. Andrew Reeves has been the very model of scholarly collaboration; he and Gabriel Byng generously shared unpublished material. A small army of friends closely proofread the manuscript before my initial submission. Any sins of commission or omission remain *mea culpa*.

I am indebted also to the archivists and librarians who have made this research possible, especially those at the University of St Andrews, the Institute of Historical Research, the Pontifical Institute of Mediaeval Studies, the University of Pittsburgh, the British Library, the Bodleian Library, the National Library of Scotland and Exeter Cathedral Archive.

Above all, I am thankful to my wife, Lucia, who married me just as this project was getting started and who coauthored Edmund and Alys Rose with me along the way. By patiently listening to my day's discoveries and perceptively seizing upon anything I had not fully thought through, she has contrived to edit every idea and passage in this book while reading almost none of it. But a decade and a half of such dinner-table conversation is the least of the sacrifices she has made to allow me

Acknowledgements

to complete this work. It is with gratitude that I dedicate this book to her.

A good wife who can find? She is far more precious than jewels.
Proverbs 31:10

Pittsburgh, Pennsylvania
Feast of St Gilbert of Sempringham, 2017

ABBREVIATIONS

Annales Monastici	H. R. Luard, ed., *Annales Monastici* (Rolls Series 36, in five vols, 1864–69).
BIHR	*Bulletin of the Institute of Historical Research* (*Historical Research* since 1987)
BRUO	A. B. Emden, *A Biographical Register of the University of Oxford to 1500* (Oxford, 1957–59).
C&S I	D. Whitelock, M. Brett and Christopher Brooke, eds, *Councils and Synods: with other Documents relating to the English Church, I: AD 871–1204* (Oxford, 1981).
C&S II	F. M. Powicke and C. R. Cheney, eds, *Councils and Synods: with other Documents relating to the English Church, II: AD 1205–1313* (Oxford, 1964).
C&YS	The Canterbury and York Society.
Chron. Maj.	Matthew Paris, *Chronica Majora*, ed. H. R. Luard (Rolls Series 57, in 7 vols, 1872–83).
Const. Ratisbonenses	I. Aramburu Cendoya, ed., *Las Primitivas Constituciones de los Agustinos-Ratisbonenses del año 1290* (Valladolid, Spain, 1966).
CPL	W. H. Bliss, ed., *Calendar of Entries in the Papal Registers relating to Great Britain and Ireland: Papal Letters, vol. I: 1198–1302* (London, 1893).
De Adventu	Thomas 'of Eccleston', *Fratris Thomae vulgo dicti de Eccleston Tractatus de Adventu Fratrum Minorum in Angliam*, ed. A. G. Little (Manchester, 1951).
DEC	G. Alberigo et al., ed., and N. Tanner et al., trans., *Decrees of the Ecumenical Councils, vol. I: Nicaea I to Lateran V* (Washington, DC, 1990).
EEA	*English Episcopal Acta*, various editors (London: 1980–, in 45 vols thus far). Cited by volume number.

List of Abbreviations

EEFP	William A. Hinnebusch, *The Early English Friars Preachers* (Rome, 1951).
Epist. Pecham	Charles Trice Martin, ed., *Registrum Epistolarum Fratris Johannis Pecham, Archiepiscopi Cantuariensis* (Rolls Series 77, in 3 vols, 1882–85).
Fasti	Diana E. Greenway et al., ed., *John Le Neve, Fasti Ecclesiae Anglicanae, 1066–1300* (London, 1968–2012, in 12 vols, cited by cathedral).
FM	Wenzel, S., ed. and trans., *Fasciculus Morum: A Fourteenth-Century Preacher's Handbook* (London, 1989).
Handlyng Synne	Robert Mannyng of Brunne, *Handlyng Synne*, ed. I. Sullens (Binghamton, NY, 1983).
Lan. Cart.	John M. Todd, ed., *The Lanercost Cartulary: Cumbria County Record Office MS DZ/1* (Surtees Society, 1997).
LAM	C. H. Lawrence, ed. and trans., *The Letters of Adam Marsh* (Oxford, 2006, 2010).
LFMB	Thomas Frederic Simmons, ed., *The Lay Folk's Mass Book; or, The Manner of Hearing Mass* (Early English Text Society, 1879).
MRH	Dom David Knowles and R. Neville Hadcock, *Medieval Religious Houses: England and Wales* (2nd edn: London, 1971).
ODNB	*The Oxford Dictionary of National Biography* (Oxford, 2004).
Ordinale Exon.	J. N. Dalton, ed., *Ordinale Exon.* I (London, 1909).
PL	J.-P. Migne, ed., Patrologiae Cursus Completus... Omnium SS. Patrum: Doctorum Scriptorumque Ecclesiasticorum ... ad aetatem Innocentii III ...: Series Latina (221 vols, Paris, etc., 1844–1903).
RACCL	C. W. Foster and Kathleen Major, eds, *The Registrum Antiquissimum of the Cathedral Church of Lincoln* (LRS, 10 vols, 1931–73).
Reg. Bronescombe	O. F. Robinson, ed., *The Register of Walter Bronescombe, Bishop of Exeter 1258–1280* (3 vols, C&YS 82, 87 and 94, 1995–2003).
Reg. Bull.	*Regula Bullata*, the bull *Solet annuere*, 1223. Printed in P. L. Oliger, ed., *Expositio Quatuor Magistrorum super Regulam Fratrum Minorum (1241–1242)* (Rome, 1950), 171–93. Cited by chapter (I–XII).

List of Abbreviations

Reg. Cantilupo	R. G. Griffiths, ed., *Registrum Thome de Cantilupo, Episcopi Herefordensis, AD 1275–1282* (C&YS 2, 1907).
Reg. Giffard	W. Brown, ed., *The Register of Walter Giffard, Lord Archbishop of York 1266–1279* (Surtees Society, 1904).
Reg. Halton	W. N. Thompson, ed., *The Register of John de Halton, Bishop of Carlisle, AD 1292–1324* (C&YS 12 and 13, 1913).
Reg. Pecham	F. N. Davis, ed., *The Register of John Pecham, Archbishop of Canterbury 1279–1292*, vol. I (C&YS 63, 1969).
Reg. Quivil	F. C. Hingeston-Randolph, ed., *The Registers of Walter Bronescombe (AD 1257–1280), and Peter Quivil (AD 1280–1291), Bishops of Exeter: with some Records of the Episcopate of Bishop Thomas de Bytton (AD 1292–1307); also the Taxation of Pope Nicholas IV, AD 1291 (Diocese of Exeter)* (London, 1889).
Reg. Romeyn	W. Brown, ed., *The Register of John Romeyn, Lord Archbishop of York 1286–1296* (Surtees Society, 1913, 1917).
Reg. St Osmund	W. H. Rich Jones, ed., *Vetus Registrum Sarisburiense alias dictum Registrum S. Osmund Episcopi: The Register of St Osmund* (Rolls Series 78, 1883, 1884).
Reg. Stapledon	F. C. Hingeston-Randolph, ed., *The Register of Walter de Stapeldon, Bishop of Exeter (AD 1307–1326)* (London, 1882).
Reg. Sutton	R. M. T. Hill, ed., *The Rolls and Register of Bishop Oliver Sutton, 1280–1299* (LRS, 8 vols, 1948–86).
Reg. Swinfield	W. W. Capes, ed., *Registrum Ricardi de Swinfield, Episcopi Herefordensis, AD MCCLXXXIII–MCCCXVII* (C&YS 6, 1909).
Reg. Wickwane	W. Brown, ed., *The Register of William Wickwane, Lord Archbishop of York 1279–1285* (Surtees Society, 1907).
Rot. Gravesend	F. N. Davis, ed., *Rotuli Ricardi Gravesend Diocesis Lincolniensis* (C&YS 31, 1925).
Rot. Grosseteste	F. N. Davis, ed., *Rotuli Roberti Grosseteste, Episcopi Lincolniensis, AD 1235–1253* (C&YS 10, 1913).
Rot. Hugonis	W. P. W. Phillimore, F. N. Davis et al., eds, *Rotuli Hugonis de Welles, Episcopi Lincolniensis AD MCCIX–MCCXXXV* (C&YS 1, 3 and 4, 1907–9).

List of Abbreviations

RTDA	*Report and Transactions of the Devonshire Association for the Advancement of Science, Literature, and Art.*
TCWAAS	*Transactions of the Cumberland and Westmorland Antiquarian and Archaeological Society.*
TRHS	*Transactions of the Royal Historical Society.*
VCH	The Victoria History of the Counties of England. Cited by county, volume and page.
Verbum Adbreviatum	Monique Boutry, ed., *Petri Cantoris Parisiensis Verbum Adbreviatum* (Turnhout, 2004).

Map 1   The Dioceses and Jurisdictions of Medieval England and Wales.
Source: Ordnance Survey, *Map of Monastic Britain North Sheet* and *Map of Monastic Britain South Sheet.*

INTRODUCTION

Pastoral Care in the Thirteenth Century

On Friday, 13 May 1250, the aged, saintly and scholarly bishop Robert Grosseteste was admitted to an audience with the pope and cardinals. In his address, he reminded the curia that Christ had suffered death out of a zeal for the salvation of souls and had sent out the Apostles to found his church in order that this salvation might be spread to all the world. Grosseteste expressed concern, however, that the hierarchy of the church, from the local parish all the way up to the men he was addressing, was losing sight of its high purpose. The cause, fountainhead and origin of this disorder, he boldly proclaimed, was the papal curia, for in committing errors themselves its members provided justification for similar misbehaviour by kings and nobles. The symptom of this disease, which he saw in his own diocese of Lincoln, was the appointment of men as rectors and vicars of parish churches for reasons that had more to do with bureaucratic convenience, political expediency and family connexions than with the real business of saving souls from damnation. Such appointees often neglected their pastoral duties, entrusting them to 'hirelings' (*mercenarii*) – the term Jesus used for incompetent spiritual guides in his Good Shepherd discourse in the Gospel of John. Grosseteste, who believed that he would be personally accountable to God for each soul in his diocese, feared for them, for himself and for the welfare of the whole church.[1]

The concerns that Grosseteste enumerated that day were characteristic of his personal convictions and local circumstances. But they were also characteristic of the Western church as a whole throughout the century at whose midpoint he stood and indeed are central preoccupations of this book. In Grosseteste's theology, the Pseudo-Dionysius' *Celestial Hierarchy* was married to the ecclesiastical hierarchy as the conduit of authority and grace.[2] The ecclesiastical hierarchy's power was not merely theoretical, however. The papacy had reached new heights of power in Grosseteste's

---

[1] Gieben, 'Grosseteste at the Curia'; Goering, 'Grosseteste at the Curia'; John 10:12–13 (Vulgate).
[2] Hoskin, *Grosseteste*, li; J. McEvoy, *The Philosophy of Robert Grosseteste* (Oxford, 1982); Wenzel, 'Deus est'.

I

day. The practice of appealing ecclesiastical cases to Rome continued its
centuries-long growth.[3] In 1213, King John had formally submitted to
papal overlordship, rendering the throne of England a papal fief.[4] Within
England, royal government was increasingly bureaucratic and documentary in nature and many of the kings' administrators were also clergy.
Bishops, aristocrats and knights were similarly served by clerks and clerics who rapidly expanded the volume of business transacted in writing.[5]
These were the writers of many of the documents upon which this book
is built.

In theory, these features led to a church and a society that were more
effectively administered, which would seem all to the good. Grosseteste
reminded the curia, however, that it came at a two-fold cost. First, people within the hierarchy disagreed over how much the superior ought to
meddle in the dealings of his inferiors rather than delegating responsibility. Grosseteste was a believer in delegation, up to a point. He personally
made official visitations of the parishes in his diocese, implying that he
did not entirely trust his inferiors, the archdeacons, rural deans and parish
priests, to act without his direct supervision.[6] And yet another of his concerns at the curia in 1250 was overreach (as he saw it) by his immediate
superior, the archbishop of Canterbury, in the latter's attempts to enter
Grosseteste's diocese and investigate local conditions himself.[7] The peren-
nial anxiety of medieval churchmen to safeguard their exemptions and
privileges made any attempt at closer supervision a potential minefield.[8]
The introduction of the new orders of friars early in the century added
another dimension to such disputes, since they were sometimes empowered by the bishop or even the pope to enter the parish church in order
to preach and hear confessions without regard for the wishes of the parish
priest, violating the delegation of pastoral authority to the local secular
clergy.[9]

The second cost was that all of these administrators somehow had to
be paid, but neither civil nor ecclesiastical structures existed to allow
for fair and regular taxation at a level that could provide their salaries.
Instead, a pope, monastery, bishop, king or noble appointed a cleric who
served him to a rectory and allowed him to take a share of the parish's
income without serving it in person. Since it was becoming progressively

[3] Cheney, *Becket to Langton*, 42–86; Sayers, *Papal Judges Delegate*.   [4] *C&S II*, 13–19.
[5] Clanchy, *Memory to Written Record*; R. Britnell, ed., *Pragmatic Literacy, East and West, 1200–1330* (Woodbridge, 1997).
[6] Hoskin, *Grosseteste*, li–lv.
[7] Gieben, 'Grosseteste at the Curia'; Goering, 'Grosseteste at the Curia'.
[8] This will be discussed more fully in Part III, particularly Chapter 8.
[9] We return to this problem repeatedly in the following pages. See in particular Chapters 3, 5 and 7.

more difficult in the thirteenth century to endow monasteries with additional land, monasteries hoping to increase their income looked instead to parochial tithes through the process of appropriation, in which the bishop to appointed the monastery itself as the rector. Such appropriations multiplied in the thirteenth century. Whether the rector was an absentee cleric or a monastery, a hired vicar or chaplain did the day-to-day work of pastoral care.[10] These were the hirelings, the *mercenarii*, of whom Grosseteste complained. Such a system was arguably the best available means of redistributing ecclesiastical wealth in a decentralised world, but 'the principles of the Gregorian Reform were difficult to reconcile with the demands of the administrative church.'[11] The parish, as Grosseteste reminded the curia, also had the material obligation to help the local poor, but the vicar's stipend was sometimes barely enough for him to live on, leaving him unable to discharge this important part of his pastoral responsibility. Indeed, one of the specific requests that Grosseteste sought from the pope in 1250 was papal authorisation to force monasteries and absentee rectors in his diocese to pay vicars a higher wage.

CURA ANIMARUM, CURA PASTORALIS

When medieval clerics referred to 'care of souls' or 'pastoral care' (terms they employed interchangeably, often simply shortened to *cura*), the literal meaning of *pastor* as 'shepherd' would have been as obvious to them as it had been to the biblical authors who so often employed the imagery of shepherding.[12] Medieval clerical authors were thoroughly familiar with these passages and cited them frequently. Each bishop carried a crozier, the shepherd's crook symbolic of his office; a silver band around Grosseteste's read, 'may you learn the rule of the prelate through the shape of this staff.'[13] Given the importance of the wool trade to the English economy, the non-symbolic, fully functional staff of shepherds, and the uses of guarding and guiding to which it was routinely put, were on display for all to see.[14]

In asserting that the care of souls was the church's chief business, Grosseteste was hardly alone. Later in the century, John Pecham,

---

[10] See Chapter 2.

[11] Burger, *Diocesan Governance*, 30; Cheney, *Becket to Langton*, 149.

[12] Select examples from *C&S II*: cura animarum: 374, 400, 408, 564, 589, 596, 702, 720; cura pastoralis: 470–71, 517, 552, 783, 808, 1016; cura: 170, 374, 519, 562, 706, 712; cura ecclesie, parochiarum or beneficiorum: 96, 298, 611, 657, 708; officium pastorale: 499, 536, 564, 609, 615, 672, 743, 756, 808; parishioners described as sheep or flock, 176, 406, 439, 589, 626, 670, 770, 783, 842, 1016.

[13] *Proceedings of the Society of Antiquaries of London*, 2nd ser. Vol. 12 (1887–89), 105.

[14] Hallam, *Agrarian History*, 755–56, 1083–84 *s.v.* 'sheep'.

archbishop of Canterbury, would insist that 'nothing in this world is more precious than the care of souls, since for this alone Christ offered his very self on the cross.'[15] Pastoral care usually dealt with individuals and local congregations, but it was also a part of the great project of the medieval Latin Church, the Christianisation of European life and thought. Pope Innocent III's summons to the Fourth Lateran Council of 1215 expressed his aspirations for that meeting, embracing the reform not only of ecclesiastical structures but of all of Catholic society.[16] In doing so, Innocent was participating in a long process that took many forms over many centuries, but he was also giving papal support to the specific theological environment in which he himself had studied, that of Paris in the later twelfth century, where keen theological minds focused on questions of immediate practical relevance to priests and parishioners.[17] If we want to see the point where this movement gained the traction it needed to transform society, a pope's thundering letter to a king might be of lesser consequence than thousands of local priests in the kingdom outlining the appointed Gospel reading to their parishioners during mass on a typical Sunday morning.[18] We should look, in other words, at pastoral care, which was intended not only to inculcate ecclesiastical ideals in the laity but also to serve them in this world and to save them in the next.

During the thirteenth century, we can see an emerging consensus on the definition of 'pastoral care'. In 1287, Pecham wrote to the parish clergy of his diocese that the *cura animarum* operated through the preaching of sermons and the celebration of the sacraments, most especially the hearing of confessions.[19] Pecham's formulation was not original and, even when other authors gave different lists of the duties of the care of souls, they fitted comfortably into this matrix. Grosseteste's friend and contemporary, the Oxford Franciscan Adam Marsh, described the pastor's three-fold office as preaching, setting a good example and administering the sacraments. The second of these was frequently discussed as preaching by example and confession would be one of the sacraments which he described as 'bestow[ing] the grace of reconciliation'.[20] Grosseteste himself wrote that 'the duty of a priest is to confect the body of Christ worthily [in the mass], to enjoin penances, and (so far as he can) to recall his flock from errors; to baptise little ones, and to anoint the sick with

[15] *C&S* II, 1078.
[16] C. R. Cheney and W. H. Semple, eds, *Selected Letters of Pope Innocent III* (London, 1953), 144–47.
[17] Baldwin, *Masters, Princes and Merchants*; and see further below in Chapter 1.
[18] Mayr-Harting calls parish priests the 'hinge-men' as the most important mediators between the local village community, on the one hand, and the wider world, including their social superiors, on the other: *Religion*, 108–10.
[19] *C&S* II, 1078–80 (=*Epist. Pecham* III, 948–49).   [20] *LAM*, 194–95; cf. 309.

extreme unction.[21] The three elements also appear in the first chapter of his statutes for parish clergy.[22] Grosseteste had given a similar definition in his address of 1250 to the papal curia:

The work of pastoral care consists not only in administration of the sacraments and saying the canonical hours and celebration of masses ... but also in the true teaching of the truth of life, in terrifying condemnation of vices, in tough and masterful cutting-off and inflexible castigation of vices when that is needed.[23]

Correction and castigation indicate confession and penance, though they also belonged to preaching. Each of Grosseteste's descriptions, even if differently ordered, fits neatly within Pecham's three-fold division.

The author of an anonymous sermon on the text *Ego sum pastor bonus* (I am the Good Shepherd: John 10:11), recorded in a thirteenth-century English Franciscan sermon collection, included as many biblical references to shepherds, sheep, wolves, pasturing and flocks as possible. The first and longest part of the sermon dwells on the pastor's responsibility to feed his sheep by word and example, not neglecting the literal feeding and clothing of the poor – for charity was both a general Christian duty and a responsibility specifically incumbent upon beneficed parish priests, as Grosseteste's address to the curia had pointed out. Secondly, the author wrote, it was necessary to feed the flock sacramentally, in the reception of Christ's body and blood.[24] Confession as such did not fit the schema of this sermon but that theme is taken up in other sermons in the same manuscript, particularly the sermon for the third Sunday in Epiphanytide, in the season of confession just before Lent, on the text *Ostende te sacerdoti* (Go, show yourself to a priest: Matthew 8:4 and Luke 5:14), a sermon concerned entirely with confession.[25]

Another description comes from the *Communiloquium*, a preacher's handbook by the Franciscan scholar John of Wales, probably dating to the 1270s. This too fits neatly with Pecham's description:

Their [priestly] office is higher than the angels, and higher even than the Mother of God: to confect the sacrament of the body of Christ; to speak prayers; to bless the gifts of God ... Their office is, furthermore, to dispense the sacraments, such as to baptise, and to catechise; to preach the word in the church; to call sinners to penitence; and to bring them before God, through the petitions of prayers, for the remission that is to be secured.[26]

---

[21] Wenzel, 'Deus est', 254. [22] *C&S* II, 268. [23] Gieben, 'Grosseteste at the Curia', 358–59.
[24] For date and provenance of this manuscript, see pp. 108–9 below. Cambridge, St John's College, MS. 255/S19, pp. 134–39.
[25] Ibid., pp. 85–93.
[26] John of Wales, *Communiloquium* 4.2.8 (British Library, Harley MS. 632); Swanson, *John of Wales*, 144.

In the 1320s, the parish priest William of Pagula used Pecham's three-fold division of the parts of pastoral care as the structure of his *Oculus Sacerdotis.*[27] Clearly by now we are dealing with a traditional commonplace.

Pecham, Marsh and (probably) the anonymous sermon author were friars concerned especially with preaching, which they placed first in their lists. In addition to formal preaching, catechesis by clergy occurred both formally and informally. Moreover, in the centuries since the first missionaries, the basic tenets of Christianity had become common knowledge passed on independently of clerical teaching. Preachers still sought to expand upon their listeners' knowledge, but as is so often the case, the preacher also reminded the congregation of what they already knew and exhorted them to act accordingly.[28]

The celebration of the sacraments referred to baptism, confirmation (performed only by bishops), the mass, the blessing of matrimony and extreme unction. The sacrament of ordination had only secondary effects for the laity in supplying them with clergy. Sacramental and liturgical pastoral care has been described as a conversation, lifting up the people's praises and petitions to God, and mediating God's blessings back to the people.[29] Liturgical and extra-liturgical devotions of many kinds were also encouraged by the clergy: devotions to particular saints, most notably Mary and the patron saint of the parish, and a variety of devotions to Jesus, especially in the form of the consecrated host at the Eucharist, continued to develop during the thirteenth century and beyond. The laity played a major role in the spread of devotions, leading by demand; but the official structures of the Church could also shape that demand, as by issuing indulgences to visitors to a shrine or by suppressing unapproved nascent cults.[30]

The practice of confession, known as the sacrament of penance, was the primary setting for individual examination, instruction and exhortation, for correction of life and training in moral thought. Our sources for confession are almost exclusively prescriptive ones in which the priest is told how to elicit and respond to confessions, though there are a few texts from thirteenth-century England that instruct the penitent on how to confess. Confession was a well-known expectation and a well-established institution in England by 1200, even if that qualitative judgement cannot be

[27] Boyle, 'William of Pagula'.
[28] J. Blair and R. Sharpe, eds, *Pastoral Care before the Parish* (Leicester, 1992); F. Tinti, ed., *Pastoral Care in Late Anglo-Saxon England* (Woodbridge, 2005); d'Avray, *Preaching*. See also Chapter 5 below.
[29] C. Burgess, 'Intersecting Spheres: The Agents of Intercession'. Paper delivered at the Harlaxton Symposium, Grantham, Lincolnshire, July 2002.
[30] Swanson, *Religion and Devotion*, 9ff. See also Chapter 6 below.

made quantitative. While confession was less obviously communal than hearing sermons or attending mass, many of the sins discussed in confessors' manuals were social in nature. The fact that Pecham singled out this sacrament ('and especially') shows how important he considered it to be.[31]

THE PROBLEM OF 'REFORM'

It has become customary to refer to the developments in thirteenth-century pastoral care as 'reform', or to single out bishops such as Grosseteste as 'reformers'.[32] It is, of course, perfectly legitimate for historians with the benefit of hindsight to describe an era or movement as having a reforming character even if people of that age did not see it as such, just as it may be fair to speak of the twelfth century as a period of renaissance, reform or even reformation even if twelfth-century intellectuals did not use those words.[33] Thirteenth-century churchmen did use the word 'reform', but we should think carefully about what they meant. Richard Poore, bishop of Salisbury, used it in the statutes he issued for his diocesan clergy around 1217, ordering his archdeacons to enforce them 'for the correction of excesses and the reform of morals'.[34] In 1237, the papal legate Otto, in a council in London, discussed the 'correction and reform' of the English Benedictines and stated that he expected bishops to set a good example of liturgical celebration in order to 'reform' their clergy.[35] A later legate, Ottobuono, summoned bishops to a council in 1268 to confer regarding the 'reform' of many matters.[36] In the preface to his 1247 diocesan statutes, Giles of Bridport, bishop of Salisbury, described canon law as directing how the church of God ought to be 'reformed' in faith and morals, noting that these statutes were part of this body of law in giving direction for 'reform and reparation', and requiring that previous diocesan and provincial statutes be rehearsed for 'correction and reform'.[37] As Giles' terms suggest, many uses of 'reform' with regard to the church at this time do not carry our modern sense of 'progress': phrases such as *ordinatum est quod status ecclesie Anglicane in statum debitum reformetur* (it was ordered that the state of the English church should be reformed to its appropriate state)[38] and *pax reformaretur* (peace was to be

[31] Murray, 'Counselling'; Cornett, 'Form of Confession'. See also Chapter 7 below.
[32] M. C. Miller, 'Reform, Clerical Culture, and Politics', in Arnold, *Medieval Christianity*, 305–22.
[33] G. Constable, *The Reformation of the Twelfth Century* (Cambridge, 1996).
[34] *C&S* II, 96; cf. 655.   [35] *C&S* II, 254, 255.   [36] *C&S* II, 744.
[37] *C&S* II, 552. Cf. the prologues to the statutes of Wells (1258) on p. 589 and of Winchester (1262 × 1265) on p. 702.
[38] *C&S* II, 694–95; for similar uses, cf. 532, 569n, 572, 585, 696, 726.

re-formed)[39] imply not the creation of something new, but the restoration of a former state (or, perhaps, restoring matters to the way they always should have been, even if they never quite were).

'Reform' and its cognates will appear below, used with care but without qualms. The primary contention of this book is that there was indeed a reform in the care of souls in thirteenth-century England, though it was confined neither to that century nor to England; and it is the primary goal of this book to illustrate the various forms that reform took. At the same time, however, as the preceding remarks suggest, we will miss our mark if we assume that thirteenth-century churchmen, particularly the ones we think of as reformers, shared a Whiggish notion of progress. They looked not forward but back, building their arguments – whether for clerical celibacy or for lay piety or for ecclesiastical liberty from the secular arm – not on aspiration but on real or imagined precedent. There does not seem, however, to be a single identifiable golden age to which they appealed: this may have been entirely *ad hoc*, thinking of a different time prior to each perceived disorder.

And there was no doubt that it was a time of disorder. English churchmen were divided by the baronial struggles against John and Henry III.[40] When Adam Marsh heard tales of great fireballs flying out of a whirlpool in the sea near Guernsey, followed by the mysterious appearance and disappearance of armed men fighting a ghostly battle, it was only natural that he should regard it as a 'portent' to be interpreted in the context of apocalyptic passages from the Gospel of Matthew.[41] Roger Bacon was convinced that he saw signs of the impending Apocalypse, as did some of his fellow Franciscans who had fallen under the influence of the prophecies of Abbot Joachim of Fiore.[42] William of Saint-Amour also argued that church reform was necessary to stave off the end times, though in his view, the friars were part of the problem, not part of the solution.[43] Grosseteste's address to the papal curia cited the schism with the Greeks, and heresy and sin among Catholics, as symptoms of the evils within the church.[44] None of these men was unusual in making associations between present disasters and the coming of Antichrist. If Muslims occupied the Holy Land, Greek Christians remained disobedient to Rome, heretics spread their errors through Mediterranean Europe, comets crossed the sky and church and state were in turmoil, these were thought by many to be the

[39] *C&S* II, 468, 527; cf. 737.
[40] Vincent, *Peter des Roches, passim*; S. Ambler, 'The Montfortian Bishops', in A. Jobson, ed., *Baronial Reform and Revolution in England 1258–1267* (Woodbridge, 2016), 139–51.
[41] *LAM*, 47.
[42] A. Power, *Roger Bacon and the Defense of Christendom* (Cambridge, 2013), 164–208.
[43] William of Saint-Amour, *De periculis*, 1–15.   [44] Gieben, 'Grosseteste at the Curia', 353.

direct results of human sin, which needed to be rooted out.[45] A reform in pastoral care was needed not just for the eternal salvation of each but for the temporal salvation of all.

The thirteenth century appears as an era of betwixt and between in the historiography of the English church, not quite belonging to the 'high Middle Ages' before it nor the 'late Middle Ages' after. The twelfth century has long been recognised as a period of intellectual and spiritual vigour in Latin Christendom; the fourteenth and fifteenth centuries are well known as an era of English lay piety, producing lay mystics and guilds, processions and plays and countless Perpendicular parish churches. It was largely in the thirteenth century that the initiative passed from the clerical hierarchy, the Church in the narrow sense, to the laity, the church in the broad sense. Yet the means by which this happened are not well understood. The use of written English for pastoral texts such as sermons gradually declined after the Norman Conquest and re-emerged in the fourteenth century. By surrendering claims on manorial churches as private property and donating some advowsons to religious houses, local lay elites yielded much control over parish churches in the twelfth century; lay peasants and townsmen once again exercised significant responsibility in their parishes in the fourteenth century with the rise of churchwardens, but we know much less about the local relationships between clergy and parishioners in the thirteenth century.[46]

This book is an attempt to recover some of these lost realities of pastoral care, the institutional church's most significant point of contact with its lay members, in England between 1200 and 1300. While important questions remain, the English church in this period has hardly been neglected. Understanding this historiographical tradition will help to contextualise this present book.

At the turn of the twentieth century, Protestant and Catholic historians still often wrote as apologists for their churches, and many of them were clergy themselves. The study of the later medieval church was a natural battleground. Protestants, especially those of Whiggish historical inclinations, saw it as an ignorant dark age from which the Reformation liberated England. To Catholics, Anglo-Catholics and Romantics,

---

[45] B. E. Whalen, *Dominion of God: Christendom and Apocalypse in the Middle Ages* (Cambridge, MA, 2010), 152–54.
[46] Cragoe, 'Written in Stone', 55–58; on the active role of the laity in maintaining church buildings during the thirteenth century, see 119–23.

however, it represented genuine Christianity; what appeared to naysayers as superstition was rather the authentic and holistic religious heritage of the English people. As we will see, the Whig/Protestant view came to predominate in English historiography. The reining in of its excesses contributed to its durability without fundamentally undermining it: despite sympathetic portrayals of the pre-Reformation English church such as Jack Scarisbrick's *The Reformation and the English People* (1984) and Robert Swanson's *Church and Society in Late Medieval England* (1989), the level of controversy generated by Eamon Duffy's distinctly Catholic *The Stripping of the Altars: Traditional Religion in England 1400–1580* (1992) shows how pervasive the Protestant view remained.

The historiographical debates of a century ago can be seen most sharply in the figures of Abbot (later Cardinal) Gasquet and his nemesis G. G. Coulton.[47] Gasquet was a prolific English writer on the later medieval church, though he 'was no scholar at all, but gathered material with a pitchfork'.[48] The material he gathered presented the pre-Reformation church, and by implication the Catholic church in general, in the best possible light. Coulton, a meticulous scholar and controversialist, called Gasquet out in a series of tracts on his errors and obfuscations.[49] As a Whig historian and a low church Anglican, Coulton had no patience for Romantic notions of a culturally superior medieval world or church. His tracts included 'The Truth about the Monasteries' ('The evidence of monastic decay, long before the Reformation, is simply embarrassing in its mass and variety'),[50] 'Priests and People before the Reformation' ('The priest, for his part, had the partial consolation of knowing that such prevaricators of tithes were destined to find their part in hell with Cain, and of proclaiming this solemnly four times a year from the pulpit'),[51] 'The Failure of the Friars' ('The friar, whom you can no more keep out of your private affairs than you can keep a fly off your plate, is often so unpopular already [by the 1260s] that the country-folk attribute the failure of their crops to the malign influence of these sons of Francis and Dominic'),[52] and 'The Plain Man's Religion in the Middle Ages' ('At the bottom of the scale, of course, the jostle for salvation was gross and frankly immoral. The vulgar caught inevitably at what was least defensible in the official religion').[53] Coulton was the founding editor of *Cambridge Studies in Medieval Life and Thought*. Hartridge, the author of one early volume

---

[47] E. Duffy, 'A.G. Dickens and the Late Medieval Church', *BIHR* 77 (2004), 99–110.
[48] C. Brooke et al., *David Knowles Remembered* (Cambridge, 1991), 51. A. Morey was more sympathetic: 'Cardinal Gasquet the Historian', *Catholic Historical Review* 15 (1929), 262–74.
[49] Powicke, *Historians*, 136–41; G. G. Coulton, *Fourscore Years: An Autobiography* (Cambridge, 1943), 317–37; G. G. Coulton, *Ten Medieval Studies* (3rd edn, Boston, 1959).
[50] Ibid., 88.   [51] Ibid., 125.   [52] Ibid., 168.   [53] Ibid., 192.

in the series, felt compelled to reassure the reader 'that never at any time have I felt myself, by weight of his authority, forced towards any conclusion at which I could not honestly arrive'.[54] Nonetheless, Coulton's view of the thirteenth century as a period of failed reform became widespread, even if often expressed in more moderate terms.[55] Another early volume in the series, G. R. Owst's *Preaching in Medieval England: An Introduction to the Sermon Manuscripts of the Period c. 1350–1450* (1926), described the century after the Black Death as 'in the Dark Ages' and identified pre-Reformation preaching with 'all that that unpopular word "Puritanism" has ever stood for, to the minutest detail'.[56]

Another book that partook of this general narrative was Marion Gibbs and Jane Lang's *Bishops and Reform, 1215–1272* (1934), which examined first the personnel of the episcopate and then the trickling down of the decrees of Lateran IV. Lang, who wrote the latter part of the book, looked for specific evidence of the impact of the Lateran decrees in English diocesan and provincial statutes and in the activity of ecclesiastical governance. She found that the Lateran Council's canons were seldom paraphrased or promulgated at all in English church legislation and concluded that few English bishops had bothered to familiarise themselves with them. She found enforcement in church governance to be just as uneven. The canons that were most energetically promulgated and enforced were those pertaining to clerical discipline, not to spiritual life. In particular, strictures against ecclesiastics taking part in secular government were ignored and widely flouted, from which she inferred that churchmen were often too busy doing the king's business to do the church's. She concluded that the spiritual revival that Innocent III had sought

had not come. On the contrary, throughout the English Church was to be seen a grosser materialism, the encroaching of the secular on the spiritual, rigidity, formalism, hostility. Most of the spiritual fervour and religious devotion seemed to have been concentrated in the friars, and although the rest of the Church regarded them indulgently and in many cases gave them active encouragement and help, it failed to absorb their simple faith or to cast off the materialism which was gradually corroding its inner life.[57]

Implementation had relied on the bishops and, despite the efforts of some, as a whole the bishops had failed. They had prioritised the wrong decrees. They ought, she believed, to have emphasised those that kept kings out of the elections of bishops and abbots and kept churchmen out of politics

[54] Hartridge, *Vicarages*, viii. [55] Heath, 'Between Reform and Reformation'. [56] Owst, 7, 94. [57] Gibbs and Lang, *Bishops and Reform*, 174.

to 'free the bishops from outside influences 'and cause them to devote all their energy to the service of the Church ... Instead, the bishops emphasized ... decrees which could not hope to stir up any spirit of enthusiasm'.[58]

There are two flaws in Lang's argument. The first is venial: Lang was a historian of her time and school. Like other English medievalists of her day, she echoed the language of the Gregorian Reform that asserted that royal and ecclesiastical government ought to be kept separate.[59] Moreover, she investigated the nexus of church and society within the strong English historiographical tradition of focusing narrowly on law and its implementation.[60] But the result is that she confined herself to legal and administrative records, which are necessary but not sufficient to support her conclusion. From this emphasis arose a second flaw, the logical fallacy of begging the question in her conclusion: 'A spiritual re-birth will never result from the enforcement of a code of law. Even if the bishops could have united together to give expression and actuality to Innocent's ideal ... it is doubtful if they could have produced any per-manent effect.'[61] She had restricted her study to the evidence of a process that she said could not bring about spiritual renewal and then accused the bishops of failing to use that process to bring about spiritual renewal. To be fair, her book predated much of the study of the literature of pas-toral care, which would enable a broader perspective. Her discovery that the Lateran decrees were so little reflected in English councils and synods is certainly interesting and surprising. But the conclusion that there was no spiritual renewal goes beyond her evidence – beyond the capacity of her evidence to determine – as if she inadvertently set up the bishops to fail.

J. R. H. Moorman's *Church Life in England in the Thirteenth Century* (1945) was a more wide-ranging and deeply researched approach to the problem, though it arrived at similar conclusions. Moorman wrote that 'The most careful legislation about the conduct of services and the performance of pastoral duties could be of little use unless the men to whom these things were entrusted were themselves animated by a keen sense of vocation and responsibility', which suggested an intention to pick up where Lang had left off.[62] Moorman accepted Coulton's criticisms of the parish clergy and analyses of structural problems in the church but he also sought to balance them through counter-examples

---

[58] Ibid., 177.   [59] E.g. Brooke, *English Church and Papacy*, 48, 186–87.
[60] E.g. F. Maitland (N. Tanner, *Inventing the Middle Ages* (New York, 1991), 74–75), T. F. Tout (Powicke, *Historians*, 41–44), A. H. Thompson (Heath, 'Between Reform and Reformation', 648).
[61] Gibbs and Lang, *Bishops and Reform*, 179.   [62] Moorman, *Church Life*, 230.

and reconsiderations, such as querying whether monastic appropriation, often viewed as bad for parish life, was much different from having an absentee rector. The Franciscans – particularly the early Franciscans – emerge as the heroes of his story. In *Church Life*, he provided a chapter with the indicative title 'The Glory of the Friars'. As for the rest of the church, one reviewer quipped that he might have more accurately entitled his book *The Shortcomings of the English Clergy and Monks in the Thirteenth Century*.[63] Moorman argued that 'Many of the parish clergy were incapable of acting as spiritual guides to their people' and that they had little capacity to preach.[64] Even the Dominicans fell short in his eyes. They 'failed in this country' for two reasons: they found no heresy in England, which he thought of as their predominant concern, and the Franciscans outdid the Dominicans in their zeal for ascetic poverty and soon also in their intellectual attainments.[65] The decline of the friars from their original purity (chronicled in his chapter 'Change and Decay', echoing Coulton's 'The Failure of the Friars') was the great tragedy that closed his book, for they alone were really suited to bring about the religious change that was needed: had they succeeded, 'the Church might have been roused from spiritual lethargy and so might have saved itself from the disastrous turmoil of the sixteenth century.'[66]

A different strain, though not a school of thought as such, emerged from F. Maurice Powicke and the circle of historians he taught or mentored. Powicke's pre-eminence at Manchester and then Oxford, combined with his interest in major ecclesiastical figures of the period, assured the subject a prominent place in research. In Powicke's 1927 Ford Lectures on Langton he had written that 'The history of the reconstruction of the Church in England after the Interdict, in accordance with the Lateran decrees, has yet to be written'.[67] Not coincidentally, he suggested the subjects of Gibbs and Lang's theses which they began to write in 1929 (thus among the earliest he supervised at Oxford) which in turn became *Bishops and Reform*.[68] Powicke's approach to the thirteenth-century English church – as also that of most of his colleagues and their students – was more sympathetic than Coulton's but lacked the Romantic affection for the friars that suffused much other work, including Moorman's. Indeed, Powicke said in his inaugural lecture at Oxford of 1929, 'The craving for an interpretation of history is so deep-rooted that, unless we have a constructive outlook over the past, we are drawn either to mysticism or to cynicism.'[69] He was an exceptionally capable palaeographer, opening

---

[63] C. E. Schrader, in *Speculum* 21 (1946), 132–34.   [64] Moorman, *Church Life*, 391, 77.
[65] Ibid., 398.   [66] Ibid., 398–401.   [67] Powicke, *Langton*, 151.
[68] Gibbs and Lang, *Bishops and Reform*, v.   [69] Powicke, *Historians*, 174.

the door to sources and source-types that previous editors had not published, and he consulted manuscripts when editions were inadequate. He collaborated with his former student Christopher Cheney in *Councils and Synods*, the definitive edition of the thirteenth-century English diocesan and provincial legislation, an undertaking so complex that it was not published until 1964, the year after Powicke's death. So indispensable is this two-volume set to the study of the thirteenth-century English church that it is cited far more than any other work in the following pages. Powicke and Cheney also independently published many studies of the thirteenth-century church, particularly the English secular clergy and ecclesiastical administration, based upon detailed examination of primary sources. The same can be said of another of Powicke's students, Robert Brentano, whose 1952 DPhil thesis would later be published as *Two Churches: England and Italy in the Thirteenth Century* (1968).

Richard Southern, a junior colleague of Powicke's at Oxford, published *The Making of the Middle Ages* in 1953. He wrote it at Powicke's behest and acknowledged that 'His influence pervades it in many ways'.[70] His study of the church in the high Middle Ages fell under two headings: ecclesiastical structures and intellectual life. Pastoral care would only become an explicit subject in later decades through his study of Grosseteste.[71] Another junior colleague of Powicke's, first at Manchester and then at Oxford, was William Pantin.[72] *The English Church in the Fourteenth Century* (1955), which Pantin dedicated to Powicke, covered three topics: 'the social and political aspects of the Church' and 'the intellectual activities and controversies that excited the Church', the same themes seen in Southern's book of two years before, but crucially also 'religious literature, such as the manuals of instruction for parish priests, the religious and moral didactic works, and the relations of these writings with the mystical writings of this period'.[73] Such works included diocesan statutes promulgated since 1215, which he viewed more favourably than had Gibbs and Lang.[74] His repeated protestations of the importance of lay piety, however, seem incongruous with the mere ten pages he allotted to the subject.[75] In the same year, 1955, Christopher Cheney delivered the Ford Lectures at Oxford, in which he examined the growth of papal power in England between 1170 and 1213. He too sought to extend his scope: 'In the past, it

---

[70] R. W. Southern, *The Making of the Middle Ages* (New Haven, CT, 1953), ix.
[71] Southern, *Grosseteste*, 225–71.
[72] J. R. L. Highfield, 'W. A. Pantin: in memoriam', *Oxoniensia* 39 (1974), iv–v.
[73] Pantin, *Fourteenth Century*, 1.
[74] Ibid., 189–95. His failure to cite Moorman's *Church Life* here or anywhere else is surprising.
[75] Ibid., 253–62.

has been treated as a question of politics or law, and answered accordingly. But there seems to be room for a broader view of the matter, to embrace the whole administration of the Church and the relations of clergy and people. This I have attempted.[76] Although he gave only eleven pages in the published version to a study of 'lay piety', he appealed to sources as diverse as church wall paintings, sermons, saints' lives and vernacular verse, categories of evidence that later historians would exploit much more thoroughly.[77] (Moorman had used such sources ten years earlier in *Church Life*, as Cheney must have been aware; and while Moorman did not include a chapter on lay piety, it was a recurrent theme throughout his book.) Moorman, Pantin and Cheney were throwing a bridge across a historiographical gap, a gap that to some extent remains: those who study the administrative and bureaucratic activities of the church are not always as familiar with its theological and devotional concerns, and vice versa. One may gauge the narrowing of that gap (accelerated by the 'Cultural Turn') by comparing the original Oxford History of England series with the New Oxford History of England. Whereas Powicke's *The Thirteenth Century* (1962) studied the church only as 'The Clergy under Two Rules of Law', *England under the Norman and Angevin Kings* (2000) by Robert Bartlett – one of Southern's doctoral students – provides sixty-seven pages on 'The Institutional Church' and forty on 'Religious Life', augmented by further analysis of religion in extensive chapters on culture, life cycle and cosmology.

A great deal of the groundwork for studying the literature of pastoral care was laid by Father Leonard Boyle, an Irish Dominican who studied under Pantin at Oxford. Boyle's DPhil thesis of 1956 focused on English pastoral texts of the early fourteenth century.[78] Over the following decades, he continued to work with such texts – for which he coined the term *pastoralia* and developed a taxonomy – and was no less at home in the records of canon law and diocesan administration. He took a broader view of diocesan statutes, seeing them not simply as local canon law but as a genre of *pastoralia*, as practical pastoral and theological instruction manuals for the priest in his parish.[79] His research gradually extended back though the thirteenth century, including articles on 'Robert Grosseteste

---

[76] Cheney, *Becket to Langton*, v.

[77] Pp. 163–74; Heath, 'Between Reform and Reformation'.

[78] L. E. Boyle, 'A Study of the Works Attributed to William of Pagula: With Special Reference to the "Oculus sacerdotis" and "Summa summarum"' (unpubl. DPhil thesis, Oxford, 1956).

[79] L. E. Boyle, '*Summae Confessorum*', in *Les genres littéraires dans les sources théologiques et philosophiques médiévales: Définition, critique et exploitation* (Louvain-la-Neuve, 1982), 227–37, at 231. The terms 'episcopal constitutions' and 'synodalia' in the table both refer to diocesan statutes.

and the Pastoral Care' (1979) and 'The Inter-Conciliar Period 1179–1215 and the Beginnings of Pastoral Manuals' (1986).[80] Furthermore, he was concerned in equal measure with the secular clergy and the mendicant friars, who have too often been studied in near isolation from one another, and as a Dominican, he countered the prevailing tendency to equate 'friar' with 'Franciscan' only. One of the world's pre-eminent palaeographers, he taught manuscript studies at the Pontifical Institute of Mediaeval Studies in Toronto before concluding his career as Prefect of the Vatican Library. Only with Boyle do all of the necessary ingredients come together for the comprehensive study of pastoral reform in thirteenth-century England, though he himself did not write such a work.

That was left to one of Boyle's doctoral students. Joseph Goering's Toronto PhD thesis of 1977 on 'The Popularization of Scholastic Ideas in Thirteenth-Century England and an Anonymous Speculum Iuniorum' gives some 190 pages to the processes through which academic pastoral theology was disseminated to parish priests and mendicant friars, in order to contextualise his analysis of the Dominican pastoral text named in his title. Neither the thesis nor an edition of the *Speculum iuniorum* has been published, though Goering has long been at work on the latter. Goering followed in Boyle's footsteps, bringing together friars and seculars, administrative records and *pastoralia*, dedicating much of his career to editions and studies of *pastoralia* from thirteenth-century England. Goering's erstwhile student Andrew Reeves has surveyed religious education in thirteenth-century England, demonstrating that Archbishop Pecham's 1281 preaching syllabus *Ignorantia sacerdotum*, far from being the 'damning' indictment of illiterate clergy that Coulton believed it to be, was rather the official codification of well-established and effective practices of teaching the faith to laypeople.[81] Cels has undermined traditional assumptions about confession to parish priests and friars.[82] Other historians have recently argued that the thirteenth-century English church's success came not in spite of its willingness to compromise but precisely because of it.[83]

Pantin recognised in 1948 that 'in the realm of religious literature we can see, in the clearest and most satisfactory way, the achievement of

---

[80] M. C. English, 'Bibliography of the Writings of Leonard E. Boyle, OP', in W. Brown and J. Stoneman, ed., *A Distinct Voice* (Notre Dame, IN, 1997), 642–57.

[81] Reeves, *Religious Education*; Coulton, *Ten Medieval Studies* (3rd edn, Boston, 1959), 233–34.

[82] M. Cels, 'Reconciling Mendicant and Secular Confessors in Late Medieval England', *JMH* 38 (2012), 225–43.

[83] Mayr-Harting, *Religion*; Tanner and Watson, 'Least of the Laity'. Thibodeaux, *Manly Priest* argues that requiring parish clergy to be celibate and restrained threatened to cut them off from parishioners, who expected them to marry, dress and act like laymen.

the fourteenth century as the logical outcome of forces at work in the thirteenth century.[84] The continuing fascination with English religious culture after 1300 requires a holistic view of the thirteenth-century English church, its place in society and how it sought to shape the religious outlook of the laity. Yet the most recent monograph to offer such a vision is the same one that Pantin could have reached for: Moorman's *Church Life*, published in 1945, never fully superseded and reprinted as recently as 2010.[85] The extensive publication of thirteenth-century ecclesiastical sources and the many investigations of particular facets of the subject have made a thoroughgoing reassessment possible, desirable and overdue. *The Landscape of Pastoral Care* is designed to satisfy this need.

THE SCOPE OF THIS WORK

If there is something distinctive about the thirteenth century, the boundary dates of 1200 and 1300 remain arbitrary. Earlier developments set the stage for the thirteenth century and must be taken into account. Since many books on later medieval English religion begin at or after the Black Death, taking this study up to that point might have been profitable; but since the density of evidence increases across the thirteenth and fourteenth centuries, the surviving evidence from the whole of thirteenth century could easily have been overwhelmed by that of just a few decades of the fourteenth. Great care has been taken not to read fourteenth-century developments back onto the thirteenth century. Fourteenth-century sources have only been appealed to when there is sound reason to believe that they represent continuities with thirteenth-century practice. Even then few date from after 1310.

Geographical coverage is limited not only to England and Wales in Parts I and II but also to a mere three dioceses (and only to parts of those) in Part III. This is a concession to limits of space and time in writing this book and ought not to suggest that pastoral care was any less dynamic or historically interesting in areas not considered here. Intellectual history is examined only in pursuit of its potential effects on the laity and their clergy. Not every aspect of the thirteenth-century English church can be covered here: church courts, visitations and patronage, for example, appear only in passing, as do the economic and internal affairs of the cloistered religious orders. 'Spirituality' is studiously avoided, not only as a potentially nebulous concept, but also because there are no windows into the souls of the laymen and laywomen who are our ultimate

---

[84] Pantin, *English Church*, 189 (published 1955, but from his 1948 Birkbeck Lectures).
[85] Although Mayr-Harting, *Religion*, nominally extends to 1272, its real focus is the twelfth century.

interest. There is, as Arnold put it, 'a kind of layperson-shaped hole in the middle of the evidence' for medieval lived religion, while Hirsh wrote of 'the impossible act of finally describing the religiousness of medieval persons'.[86] We are outside the literate cloister and too early for the conventional lay piety of the Paston letters or the unconventional lay piety of a Margery Kempe.[87] Much as we should like to know about the sheep themselves, this is predominantly a study of the practice of shepherding.

Part I of this book, 'Pastors and People', begins in Chapter 1 with the foundations that had been established for pastoral care in England by the year 1200. Energetic co-operation between churchmen and laity for the improvement of pastoral care was decidedly not a creation of the Fourth Lateran Council of 1215. The truth is the converse: Lateran IV's decrees enshrined in canon law the pastoral principles that were already gaining momentum.[88] It came at a crucial time, for Pope Innocent had laid England under interdict from 1208 to 1214, and his victory over King John came at great cost to the English church. The need to rebuild in the wake of the interdict gave a greater urgency to Archbishop Langton and his suffragans than they might have felt otherwise. Chapter 2 will turn our attention to the social contexts in which parish clergy operated, which established their local status but also brought them face to face with parishioners who knew their priests' personal failings and the limits of their moral authority. Chapter 3 will follow the introduction of the orders of mendicant friars to England and to individual towns, as a new class of pastorally active clergy who supplemented but also potentially challenged the parish clergy. These two chapters will also consider the much-debated question of the educational levels of the parish clergy and the friars, how well prepared they were for their tasks and how this may have influenced lay respect for and response to their pastors' attempts to shepherd them. Chapter 4 will address the particular pastoral contributions of monks and regular canons, as well as activities of nuns and anchoresses that may be described as pastoral.

Like William of Pagula's *Oculus sacerdotis*, Part II of this study ('The Processes of Pastoral Care') will follow Pecham's three-fold description of the care of souls. Chapter 5 will turn to preaching and catechesis, including both the homily and the development of the structurally complex *sermo modernus* associated with friars and other educated preachers. In addition

---

[86] Arnold, *Belief and Unbelief*, 22; J. C. Hirsh, *The Boundaries of Faith: The Development and Transmission of Medieval Spirituality* (Leiden, 1996), 3.

[87] J. T. Rosenthal, *Margaret Paston's Piety* (New York, 2010); J. C. Hirsh, *The Revelations of Margery Kempe: Paramystical Practices in Late Medieval England* (Leiden, 1989).

[88] Cheney, *Becket to Langton*, 175–76.

to knowing their faith, laypeople were expected to practice it, both corporately and individually. The most visible corporate expression was the Sunday or feast-day mass, which is the focus of Chapter 6. Here we will try to tease out what churchgoing meant to, and did for, lay parishioners, particularly as a parochial body. Chapter 7 will attempt to follow the priest into the most intimate of pastoral encounters, the confession, in which he was to probe the penitent's conscience.

Part III, 'The Landscape of Pastoral Care', will address a serious problem in studying the medieval church, even within the limited scope of thirteenth-century England: its heterogeneity. Local customs and the physical landscape shaped the agrarian economy and, with it, much else. The country was socially, economically, culturally, linguistically and indeed spiritually diverse, among clergy and laity alike. Parishes' institutional and social organisations exhibited great variety.[89] Clerical aims were as diverse as lay ones: St Gilbert of Sempringham, whose solicitude for women's spiritual lives led him to found a new religious order for them, and Bogo de Clare, who reaped vast wealth from the church with little apparent interest in serving parishioners, both doubtless thought of themselves as successful English parish clergy.[90] Some bishops considered the friars a necessary supplement to the parish clergy, while others argued that they critically undermined the parish priest's ability to do his job.[91] As this implies, parishes did not have a monopoly on lay religious life. There were other loci of devotion, such as shrines; other agents of intercession, such as monasteries; and other sources of pastoral care, such as friars; all existing in parallel with one another and within the context of the parish system.[92] Pastoral care and religious devotion were composites and, if we do not study them as such, we cannot understand them as contemporaries did. Moreover, because the particular blend of these elements varied from place to place, we cannot hope to appreciate the diversity of lived religion without exploring the myriad of possible combinations of elements and their synergistic interactions as found at specific locales across the English landscape. A comparative analysis of parochial religious life in two districts, for example, would be defective if one failed to note their relative distances to houses of friars.

Chapter 8, 'Towards a Geography of Pastoral Care', will explore these themes more extensively to lay the foundation for the geographical case

---

[89] Burgess and Duffy, eds, *The Parish*.
[90] R. Foreville and G. Keir, ed. and trans., *The Book of St Gilbert* (Oxford, 1987); Hartridge, *Vicarages*, 155; Thompson, 'Pluralism'.
[91] See below, particularly in Chapters 5 and 7.
[92] G. Rosser, 'Parochial Conformity and Voluntary Religion in Late-Medieval England', *TRHS* 6th s. 1 (1991), 173–89.

studies to follow. Chapter 9 contrasts the administrative structures of England's two provinces, Canterbury and York, with a view to the archbishops' capacities for encouraging or enforcing developments in pastoral theology and canon law. Lang's thesis that the canons of Lateran IV were seldom enforced is not overturned but circumnavigated, for such developments are frequently to be found outside those canons. Chapter 10 takes on Grosseteste's great Diocese of Lincoln, with some nineteen hundred parishes and the most thorough documentation of any English diocese in the century. The size of the diocese makes it impossible to study its internal dynamics comprehensively, so the counties at the opposite ends of the diocese – Lincolnshire and Oxfordshire – will be subjected to particular scrutiny. Chapter 11 takes us to the Diocese of Exeter in the far south-west and Chapter 12 to Carlisle in the far north-west, both being regions with a considerable proportion of upland rather than arable, which, as we shall see, affected the structures and practices of the church, and therefore pastoral provision, in ways that differed both from Lincoln and from one another.

The aim of *The Landscape of Pastoral Care* is to provide guiding principles and an organisational schema in which other local case studies of the English church, whether published in years past or still to be written, may find a place in comparative dialogue. Nor are the diocesan case studies here all commensurable, for the types of surviving evidence differ from place to place and do not always allow for neat comparisons by identical criteria. Nevertheless, within these studies, we can begin to see pastoral care's 'landscape' in both the literal and figurative senses of that word. And if – as Pecham, Grosseteste, Marsh and others claimed – the *cura animarum* was the ultimate purpose of the Church Militant, then arguably even its administrative and bureaucratic activities should be measured by that yardstick.

SOURCES

The shift from memory to written record described by Clanchy is very visible in the sources used in this study.[93] At the beginning of the century, no English bishop kept a register of *acta* or correspondence; by the end of the century, many (perhaps most) did.[94] For the period prior to registration in each diocese, the British Academy has published bishops' charters and other records in the *English Episcopal Acta* series, though unregistered *acta* dating from the period after registration begins

---

[93] Clanchy, *Memory to Written Record.*   [94] Smith, *Guide.*

have not been collected.[95] The cartularies of religious institutions, both monastic and secular, include material illustrative of their direct and indirect involvement in pastoral care. Few visitation records survive from the thirteenth century, but those that do provide invaluable snapshots of specific churches on specific days and demonstrate the processes of enforcement and supervision.[96] Papal bulls could be universal in scope, but many papal letters specifically addressed a local condition. Diocesan and provincial legislation is an invaluable resource.[97] It expressed each prelate's priorities for enforcement and provided parish clergy with broad pastoral instruction. It also allows us to gauge the similarities and differences among dioceses in their pastoral provision. Other instructional works on pastoral care include catechetical material and instruction manuals on how to preach a sermon or hear a confession, as well as liturgical books, while chronicles offer a variety of illuminating details ranging from characters of bishops to attitudes towards the mendicant friars. The friars also created records. At the international level, each order had its Rule as well as the constitutions and amendments laid down by successive general chapters. A long series of papal bulls were issued in an attempt to regulate the overlapping pastoral responsibilities of friars and secular clergy.[98] Each quasi-national mendicant province also made its own regulations, though few survive from England. More prominent are the preaching handbooks, confessors' manuals and general pastoral-theological treatises created and used by these orders.

Secular records have been used as well, from those of royal courts to those of manor courts, but not nearly as heavily as ecclesiastical records. That is not because they have nothing to say on the subject but rather because church business with a bearing on pastoral care is thinly spread among a great deal of other material. Many local sources, such as records of manorial courts, remain unpublished, and in any event will only divulge their fullest secrets to the researcher willing to follow a given locality over many years to reconstruct a village's internal dynamics. Thousands of miscellaneous charters await detailed inspection in the British Library alone. For now, 'The medieval English church and clergy as recorded in secular sources' remains a desirable book awaiting an industrious author.

---

[95] *EEA*, vols 1–45 (to date).
[96] Several larger sets of records have been published, but numerous smaller ones and incidental mentions have not. Forrest, 'Visitation'.
[97] *C&S I* and *C&S II* include all surviving English legislation for the thirteenth century.
[98] Lawrence, *The Friars*, 152–65.

PART I

Pastors and People

Chapter 1

GROWTH, CRISIS AND RECOVERY

The Twelfth and Early Thirteenth Centuries

The reform movement associated with Pope Gregory VII (r. 1073–85) aimed to purge the church of practices that the hard-line pope and his followers viewed as abuses, most notably lay interference in the elections of prelates. Concurrent developments helped to set the stage for the following centuries. The Normanisation of England after 1066 brought the country more into the Continental world, with most new abbots and bishops being of Norman stock. England participated, too, in the pan-European trends of demographic, economic and urban growth. It was a more orderly world than that of previous centuries despite the civil war between Stephen and Matilda. The weakening of royal power during that episode of unrest allowed unprecedented freedom to reform-minded bishops. The intellectual flourishing that Haskins christened 'the renaissance of the twelfth century', with loftier ideals in the cloister and greater learning among the clergy, was as evident in England as anywhere else. Together, these factors enabled the English church to grow in stability, wealth, influence and piety across the eleventh and twelfth centuries, with clergy and laity working together for reform and improvement of local churches.[1] The immense monetary investment in the building of parish churches across the country testifies to growing wealth, population and piety, while the particularly large number of anchorites and anchoresses reflects not only sufficient resources to support unproductive members of the population but also the motive to flee an increasingly commercial society.[2]

---

[1] Brooke, *English Church and Papacy*, 175–90; F. Barlow, *The English Church, 1066–1154* (London), 95–103; Bartlett, *Norman and Angevin Kings*; S. Hamilton, *Church and People in the Medieval West* (London, 2013); Barrow, *Secular Clerics*; C. H. Haskins, *The Renaissance of the Twelfth Century* (Cambridge, MA, 1927); Firey, *Penance*; J. Blair, ed., *Minsters and Parish Churches: The Local Church in Transition, 950–1200* (Oxford, 1988); J. Blair and R. Sharpe, eds, *Pastoral Care before the Parish* (Leicester, 1992); Thomas, *Secular Clergy*, 323–42; C. Cubitt, 'The Institutional Church' and 'Pastoral Care and Religious Belief', in P. Stafford, ed., *A Companion to the Early Middle Ages: Britain and Ireland, c. 500–c. 1100* (Chichester, 2009), 376–94, 395–413; F. Tinti, ed., *Pastoral Care in Late Anglo-Saxon England* (Woodbridge, 2005).
[2] Mayr-Harting, *Religion*, 6–7, 98–124.

The ideals that arose in the eleventh- and twelfth-century cloister, such as the spirituality behind the meditations of Anselm of Canterbury and the sermons of Bernard of Clairvaux, did not remain a monastic preserve. Affective devotion focused the emotions on the sufferings of Christ.[3] The aim of such devotion was to school the emotions into a proper piety. Compassion for the Crucified called the worshipper to consider the reason for the crucifixion: his or her own guilt. True compassion, therefore, should lead to an aversion to sin. As a monastic prayer from the turn of the twelfth century articulated it,

Drive out from me, o Lord, despondency of mind, and increase compunction of heart. Shrink my pride, and perfect in me true humility. Awaken weeping in me, and soften my hard and stony heart ... Give me tears from your emotion (*ex tuo affectu*), which are able to loosen the bonds of my sins.[4]

Such affective devotion came to influence popular piety through a number of intersecting channels, some of which are better understood than others. The Augustinian Canons, a new cloistered order that nonetheless engaged in pastoral work, are often credited with spreading monastic piety among the twelfth-century laity.[5] The scholarly canons of St-Victor at Paris fostered affective piety; their writings would be influential in the spiritual outlook of the friars, who, as is well known, regularly preached and heard confessions in the thirteenth century and beyond.[6] Historians are working to understand the relationship between affective devotion on the one hand and concepts of selfhood and the history of the emotions on the other.[7] We do not yet know how far these emotional and philosophical trends originated among monks, nuns, canons and scholars; how far the clergy were being carried forward on a cultural current; and to what extent the answers would differ from one place to another. England was not identical with France or Italy in its lay culture or in the ecclesiastical structures through which affective devotion could be disseminated. All indications, however, are that affective devotion was a widespread feature of lay religious expression in England after 1200.

---

[3] Ross, *Grief of God*.   [4] T. H. Bestul, ed., *A Durham Book of Devotions* (Toronto, 1987), 44–45.
[5] E.g. J. Leclerq et al., *The Spirituality of the Middle Ages* (London, 1968).
[6] Affective piety, drawing on both monastic and scholastic traditions, is prominent in the sermons of the early Franciscan Anthony of Padua (d. 1231): Anthony of Padua, *Sermones*. For friars as preachers and confessors, see below. On Franciscan preaching and the emotions, see Campbell, 'Franciscan Preaching in Thirteenth-Century England'.
[7] S. R. Kramer, *Sin, Interiority, and Selfhood in the Twelfth-Century West* (Toronto, 2015); S. McNamer, *Affective Meditation and the Invention of Medieval Compassion* (Philadelphia, 2011).

While minsters serving large districts with outlying chapels could still be found in thirteenth-century England, by and large the landscape had been filled in by more conventional parishes.[8] These constituted the church's institutional existence in each lay community and naturally attracted the attention of prelates concerned with the oversight of their flocks. While bishops might perambulate and preach, it was through the constant, stable existence of the local church with its local priest that the population could be effectively reached, taught, exhorted and disciplined. Parish life at the end of the twelfth century was not yet everything that reform-minded churchmen wanted it to be. Married priests still handed on their benefices to their sons.[9] Where rectors were absentees, vicarages were seldom formally established, and those that existed 'were but sporadic attempts to provide for the proper payment of ministers who should perform the regular service of the churches'.[10] It may well be that preaching was intermittent, divine service was not everywhere regular or well attended and laypeople were lax about confessing their sins.[11] Yet because the local church and its ideals already existed, even if manifested imperfectly, those churchmen who shared visions of pastoral renewal and efficient administration were widening and improving existing roads, not blazing new trails in the wilderness.

LATERAN III AND PETER THE CHANTER

The Third Lateran Council, which met in March 1179, indicates the growing impulse for reform in the Latin Church. More than one-third of its canons would be applicable to pastoral care in an English context. Bishops were charged with ordaining to the priesthood men over twenty-five years of age only, and of good learning and character; the procedure for excommunications was clarified; benefices were not to be left vacant for more than six months; incontinent priests were commanded to surrender either their mistresses or their benefices; pluralism and non-residence were curtailed; gifts to parish churches (such as liturgical ornaments) had to be kept by the churches and not sold by the priest to his profit; quick settlement was required in disputes over rectories; each cathedral was to

---

[8] Pounds, *English Parish*, 3–152. For examples of surviving minsters, see Chapter 11 below.

[9] Thibodeaux, *Manly Priest*, 64–85; E. U. Crosby, *The King's Bishops: The Politics of Patronage in England and Normandy, 1066–1204* (New York, 2013), 52–55.

[10] Hartridge, *Vicarages*, 30–35.

[11] Mayr-Harting, *Religion*, 118, 124. It is curious that surviving synodical decrees in *C&S* I concerning these topics date from before the Conquest and from the later twelfth century, but few from in between.

support a *magister* to teach its chapter and poor scholars without charge; and provisions were made to facilitate the founding of hospitals and leper colonies.[12] While not a comprehensive programme of reform by later standards, the canons, when followed, will have raised the bar for the practitioners of pastoral care at the parish level, offered some of them some access to further education, prevented some abuses of their position and ensured that they were present to minister to their flocks.

It was after the Third Lateran Council that handbooks on pastoral care designed for parish clergy began to appear. Boyle ascribed this timing not only to the Council but also to the awareness that the growing body of theology on the sacraments needed to be disseminated, the recognition that the parish clergy were a valuable component of the church's mission who needed access to the fruits of scholarship and the development of the *summa* as a genre conducive to mediating the supply to the demand.[13] The influence of the practical theologian Peter the Chanter (d. 1196) in Paris was great, and English students and colleagues of his returned to their homeland or sent writings there.[14] Robert of Flamborough and Thomas of Chobham both drew inspiration from his work in writing their treatises on penance around the time of Lateran IV.[15] Stephen Langton, who would be elected archbishop of Canterbury in 1205, was probably his student and was certainly of one mind with Peter on pastoral theology.[16] He quoted Peter's *dictum* that 'Christ is heard in well-lettered clerks, but is found in good-living peasants.'[17] Odo de Sully, bishop of Paris (1196–1208), issued an extensive set of diocesan statutes that drew upon, or at least were in concord with, recent theologians and canonists, including Alain de Lille and Gratian, and shared Peter's emphasis on pastoral care.[18] Odo's statutes were the principal source of the diocesan statutes that Langton and his one-time Paris student Richard Poore issued in the dioceses of Canterbury, Salisbury and Durham, which in turn were echoed to a greater or lesser extent in many other English dioceses.[19] If, as Lang showed, the canons of Lateran IV were not the fountainhead of English episcopal statutes, it is in part because that distinction belongs to Odo's Paris statutes. Jacques de Vitry described western Europe as being awakened from its sloth and torpor by the bright dawn of Parisian theologians and those who disseminated their vision.[20] Naturally, this must

[12] *DEC*, 212–22. [13] Boyle, 'Inter-Conciliar Period'.
[14] Baldwin, *Masters*; A. J. Andrea, 'Walter, Archdeacon of London, and the "Historia Occidentalis" of Jacques de Vitry', *Church History* 50 (1989), 141–51.
[15] Baldwin, *Masters* I, 48–59. [16] Baldwin, *Masters* I, 25–31. [17] Powicke, *Langton*, 58.
[18] O. Pontal, ed., *Les statuts synodaux Français du XIIIᵉ siècle, Tome I: Les statuts de Paris et le synodal de l'Ouest* (Paris, 1971).
[19] Cheney, *Synodalia*; *C&S* II, 23–36, 57–96. [20] Hinnebusch, ed., *Occidentalis*.

be understood as the overdrawn rhetoric of reformist propaganda, but it clearly had some basis in fact.

It was, however, a slow and experimental beginning, for 'there was precious little available by way of *pastoralia* to the ordinary, run-of-the-mill priest in his *cura animarum* before about 1200.'[21] The *Gemma Ecclesiastica* of Gerald of Wales (ca. 1197), a work heavily indebted to Peter the Chanter's *Verbum Abbreviatum*, was still too long, too demanding and too expensive for the great mass of parish clergy, its purported readership.[22] Other texts were more accessible, to varying degrees. The verse sermon cycle *Ormulum* (1150 × 1180?) was written in idiosyncratic English; Angier, canon of St Frideswide, Oxford, created a French verse translation of the *Dialogues* of Gregory the Great.[23] Towards the end of the twelfth century, the Augustinian Canon Guy of Southwick composed a tract on confession at the behest of the bishop of Hereford.[24] The Trinity and Lambeth Homilies, dating from the late twelfth or early thirteenth century, appear to be (at least in part) renderings into English from Latin originals and reflect twelfth-century Latin homiletic developments. The extent of their circulation and use is not known, and each collection exists in a single manuscript copy; but the fact that they have several sermons in common suggests that they are the only extant members of a larger family of manuscripts.[25] The sermon collection of Maurice de Sully, bishop of Paris from 1160 to 1197, circulated freely in England, not only in Latin but also in an early French translation.[26] Odo of Canterbury, abbot of Battle (d. 1200), wrote numerous scriptural commentaries and sermons and was commended by his biographer for his gift in making his ideas understood 'for the edification of listeners, sometimes in Latin and sometimes in French, frequently speaking publicly for the edification of the humble (*rudis*) in their common [English] mother tongue'.[27] None of his surviving sermons is explicitly addressed to laypeople, but several are addressed to those hearing non-monastic confessions and are in keeping with later twelfth-century penitential theology.[28] Perhaps his monks sometimes heard lay confessions, but Odo preached to secular clergy in at least one diocesan synod, a more likely audience for his teachings on

---

[21] Boyle, 'Inter-Conciliar Period', 46; see also Rubin, *Corpus Christi*, 86.

[22] This may explain why it exists in only one manuscript (Sharpe, *Handlist*, 135). On Gerald's use of Peter, see E. M. Sanford, 'Giraldus Cambrensis' Debt to Petrus Cantor', *Medievalia et Humanistica* 3 (1945), 16–32.

[23] J. Wogan-Browne, 'Time to Read: The Case of Angier of St Frideswide', in Gunn and Innes-Parker, *Texts and Traditions*, 62–77.

[24] Wilmart, ed., 'Guy de Southwick'.   [25] Millet, 'Pastoral Context'; Millet, 'Discontinuity'.

[26] Reeves, *Religious Education*, 74–87.

[27] E. Searle, ed. and trans., *The Chronicle of Battle Abbey* (Oxford, 1980), 306–9.

[28] C. de Clerq, ed., *The Latin Sermons of Odo of Canterbury* (Brussels, 1983), 278–307, 312–15.

penance.[29] William de Montibus (d. 1213), who had taught theology as a colleague of Peter the Chanter at Paris, returned to his native Lincoln in 1194, where he taught, preached and wrote practical pastoral instruction at a level suitable to the needs of parish clergy, as attested by the large number of surviving manuscripts of his works. William's *Numerale*, for example, written as a basic introductory text to theological study, covered in simple terms and with numeric mnemonic devices the three parts of penance, the four cardinal virtues, six things to attend to when visiting the dying, the seven capital vices, the Ten Commandments and the twelve articles of faith, among many other numeric lists of subjects a parish priest needed to know.[30] William's student Samuel Presbiter compiled extracts from the writings of Gregory the Great in two versions, one in prose and one in verse.[31] The Crusade-preaching manual written by Master Philip of Oxford around 1213–14 was also shot through with the new Parisian pastoral and sacramental theology, particularly of penance and transubstantiation, explained in simple terms appropriate for teaching to the laity and lower clergy.[32] Only a few of these works (particularly those of Maurice de Sully and William de Montibus) can be shown to have had a wide circulation.[33] Nonetheless, they demonstrate that theologians were setting their minds to the task, and we must wonder how much else they wrote that is now lost.

Local legislation was another effective way of disseminating ideas, its prescriptions and proscriptions often given theological glosses. The Fourth Lateran Council of 1215 was to be followed in England by a deluge of diocesan constitutions. But some important diocesan and provincial constitutions preceded Lateran IV, based on Lateran III and the works of twelfth-century canonists, strengthening the papacy-to-parish channel that would direct future reforms in pastoral care and ecclesiastical governance. In a council at York in 1195, Archbishop Hubert Walter of Canterbury, acting as a papal legate, issued canons – whether for the Northern Province or only the Diocese of York is not clear – regarding clerical behaviour and discipline, including pastoral care. The first canon deals with the proper celebration of the mass, the second with bearing the consecrated host to visit the sick, the fourth with the mass and penance, canon five with the number of godparents, canon six with baptism and penance and canon seven with eucharistic vessels, while canon fifteen addresses public penance for those commonly suspected of a sin. Although only

[29] Ibid., 318–20.   [30] Goering, *William de Montibus*, 227–60.
[31] Samuel Presbiter, *Notes*; Goering, *William de Montibus*, 504–14; Sharpe, *Handlist*, 600–601.
[32] Cole, *Preaching of the Crusades*, 110–27.
[33] Reeves, *Religious Education*, 74–87; Goering, *William de Montibus*.

one injunction was the direct result of Lateran III, there was other new material in these chapters, and they helped to establish what would become an important means of reform: using local legislation to spread pastoral ideas and raise standards. The York council was attended by the rectors of York Diocese and their superiors, the officials (presumably meaning archdeacons) and rural deans, so the dissemination of these directions for pastoral care was direct to many of its practitioners. Vicars and chaplains could have received the directions either from their rectors or from their archdeacons or rural deans.[34]

Walter held another council in September 1200, this time as archbishop in his own Province of Canterbury, in which he met with monastic officials and ten bishops of his province.[35] Its dissemination to parish clergy was dependent upon the bishops' co-operation. Unlike the York canons, the canons issued here directly reflect decrees of Lateran III and other recent developments in canon law; like the canons of 1195 and thirteenth-century diocesan statutes, they dealt with clerical behaviour and the sacraments. To prevent churches being served by starveling vicars, any church worth less than three marks per year had to be served in person by the rector. The canon on penance reflects developments in twelfth-century theology, specifically Gratian's *De penitentia*, by insisting that the priest diligently inquire into the circumstances of sin and the penitent's devotion.[36] A short set of what appear to be diocesan statutes based on them, written 1200 × 1215, follows them in one manuscript.[37] Unlike Walter's two provincial councils, but like most thirteenth-century diocesan statutes, this unknown bishop included a chapter on preaching, requiring priests to teach their parishioners frequently in their mother tongue the Lord's Prayer, the Apostles' Creed and the general confession used during the mass.

Reforming legislation had now been promulgated by Archbishop Walter in both English provinces by the turn of the thirteenth century, with the aim of improving pastoral care of the laity. In York Diocese, and possibly its neighbours, Durham and Carlisle dioceses (the three constituting the Province of York in England), the thirteenth century began with a short set of directions for pastoral care being placed directly into the hands of parish clergy, while Canterbury Province was given a more extensive and up-to-date set of directions that may or may not have been disseminated in its original form to parish clergy at the time. It

---

[34] *C&S* I, 1042–52.   [35] *C&S* I, 1055–70.
[36] A. A. Larson, ed. and trans., *Gratian's* Tractatus de penitentia: *A New Latin Edition with English Translation* (Washington, DC, 2016), 8–10, 246.
[37] *C&S* I, 1057–58, 1070–74.

is clear, however, that it did have longer-term effects, since bishops over the ensuing decades mediated the principles of its canons to the pastors of their dioceses through their own diocesan constitutions and through individual injunctions to diocesan officials to pass on to parish clergy.[38]

INTERDICT

The progress of English ecclesiastical reform was not to be smooth. On 23 March 1208, Pope Innocent III placed all of England under interdict because in 1206 King John had refused to accept the papal nominee Stephen Langton as Hubert Walter's successor to the See of Canterbury. For six years, various duties involved in pastoral care, including most services in parish churches, were forbidden. There was some confusion regarding precisely which duties were permitted, which were prohibited and which were done in practice.[39] At first, parish priests could have made decisions in their own parishes if they lacked specific instructions from the bishop, or may even have covertly disregarded some prohibitions. In any case, baptism, widely considered the most necessary of sacraments for salvation, was still permitted, though it may have taken place in houses instead of in the parish church, and from 1212 clergy were allowed to give the consecrated host to the dying.[40] This required that hosts be consecrated at private masses. Monasteries could not admit laypeople to their masses but they did not cease to function; they continued to receive donations, pray for the living and the dead and undertake building works.[41] Some received pilgrims and supplicants at their saints' shrines.[42] Despite the interdict, many devotional practices could continue, including outdoor preaching and processions, prayers, fasts, confession and penance, the imposition of ashes on Ash Wednesday and adoration of the Rood outside the church building on Good Friday.[43] Those who could afford it might travel abroad: the interdict was imposed geographically on England, not personally on the English.[44] Schools for clergy do not appear to have closed.[45] Since the supervisory structures of the church

---

[38] Cheney, *Synodalia*; *C&S II*.

[39] P. Clarke, *The Interdict in the Thirteenth Century* (Oxford, 2007), 130–68; T. M. Parker, 'The Terms of the Interdict of Innocent III', *Speculum* 11 (1936), 258–60; Vincent, *Peter des Roches*, 82–84; Cheney, *Innocent III*, 305–13; Cheney, 'King John'.

[40] Cheney, *Innocent III*, 329. The change was from allowing the dying only to gaze upon the host ('spiritual reception') to permitting physical reception.

[41] Vincent, *Peter des Roches*, 81–82.   [42] Cheney, 'King John', 316.

[43] C. R. Cheney, 'A Recent View of the General Interdict on England', *Studies in Church History* 3 (1966), 159–68, at 162.

[44] William de Montibus died in Scotland in spring 1213; Goering suggests that he had gone there from Lincoln to celebrate Easter: Goering, *William de Montibus*, 26.

[45] Goering, *William de Montibus*, 25.

were weakened, local enforcement was presumably spotty. Nonetheless, the interdict was felt in all corners of England by all Christian inhabitants for flouting it could not have gone unnoticed for long. Even Peter des Roches, King John's loyal bishop of Winchester, who stayed at the king's side throughout the interdict, is not known to have flouted its terms or allowed others to do so.[46]

Some of the problems created by the interdict may be reflected in the diocesan statutes issued by Langton during the year between his acceptance by John and the lifting of the papal sentence. Clerical celibacy, which probably became far more problematic under a weakened hierarchy, received particular attention.[47] The collection of tithes was to be *renewed*, which suggests a lapse; parishioners may have been loath to give full payment to clergy who could offer them limited services.[48] Perhaps this drove clergy to sell or pawn church-owned valuables.[49] Laypeople were forbidden to attend markets on Sundays or feast days when they ought to be in church, an old problem doubtless intensified by the long-term closure of churches.[50] In August 1213, Langton preached a sermon at St Paul's to explain to the laity why the interdict was not yet lifted, which suggests that some were getting impatient.[51] The necessary terms were fulfilled by the beginning of July 1214 and the clergy could get back to work for the laity, administering the sacraments, pronouncing absolution of sins, publicly celebrating the mass, having the ground consecrated in which friends and relatives had been buried and blessing marriages contracted in those years.[52]

Yet church administration had been severely disrupted, and recovery would be slow. The system of papal judges-delegate, by which the papacy referred cases back to selected committees of competent English clergy for resolution, had broken down completely by 1210 after several years of trouble.[53] Peter des Roches was the only bishop left in England; all the others had fled abroad in 1209.[54] The unrest had led to the quashing of numerous episcopal elections and the difficulty of calling new ones, which had prolonged vacancies: Exeter was without a confirmed bishop from 1206 to 1214; Chichester, from 1209 to 1215; Durham, 1208 to 1217; Coventry, 1208 to 1214; Lincoln, 1206 to 1209; Worcester, 1212 to 1214, followed by new bishops in 1216 and 1218; York, 1212 to 1215; Bangor, 1213 to 1215; Carlisle, 1214 to 1218; Ely, 1215 to 1220. Other dioceses added to the high turnover rate: Norwich, Rochester and St Davids

---

[46] Vincent, *Peter des Roches*, 82–83.   [47] *C&S* II, 25–26; Cheney, *Becket to Langton*, 14–15, 137–38.
[48] *C&S* II, 33.   [49] *C&S* II, 29.   [50] *C&S* II, 35.
[51] Cheney, *Innocent III*, 348–49.   [52] *C&S* II, 36–38; Cheney, 'King John', 299.
[53] Sayers, *Papal Judges Delegate*, 268–70.
[54] Vincent, *Peter des Roches*, 74–88. For the dubious exception of Carlisle, see Chapter 12 below.

all received new bishops between 1213 and 1215.[55] Each new election required royal assent, taking possession of temporalities of the see, the archbishop's confirmation, a profession of obedience to the archbishop, consecration, taking possession of the spiritualities of the see and assembling a body of household clerks and servants to undertake administration. Kings chronically dragged out vacancies so that they or their favourites could pocket the revenues of the temporalities of the diocese for as long as possible and even plunder its moveable assets. In the best of times, it could take a bishop a year or more from the date of his election to when he firmly held the reins of his new diocese; and these were hardly the best of times. The papal legate Guala (1216–18) was empowered by the pope to nominate bishops to vacant sees, whom the cathedral chapters were then obliged to elect.[56] The English church could ill afford further wrangling over vacant bishoprics.

Since one of the duties of bishops is ordination, England would have been desperately short of priests. The backlog must have been immense: it was not uncommon for a bishop to ordain several hundred clergy every year.[57] Men may have been appointed by patrons and inducted by archdeacons as vicars or rectors, but most would have remained in lower orders unless they went abroad for ordination or were ordained in England by episcopal vicars.[58] War and unrest continued until John's death in 1216 and Langton was suspended by Innocent III from September 1215 for failing to excommunicate John's enemies when ordered to do so. The suspension was cancelled early the next year, but Langton did not return to Canterbury until May 1218.[59] Lang characterised the aftermath thus:

A difficult and arduous task lay before the bishops ... They must not only reorganize and reform but they must endeavour to raise both clergy and laity from the lethargy into which they had fallen and inspire them anew with a spirit of zeal and enthusiasm in the service of their religion ... They did not, however, lack guidance and advice in the work they were to do. On the contrary, a whole

---

[55] E. B. Pryde et al., ed., *Handbook of British Chronology* (3rd edn, London, 1986), 227–97, *passim*; for fuller details, see relevant volumes of *Fasti*.

[56] Harvey, *Episcopal Appointments*, 109.   [57] Logan, *University Education*, 3–4.

[58] C. R. Cheney, 'The Earliest English Diocesan Statutes', *English Historical Review* 75 (1960), 1–29, at 13, and Goering, *William de Montibus*, 24–25, show some ecclesiastical administration still going on, though Goering may be mistaken to attribute any of the records of institutions in *Rot. Hugonis* I to the interdict period: D. M. Smith, 'The Rolls of Hugh of Wells, Bishop of Lincoln 1209–1235', *BIHR* 45 (1972), 155–95. For near-contemporary evidence of ordination by foreign bishops, see Gerald, *Opera* III, 368; *C&S* II, 147; *Reg. St Osmund* I, 313. Ordination was not explicitly prohibited under the terms of the interdict; the archbishop of Armagh was acting as vicar in Exeter and Worcester in 1207: E. B. Pryde et al., ed., *Handbook of British Chronology* (3rd edn, London, 1986), 334.

[59] *C&S* II, 46–47.

programme of reform had been drawn up in a General Council of the Church, held in 1215, the many decrees of which it was their duty to enforce.[60]

LATERAN IV AND RECOVERY

Pope Innocent III promulgated a summons in April 1213 for an ecumenical council to meet at the Lateran Basilica in November 1215,

for the extirpation of vices and the planting of virtues, the correcting of excesses and the reform of customs, the elimination of heresies and the strengthening of faith, the settling of discords and the establishing of peace, the curbing of oppressions and the fostering of liberty; for Christian princes and peoples to hasten to help and support the Holy Land – to be attended to equally by the clergy and the laity – along with other reasons too numerous to list individually.[61]

The breadth of the Council's decrees would reflect the breadth of its intent, ranging from the theology of the Trinity and the sacraments to the procedures for electing abbots and bishops, from church-state relations to crusade preparations. In particular, the Council considered many issues directly related to pastoral care. Since Innocent and other influential prelates had studied at Paris, Peter the Chanter's school of practical, moral and pastoral theology determined their approach.[62] The most celebrated pastoral canon of the Council is canon 21, *Omnis utriusque sexus fidelis*, which enjoined that 'All the faithful of either sex … should faithfully confess their sins alone to their own priests at least once a year' in preparation for receiving the Eucharist at Easter.[63] This was not entirely novel, as some older authorities had required the confession-satisfaction-reception of Eucharist pattern to be observed leading up to Christmas and Pentecost as well,[64] making *Omnis utriusque* a relaxation. Some English bishops continued to enjoin the older, thrice-yearly form.[65]

While diocesan chanceries may have had copies of the Council's canons, parish priests did not.[66] It was the responsibility of the bishops to

---

[60] Bartlett, *Norman and Angevin Kings*, 66–67; Gibbs and Lang, *Bishops and Reform*, 94–95.

[61] C. R. Cheney and W. H. Semple, eds, *Selected Letters of Pope Innocent III* (London, 1953), 144–47.

[62] N. Tanner, 'Pastoral Care: The Fourth Lateran Council of 1215', in G. Evans, ed., *A History of Pastoral Care* (London, 2000), 112–25, at 123; A. Murray, 'Confession before 1215', *TRHS* 6th s. 3 (1993), 51–81, at 63–64.

[63] *DEC*, 245.

[64] E.g. Gratian, *Decretum* (PL CLXXXVII, 1738–39); A. Morey, *Bartholomew of Exeter, Bishop and Canonist* (Cambridge, 1937), 271; *C&S* II, 32.

[65] *C&S* II, 72–73, 236–37, 639; and see Chapter 7 below.

[66] The pastoral canons were included in the Decretals of Gregory IX, Liber V. We find these in the possession of bishops (e.g. C. M. Woolgar, ed., *Testamentary Records of the English and Welsh Episcopate* (C&YS 102, 2011), 76), but not one parochial copy was noted in the whole Diocese of Ely in the thirteenth or fourteenth centuries: Feltoe and Minns, ed., *Vetus Liber*.

publish and enforce applicable developments in canon law to the clergy of their dioceses: the Council directed archbishops to hold annual councils with the bishops of their provinces, 'in which, diligently and with fear of God, let them correct excesses and reform morals, repeating canon law, especially that which is ruled in this General Council ... and what they rule, let them cause to be observed, publishing them in episcopal synods to be held annually in every diocese.'[67] Compliance was not immediate. The first known diocesan statutes to follow the Council are those of Richard Poore at Salisbury, 1217 × 1219, and the first provincial council in England after Lateran IV was the Council of Oxford of April 1222. But the spirit of the injunction was followed with increasing frequency from the 1220s to the 1280s in several sets of provincial canons (in Canterbury Province only) and many sets of diocesan statutes, with at least one set issued for all but two English dioceses.[68] Surprisingly few of the Lateran canons were quoted directly in English statutes; as we have seen, Lang concluded that most English bishops were aware of the Lateran decrees in a vague and second-hand way only.[69] Rather than promulgating the precise instructions of Lateran IV, provincial and diocesan legislation promoted more generally the reformist impulses and pastoral concerns that predated 1215 and had animated Innocent's decrees.

Moreover, the reduction of royal influence in episcopal elections following John's submission led to the greatest electoral freedom the English cathedral chapters would see in the Middle Ages. This gave greater opportunities for theologians and men experienced in diocesan administration to be elevated to a bishopric, while the obvious need to rebuild the church after the interdict allowed these bishops to press for more far-reaching reforms than they might have achieved otherwise.[70] The bishops and their statutes will be considered individually under their appropriate provinces and dioceses in Part III, especially for the local variation reflected in them or created by them, but the degree of similarity is sufficient to illustrate the range of possibilities in preaching, liturgy and confession. First, however, we must consider the social contexts in which parish priests operated and then witness the arrival of a new class of clergy who would be the parsons' coadjutors, and perhaps also their rivals: the friars. This will be followed by an investigation into the pastoral activities of monks and canons regular.

[67] *DEC*, 236–37.
[68] Rochester and Hereford have no known sets of diocesan statutes, nor do any of the four Welsh dioceses, but there are also two surviving sets from the 1220s that cannot be assigned to any particular diocese and probably came from two of these six: *C&S II*, 139–54, 181–97.
[69] Gibbs and Lang, *Bishops and Reform*, 105–30.
[70] Binski, *Becket's Crown*, 62–70; Harvey, *Episcopal Appointments*, 1–8.

Chapter 2

PARISH CLERGY

English local society at its lowest level was defined by a variety of types of jurisdictions, including the town, the township or vill, the manor and the parish. Theoretically, these represented different ways of describing the same plot of land inhabited by a community of people who belonged to one lord, one church, one village; but in practice this was not always the case.[1] In some rural regions, especially to the north and west, inhabitants lived in dispersed hamlets and farmsteads. While groups of these scattered settlements would still be classified as vills, there was nothing we would call a village.[2] A manor could comprise several whole townships, or parts of one or more. A rural parish might comprise one or more whole or partial manors each of which in turn might comprise one or more whole or partial townships; if it was large it was likely to be subdivided, with those in more distant corners attending chapels-of-ease. An urban parish could take in part of the town's suburban and rural hinterland. Most towns founded after the Conquest, such as Wells or Boston, were served by a single large parish, making for a community much too populous for anyone to know everyone else. This suggests that parishioners found smaller loyalties in their trades and neighbourhoods. Older towns were divided into multiple parishes whose boundaries had little significance for secular jurisdiction or economic activity. The parish, therefore, was not the only focal point of local collective identity. According to Reynolds, 'an essential attribute of any local group which was perceived as a group was the right and duty to participate in its own government'. This attribute might seem to belong more to the manor court than to the parish congregation but self-organisation among the laity was already a familiar characteristic of parish life in thirteenth-century England. Where parochial boundaries

---

[1] In the East Midlands, for example, the vill was commonly identical with the parish, and settlements were mostly nucleated villages, but even here the vill/parish was commonly subdivided among manors by the thirteenth century. C. Lewis, P. Mitchell-Fox, and C. Dyer, *Village, Hamlet and Field: Changing Medieval Settlements in Central England* (Manchester, 1997), 54, 69–71, 108, 132, 148, 184.
[2] Dyer, *Everyday Life*, 3–4; but cf. G. Astill, 'Rural Settlement: The Toft and the Croft', in G. Astill and A. Grant, eds, *The Countryside of Medieval England* (Oxford, 1988), 36–61.

coincided with those of the town, township or manor, the convergence of the residential, economic, juridical and spiritual realms into one set of boundaries led to a particularly close intertwining of the lives of the people who lived there.[3]

Where members of the same parish answered to different manorial courts, or where neighbours across the street attended different churches, parishioners would be required *ipso facto* to distinguish in practice what loyalties they owed to the parish and what to each other institution that claimed them. Even in these circumstances, though, entirely disentangling parochial life from other concerns was unlikely to be easy, particularly where finances were concerned. Even the most impious layman owed tithes and dues to his parish: Edward I confirmed that ecclesiastical courts had the right to compel lay payments not only of tithe but also for mortuary dues, maintenance of church and churchyard, the supply of necessary books and ornaments and customary oblations.[4] Bishops struggled to suppress scot-ales, drinking parties or taverns held by various officials to their own profit, attendance at which might be effectively compulsory. Some of these were held by clergy to exact money from parishioners, possibly the ancestor of the late medieval church-ale held to plenish the fabric fund.[5] Rural churches were typically endowed with land called the glebe, ranging from a few acres to a holding several times that of a typical peasant. Some clergy held additional land as well. The priest could (and sometimes did) farm personally, but he was more likely to rent his land to neighbours or hire them to work it.[6] Animals owned by the rector or vicar were rented out for their milk, wool and offspring, as were animals that had been given to the church for the perpetual support of a candle before a specified image.[7] The layperson who farmed the rector's land or

---

[3] Richardson was mistaken in stating that 'for the most part, the parish was co-extensive with the manor' in this period: 'Parish Clergy', 90. Cf. D. M. Palliser, 'Introduction: The Parish in Perspective', in S. Wright, ed., *Parish, Church and People* (London, 1988), 5–10; S. Reynolds, *Kingdoms and Communities in Western Europe* (2nd edn, Oxford, 1997), 102; Mayr-Harting, *Religion*, 99; Ault, 'Village Community'; R. Britnell, *Britain and Ireland, 1050–1530: Economy and Society* (Oxford, 2004); Pounds, *English Parish*, 3–4, 134–35; Shaw, *Creation of a Community*. For internal organisation, see Byng, *Church Building*.

[4] *C&S* II, 974–75.

[5] The thirteenth-century evidence is mostly inconclusive, as bishops' statutes focus on forbidding the holding of scot-ales without discussing who would hold them (or only mentioning secular officials), or on forbidding laity to announce scot-ales in church and clergy to announce them at all: *C&S* II, 36, 64, 93, 174, 195, 203, 274, 311, 416, 432, 560, 604. A few specifically forbid clergy from *holding* scot-ales: ibid., 214, 480. See also Dyer, *Everyday Life*, 5–6.

[6] Ault, 'Village Community', 197–200; Richardson, 'Parish Clergy', 108–10; G. C. Homans, *English Villagers of the Thirteenth Century* (New York, 1941/1960), 385; A. T. Bannister, ed., 'A Transcript of the Red Book: A Detailed Account of the Hereford Bishopric Estates in the Thirteenth Century', *Camden Miscellany XV* (London, 1929), 23; Cheyney, trans., 'English Manorial Documents', 4–5.

[7] Sparrow-Simpson, *1297 Visitations*; Ault, 'Village Community', 210–14.

leased the church's sheep, who drank the vicar's ale and in due course was buried by the parish sexton, helped to finance the parish's religious life, whether he liked it or not.

While the rector may have been a non-resident cleric or a distant monastery, the man charged with the cure of souls typically lived in a house close to his church and parishioners and was involved in all aspects of local life.[8] Many beneficed parish clergy came from the free peasantry and were of local origin, from the same county if not from the same parish; these were part of the social fabric long before they took orders.[9] The unbeneficed assistant clergy were even more likely to be local men, as, for example, was William, chaplain of King's Ripton, who held three acres in that same manor inherited from his father and who in his final illness sold another parcel of land to a local family for the use of their two boys.[10] Sons of serfs could not be ordained unless their lords granted manumissions but these could be had for a fee, allowing young men to go away to school and take orders.[11] The lord who freed a serf possibly expected him to return to serve his native parish.[12] At the other end of the local social scale, ordination was a respectable option for younger sons of knights and gentry. Where a secular lord was patron of a parish church with a suitable income, he was likely to prefer his own flesh and blood, who would bring lordly bearing and expectations of deference.[13] He might or might not bring expertise. Mayr-Harting suggests that 'lay patrons in general evidently cared as much as anyone about the suitability of priests in their churches, for their families would lose face' if they appointed an unworthy priest; though it may be countered that, of the twenty-one parish clergy cited in Grosseteste's register for inadequate learning, three shared their patron's surname, one of them explicitly being the patron's son.[14] The priest who was a long-established and fully integrated part of the local social fabric knew his people well but this was

---

[8] Hallam, *Agrarian History*, 915–20; Pounds, *English Parish*, 59, 128–46; Richardson, 'Parish Clergy'; French, *People of the Parish*, 20–27.

[9] Robinson, *Beneficed Clergy*, 21; C. H. Lawrence, 'The English Parish and Its Clergy in the Thirteenth Century', in P. Linehan and J. Nelson, eds, *The Medieval World* (London, 2001), 648–70, at 654–55; Pounds, *English Parish*, 164.

[10] Maitland, ed., *Select Pleas*, 125–27.

[11] *C&S* II, 24–25, 60, 186, 228; Richardson, 'Parish Clergy', 118; Olson, *Mute Gospel*, 134.

[12] On assistant clergy, see Richardson, 'Parish Clergy', 90–92; Moorman, *Church Life*, 52–58; Thompson, *English Clergy*, 122–24; W. G. Hoskin, *The Midland Peasant: The Economic and Social History of a Leicestershire Village* (London, 1957), 73n.

[13] N. Orme, *From Childhood to Chivalry* (London, 1984), 36–41, 66–71; Robinson, *Beneficed Clergy*, 17–21.

[14] Mayr-Harting, *Religion*, 117; Hoskin, *Grosseteste*, nos. 218, 735, 736. The trend can also be seen in *Rot. Hugonis*.

a two-edged sword. The statutes of Salisbury, Canterbury and Durham inveighed,

We enjoin upon priests, on peril of their souls, that in exercising their duties they do not follow their personal motives, such as grudges, hatred, or carnal affections. Rather, let them be prudent and provident, so that they may not by any means outrage those subject to them in their appropriate obedience, which we know sometimes happens. In a financial dispute, priests may not forbid anyone from communion on their own authority.[15]

Other clergy had no connexion to their parishes before their appointments and might have precious little thereafter. The king as well as monastic and aristocratic patrons had a plethora of clergy who served them in various capacities and whom they wished to reward with benefices.[16] Master Ralph of Collingham, a secular clerk who served Peterborough Abbey, was given a pension of one hundred shillings in the 1220s to augment his benefice for as long as he served the abbey faithfully or attended the schools by their leave, until they could provide him with a richer benefice: this they managed to do in the next decade.[17] Some canons and dignitaries at secular cathedrals and collegiate churches were supported by prebends that were nominal rectories of parish churches; they might occasionally visit to ensure order, exercise jurisdiction and collect fees but they were not expected to be resident there.[18] By the thirteenth century, the bishop's growing retinue of clerical administrators was no longer identical with the cathedral body as it once had been: bishops now needed to support their bureaucrats with additional parish benefices.[19] Such men were often the most capable clergy around but they were occupied much of the time by the needs of their patrons.

The parish priest's status was determined by, and reflected in, the level of his income. On the basis on tithe and glebe income, Ault described the rural parson as 'one of the important landholders' with the status of a rich peasant.[20] As a general rule, rectors were better paid than vicars but there was little practical difference between a rectory with care of souls (i.e. without a vicarage, where the rector was expected to serve the parish in person) and a vicarage with a comparable stipend.[21] Dyer compared rectors with knights, vicars with lesser gentry and upper peasantry,

[15] *C&S* II, 92.   [16] Gemmill, *Nobility and Patronage*, 68–97.
[17] Brooke and Postan, eds, *Carte Nativorum*, no. 536 (1222 × 1226). The abbey presented Ralph to the church of Stanwig in 1225 (probably the original benefice) and then to the church of Kettering in 1233: *Rot. Hugonis* II 124, 173, 221, 264.
[18] Thompson, *English Clergy*.   [19] Burger, *Diocesan Governance*.
[20] Ault, 'Village Community', 199.   [21] Fizzard, *Plympton*, 179–95.

40

and unbeneficed clergy with cottars.[22] Allowing for considerable ranges of status and income within each group, this is a reasonable equivalence. The average rectory with care of souls was worth about £10 (15 marks).[23] The *inquisiciones post mortem* in the first half of the fourteenth century gave the mean value per reported manor at just over £19; nearly half of all manors were worth less than £10, with a mean within that group under £5.[24] Even if a rectory was comparable to a manor, however, the average rector was not as wealthy as the average knight or member of the greater gentry. Some clergy held multiple benefices but probably not as many as the lords who held multiple manors. Just as the lord was required to make substantial expenditures on his manor, such as supporting his servants, maintaining his hall and providing for the poor, a vicar or rector with the care of souls often had to support assisting clergy out of that income and was expected to provide charity to the poorest parishioners. The rector was also responsible for maintaining the chancel.[25] These obligations might consume much of the priest's or lesser lord's income, but the ways in which they spent their income reinforced their social standing.

The minimum salary for a vicar was set by the Council of Oxford in 1222 at five marks, about the same as a carpenter's wages.[26] Many vicars received more than the minimum. Vicarages ordained in Chichester Diocese during the thirteenth century range in value from seven to perhaps as high as thirty-five marks.[27] Some vicars received less, even when their vicarages were ordained after 1222.[28] In most cases, the vicar's stipend, even if described as having a certain value, represented not a cash payment but the estimated worth of a certain share of the tithes and offerings (different from parish to parish) and often the provision of a house. The real value would rise and fall from year to year, based on the productivity of the parish and the market value of the vicar's share. The vicarage of Newchurch (Kent) was found to be inadequate in the 1290s because land that had formerly been pasture, providing tithes to the vicar, had now been put to the plough, and the tithe of grain went to the rector.[29] Under such conditions a bishop could order an 'augmentation' of the vicarage,

[22] C. Dyer, *Standards of Living in the Later Middle Ages: Social Change in England c. 1200–1520* (Cambridge, 1989), 20–22.
[23] Logan, *University Education*, 70–71.
[24] Campbell and Bartley, *Eve of the Black Death*, 80–83; Dyer, *Standards of Living*, 10–15.
[25] Richardson, 'Parish Clergy', 97–98; Moorman, *Church Life*, 59–67.
[26] Logan, *University Education*, 70–71.
[27] *EEA* 22, nos. 16, 69, 83, 116. No. 16 is the ordination of a vicarage at Icklesham (Susx.) with tithes estimated at twenty marks; no. 116 augments this with a cash pension of fifteen marks.
[28] Richardson, 'Parish Clergy', 100–101, 112–15.
[29] Woodruff, 'Visitation Rolls', 158.

a renegotiation to raise the vicar's income: one of Grosseteste's requests at the papal curia was the authority to enforce augmentations against monastic houses, an authority that he received and put into effect.[30]

The thirteenth century was the age of the growth of vicarages, in part because of the large number of rectories appropriated by religious houses between 1200 and 1300. It was nothing new for parish churches to give a share of their tithes to religious houses, nor for rectors to be pluralists or absentees. Such churches cannot have been entirely unserved in the twelfth century: much of the time at least, chaplains served them. But it was rare for those chaplains to have security of tenure and, without official oversight, at least some of them were underpaid by monastic or absentee rectors.[31] The system of vicarages in England had begun to develop organically in the later twelfth century, before Lateran IV's Canon 32 required that vicars be given security of tenure and a suitable stipend.[32] The canons of St Paul's Cathedral voluntarily ordained vicarages in their appropriated churches as early as 1181.[33] Hugh of Wells, bishop of Lincoln from 1209 to 1235, was an energetic enforcer of the Lateran canon, ordaining at least three hundred vicarages, only a few of which appear to be restatements of existing arrangements.[34] The codification of a vicarage where an informal arrangement had previously obtained should have provided a more stable environment for pastoral care. What is less certain is whether the rapidly increasing number of parishes appropriated to religious houses and secular collegiate churches during the thirteenth century more than offset that gain. Religious houses could be extortionate and careless. Where a church formerly served by its rector was appropriated, the parishioners were probably worse off because more resources were flowing out of the parish, assuming that the previous rector had been residing and fulfilling his duties (such as poor relief), which was not always the case.[35]

If a parish already served by a vicar was appropriated to a religious institution, the parish might actually end up better off. The bishop had leverage at the outset: he could refuse to allow the appropriation unless the institution agreed to increase the value of the vicarage or serve the parish in some other way, such as guaranteeing poor relief or paying the synodal dues. Grosseteste allowed Oseney Abbey in Oxford to

[30] Hartridge, *Vicarages*, 51–53.
[31] Bishop William de Vere of Hereford (1186–98) was unusual in specifying that appropriating monasteries must give vicars security of tenure and a suitable income: J. Barrow, 'A Twelfth-Century Bishop and Patron: William de Vere', *Viator* 18 (1987), 175–89, at 184.
[32] Hartridge, *Vicarages*, 1–35, 209–17; *C&S* I, 1049; *EEA 16*, xxx–xxxiv; *EEA 17*, xlix–liii.
[33] W.H. Hale, ed., *The Domesday of St Paul's of the Year MCXXII* (Camden Soc. No. 69, 1858), 146–52.
[34] Hartridge, *Vicarages*, 38, and see Chapter 10 below.   [35] E.g. Woodruff, 'Visitation Rolls'.

42

appropriate the church of Fulwell but required it to pay two marks per year from its revenues to support poor scholars at Oxford.[36] Reluctantly permitting Westminster Abbey to appropriate the church of Ashwell, he ordained a vicarage there worth forty-three marks.[37] Moreover, an absentee rector could be hard to track down. When Nicholas of St Albans was instituted rector of Wadenhoe (Northamptonshire) in 1242, he was warned that it might be a temporary arrangement, for the previous rector, Richard de Munteni, was merely missing and presumed dead, and might return to reclaim his rectory.[38] Perhaps he did so: when a new rector was instituted in 1261, the church was said to be vacant by the death of Richard, not of Nicholas.[39] This was apparently a common enough problem for the papal legate Otto to promulgate a canon concerning it in 1237. It sometimes happens, he said, that an absentee is rumoured to have resigned or died and another cleric inveigles his way into the benefice; when the original rector comes back, the intruder says 'I don't know you' and slams the door in his face.[40] By contrast, when the archdeacon of Worcester visited the parish of Brailes (Warwickshire) in 1280 and found numerous 'intolerable defects' that were the fault of the rector, he knew that the rector would be found twenty-three miles to the north, because the rector was Kenilworth Priory.[41] Monasteries seldom wander off.

The priest, by virtue of his position and his orders, had a great deal of local prestige, which was necessary for the carrying out of his duties.[42] A vicar shared some of the parish's prestige with the rector, who in some cases had appointed him; a hired chaplain could claim the prestige of priestly orders but not of wealth or beneficed status. It appears that all secular priests, regardless of job title, were given an honorific: *Dominus* (Lord) in Latin, *Pere* (Father) in French, with the English *Sire* encompassing both meanings.[43] In many cases, the man who administered the church's services – offering the sacrifice of the mass, baptising infants into the community of salvation, binding and loosing sins, praying the dead through purgatory – also exacted the church's fees and tithes for doing so.[44] He carried the keys to the parish church, often the only communal

---

[36] Hoskin, *Grosseteste*, no. 1210 and n.   [37] Hartridge, *Vicarages*, 52; Hoskin, *Grosseteste*, no. 2082.
[38] Hoskin, *Grosseteste*, no. 777.   [39] *Rot. Gravesend*, 100.   [40] *C&S* II, 249–50.
[41] British Library, Add. MS. 47677, f. 231r.   [42] Goering, 'Popularization', 74, 92–93, 100–104.
[43] Latin: e.g. Harvey, ed., *Records of Cuxham*, no. 612; and bishops' registers, *passim*. French: T. Hunt, ed., and J. Bliss, trans., *'Cher Alme': Texts of Anglo-Norman Piety* (Tempe, Arizona, 2010), 314–15. English: 'sire prest', C. d'Evelyn and A. J. Mill, eds, *The South English Legendary* (London and Oxford: Early English Text Society, 3 vols, 1956–59), II 678; *Oxford English Dictionary, s.v.* 'sire (n.)' 1b, 'sir (n.)' 4.
[44] Thomas, *Secular Clergy*, 61–71; Ault, 'Village Community', 207–9; R. N. Swanson, 'Profits, Priests and People', in Burgess and Duffy, eds, *The Parish*, 146–59.

meeting-place and monument.[45] The priest had spiritual authority over every resident of the parish and connections with the clerical network that extended across Western Christendom. He had been appointed by the patron, often a king, noble, knight, bishop or ecclesiastical corporation (any of which might also be lord of the manor) and had been ordained by a bishop who might be a magnate of the kingdom and a prince of the church.[46] The priest's ecclesiastical superiors hoped for him to maintain his parishioners' respect by conspicuous holiness of life, though he and his parishioners might have had other expectations. Clerical concubinage, still widely considered an acceptable form of marriage, was never fully eradicated and sympathetic parishioners often neglected to mention it to their bishop or archdeacon unless questioned under oath.[47] But parishioners scandalised by this or some other failing of their priest were actively enlisted by a church hierarchy keen to root out irregularities. The rector of Gedding (Suffolk) was reported, probably by parishioners, to have ignored the poor of the parish and gone away with Magga, step-daughter of Sir Adam fitz Hugh. In extreme cases, laypeople were willing to mete out direct justice themselves.[48]

While benefit of clergy notionally exempted the cleric from criminal prosecution in secular courts, and Lateran IV prohibited him from participation in trial by ordeal, he could find himself a plaintiff, defendant or compurgator in civil suits.[49] In 1278, the vicar of St Ives was fined in the manorial court of the abbot of Ramsey for unlawfully cutting the abbot's willows, while the township of Hemingford admitted that

---

[45] Pounds, *English Parish*, 371–73.

[46] Thomas, *Secular Clergy*, 87–116. It is difficult to say whether greater prestige attached to those ordained by the greatest bishops than to those ordained by minor or foreign ones.

[47] J. Goering, 'The Changing Face of the Village Parish II: The Thirteenth Century', in J. A. Raftis, ed., *Pathways to Medieval Peasants* (Toronto, 1981), 323–32; Mason, 'A Truth Universally Acknowledged', 175–76; R. N. Swanson, 'Problems of the Priesthood in Pre-Reformation England', *English Historical Review* 105 (1990), 845–69; Thomas, *Secular Clergy*, 154–89; Thibodeaux, *Manly Priest*; *C&S* II, 312–13; Richardson, 'Parish Clergy', 120–23; Forrest, 'Visitation'.

[48] A. Gransden, 'Some Late Thirteenth-Century Records of an Ecclesiastical Court in the Archdeaconry of Sudbury', *BIHR* 32 (1959), 62–69; B. R. Kemp, 'Informing the Archdeacon on Ecclesiastical Matters in Twelfth-Century England', in M. J. Franklin and C. Harper-Bill, eds, *Medieval Ecclesiastical Studies in Honour of Dorothy M. Owen* (Woodbridge, 1995), 131–49; Carlin and Crouch, ed., *Lost Letters*, nos. 71–73; and in Stansbury, *Companion to Pastoral Care*, the following: W. J. Dohar, 'The Sheep as Shepherds: Lay Leadership and Pastoral Care in Late Medieval England', 147–71; M. Armstrong-Partida, 'Conflict in the Parish: Antagonistic Relations between Clerics and Parishioners', 173–212; and B. A. Barr, 'Three's a Crowd: Wives, Husbands and Priests in the Late Medieval Confessional', 213–34.

[49] P. A. Bill, 'Five Aspects of the Medieval Parish Clergy of Warwickshire', *University of Birmingham Historical Journal* 10 (1965), 110; E. P. Cheyney, 'English Manorial Documents', 23; J. A. Raftis, *Warboys: Two Hundred Years in the Life of an English Mediaeval Village* (Toronto, 1974), 248–49; Richardson, 'Parish Clergy', 110–11; Hyams, *Rancor*, 55.

animals belonging to the whole township had destroyed an acre of the same vicar's peas the year before and that they had not yet made amends.[50] As the whole township was implicated, we may wonder whether the animal trespass on the vicar's field was symptomatic of deeper strife. On one eventful day in 1296, William the chaplain pledged for his brother Henry, accused of trespass. William then pleaded innocent to defaming the lord's butler and was told to return with six clergy as compurgators. Finally he left the court in contempt when he was convicted of breaking the lord's hedges and stealing his poultry. For the last crime the court ordered his chattels to be distrained until he should pay.[51] Walter, parson of Hartfield, was accused in 1268 of joining with fourteen others to commit trespass and theft; when he repeatedly failed to come to court but was found to have no property in lay fee to distrain, the sheriff was ordered to arrest him.[52] We do not know if these punishments were effective, since the power of the rector or vicar could make it difficult to bring him to heel if he remained obstinate.[53] Master Adam, rector of Cuxham, was accused in November 1295 of unjustly selling nine feet of the lord's demesne and harvesting two bushels of the lord's grain but, as he was not present, he was distrained to come and answer at the next court. He did not come at the subsequent courts of April 1296 or May 1297, and the court of June 1298 again distrained him to do fealty. We hear no more of this case in the subsequent rolls and are left to guess whether he settled out of court or the lord of the manor – Merton College, which had also appointed Master Adam, a former fellow of the College, to the living – conceded defeat.[54] In either case, Merton, as both patron of the church and lord of the manor, struggled to get the rector it had appointed to answer for direct damage to his own college's purse. It must have been more difficult for a peasant aggrieved by a rector to get justice in a manor court when the lord himself had appointed a close friend or relation to the living.

On the other hand, a pious and dutiful parson might find himself *persona non grata* to his parishioners precisely for obeying his superiors. Scrupulosity in reporting parishioners' infractions to higher authorities was unlikely to make the priest very popular. If parishioners turned against him, they could cause no end of petty trouble: John de Wylminton was accused in 1294 of impeding the vicar from cultivating land, playing truant from church and keeping back church dues. Delaying tithe

---

[50] Maitland, ed., *Select Pleas*, 89–90.   [51] Maitland, ed., *Select Pleas*, 164, 172–73.
[52] S. Stewart, *Royal Justice in Surrey, 1258–1269* (Surrey Record Soc., 2013), nos. 39, 85, 90.
[53] Ault, 'Village Community', 200–204.   [54] Harvey, ed., *Records of Cuxham*, 614–17; *BRUO* 1999.

payments and heckling during sermons were also familiar strategies.[55] Some bishops required their clergy to work for reconciliation among estranged parishioners; but an arbitrator needs the trust and goodwill of both parties.[56] The successful parish priest was probably the one most capable of navigating the conflicting expectations of his bishop and archdeacon, his parishioners and perhaps his patron. The results might not always satisfy clerical reformers but even a saintly priest who pushed counsels of perfection too hard might alienate his flock.[57] As a student of William de Montibus wrote, if preaching is rare, it does not suffice, but if it is too persistent, it grows contemptible (*vilescit*).[58]

EDUCATION AND LITERACY

Another source of clerical prestige was literacy, though this is more difficult to measure than land tenure or litigation. We may presume that local clergy, particularly in the countryside, were among the most literate men in the parish. Their duties required them to be. Yet the seminary system lay centuries in the future. As we will see in the following pages, the church provided a variety of opportunities for learning, both before and after assuming a parish benefice.[59] Clergy, or aspiring clergy, were expected to take advantage of those opportunities until they were capable of performing their duties. Bishops were expected in turn to make sure that each aspiring cleric had done so, a responsibility that they and their officers exercised at ordination, institution and visitation.

The minimum level of functional Latin for ritual purposes, which is what some clergy had, was not enough to allow the cleric to construe Latin sentences so as to expound the day's Gospel lesson from the pulpit or make use of the new instructional texts on hearing a confession.[60] The pastoral reform project could have little effect on the local parish if the priest could not read the manuals and mandates that came his way. The fact that such texts were being created indicates that bishops believed that some parish clergy could read them but, since we can only guess at how many, that line of reasoning can only take us so far. Historical debates over the moral and intellectual quality of the medieval parish clergy remain unresolved. Some historians have been

---

[55] Woodruff, 'Visitation Rolls' at 162 for John, and *passim* for others withholding dues; J. Berlioz and M. A. Polo de Beaulieu, 'The Preacher Facing a Reluctant Audience according to the Testimony of *Exempla*', *Medieval Sermon Studies* 57 (2013), 16–28; Reeves, *Religious Education*, 77; Ault, 'Village Community', 206–9.

[56] *C&S* II, 64, 231.   [57] E.g. Fulk de Neully: Cole, *Preaching of the Crusades*, 90–91.

[58] Samuel Presbiter, *Notes*, 90.   [59] For the period to 1200, see Barrow, *Secular Clerics*, 170–235.

[60] *Reg. St Osmund* I, 304–7.

willing to accept reformers' laments about the parish clergy at face value.[61] However, when we consider both the education offered to the parish clergy and the level of ability demanded of them, what primary sources do not say often tells us more than what they do. Against the few clergy cited for poor education, for instance, we must set the vast majority who were not. The more positive views advanced by Denton, Dohar and Clanchy stand on firmer ground.[62]

Ecclesiastical pragmatic literacy began with phonetic literacy, the ability to look at the Latin of liturgical texts and speak the words aloud. This would be both less and more challenging than a child's learning to read English today: Latin is pronounced as spelt but the medieval reader also had to contend with an elaborate system of abbreviations. The precise appearance of the abbreviations, just like the letters of the alphabet, varied from the hand of one copyist to the next, and the priest was expected to use at least half a dozen liturgical books in the course of an ordinary Sunday, no two of which were likely to be in the same hand. The second step was what we normally think of as 'literacy', the ability to parse the grammar and translate the words. A visitation record from 1222 showed that a chaplain might function at the altar despite a comically deficient grasp of Latin grammar. The visitors, led by the dean of Salisbury, considered such ignorance intolerable, wryly quipping *sufficienter illiteratus*.[63] A third requirement, which went beyond what lay administrative clerks were required to learn, was the ability to read music and to sing the liturgies. In 1277, the bishop of Hereford examined a candidate for ordination and ordered him to spend the next year studying singing.[64] 'Reading' or 'song' schools taught the rudiments of literacy and music to boys.[65] A boy who decided young to become a cleric might enter one of these schools. In the dioceses of Worcester, Lincoln, Winchester, Wells, Carlisle, York and Exeter, parish churches within reasonable proximity of schools were obliged, if they had the means, to support a junior clerk as holy-water bearer, with duties on Sundays and festivals only, enabling him to pursue studies leading to parish ministry.[66] The vicar of Spalding was required to support two of these and was reprimanded by his bishop in 1282 for keeping only one.[67] Schools in which boys and youths could

[61] C. H. Lawrence, 'The English Parish and Its Clergy in the Thirteenth Century', in P. Linehan and J. Nelson, eds, *The Medieval World* (London, 2001), 648–70.
[62] J. H. Denton, 'The Competence of the Parish Clergy in Thirteenth-Century England', in C. Barron and J. Stratford, eds, *The Church and Learning in Later Medieval Society* (Donington, 2002), 273–85; Dohar, '*Sufficienter litteratus*'; Clanchy, *Memory to Written Record*, 242–48.
[63] *Reg. St Osmund* I, 304–8.   [64] *Reg. Cantilupo*, 124.   [65] Orme, *English Schools*, 60–62.
[66] *C&S* II, 174, 309, 606, 713, 1026–27; *Reg. Sutton* III, 104–5.
[67] British Library, Add. MS. 35296, f. 288r–v.

learn these skills before ordination were well established in England by the thirteenth century and continued to flourish in an age of growing demand.[68]

Likewise, a boy who had an early education from some other source might decide to become a cleric, for his literacy would give him a head start. Choristers were supported and taught at secular cathedrals and other collegiate churches.[69] A school was attached to St Mary's collegiate church in Warwick in the 1120s; in the early fourteenth century, the offices of the grammar master (who would teach from Donatus' Latin grammar) and the music master (who would teach first letters from the psalter as well as singing and music) were clarified.[70] Exeter's cathedral choristers were taught morals and behaviour as well as music.[71] Once a boy's voice changed, he could continue his musical training and liturgical experience as a 'secondary' in the choir until he was old enough to take higher orders.[72] Smaller and less formal schools were probably offered by many parish clergy in the countryside as well.[73] A few secular clergy had been educated as novices or boys at religious houses without taking vows, such as Walter de Merton, founder of Merton College and bishop of Rochester, who probably began his education at Merton Priory and was presented by them to his first benefice.[74] But monastic houses also recruited secular clergy to their own ranks and may have been a net drain on educated parish clergy.[75]

In addition to formal education in the reading or singing school, an aspiring cleric could learn by assisting the parish priest. A boy could be entrusted to an ecclesiastical household for upbringing, as was William de Montibus, whose youthful years in the household of Gilbert of Sempringham were apparently deeply formative.[76] The existence of vicarages worth more than the minimum of five marks suggests an expectation

---

[68] Orme, *English Schools*, esp. 167–93; Orme, *West of England*; P. Damian-Grint, *The New Historians of the Twelfth-Century Renaissance* (Woodbridge, 1999), 32–33; T. Hunt, *Teaching and Learning Latin in 13th-Century England* (Cambridge, 1991).

[69] Edwards, *Secular Cathedrals*, 166–68.

[70] C. Fonge, ed., *The Cartulary of St Mary's Collegiate Church, Warwick* (Woodbridge, 2004), nos. 20–21, 5.

[71] *Reg. Bronescombe* III, 67; Orme, *West of England*, 45; *RACCL* II, 391, 405, 429, 442–77.

[72] N. Orme, 'The Medieval Clergy of Exeter Cathedral, II: The Secondaries and Choristers', *RTDA* 115 (1983), 79–100.

[73] Orme, *English Schools*, 64–67; Moorman, *Church Life*, 102–9.

[74] G. H. Martin and J. R. L Highfield, *A History of Merton College, Oxford* (Oxford, 1997), 4–5; N. Orme, 'The Augustinian Canons and Education', in J. Burton and K. Stöber, eds, *The Regular Canons in the Medieval British Isles* (Turnhout, 2011), 213–32; D. Knowles, *The Monastic Order in England* (2nd edn, Cambridge, 1976), 491–92.

[75] E.g. *Rot. Gravesend*, 109.

[76] J. Goering, 'The Thirteenth-Century English Parish', in J. Van Engen, ed., *Educating People of Faith* (Grand Rapids, MI, 2004), 208–22, at 210–11; Goering, *William de Montibus*, 8–10.

that the vicarage was to support assistant clergy as well.[77] The vicar or rector who took on junior clergy might well be their relative.[78] The higher echelons of the English church were populated by clerical families and the lower levels may well have been too. Gerald of Wales was prompted in his early education by his uncle, who was a bishop, and some of his episcopal clerks.[79] On the Continent, John of Parma, Minister General of the Franciscan order from 1247, had been educated by his uncle, a parish priest; Dominic Guzman, founder of the Dominican order, had been handed over by his parents at an early age to be taught by his uncle, a rural dean.[80] Some early modern English episcopal registers show a vicar or rector having his son licensed as his own parish curate and we should not assume that such low-level nepotism was unknown in the thirteenth century, when curacies were not apparently subject to episcopal licence.[81] Clergy continued to have *de facto* marriages and children. Their sons might enter the family trade once their illegitimacy had been dispensed by the bishop and, although they were canonically barred from succeeding to their fathers' benefices, they sometimes did so anyway, openly or under the guise of 'nephews'. Despite official disapproval, some may have been well-qualified parish clergy by virtue of their upbringing in a clerical household.[82] *Handlyng Synne* told a tale of a priest who had four sons by his lifelong concubine, all four of whom he sent to school and all four of whom in due course became priests.[83] In default of a clerical relative or willing local priest, teachers could be hired to train up a boy or young man for the priesthood. This can be seen in action when bishops, reluctant to refuse the wishes of a magnate presenting to a rectory or vicarage despite the candidate's being underage or not yet ordained, instituted the presentee with the proviso that he and his church would be under the tutelage of a *magister*.[84]

Under the canons of the Third Lateran Council (1179), men could not be ordained deacons or priests without 'title', such as a vicarage, rectory, chaplaincy or assistantship to provide a means of support, or the bishop would be obliged to support them himself. Innocent III extended this to subdeacons in 1198, a provision Archbishop Hubert Walter included in his Canterbury provincial statutes in 1200. In practice, many titles were

---

[77] See above, p. 41.   [78] Barrow, *Secular Clerics*, 115–57.

[79] H. E. Butler, ed. and trans., *The Autobiography of Gerald of Wales* (Woodbridge, 2005), 35–37.

[80] Moorman, *Franciscan Order*, 112; Vicaire, *Dominic*, 23.

[81] To be observed, for instance, in the Diocese of Hereford in the eighteenth and nineteenth centuries: Herefordshire Record Office, MS. series AL 19/ and CA 19/, *passim*.

[82] Thibodeaux, *Manly Priest*, 66–67, 81–82; J. Raine, ed., *The Historians of the Church of York and Its Archbishops*, vol. III (London, 1894), 115.

[83] *Handlyng Synne*, ll. 7981 et seqq.   [84] Gemmill, *Nobility and Patronage*, 59–60.

either meaningless or unconnected to parish churches.[85] Nonetheless, many clerks, subdeacons and deacons were attached to churches in which they had ceremonial roles.[86] As each worked his way up, he would assist in the parish liturgy in numerous ways, such as bearing candles and incense. A subdeacon could read the Old Testament lesson and explain it to the people; as a deacon, he would be responsible for reading or singing the Gospel at mass and was permitted to preach on it.[87] Liturgies required switching back and forth among several books or several parts of the same book; deacons may have been called upon to hold books and turn pages to free the priest's hands for the manual actions of the mass. Following the words as the priest read them would improve his phonetic literacy and, if the text was noted and sung, his musical literacy as well. He would need some comprehensional literacy in order to read the rubrics and find the appropriate pages and passages. If a priest found his assistant's literacy inadequate, he would have to do some teaching himself, unless a suitable school was close by. Such assistant clergy aspired to vicarages, chaplaincies and rectories of their own, and few could have been as incompetent as the infamous chaplains in the 1222 Salisbury visitation. Somewhere and somehow between first tonsure (preceding ordination to minor orders) and becoming a parish priest, functional competence had been acquired and, especially in areas distant from schools, much of this must have been through apprenticeship.

This practice had many advantages. Working within the existing, geographically dispersed, structures of the church, it reduced the need for central institutions. It provided hands-on learning. A junior cleric might also learn from more than one priest. This cross-fertilisation circulated knowledge socially and institutionally and perhaps helped to create a collective, if heterogeneous, *mentalité* among the secular clergy. This could be guided and informed from above by instructional literature on pastoral care. A cleric of reasonable literacy and learning could mediate the content of these works to other clergy who could not digest or purchase them for themselves. As ideas became accepted and embedded in the common knowledge of the clergy, and through them that of the laity, they became part of the underlying assumptions by which society operated, the Christianising of fundamental customs and habits, which was the great project of the medieval church.

Clerical apprenticeship was not a complete educational system. It could not provide the junior cleric with more knowledge than the

---

[85] *DEC*, 214; *C&S* I, 1064; Cheney, *Innocent III*, 82n.

[86] S. Townley, 'Unbeneficed Clergy in the Thirteenth Century', in D. M. Smith, ed., *Studies in Clergy and Ministry in Medieval England* (York, 1991), 38–64; Mayr-Harting, *Religion*, 268.

[87] Wenzel, 'Deus est', 254.

priest(s) he assisted. Many of the men appointed to vicarages or benefices were not even deacons yet, as bishops' registers testify, and so probably had less experience, especially at the altar. Several options remained for men whose learning was still insufficient after ordination and institution to a benefice. One solution was to hire a private teacher.[88] This might be as simple as engaging a more literate cleric to give remedial lessons: Grosseteste recommended that priests with too little Latin to interpret the Gospel should consult more literate neighbouring priests.[89] Parish clergy could also be granted licences to be absent from their benefices for a period of time to study at a school, so long as they could provide a hired chaplain in their absence.[90] Although this is best known in the form of the 1298 papal constitution *Cum ex eo*, there were long-established precedents.[91]

While some university-educated clerics had their eyes set on climbing the ecclesiastical ladder, which would have taken them away from parochial ministry, we should not assume that all wished to do so.[92] Even if they succeeded, this was not always a loss. The church could not function without a capable bureaucracy, including rural deans, archdeacons' officials, bishops' clerks, and a host of serving priests who could be called away from their parishes from time to time as qualified *ad hoc* deputies.[93] Service as chaplain to a noble household was still the care of souls. Furthermore, many hoping to ascend the career ladder doubtless remained parish clergy for lack of opportunities. Around 1254, Adam Marsh OFM recommended two *magistri* as candidates for institution to Kemsing, Kent, with the clear understanding that he was proposing men who could carry out the care of souls.[94] We cannot imagine that the clergy approved for *Cum ex eo* licences from the dioceses of Bath and Wells, Exeter and Lincoln in the early fourteenth century, at a rate of about twenty per year in each diocese, all secured sinecures.[95] Nor were educated parish clergy confined to the end of the century. Just across the Channel in Poitou, Master Radulphus Ardens ('fiery Ralph'), the author of a wide-ranging and sophisticated *Speculum universale*, wrote up a cycle of sermons that he had preached to his own parishioners in the late twelfth

---

[88] Hoskin, *Grosseteste*, nos. 735–37 (=*Rot. Grosseteste*, 198).
[89] Gieben, 'Grosseteste on Preaching', 112.
[90] *Reg. Cantilupo*, 125; *Reg. Swinfield*, 545; *Reg. Quivil*, 375.
[91] Haines, *Ecclesia Anglicana*, 129–55; Logan, *University Education*.
[92] J. Dunbabin, 'Careers and Vocations', in Catto, ed., *Oxford Schools*, 565–605.
[93] Burger, *Diocesan Governance.*   [94] *LAM*, 562–63.
[95] L. E. Boyle, 'The Constitution *Cum ex eo* of Boniface VIII', *Mediaeval Studies* 24 (1962), 236–302; Logan, *University Education*, 37. In the case of Lincoln, this figure is only the number of clergy licensed for the first time; there were also, on average, a further nine licenses per year given to extend the period of leave for clergy whose licenses were expiring.

century.[96] His contemporary, Fulk de Neuilly, also a serving parish priest, became so frustrated with his own lack of education that he spent each week at the schools in Paris, studying with Peter the Chanter himself, and returned each Sunday to his parish a few miles away to teach and preach what he had learned.[97] We only know about Fulk because his passionate preaching made him famous. Many less charismatic priests may have sought out education in a similar way without attracting the attention of a Jacques de Vitry to record them for posterity: in fact, after naming famous preachers who picked up where Fulk left off, Jacques added that there were many others.[98] Around 1207, the Parisian theologian Robert Courçon wrote that the parish priests were hammering at the gates of (academic) theology, demanding solid food.[99] Perhaps this was not groundless rhetoric.

Not every rector, vicar and chaplain had the resources or opportunity to attend a university or hire a private master. There were three situations where he might have free access to teaching: cathedral schools, houses of friars and the teaching at archidiaconal lectures. The first two were more accessible to those who lived near such an establishment, while the third would be routine and compulsory. The Third and Fourth Lateran Councils (1179 and 1215) ordered that each cathedral or great church should support a master to offer free teaching. The chancellorship of English secular cathedrals had grown out of the office of *archischola* or *magister scholarum*, generally in the twelfth century. Edwards has offered substantial evidence of intellectual life and pedagogy at most English secular cathedrals before and throughout the thirteenth century.[100] At the beginning of the century, for instance, Lincoln had its chancellor William de Montibus and Salisbury had its subdean Thomas of Chobham, both of whom taught practical theology to parish clergy.[101] Some other great churches supported schools (such as Bury St Edmunds and Northampton), growing to several dozen by the end of the century, though not all were free of charge.[102] Parish clergy were welcome to attend the in-house theology lectures in friars' convents, though these were given in Latin and probably over the heads of those parish clergy who needed them the most.[103] Of greater consequence, however, was that parish clergy could attend the vernacular sermons of friars just as easily as the laity could, learning

[96] C. P. Evans, ed. and trans., *Radulphus Ardens: The Questions on the Sacraments* (Toronto, 2010), 5.
[97] Hinnebusch, ed., *Occidentalis*, 95–101.   [98] Ibid., 102–3.
[99] Boyle, 'Inter-Conciliar Period', 47.   [100] Edwards, *Secular Cathedrals*, 177–205.
[101] *DEC*, 220, 240; Goering, *William de Montibus*; F. Morenzoni, *Des Écoles aux Paroisses* (Paris, 1995).
[102] Butler, *Jocelin of Brakelond*, 95.
[103] Mulchahey, *First the Bow*, 50–51; Roest, *Franciscan Education*, 7n, 284, 327; Şenocak, *Poor and the Perfect*, 237–42.

homiletic technique alongside theological content. In the dioceses of Salisbury, Canterbury, Lincoln, Worcester, Durham, Chichester and York, the archdeacons or rural deans seem to have had an established teaching role by mid-century. At York, the statutes were to be expounded in each rural deanery every time it had its local chapter meeting; at Salisbury, Durham and Canterbury, the archdeacons were to lecture at their annual archdeaconry chapters on the creedal statement of Lateran IV.[104] In 1237, the papal legate Cardinal Otto ordered the archdeacons of both provinces zealously to teach the parish clergy about the sacraments in rural deanery chapters.[105] Since all rectors, vicars and chaplains were generally expected to attend these meetings, the lectures would have been an excellent vehicle for broad dissemination of knowledge and instruction for clerical behaviour and pastoral care, though, if they were given in unglossed Latin, those most in need of instruction would have been left behind. In the prologue of his *Gemma Ecclesiastica*, Gerald of Wales, archdeacon of Brecon, wrote to his parish clergy that, since he was absent from them, he was setting down in writing the important information about which they were wont to question him when he was present. Despite the fact that Gerald probably intended this claim to impress Innocent III (whom he would soon be petitioning to create him the first archbishop of Wales), this suggests that parish clergy could receive informal education from their overseers.[106] Writing in mid-century, Adam Marsh, the brother of one archdeacon and a correspondent of many, assumed that teaching the parish clergy was part of the archidiaconal office.[107]

Once a cleric was sufficiently literate, a growing literature was available to instruct him in the care of souls: *pastoralia*. While Boyle considered these to have been rare before 1200, Stansbury notes that sermon and homily collections in Latin and the vernaculars had been circulating in England for centuries and the priest could learn from them as he taught.[108] Much the same could be said of liturgical books. To judge from surviving manuscripts, the most ubiquitous *pastoralia* among thirteenth-century parish priests, after liturgical books, were synodal statutes, rules laid down by bishops for the running of their dioceses and (in theory) put into the hands of every rector, vicar and chaplain in the diocese. One set of parish visitation records from 1297, mostly from London Diocese, showed churches holding various combinations of four different pieces of diocesan and provincial legislation: at least in this area, the

[104] *C&S* II, 61, 496.   [105] *C&S* II, 246–47.   [106] Gerald, *Opera* II, 5–6; Bartlett, *Gerald.*
[107] *LAM*, 194–95; W. E. Black, 'The Medieval Archdeacon in Canon Law' (unpubl. PhD thesis, University of Toronto, 2008), 188–89.
[108] R. Stansbury, 'Preaching and Pastoral Care in the Middle Ages', in Stansbury, *Companion to Pastoral Care*, 23–39.

information in local legislation was reaching the practising clergy.[109] These texts distilled what the bishop considered the most salient points of canon law and theology and passed them on in a practical and accessible form. Since a considerable part of a parish priest's duties lay in the administration of the sacraments, instructions and theology regarding them usually constituted a bishop's foremost concern. The most difficult of sacraments was penance, both an art and a science, and some bishops took to appending tracts on the subject to their statutes. When Bishop Walter Cantilupe of Worcester did so in 1240, he added strong inducement. At archidiaconal chapters, parish clergy would be called upon without warning to read aloud his statutes and tract on penance and the archdeacon would explain any difficulties. If a cleric's literacy were insufficient, it would be found out at once. If he did not arrive with both a copy of the documents and a satisfactory knowledge of their contents, he was subject to the hefty fine of half a mark – 10 per cent of the minimum annual stipend for vicars.[110] Getting their information into the hands and heads of the pastors was clearly important to many bishops and commentary on their constitutions probably formed the meat of many archidiaconal lectures.

A broad range of other *pastoralia* was composed and circulated. Some were short, simple tracts on such subjects as the mass or the seven sins. A step higher were longer treatments of aspects of pastoral care, such as Cantilupe's tract on penance or some of Grosseteste's penitential handbooks. These demanded greater literacy of the reader, but Grosseteste and Cantilupe believed that at least some parish clergy could understand them. Other works were more challenging still. One was a *summa* on penance by Thomas of Chobham, subdean of Salisbury Cathedral and sometime student of Peter the Chanter at Paris. Running to 572 pages in the modern printed edition, this work examines hundreds of potential cases of moral theology in order to aid the priest in hearing lay confessions. A legal text on penance produced at the same time, Robert of Flamborough's *Liber Poenitentialis*, was shorter but in the same league.[111] Very few parish priests could even afford copies of these works, much less digest them. These were at the high end of the spectrum of works that aimed to benefit pastors directly and were probably of greater use to diocesan penitentiaries and archdeacons than to parish clergy but, through their teaching office, higher clergy could communicate the salient points to

---

[109] Sparrow-Simpson, *1297 Visitations*. Copies owned personally by the clergy would not have been noted, so visitation records are likely to under-report the presence of synodal statutes.
[110] *C&S* II, 321.
[111] Thomas of Chobham, *Summa Confessorum*; Robert of Flamborough, *Liber*.

parochial clergy. Some parish clergy were qualified to digest the more challenging works themselves, if we may take the title *magister* as a reasonable proxy for such ability. As we shall see in Chapter 10, there was a profusion of university graduates in Oxford-area churches, not only holding benefices but apparently serving them in person. *Pastoralia* were increasingly available at all levels throughout the thirteenth century, enabling any literate priest to advance his education further, to the limits of his motivation, opportunity and mental ability.

Perhaps the greatest teacher was experience. While experience might not teach much doctrine, it must have taught most of what parish clergy knew about hearing a confession, celebrating the sacraments and putting together a homily that would suit the needs and the attention spans of his congregation. The ability to give practical and spiritual direction on such topics as prayer, fasting, abstinence, sobriety, forgiveness, devotion and the choosing of the cardinal virtues over the deadly sins may have depended as much on practice as on books. While many books and tracts could give inspiration and wise guidance to clergy – and some of these would be translated into the vernacular for lay use in the next two centuries – they could only be aids to practice.

Each cleric was also expected make his confession several times per year to a penitentiary, a priest appointed by the bishop for that purpose.[112] As with the laity, confession served both educative and formative functions. As specialists in hearing clerical confessions, the penitentiaries would have been men educated in the aspects of canon law and theology that were particularly applicable to hearing the confessions of the clergy. In some dioceses, the same penitentiaries were charged with hearing lay penitential cases that belonged to the bishop's jurisdiction. In their necessary education, the penitentiaries would have learned of other developments in doctrine and canon law relevant to the sacrament of penance, passing these along to clerical penitents. The lessons of tomes too erudite or unwieldy for use by parish clergy would be taught in this applied form, demonstrating how to hear the confessions of the laity. As confessors' manuals in the twelfth and thirteenth centuries paid increasingly explicit attention to inward intentions, the cleric may have faced progressively more pointed questions of motive, not only calling for him to search his own conscience but also showing him how to search the consciences of others. When a cleric confessed to thoughts, words and deeds that elicited disciplinary action, he might have the bodily experience of blushing or some other reaction due to shame and reticence while confessing, and would undergo the bodily experience of undertaking the

---

[112] E.g. *C&S* II, 75; Haines, *Ecclesia Anglicana*, 39–52.

penance assigned; this discipline of obedience could result in a psycho-somatic aversion to repeating his error, the sum of which was expected to constitute character formation.[113]

The importance ascribed to the character formation of pastors by lead-ing churchmen can be seen in Richard Poore's admonition that the spir-itual health of the laity is dependent upon *conversatione sacerdotum* (the words and deeds of priests) who can lead people into sin just as well as out of it.[114] The theme of preaching by both word of mouth and example of life appears in such varied places as Thomas of Chobham's *Summa de arte praedicandi* of the 1220s, Friar John of Wales' *Communiloquium* of some fifty years later and a university sermon preached at Oxford in the 1290s; Chobham even argued that it was better for a priest to live well and not preach at all than to preach well and live badly.[115] Adam Marsh advised Grosseteste against instituting a presentee to an parish benefice, despite Marsh's assertion that he was a scholar of good morals and a personal friend of his, as he was 'presented without due consideration ... [and] in no way adequate' to this particular task.[116] The presentee in question was none other than Oliver Sutton, who would later become dean and then bishop of Lincoln. Marsh did not elucidate Sutton's shortcomings, though he referred to his youth, but Marsh's concern that the parish-ioners' salvation was at stake – and, therefore, so was Sutton's – accentuates the importance of intangible qualifications.

Marsh's letter to Grosseteste also illustrates the other side of the equa-tion: if the aspiring cleric was responsible for acquiring the necessary education, the bishops and archdeacons were charged with finding out which candidates had met that challenge. Lateran IV required bishops to ensure that candidates for ordination were capable of celebrating rites and sacraments. Any man being ordained for, or instituted to, parish min-istry was to be examined by the bishop, an archdeacon or some other official at each step.[117] Full examination covered legitimate birth (or dis-pensation for illegitimacy), sufficient age and maturity, moral character and education.[118] Both Gerald of Wales, around 1218, and a diocesan statute of the early 1220s noted that men rejected by English bishops sometimes sought orders from Irish, Scottish and Welsh bishops who

[113] Thomas of Chobham, *Summa Confessorum*. As subdean of Salisbury, Thomas was also the bishop's penitentiary. See further in Chapter 7 below.
[114] *C&S* II, 62–63.
[115] Thomas of Chobham, *Summa de Arte*, 24–27; John of Wales OFM, *Communiloquium* 4.4.4–5 (British Library, Harley MS. 632); Worcester Cathedral Library, MS. Q.46, ff. 171v–173r.
[116] *LAM*, 34–37.   [117] *C&S* I, 423–27; *C&S* II, 246–47.
[118] *C&S* II, 147; Dohar, '*Sufficienter litteratus*'; L. Boyle, 'Aspects of Clerical Education in Fourteenth-Century England', in Boyle, *Pastoral Care*, IX.

often ordained without sufficient examination: this suggests that examination was already commonplace in England at this date.[119] There were many potential examinations to pass before beginning full parish ministry – the ordinations of first tonsure, acolyte, subdeacon, deacon and priest, at the receipt of a benefice and perhaps during a visitation of the parish or an archidiaconal or ruridecanal chapter – and these narrowed the gaps through which unsuitable candidates could slip. The register of John Pecham, archbishop of Canterbury, indicates examination before ordination.[120] In 1296, Bishop Sutton of Lincoln gave dispensation to a priest to serve despite having been ordained by another bishop without Sutton's permission but allowed him to say only three particular masses for the next year; he was ordered in the meantime to study grammar, the canon of the mass 'and other things that pertain to your duty' and to return to be examined on them at the year's end.[121]

Lateran IV did not require it, but English bishops also examined men presented to benefices before instituting them. The bishops of Lincoln and Salisbury rejected clergy presented to benefices in the later 1210s for insufficient literacy, the earliest known cases in England of effective episcopal vetoes of a patron's presentee. This suggests that some standard existed and that most other presentees met it. The Council of Oxford (1222) added that priests should also have a sound understanding of the words of the canon of the mass and of baptism and that they should be able to teach the latter to the laity in the vernacular.[122] At Lincoln, Grosseteste's register only mentions examination at institution when a deficiency was discovered, which suggests that most entries reflect satisfactory candidates; and Adam Marsh OFM, whose condemnations of the parish clergy were as shrill as any in England in his day, commended Grosseteste's examinations for their strictness.[123] Sometimes a cleric who failed would be allowed to re-sit his examination, as in the cases of two men instituted by Grosseteste each with the proviso 'let him come at the feast of St Michael to be thoroughly examined regarding the Ten Commandments, the seven sacraments and the seven sins with circumstances'.[124] This was exceptional but the occasional recalling of candidates for further examination, because of the study it motivated, possibly transformed

[119] Gerald, *Opera* III, 368; Bartlett, *Gerald*, 219; *C&S* II, 147.   [120] *Reg. Pecham*, 184.
[121] *Reg. Sutton* V, 184; Lincolnshire Archive Office, Episcopal Register I, f. 149r–v.
[122] *DEC*, 248 (cf. Gratian, *Decretum*, PL CLXXXVII, 207–12); *Rot. Hugonis* I, 101 (ca. 1217 × 1218); *Curia Regis Rolls of the Reign of Henry III*, vol. 8 (London, 1938), 185, 282; ibid. vol. 9 (London, 1952), 196–98; Cheney, *Becket to Langton*, 136–39; *C&S* II, 115.
[123] *LAM*, 104–9.
[124] Hoskin, *Grosseteste*, no. 1438 (=*Rot. Grosseteste*, 416–17). For a case in which examination caught an unworthy priest, see *LAM*, 54–55, 62–73.

some of the less qualified candidates into some of the better-qualified priests. The duty of sifting out unsuitable candidates before institution was delegated to archdeacons in many dioceses.[125] In 1287, the bishop of Exeter ordered his archdeacons to search out clergy whose literacy was defective – even those already instituted to benefices – and denounce them to him.[126]

Until the 1220s, the only ecclesiastical competitors the parish clergy had for prestige were nuns, monks, canons and the occasional hermit or anchoress.[127] Medieval society fitted the pattern that Hofstede described as a 'high power distance culture', one in which the powerful are made conspicuous by visible cues.[128] One of the aims of the Gregorian Reform and its outworking over the following centuries was to increase the perceived distance between priest and layman, and diocesan statutes show the bishops' concern for parish clergy to demarcate themselves from the laity in a variety of ways.[129] Voluntary poverty was not one of them. The arrival of the friars, with their higher education, more anonymous and more nuanced confessions, and more austere manner of life, can only have challenged the parish priests' prestige, potentially disrupting the pastoral duties that depended on the community's respect.[130] For, while friars were materially poor and thus did not display power by conspicuous consumption as a lord or rector might, by the fact that their poverty was voluntary they could lay claim to another recognised type of power: ascetic sanctity. In any competition between the parish clergy and the friars, we find them both acknowledging the necessity of prestige for the pastoral mission and competing before the audience of the laity using two very different models of sacred authority. In high power distance cultures, the inferior party may seek to close the distance between himself and his superior by imitation and the friars often repeated ecclesiastical tropes of preaching by setting a good example, thereby indicating a hope to be imitated. Social order depended upon conformity, especially to the 'master values' of local life.[131] The church, no less than lay elites, clearly identified and promoted its master values and much of pastoral care was aimed at encouraging conformity to them. But conformity to *which* norm? Quite apart from the verbal content of their sermons and confessions, friars were setting a different example. By visibly modelling monastic asceticism while circulating through the world, they were inviting laypeople to emulate asceticism in a way that more cloistered orders would have found difficult to

---

[125] *C&S* II, 313, 429–30, 487, 608–9, 1017–18.   [126] *C&S* II, 1017.   [127] License, *Hermits*, 150–58.
[128] G. H. Hofstede, *Culture's Consequences* (2nd edn, London, 2001); Shaw, *Necessary Conjunctions*, 36–44.
[129] Thomas, *Secular Clergy*, 17–36.   [130] Goering, 'Popularization', 103–4, 110–12.
[131] Shaw, *Necessary Conjunctions*, 48–49.

copy. The parish clergy and the friars, then, offered the laity not just a choice of preachers and confessors but also a choice of models of the pursuit of sanctity to which they might aspire.

At no time, however, were friars evenly distributed across England. Their convents were urban or suburban and, as they moved in and took root, their settlement followed patterns that have not hitherto been explored. This, too, was a factor in the geography of pastoral care. By 1300, a town such as Oxford or London, home to friaries since the 1220s, had experienced generations of constant exposure to mendicant life and pastoral care, while mendicant convents were still recent arrivals in other towns. To assess pastoral care in actual contexts, we shall need to consider the geography and chronology of mendicant settlements.

The Coming of the Friars

Map 2 The Houses of Friars in England and Wales, 1300.
Sources: Ordnance Survey, *Map of Monastic Britain North Sheet* and *Map of Monastic Britain South Sheet*; B. P. Hindle, *Medieval Roads and Tracks* (Oxford, 2016); O'Carroll, *Grosseteste*, 324–25; *MRH*, 212–50; Egan, 'Carmelite Houses'.

Chapter 3

THE COMING OF THE FRIARS

The English parochial system, though paralleled elsewhere, arose and evolved in an English context. The friars arose in the Mediterranean world, spread to England and developed different accommodations to English culture. There were, for example, none of the lay confraternities that grew up around the friars in southern Europe. The profit economy of Italy against which Francis reacted, and the heresies against which Dominic preached, were not prominent features of English society.[1] Like the religious orders that had come to England in the previous century, however, the friars quickly became naturalised parts of the social and religious landscape. They also constituted centralised networks of communication that connected the papacy and Paris to the pastorate and parish, networks that were largely independent of the existing structures of the secular church.[2]

The mendicant orders originated independently of one another and for different reasons but each order was also embedded in the religious movements sweeping Latin Christendom in the twelfth and thirteenth centuries. The similarities between the orders are marked, since both sought to follow the new concepts of *vita apostolica*, imitation of the life of the Apostles.[3] Both orders were committed to seeking support through begging rather than endowments; both lived in convents but circulated among the common people more readily than monks did, where they aimed to teach by setting a visible example. They became more similar as time went on: the Dominicans were probably prompted to higher standards of ascetic poverty by the Franciscans, while the Franciscans quickly evolved from a lay movement into an educated clerical order like the Dominicans.[4]

---

[1] Brentano, *Two Churches*.   [2] D'Avray, *Preaching*.
[3] Little, *Religious Poverty*; Rivi, *Francis*; Brooke, *Coming of the Friars*, 40–90; Vicaire, *Dominic*, 199–200.
[4] Şenocak, *Poor and the Perfect*, denies that the Franciscans simply copied the Dominican education system.

Dominic Guzman founded his order primarily to stem the tide of heresy but preaching to orthodox Catholics was also part of the Dominians' mission from the start.[5] Best known as Dominicans or as Blackfriars, from their black habits, they took the title of *Ordo fratrum praedicatorum*, Order of Friars Preachers (abbreviated OP). The mission of preaching and teaching required the Dominicans to be a priestly order.[6] Moorman assumed that the Dominicans faced a crisis in England because of the lack of organised heresy there but neither evidence nor reason supports this conclusion.[7] Even among English clergy and laypeople, medieval 'popular religion' accommodated heterodoxy.[8] Nor were Dominicans concerned only with mistaken belief. A major target of their preaching was *accidia*, spiritual sloth or lethargy. Combating this capital vice required more than catechesis: it called for moral exhortation.

Tugwell concluded that 'in the thirteenth century ... one is hard-pressed to find any [Dominican] spiritual books at all, let alone "spiritual classics"'.[9] However, this may be because the modern semantic field of 'spiritual classic' is too narrowly based on monastic spirituality, in which *lectio*, reading of scripture and other Christian texts, led to *ruminatio*, literally 'chewing-over' the text, and finally *contemplatio*, contemplation. This had been reformulated by Peter the Chanter: *lectio* led to *disputatio*, schoolroom argumentation, a communal sort of rumination, which led in turn to *praedicatio*, preaching.[10] The result was not the introspection one normally associates with 'spiritual' writings but an outwardly directed spirituality aimed at public rather than private enlightenment. The early Dominicans adopted such a missionary spirituality, and this new triad of spiritual exercises would remain central to their vocation.[11]

By contrast, Francis of Assisi did not set out to found a religious order.[12] Yet, once new brothers found him, he was careful to seek approval from Innocent III.[13] He emphasised humility by adopting the official name *Ordo fratrum minorum*, Order of Friars Minor (Minorites or OFM). Their habits were grey or brown, leading to the nickname Greyfriars. Where the Friars Minor proved most successful was in adopting, popularising and directing existing trends in popular devotion.[14] Most of these, such as the preaching of repentance, the Apostolic Life, emphasis on the earthly life

[5] Vicaire, *Dominic*, 80–114, 164–72; Brooke, *Coming of the Friars*, 94.
[6] *EEFP*, 333–37.   [7] Moorman, *Church Life*, 398.
[8] Biller, 'Intellectuals'; L. Smoller, '"Popular" Religious Culture(s)', in Arnold, *Medieval Christianity*, 340–56; and D. Weltecke, 'Doubts and the Absence of Faith', in ibid., 357–74.
[9] Tugwell, *Early Dominicans*, 1.   [10] *Verbum Adbreviatum*, 9.
[11] *EEFP*, 279, 332; Tugwell, 'Second Distinction', 128–31; Vicaire, *Dominic*, 178, 197.
[12] Little, *Religious Poverty*, 146; Moorman, *Franciscan Order*, 1–9; M. Robson, *The Franciscans in the Middle Ages* (Woodbridge, 2006), 10–21.
[13] Moorman, *Franciscan Order*, 15–19.   [14] Brooke, *Coming of the Friars*, 38, 48–88; Rivi, *Francis*, v.

and death of Jesus and Mary and the imitation of Christ, were important features of the religious landscape of the day shared by the Dominicans and others.[15] To focus too much on Francis himself and his intentions would be to miss the point. English recruits to the Order spoke in terms not of the imitation of Francis but rather of the imitation of Christ manifested in obedience to the Rule and the Order.[16]

Keeping this in mind helps to solve what would otherwise be a significant puzzle: it is extremely rare to find any traces of differences between the Franciscan and Dominican orders reflected in their thirteenth-century *pastoralia*.[17] The distinctions between the orders that attract the most scholarly attention are in high theology and philosophy, or over niceties of what constituted true evangelical poverty.[18] Laypeople receiving pastoral care from friars probably knew little and cared less about such matters. We seldom see laypeople exhibiting preferences among mendicant orders. The wills of laity and sympathetic secular clergy, perhaps our closest approximation, often show equal bequests to both orders and even to the later Carmelite and Austin orders (introduced below), which suggests equal esteem.[19]

THE COMING OF THE FRANCISCANS AND DOMINICANS TO ENGLAND

The General Chapter of the Dominican order of 1221 dispatched thirteen brethren – one over the minimum number for a canonical community – to England. They arrived in early August, probably on the fifth, the day before Dominic's death.[20] Writing early in the fourteenth century, the English Dominican Nicholas Trivet reported that bishop Peter des Roches of Winchester accompanied them to Canterbury and presented them to Archbishop Langton. Hearing that they were called preachers,

---

[15] K. Emery and J. Wawrykow, eds, *Christ among the Medieval Dominicans* (Notre Dame, IN, 1998).

[16] A. Power, 'The Problem of Obedience among the English Franciscans', in M. Breitenstein et al., eds, *Rules and Observance: Devising Forms of Common Life* (Berlin, 2014), 129–67.

[17] David d'Avray notes that he has never seen any difference between Franciscan and Dominican sermon texts (personal correspondence and conversation, Dec. 2006–Jan. 2007). Without additional evidence, it is often impossible to determine even whether the sermon was written by a friar at all.

[18] Little, *Studies*; Lawrence, *The Friars*.

[19] Some testators gave the Carmelite and Austin friars (discussed below) the same amounts as those bequeathed to the Franciscans and Dominicans. J. Raine, ed., *Wills and Inventories ... of the Northern Counties of England* (Surtees Soc., no. 2: London, 1835), 6–25. In 1283, Christiana de Bennington left a larger sum to Lincoln's Franciscans than to the Dominicans, Carmelites and Austins but specified that it was for the use of the Franciscan Geoffrey Samson, whom we may infer was her confessor: C. W. Foster, ed., *Lincoln Wills, vol. I: 1271–1526* (Lincoln, 1914), 2.

[20] *EEFP*, 2.

Langton directed their leader, Gilbert of Fresney, to preach in his stead in a church that very day. Finding himself so edified by Gilbert's sermon, Trivet modestly tells us, the archbishop retained his approval for their order throughout his life. The Dominicans passed from Canterbury via London to Oxford, reaching it on 15 August. There they had copious success in attracting learned men and promising adolescents into their order, enough to found a house in London by 1224 followed by ones at Norwich in 1226 and York in 1227.[21]

An earlier and more detailed account describes the arrival of the Minorites, the *De adventu fratrum minorum in Anglie* of Thomas 'of Eccleston', completed ca. 1258–59.[22] While he is sparing with dates, other sources have enabled historians to construct a temporal framework for much of Thomas' narrative, which A. G. Little judged to be accurate and trustworthy.[23] Franciscans first arrived in Britain at Dover on 10 September 1224 under the leadership of Agnellus of Pisa.[24] They were only nine in number, four clerics and five laymen. Three of the clerics, including the only priest, were English; none of the lay brothers was. Like the Dominicans, they went directly to Canterbury, probably to seek official approval.[25] Not constrained by a minimum community size, the group split: four (including two English clerics) set off for London, while the others settled in a local priests' hospice, which would continue to house the Canterbury Minorites until 1268.[26] The friars who arrived in London stayed with the Dominicans for fifteen days until they acquired their own lodgings.[27] Before the year was out, the two English clerical friars set off for Oxford, where again the Dominicans hosted them until they found lodgings; presumably this reflected successful recruitment in London.[28] The Franciscans had thus established themselves in the ecclesiastical, governmental and intellectual centres of the kingdom within four months.[29]

The first settlement patterns reflect fundamental differences between the orders, especially in the early years. The Dominicans needed twelve brothers to establish a convent.[30] Although they travelled in pairs in their apostolic activity, they also maintained the common life of canons regular and so preferred larger convents.[31] Early Franciscans had no such intentions of stability or canonical observance and tended to break off into

---

[21] Trivet, *Annales*, 209; *EEFP*, 365, 442. For the most up-to-date data on Dominican house foundations, see O'Carroll, *Studies*, 59.
[22] *De Adventu*, xxii.   [23] Ibid., xxv.   [24] Ibid., 3.
[25] Ibid., 3–6; *C&S* II, 33–34. Langton's whereabouts in September are unknown. Major, *Acta*, 167.
[26] *MRH*, 224; C. Cotton, *The Grey Friars of Canterbury* (Manchester, 1924).
[27] Kingsford, *Friars of London*, 15; *De Adventu*, 9.   [28] *De Adventu*, 9, 12–18.
[29] D. Jeffrey, *The Early English Lyric and Franciscan Spirituality* (Lincoln, NB, 1975), 169.
[30] Denifle, 'Constitutiones', 221.   [31] *EEFP*, 275.

small groups. Although this practice later changed, it allowed for rapid dissemination of Franciscans in these early years. However, at least some of this may be an illusion.[32] Three Dominicans were sent to London in 1221.[33] The foundation date of 1224 for that house thus reflects the point at which the number of friars reached a dozen and the General Chapter was able to grant official recognition. Continental evidence, too, shows Dominicans as pastorally active in a locality for some time before the official foundation of a convent.[34] Eccleston's and Trivet's reporting may have respectively revealed and obscured this pattern in England. Nonetheless, after 1220 an established convent was probably reluctant to drop its numbers below twelve to send friars out to found another house. If three Dominicans were sent to London in 1221, the Oxford convent was already experiencing success in recruitment. This chapter of the Dominican constitutions requiring a convent to have twelve brothers and a lector would have a crucial damping effect on the multiplication of Dominican houses.[35] By 1235, when the Franciscans founded their twenty-fourth convent, the Dominicans only had ten.[36] The greater distribution of Franciscan influence even at the end of the century can be seen by mapping the location of the priories of the four main mendicant orders, which shows not only that the Franciscans had more convents – and therefore, by one estimate, 2,420 brothers in England in 1300 as opposed to 1,887 Preachers[37] – but also that there was not a single town in England in 1300 with two or more friaries of the four main mendicant orders where one of those was not Franciscan. The same difference in growth rates can be seen in France and Hungary, probably for the same reasons.[38]

Plotting the spread of convents on a map reveals a further difference in settlement patterns: from the start, the Franciscans tended to keep their

[32] K. J. Egan, 'Dating English Carmelite Foundations', P. Fitzgerald-Lombard, ed., *Carmel in Britain, Volume I: Essays on the Medieval English Carmelite Province* (Rome, 1992), 120–42.

[33] *MRH*, 217.

[34] Vicaire, *Dominic*, 187 *et seqq.*, *passim*. In the same year, only five brethren were dispatched to Hungary. Vicaire even doubted Trivet's claim that thirteen were sent to Oxford on the grounds that the minimum number of twelve was a later addition to the constitutions (526). Tugwell, however, has since dated the relevant section of the constitutions (Dist. II c. 23a) to 1220 and argues that the wording of Jordan of Saxony's contemporary report of the 1221 General Chapter makes clear reference to the group sent to England as a 'convent' in keeping with the constitutions as they then stood: Tugwell, 'Second Distinction', 112–16.

[35] Tugwell dates this as well to 1220: 'Second Distinction', 112–16.

[36] O'Carroll, *Grosseteste*, 324–25.

[37] Moorman, *Church Life*, 411. Hinnebusch estimated that in the first quarter of the fourteenth century, there were on average 1,795 Dominicans in England (*EEFP*, 274–75), while Little calculated an average of 1,900 Franciscans in the period 1289–1339: Little, *Studies*, 69–71.

[38] R. W. Emery, *The Friars in Medieval France* (London, 1962), 3; E. Fugedi, 'La formation des villes et les ordres mendiants en Hongrie', *Annales É. S. C.* 25 (1970), 966–73; Lawrence, *The Friars*, 103–4.

houses close to one another, while the Dominicans dispersed themselves widely.[39] The first six Franciscan convents, settled in 1224–26, were a horseshoe curve: Canterbury, London and Oxford (1224), Northampton (1225), and Cambridge and Norwich (1226). The furthest distance between any two in the chain, as the crow flies, was fifty-eight miles between Cambridge and Norwich but these were both close to the Icknield Way (the Greenway), facilitating travel between them. In 1233 a convent settlement was attempted at Bury, which would have provided a convenient way-station roughly halfway in between but the opposition of the monks there prevented a stable settlement for thirty years.[40] London and Canterbury were likewise connected directly by Watling Street, part of the Roman road network. This ring was followed by a cluster further west, Worcester, Hereford, Bristol and Gloucester (1227–34), which were joined by another arc (Coventry, Leicester, Stamford, King's Lynn) to Norwich by about 1230, none above forty miles from another and most rather closer. By 1232 this outer orbit also included Salisbury and Chichester, bringing to six the number of cathedral cities settled by the Franciscans.[41] The Franciscans then aimed north. Around 1230 they settled at Lincoln and York, pressing further north in the next three years to Carlisle, Roxburgh and Berwick-upon-Tweed. All of these were along the Roman Ermine Street (except Berwick, downstream of Roxburgh by the Teviot and the Tweed). These were joined by a settlement at Durham around 1239 which decamped to Hartlepool in 1240.[42] The two concentric rings and the northern arm are so orderly as to suggest deliberate planning. Settlement in the decade 1235–45 again follows a pattern. Until 1234, Franciscan convents were almost invariably settled inland. Over the following decade, Franciscans settled at Ipswich and Colchester on the east coast (by 1237), towns on or near the south coast were settled from Romney to Exeter, and five convents were established on the north-east coast from Boston up to Haddington, east of Edinburgh. Meanwhile, a strung-out cluster of houses cut diagonally across the earlier concentric arcs, running from Ipswich and Colchester to coastal Llanfaes, the first Franciscan house in Wales (1245).

There was an apparent hiatus in Franciscan settlement from 1245 to around 1257 or 1258, when Richmond was settled. It is possible that

[39] For dates of the foundation of Franciscan and Dominican houses, see O'Carroll, *Grosseteste*, 324–25 for the most recent data, and *MRH*, 212–50 for greater detail. At least twenty of the Franciscan convents' dates (but none of the Dominican ones) reflect first mention of a convent, which may be older.
[40] *MRH*, 224; *Annales Monastici* III, 134; Little, *Papers*, 219.
[41] *MRH*, 224, improves on Little's date of 'by 1243' copied by O'Carroll, *Grosseteste*, 324–25.
[42] *MRH*, 221, 225. Berwick is omitted from *MRH* because it was in Scotland: see Little, *Franciscan Papers*, 221.

the Minorites, carried on by momentum, had overreached their numbers: some dozen houses had been settled in 1240 to 1245 alone. This is also the period when the order tightened its admission standards, which shrank the number of recruits dramatically. However, there may not have been so much of a chronological gap. Friar Thomas recorded that in 1256 there were forty-four convents in the English province totalling 1,242 Friars Minor.[43] If Thomas' figure was accurate, then forty-four Franciscan convents had been settled in thirty-two-year period from 1224 to 1256 but only eleven more would follow in the forty-four years from 1256 to 1300.[44] The list of later, or possibly later, settlements shows expansion in densely populated areas: up to five in East Anglia; settlements along roads between other convents (Dorchester, Doncaster, Richmond); and new convents in more remote areas (Bodmin in Cornwall, Cardiff and Carmarthen in Wales, Preston in West Yorkshire, Dumfries and Dundee in Scotland).[45] By 1256, and possibly by 1245, Britain was already approaching the saturation point for Franciscan settlements. However, if Moorman's estimate of 2,420 Franciscans in England and Wales around 1300 is accurate, the order would nearly double in membership between 1256 and the end of the century; even Little's more conservative estimate of 1,900 shows a 61 per cent increase in manpower distributed over a 25 per cent increase in the number of convents.[46] The average population of Franciscan convents was on the rise.

The English Dominicans' settlement pattern, rather than the close networks established by the early Franciscans, aimed at diffusing their presence more widely. Both orders settled in remote Carlisle in 1233 but, if we compare the sequences of convent foundation rather than the years, it was the Dominicans' eighth or ninth house and about the twentieth for the Franciscans. Exeter was settled in 1232 by the Dominicans, their sixth or seventh convent; as we have seen, the Franciscans did not get so far southwest until perhaps as late as 1240, when they already had around thirty other houses, mostly clustered in the Midlands. Although both orders settled Norwich in 1226, the Franciscans' nearest neighbour then, as noted, was Cambridge, 58 miles west; the nearest Dominican priory was London, 100 miles as the crow flies, around 125 miles by major roads. The

43 O'Carroll, *Grosseteste*, 324–25; Little, *Papers*, 217–29; *De Adventu*, 11. Little suggested Bodmin, Boston, Dorchester, Preston and Yarmouth, but these are conjectural (*De Adventu*, 111). One manuscript gives forty-nine, not forty-four.
44 Moving the foundation near Bury from 1233 to after 1256 and subtracting Romney, which failed ca. 1287: *MRH*, 226.
45 For Scottish houses north of the Forth, see W. M. Bryce, *The Scottish Grey Friars*, vol. I (Edinburgh, 1909), 199, 219.
46 Moorman, *Church Life*, 411; Little's figure was an average for the period 1289–1339: Little, *Studies*, 69–71.

closest pair of Dominican priories founded before 1234 were Oxford and Northampton, only around thirty-five miles apart, but Oxford was the first house founded in this period and Northampton either the penultimate or the last, and Northampton was already a seat of learning where the Dominicans could both study and recruit.

As with the Franciscans, the Dominicans' initial settlement pattern suggests planning, but a very different plan. Having already spread out around the country, the Dominicans from 1235 to 1245 mostly filled gaps in the settlement pattern, again aiming at greater distances between houses than seen on the Franciscan map. With fewer houses being founded in that decade (twelve Dominican convents as opposed to around twenty Franciscan ones) in the same area of land, the average distance is greater as a matter of mathematical necessity; nonetheless, it is as if Dominican settlements were determined by consciously searching out a void on a map and placing a priory as far as possible from all neighbouring priories. Much the same could be said of the foundations from 1246 to 1260 including three further priories in Wales (Cardiff having been settled in 1242) and one at Truro in Cornwall. During this latter period the Dominicans surpassed the Franciscans in the rate of multiplication of convents, settling in twelve towns as compared to about six.

The years from 1260 to that of the last Dominican settlement of the century – Boston, 1288 – show dispersal (Lancaster, Yarm, Brecon) but also some much closer foundations: Chichester (1278)[47] is not ten miles from Arundel, Ipswich (1263) is eighteen miles from Sudbury, and Yarmouth (1267) the same from Norwich. Dominicans had already settled in almost all parts of the country; now they turned to the remaining towns that could support them and provide sermon audiences. With this progression of increasingly close settlement, the hinterlands of Dominican convents shrank and the potential for coverage of the countryside within each hinterland became denser.

THE SMALLER ORDERS

The Franciscans and Dominicans had been in the British Isles for some twenty years before they were joined by two orders of hermits, the Order of Hermits of St Augustine (Austins, OESA)[48] and the Order of Hermits of Mount Carmel (Whitefriars, OCarm). Over the ensuing years, both of

---

[47] Misprinted in O'Carroll, *Grosseteste*, as 1288, which would put it out of chronological order. *MRH*, 214 gives *ante* 1280.

[48] Throughout this book, Augustinian Canons (OSA) are referred to as 'Augustinians', while members of the eremitical/mendicant order (OESA) are called 'Austins'. These terms are technically interchangeable, but I follow this established convention for clarity.

these orders also developed into orders of mendicant friars and took on pastoral work, though both also retained hermitages and some eremitical aspects of life.[49] Both orders flourished chiefly in the fourteenth century. It is difficult to assess their pastoral activities in the thirteenth century because of limited evidence and we must not read fourteenth-century developments back onto the thirteenth century but their success in recruiting members and securing support for new foundations – a combined total of about fifty by 1300 – testifies to some level of impact.

The Carmelites arose as hermits on Mount Carmel in the Latin Kingdom of Jerusalem and were brought to England by Richard, earl of Cornwall, upon his return from crusading in 1241.[50] Within two years, the hermits had settled sites at Aylesford and Lossenham in Kent, Hulne in Northumberland and Burnham Norton in Norfolk.[51] These settlements reflect the Carmelites' eremitical period: from the fact that none of these locations ever had a second friary of another order, we may deduce that they were not very urbanised. However, in 1247, Innocent IV sanctioned minor alterations in the Carmelite Rule at the request of the leadership of the order. While some aspects of eremitical life remained, such as living and praying in separate cells, excursions for begging were now sanctioned and the next year the new house at Cambridge reached an agreement with a local parish church over administration of the sacraments to parishioners. In 1252 the pope confirmed their right to build churches with cemeteries and bells, while preaching and hearing confession were authorised by another bull the following year.[52] Their transformation into a pastoral mendicant order was well underway and their pattern of settlements reflects this. Of the nineteen English houses founded between 1247 and 1277, seventeen were in towns that already had both Franciscan and Dominican convents. Only after settling in these major centres did they return to founding houses in smaller and more remote towns. By 1300 they had twenty-seven houses in England and Wales, four in Scotland and nine in Ireland.[53]

[49] K. J. Egan, 'The Spirituality of the Carmelites', in Raitt, *Christian Spirituality*, 51–62, at 53; Hackett, 'Spiritual Life', 429–34.

[50] Andrews, *Other Friars*, 7–14; A. Jotischky, *The Carmelites and Antiquity* (Oxford, 2002); and A. Jotischky, *The Perfection of Solitude* (University Park, PA, 1995).

[51] *MRH*, 232–33.

[52] A. Staring, 'Four Bulls of Innocent IV: A Critical Edition', *Carmelus* 27 (1980), 273–85, at 282–85; M. H. Laurent, 'La Lettre "Quae Honorem Conditoris" (1er Octobre 1247)', *Ephemerides Carmeliticae* (1948), 5–16; Andrews, *Other Friars*, 14–17; K. J. Egan, 'The Carmelites Turn to Cambridge', in P. Chandler and K. J. Egan, eds, *The Land of Carmel* (Rome, 1991), 155–70, at 163.

[53] Egan, 'Carmelite Houses', 2; R. Copsey, *Carmel in Britain, Volume III: The Hermits from Mount Carmel* (Faversham, 2004), viii; Andrews, *Other Friars*, 23–24.

The Austin (Augustinian) Friars originated as several groups of hermits, mostly Italian, united in 1256 under the Rule of St Augustine.[54] Separate groups of proto-Austins arrived in England in the years 1248–52, establishing themselves at Clare (Suff.) and Woodhouse (Kent).[55] As with the early English Carmelite houses, these were not in urban environments; in neither location was there ever a second friary. These groups probably spent the next few years living as hermits, though the same is probably not true of the brothers who settled in London in 1253. The union of 1256 also changed the terms of the Austins' life: henceforth they would be mendicant friars.[56] Like the Carmelites, they were soon permitted to hear lay confessions and there is evidence that they did so.[57] The change in settlement patterns after 1256 is similar to that of the Carmelites after 1247, with a series of convents settled in towns that already had at least Franciscan and Dominican houses already, and sometimes Carmelite ones as well. By 1300, they had twenty-two houses in England.[58]

FRIARS AND TOWNS

Although the different orders of friars show different settlement patterns, it is clear from the foregoing that they shared one important feature: they settled in, or immediately outside, towns. While acknowledging that rural populations were just as much in need of their pastoral care, they nonetheless justified this practice on the grounds that it was easier to gather an audience for a sermon in a town and preaching to a large audience is more efficient than preaching to a small one.[59] At the time of Domesday, around 10 per cent of the English population was urban; by 1300, that had risen to 15 to 20 per cent.[60] If by the end of the century every English town had at least one friary and if we add each town's suburbs and nearby countryside, it is fair to estimate that at least one-fifth of the English population lived within half an hour's walk of a house of friars.[61]

The expansion plans of the friars were not the only criterion determining in which towns they settled. They also needed the support of

---

[54] Lawrence, *The Friars*, 98; Roth, *Austin Friars* I, 13–17; van Luijk, *Bullarium*, 128–30.
[55] Roth, *Austin Friars* I, 18–21; *MRH*, 200–203.
[56] E. Ypma, 'Les études des Augustins et leur installation dans le Midi', *Cahiers de Fanjeaux* 8 (1973), 111–31, at 111–12.
[57] See pp. 146–47 below.   [58] *MRH* 200–203.   [59] d'Avray, *Preaching*, 30–31.
[60] R. Britnell, *Britain and Ireland, 1050–1530: Economy and Society* (Oxford, 2004), 74.
[61] Historians continue to debate what distinguished a town or urban settlement from a large village. Sometimes the presence of a house of friars is itself used as a determinant.

the local laity and churchmen who made mendicant life possible. Both forces are visible in the historical record. Friars were invited to settle in certain locales and sometimes the inviters had to wait for some time until a sufficient number of friars could be raised. Peter des Roches attempted to found a Dominican convent at Portsmouth in 1225. The reason for the failure is not indicated but, given the early date, it may be that not enough friars were available.[62] Some settlements attempted by the friars failed for lack of support or from the opposition of vested clerical interests. The monks of St Edmund's Abbey prevented a Franciscan settlement at Bury for a generation and the migration of the Franciscans of Durham to Hartlepool in 1239–40 was probably a result of ecclesiastical opposition or insufficient material support. It is likely that there were other failed attempts of which no record now exists.[63]

On the other hand, some bishops were clearly keen to attract the friars to their dioceses and may have welcomed incursions. If Peter des Roches attempted to found a Dominican convent in Portsmouth and they did settle in his cathedral city of Winchester by 1235, then he was probably supportive of London Dominicans crossing the diocesan boundary, the Thames, on the north bank of which they dwelt, to minister in Southwark and other areas.[64] Elsewhere, a deanery in the northern suburbs of Gloucester, surrounded by the Diocese of Worcester, was a peculiar of York Diocese; the Carmelite house there was apparently in the peculiar while the Franciscans and Dominicans were in Worcester Diocese but there is no reason to imagine that they never crossed these boundaries.[65] In the landscape of pastoral care, borders could be supremely important, such as when parishioners annually 'beat the bounds' of the parish to demarcate precisely where they lay, but not all such delineations were equally important.[66] Friars' ministry required mobility and, while only a minority of friars in a given house were pastorally active at any time, they could and did range beyond the towns and suburbs where they had settled, creating a pastoral hinterland.[67]

NOVITIATES

Like a parish priest, a friar was viewed as a man to be formed, not just a mind to be filled; but, for the friar, the process was much more

---

[62] *EEFP*, 107–8.

[63] *MRH*, 221, 224; *Annales Monastici* III, 134; Little, *Papers*, 219. Little printed a charter of ca. 1250 referring to an otherwise unknown Franciscan house at 'Wluerenston': *Papers*, 228–29. On the process of settlement, see also *EEFP*; *De Adventu*, 20–24; *Chron. Maj.* III, 332–34.

[64] *EEFP*, 107–8, 20–55. [65] *VCH* Gloucester II, 48; *Reg. Giffard*, 92–93; *MRH*, 216, 225, 235.

[66] Duffy, *Stripping of the Altars*, 136–39. [67] See Chapter 8.

systematic. The Franciscan and Dominican novitiate programmes included the reading of spiritual classics as part of religious formation, in which they resembled monastic novitiates. Much of this material originated among monks or canons regular, particularly the Cistercians and Victorines, but both orders added material specific to themselves.[68] Dominic himself wrote the chapter of the Dominican constitutions concerning the novice-master. In common with other novitiates, this programme focused on teaching the novice submission, humility and other habits necessary for regular life. Novices were to be taught the careful handling of books and 'how fervent they ought to be in preaching at the right time.' This could best be taught by exposing them to frequent sermons, which would remain part of the quotidian round for the rest of their lives.[69] Likewise, frequent confession to their novice-masters would give novices a clearer idea of how to hear the confessions of the laity in due course. The Franciscan *Regula Bullata*, the Rule of 1223, indicated a novitiate of one year, though it gave no details of what was to occur during that year beyond determining the novice's clothes. After Francis' death, his order both became more clerical and began accepting adolescents; for a time, the novitiate was a period of theological instruction to enable the younger postulants to catch up with their more experienced peers. Novice-masters appeared by 1240, along with a programme devoted to 'personal transformation ... gearing the novices towards poverty, humility, obedience, self-negation and the love of God' rather than education *per se*. In 1260, the Franciscan constitutions would forbid engaging in study or assigning books of study to novices: they were to read only 'writings of edification'.[70] Though basic literacy was already assumed, spiritual formation thenceforth had to precede further theological study. Both the Carmelites and the Austins also developed novitiates lasting one year; less is known about their development before the fourteenth century but the primary concern was for spiritual formation, for the postulant to test his own commitment to the order's way of life and for the professed friars of the order to determine his preparedness to commit the rest of his life to service and life among them.[71]

---

[68] Roest, *Franciscan Education*, 248–50; Humbert, *Opera* II, 213–33; Mulchahey, *First the Bow*, 101–14; Bonaventure, *Opera* VIII, 475–90; Monti, ed., *Bonaventure's Writings*, 78n, 145–48.

[69] Vicaire, *Dominic*, 209; Denifle, 'Constitutiones', 201; d'Avray, *Preaching*, 35; Mulchahey, *First the Bow*, 75–129; Humbert, *Opera* II, 213–33.

[70] Little, *Religious Poverty*, 159; Sbaralea, *Bullarium Franciscanum* I, 6; *Reg. Bull.* II; Roest, *Franciscan Education*, 239–44; Bonaventure, *Opera* VIII, 450–51. This portion of the earlier constitutions of the order is lacking. C. Cenci, ed., 'De Constitutionibus Praenarbonensibus', *Archivum Franciscanum Historicum* 83 (1990), 50–95.

[71] Andrews, *Other Friars*, 41–42, 122–24.

EDUCATION AND FORMATION

As we have seen, the Franciscans and Dominicans settled in Oxford shortly after arriving in England; both found it fertile ground for recruiting. In the winter of 1229–30, Jordan of Saxony, Master-General of the Dominican order, visited Oxford and preached to a university audience on 11 November. His sermon included the following exhortation:

> To be perfect, as the clergy ought to be since they are elected to the portion of God, good conscience born of charity is not enough. Rather, it is proper that one should attract others to good deeds through holy behaviour and a good example; and this is especially appropriate for parish priests.

Perhaps Friar Jordan intended this sermon as a good example of holy behaviour that might attract others to good deeds, specifically joining the Order of Preachers and putting their education, paid for by the tithes of the poor, to better use than furthering their academic careers – which he compared to the devil's temptation of Jesus at the pinnacle of the temple. This was a recruiting sermon and we know that Jordan was actively recruiting in his time at Oxford.[72] He also met Grosseteste, who around this time became lector to the Oxford Franciscans.[73] While Francis may have had some reservations about his friars becoming learned, Grosseteste did not.[74] According to Friar Thomas, who joined the Franciscans at Oxford around 1230 and may have studied under Grosseteste personally, 'under him, within a brief time, they made inestimable progress both in academic arguments and in subtle moralities suitable for preaching.'[75]

The timing of Jordan's visit and Grosseteste's enlistment was no coincidence. A violent town-gown dispute at Paris in the spring of 1229 had resulted in its university being temporarily disbanded and its scholars migrating to other locales. Friar Thomas records that during this dispersal several English scholars who had joined the Franciscan order at Paris made their way to Oxford. He himself was then a secular student at Paris; he joined the order after coming to Oxford at this time.[76] It was natural that both the newly arrived Paris Franciscans and their newly recruited Oxford brethren would then seek a teacher. Jordan typically spent Lent preaching and recruiting at Bologna or Paris. This visit to England's chief

---

[72] Little and Douie, 'Sermons of Jordan of Saxony', 4, 10, 12; *EEFP*, 264.

[73] *De Adventu*, 48; Little, *Grey Friars in Oxford*, 29–30; J. Goering, 'When and Where'; S. Gieben, 'Robert Grosseteste and the Evolution of the Franciscan Order', in J. McEvoy, ed., *Robert Grosseteste: New Perspectives* (Turnhout, 1995), 215–32; Luard, ed., *Grosseteste Epistolae*, 131–33.

[74] On the transformation of the Friars Minor into an educated clerical order, see now Şenocak, *Poor and the Perfect*, and Roest, *Franciscan Learning*.

[75] *De Adventu*, 27–33, 48; *BRUO*, 623–24.

[76] *Chron. Maj.* III, 166–69; *De Adventu*, 27–33; *BRUO*, 623–24.

university town was following the academic herd and presumably he stayed to preach at Oxford in Lent 1230.[77] These circumstances would breed competition in recruitment and Grosseteste's invitation to teach the Franciscans should probably be seen in this light. Thomas, for one, might otherwise have joined the Dominicans.

As Jordan suggested in his Oxford sermon, the Friars Preachers had a clear idea of the purposes of study, which he also hoped would be adopted by listeners who did not join his order. According to the prologue to the Dominican constitutions of 1220,

> Our order is recognized to have been instituted from the beginning especially for preaching and the salvation of souls, and our study ought to aim principally and ardently at this, the highest task: that we should be able to be useful to the souls of our neighbours.[78]

Humbert of Romans OP noted that, while a friar out preaching missed the theology lectures in the convent, 'if such study is not directed to the doctrine of preaching, of what use is it?'[79] Robert Kilwardby OP, Oxford scholar, English Provincial Prior and future archbishop of Canterbury, described the purpose of Dominican education as 'to prepare persons and fit them for the salvation of souls; and, those prepared being fit both in life and in knowledge, to appoint them to the conversion of sinners'. The standard of the Constitutions was reiterated throughout the thirteenth century.[80]

Franciscans showed similar convictions.[81] Grosseteste is well known for his uncompromising insistence on the primacy of the care of souls and this attitude may have recommended him to Agnellus of Pisa. While studying and teaching in the liberal arts, Grosseteste was pursuing theology in order to write practical manuals for confessors.[82] Roger Bacon considered his fellow Franciscan Adam Marsh a great philosopher, yet Marsh's letters, his sole surviving writings, chiefly reveal a profound solicitude for the care of souls.[83] When the Franciscan John Pecham, like Kilwardby, a scholar, English Provincial Minister of his order and future archbishop of Canterbury, was sparring with Kilwardby over the relative merits of their orders, Pecham concurred with Kilwardby's statement on

---

[77] *EEFP*, 264; Little and Douie, 'Sermons of Jordan of Saxony', 5.

[78] I have translated 'studium' here as 'study' rather than 'concern' because the same word is used a few lines earlier in its unequivocally academic sense. Denifle, 'Constitutiones', 194, dated by Mulchahey, *First the Bow*, 3.

[79] Humbert, *Opera* II, 432.   [80] Pecham, *Tractatus Tres*, 128; Mulchahey, *First the Bow*, 57–67ff.

[81] Roest, *Franciscan Education*, 3, 123.   [82] Goering, 'When and Where'.

[83] Bacon, *Opera*, 70; *LAM*.

the purpose of education. As archbishop, Pecham wrote that 'nothing in this world is more precious than the care of souls, since for this alone Christ offered his very self on the cross.'[84]

In the first third of the thirteenth century, Oxford had a native tradition of learning that was not entirely dependent on Paris.[85] Nonetheless, although the English scholastic enterprise retained some distinctive features, it was increasingly drawn into the orbit of Paris for theology and Bologna for canon law. Both Preachers and Minorites made Paris the hub of their educational systems and constructed spokes that directed the energy of Parisian pastoral theology and Bolognese pastoral law to the brothers who preached to and shrove the laity. Paris was already the centre of developments in preaching methodology and sermon publication.[86] It was at Paris that daily lectures on the Bible were first displaced by ones on Peter Lombard's *Four Books of Sentences*, which Oxford eventually followed.[87] The Paris Dominican Hugh of St-Cher's *Postillae in totam Bibliam* was designed as a useful handbook for conventual lectors and for sermon composition; it quoted other Paris scholars often, especially Stephen Langton, and it circulated among English friars.[88] Robert Bacon had probably studied in Paris before joining the Dominicans as a regent master in theology at Oxford; he lectured for several years to the Oxford Dominicans, and the English Dominican Richard Fishacre incepted under him.[89] Among Franciscans, Richard Rufus of Cornwall (the first Oxford Franciscan lector to teach from Lombard's *Sentences*) bounced back and forth between Paris and Oxford; John Duns Scotus did the same with a spell in Cambridge; and Roger Marston went from Paris to Cambridge to Oxford.[90] The learning of Raymond of Peñaforte, a Bolognese doctor of canon law who joined the Dominicans, had a substantial impact on pastoral care in England in the thirteenth century: his canonical work on the sacrament of penance, the *Summa de casibus penitentiae*, was officially sanctioned reading material in the Dominican order and was also used by Franciscans.[91]

---

[84] Pecham, *Tractatus Tres*, 128–29; *C&S* II, 1078.
[85] B. Smalley, *The Study of the Bible in the Middle Ages* (2nd rev. edn, Oxford, 1952), 316–26; Southern, *Grosseteste*.
[86] d'Avray, *Preaching*.
[87] J. McEvoy, *Robert Grosseteste* (Oxford, 2000), 160–71; Roest, *Franciscan Education*, 126–27.
[88] Mulchahey, *First the Bow*, 486–88; Humphreys, *Friars' Libraries*, 210–11, and note other Parisian works there; Bannister, 'Manuscripts of the Cambridge Friars', 126–27.
[89] B. Smalley, 'Robert Bacon and the Early Dominican School at Oxford', *TRHS* 4th s. 30 (1948), 1–19, at 8; Trivet, *Annales*, 229–30; *Chron. Maj.* IV, 244.
[90] Moorman, *Franciscan Order*, 244, 254, 251; *BRUO*, 1604–5; 607–10; 1230–31.
[91] *EEFP*, 335; for use by a Franciscan author, *FM* in index *s.v.* 'Raymundus'.

The mendicant educational systems mediating between the *studia generalia* – the scholarly university convents – and the ordinary convent schools, where rank-and-file friars received lifelong education, enabled a dissemination of learning from the master in the classroom to the preacher in the pulpit. Nor were the scholars entirely insulated from pastoral work: from the Oxford convent, the twenty-two Franciscans presented to the bishop of Lincoln in 1300 to be licensed to hear confessions included not only two doctors of theology (who were licensed) but also other budding academics, including the young John Duns Scotus (who was not).[92] A hierarchy of schools addressed themselves to training conventual lectors, training those who in turn trained conventual lectors, and so on.[93] From 1220, every Dominican convent officially required a lector and the first Preachers who arrived in England in 1221 doubtless included one. Humbert of Romans observed that many good men never would have become Dominicans if they had not been able to continue to study, and the Preachers who set out for Oxford, a university town, surely knew that their recruiting success depended upon the teaching that they offered.[94] In addition to competition in recruiting, Grosseteste's invitation to teach the Oxford Franciscans may reflect pressures from students who were joining the order. From that time we can trace the spread of lectors in English Franciscan convents. By 1238 there were at least seven lectors spread among about twenty-eight convents (25 per cent); by 1256, there were thirty-four lectors among forty-nine convents (69 per cent); by 1300, nearly all of the fifty-three houses had lectors.[95] The level of education among ordinary Franciscan friars was on the rise during the century and may have been higher than these numbers suggest. Even a convent without a lector was likely to include friars who (like Thomas) had studied before joining the order or who had spent time since in a convent with a lector.

In both Dominican and Franciscan convents, the courses were geared towards producing and polishing pastors. On weekdays, friars of both orders could expect to spend several hours in lectures, sermons, disputations and individual study, which replaced much of the manual work of monastic life and, to some extent, *lectio divina*.[96] Our evidence of thirteenth-century mendicant libraries suggests that the collections were

[92] Little, *Grey Friars in Oxford*, 63–64; Little, *Papers*, 235.
[93] Roest, *Franciscan Education*; Mulchahey, *First the Bow*; O'Carroll, *Studies*, 35–74; M. O'Carroll, 'The Educational Organisation of the Dominicans in England and Wales, 1221–1348', *Archivum Fratrum Praedicatorum* 50 (1980), 23–62.
[94] Humbert, *Opera* II, 28.   [95] Roest, *Franciscan Education*, 83; *De Adventu*, 49–50.
[96] D. Flood, 'Franciscans at Work', *Franciscan Studies* 59 (2001), 21–62; Roest, *Franciscan Learning*, 51–82.

designed to support pastoral and theological education.[97] Dominican convents often included study cubicles.[98] The Dominicans reduced the liturgy to its bare bones to allow more time for study and lectors and students could be dispensed from attending the lesser services and other duties to facilitate their work.[99] The Franciscans were tempted to do the same, though John Pecham obstructed such attempts among English Franciscans.[100] Training friars to be pastors required that they be taught both how to preach and how to hear confessions. Mendicant preaching included both catechesis and moral and devotional instruction. Any of the instruction available in the convent, verbal (sermons, lectures, liturgy) and textual (theological, devotional and instructional works), was potential material for preaching. At least among the Franciscans, lectors of ordinary convents produced most of the practical pastoral manuals used by their friars.[101] Friar Thomas described Grosseteste's lectures as including 'subtle moralities suitable for preaching'.[102] In Dominican convents, the lectures taught doctrine while other academic exercises taught moral theology.[103] The constant round of sermons in the convent would provide object lessons in preaching, while friars seeking further guidance could turn to model sermon collections and *artes predicandi*, instructional texts on preaching.

The literature used and produced to help the *fratres communes*, the common friars, in hearing confessions was extensive. Guillaume Peyraut's *Summa de vitiis et virtutibus* was one of the standard texts that Humbert of Romans OP recommended that every Dominican convent librarian keep in a readily accessible place; another was Raymond of Peñaforte's *Summa de casibus penitentiae*, which first appeared in 1225 and was used in the convent classroom.[104] It is less clear what texts English Franciscans used in learning to hear confessions. But Grosseteste had written several manuals on confession before he began to teach the Franciscans

[97] Humbert, *Opera* II, 263–66; K. W. Humphreys, *The Book Provisions of the Medieval Friars* (Amsterdam, 1964); Humphreys, *Friars' Libraries*; M. R. James, 'The Library of the Grey Friars of Hereford', in A. G. Little et al., eds, *Collectanea Franciscana I* (Aberdeen, 1914), 114–23; Bannister, 'Manuscripts of the Cambridge Friars'; N. R. Ker, ed., *Medieval Libraries of Great Britain* (2nd edn, London, 1964), together with A. G. Watson, *Medieval Libraries of Great Britain: Supplement to the Second Edition* (London, 1987); *EEFP*, 180–86; Jones, 'Monastic Libraries'.

[98] *EEFP*, 164–76.   [99] Denifle, 'Constitutiones', 194.

[100] B. Thompson, 'The Academic and Active Vocations in the Medieval Church: Archbishop Pecham', in C. M. Barron and J. Stratford, eds, *The Church and Learning in Later Medieval Society* (Donington, Lincolnshire, 2002), 1–24.

[101] Roest, *Franciscan Education*, 96–97. The Franciscan preaching handbook *Fasciculus Morum* apparently originated in a convent setting: Wenzel, *Verses in Sermons*, 50.

[102] *De Adventu*, 48.   [103] Mulchahey, *First the Bow*, 140–41; Humbert, *Opera* II, 254.

[104] Humbert, *Opera* II, 265; L. E. Boyle, 'Notes on the Education of the *Fratres Communes*' in Boyle, *Pastoral Care*, 259–63; Mulchahey, *First the Bow*, 200–203.

and by far the most popular of these, *Templum Dei*, was probably written by 1225. The Friars Minor were becoming a more clerical order at this time, enabling them to hear the confessions of the laity. It was the perfect time to enlist the services of someone who could teach them how to do so.[105]

In her recent study of Franciscan education, Şenocak has questioned whether the Franciscan *studia* system in particular, but also its Dominican counterpart and the theology faculties of the universities more broadly, were really as well suited for training preachers and confessors as they claimed to be. She argues that both of these orders, and particularly the Franciscans, established themselves at the universities before they had the pastoral mission later used to justify study there; that other criteria (including competing for recruits and striving for prestige) were at least as important as pastoral care; that many of the educational elite scorned the grunt-work of actual pastoral care and could not help but pass on that ethos to their students; that effective preaching did not require such extensive training in any case; and that lectorship became a privileged status to be sought without necessarily undertaking the corresponding responsibility to teach.[106] These are all compelling arguments, closely argued from ample evidence, and a necessary corrective to a rose-tinted view. However, if the mendicants' educational systems above the level of the ordinary convent were not solely optimised for pastoral training, that does not require us to infer that the common brothers trained in the convent school were poorly prepared. It would also go too far to assume that the university-trained friars' literary creations were irrelevant to pastoral care. The only surviving copy of the *Summa de sacramentis* of the Oxford-trained Franciscan lector Henry of Wodestone, a work heavily indebted to Bonaventure (the scholarly Franciscan *par excellence*), is not a library volume but a *vademecum*, a small pocket-book about three by four inches in size made for carrying on the road.[107] Wodestone's other major source was a similar tract, the *Summa iuniorum* written by the Oxford Dominican lector (and later English provinicial prior) Simon of Hinton, a copy of which is bound together with it in the same *vademecum*. The *Summa iuniorum*, according to its editor, was probably written to help new Dominicans prepare for the Order's internal examination for licensing as a preacher and confessor. This may also have been the case with Wodestone's *Summa de sacramentis*. The existence of both in *vademecum*

---

[105] J. Goering, 'When and Where', 29; Grosseteste, *Templum*. For an English Franciscan's use of *Templum Dei*, see *FM*, 356–61.

[106] Şenocak, *Poor and the Perfect*.

[107] Bodleian Library, Laud Misc. MS. 2; R. Mokry, 'Henry Wodestone's *Summa de Sacramentis*'.

form, however, suggests that they could also be used for direct catechetical instruction in the field. Simon's *Summa* was very practical in nature. It covers the twelve articles of the Creed, the seven petitions of the *Paternoster*, the Decalogue, the seven sacraments, the seven virtues, the gifts of the Holy Spirit and the eight beatitudes. Whatever was happening in the *studia generalia* of Oxford and Paris, the evidence points towards a pastorally oriented education for the pastorally active friars.[108]

Like the Franciscans, the Carmelites originated as a predominantly lay order in which education was not paramount. As their order developed from one of lay hermits to one of clerical mendicant friars, this was recognised, from both outside and inside the order, as a defect; they needed to be equipped for pastoral duties. This parallels the experience of Franciscan clericalisation and education, although the Carmelite process began decades later, followed its own course and perhaps proceeded more slowly. For the Carmelite order, however, education would be essential for something even more basic than preparation and recruitment: survival. The Second Council of Lyons (1274) aimed to curtail the expansion of mendicant orders, enforcing Lateran IV's decree that no new religious orders should be allowed after 1215. The Franciscan and Dominican orders were exempted, according to the Council, because of their evident usefulness to the church, while the Carmelites and Austins were left in limbo, pending further papal decisions. Other orders, the Pied Friars and Friars of the Sack, were suppressed in 1274. An example had been made. On a canonical level, the Franciscan and Dominican exemption was really because both could claim that they had been founded, and received papal approval, prior to Lateran IV, but the utility argument may have been brought out because the Carmelites and Austins could make varying degrees of the claim to predate 1215. The Austins followed the same Rule of St Augustine used by the Dominicans and the Augustinian Canons and had evolved from various groups of Italian hermits, some of which predated 1215. The first Carmelite rule came from the early thirteenth century and the earliest traceable Carmelite hermits from the twelfth. While both orders could thus lay some claim to sufficient age, the shifting of the argument to utility hung a different Damoclean sword over them. Without a serious investment in education to make them useful, both orders were doomed to extinction along with the Sack and Pied Friars. As with their pastorate, their intellectual flourishing came largely in the fourteenth century but they had apparently proved themselves by 1298, when Boniface

---

[108] B. Roest, *Franciscan Literature of Religious Instruction before the Council of Trent* (Leiden, 2004), 318–19; Carroll-Clark, 'Practical Summa'.

VIII finally extended the exemption from suppression to both of these orders.[109]

It may not be coincidental that one of the Carmelites' earliest English houses was at Cambridge, just as Franciscans and Dominicans established Oxford convents immediately upon reaching England. Recruiting educated clerics would help in their project of establishing an internal education system for the existing brothers comparable to what the larger mendicant orders already had. The Austins, while behind the Dominicans and Franciscans in terms of developing an educational system, were ahead of the Carmelites. Their General Chapter was making provisions for students, books and examination in literacy as early as 1281, while, according to the Constitutions of 1290, which describe in detail a hierarchy of *studia*, the study of theology was central to the order's purpose. The fact that Augustine of Hippo, whose Rule they followed and to whose cult they were particularly devoted, was famed as an intellectual rather than as a hermit or mystic, perhaps made academic pursuits seem a more natural expression of their way of life than some early Carmelites or Franciscans had found them. By the end of the century, the Carmelites and Austins had achieved numerical parity with one another both at Oxford and at Cambridge, a level just above half of the Franciscan and Dominican populations.[110]

Neither the parish clergy nor the monks and canons regular, to whom we shall turn next, had educational systems as thorough as those developed by the friars. The monks did, however, share a long tradition of the novitiate – indeed, they had invented it many centuries before. They also shared with the friars communal life and communal discipline. A parish priest might get away with skipping or rushing through the canonical hours; a friar, monk or canon generally could not. The monks' and canons' advantage over the mendicant orders was their greater antiquity. They occupied a well-defined space not only in ecclesiastical but also in social, familial and economic structures. As we shall see, their interactions with the outside world were not the same as those of the friars but some of their activities were decidedly pastoral in nature.

---

[109] Andrews, *Other Friars*, 17–21.

[110] Ibid., 37–44, 148–62; *Analecta Augistiniana* II (Rome, 1907), 249–51; A. Zumkeller, 'The Spirituality of the Augustinians', in Raitt, *Christian Spirituality*, 63–74; D. Gutiérrez, *The Augustinians in the Middle Ages, 1256–1356* (Villanova, PA, 1984), 60–61; *Const. Ratisbonenses*, 110–21; D. Gutiérrez, 'Ermites de Saint-Augustin', in M. Viller et al., eds, *Dictionnaire de Spiritualite Ascetique et Mystique: Doctrine et Histoire*, vol. IV (Paris, 1961), 983–1018; Hackett, 'Spiritual Life', 433.

Chapter 4

MONKS AND CANONS REGULAR

It is a truism that monasticism was a vital part of the medieval church. In England, there were even monastic cathedral chapters, which were rare on the Continent.[1] Over many centuries, monks had created and refined the texts and ideas that would form the bedrock of *pastoralia* used by pastors of the laity, most notably Gregory the Great's *Liber de regula pastoralis*. Despite their cloistered lives, we can see them engaging in lay pastoral care both before and after the thirteenth century but how far they did so in the thirteenth century itself represents a gap in our knowledge.[2] What evidence we have is typically local, sporadic and ambiguous and one must resist the temptation to generalise beyond it. If there was a temporary withdrawal, the reasons for it are unclear. After 1225 or so, clerics interested in joining a religious order and administering pastoral care to the laity might find the orders of friars more attractive, as might laypeople who wanted to receive pastoral care from the religious; but our evidence for pastoral care by the religious orders seems to peter out before the friars had the critical mass to displace them.

Did monks and canons regular perform pastoral functions during the thirteenth century analogous to those of parish priests and friars? We shall see that they occasionally did but also that this is not the ideal question to pursue. Rather, we must ask such questions as these: what roles can we see monks or canons occupying that contributed to pastoral care? What benefit did the laity believe that their souls received, whether directly or indirectly, from religious houses and their inhabitants? Were there differences among religious orders in the frequency or manner in which they dispensed pastoral care?

The flexible Rule of the Augustinian Canons (OSA) did not preclude pastoral activity. The Dominican and Austin friars, who undertook

---

[1] *Fasti* Monastic.
[2] C. Muessig, ed., *Medieval Monastic Preaching* (Leiden, 1998); J. Greatrex, 'Benedictine Monk Scholars as Teachers and Preachers in the Later Middle Ages', in J. Loades, ed., *Monastic Studies II. The Continuity of Tradition* (Bangor, 1991), 219–25.

pastoral work, followed the same Augustinian Rule as the canons did. So did the Premonstratensian canons, whose ascetic withdrawal from the world was modelled on that of the Cistercians. It has long been supposed that Augustinian Canons accepted pastoral care of the laity as part of their mission but evidence from thirteenth-century England is surprisingly sparse.[3] Many Augustinian houses had been created in the twelfth century by the regularisation of minsters and other houses of secular canons which had had a pastoral function. The southern English Augustinian foundations in the period 1100–1135 were typically urban, perhaps aiming at ministering to the growing populations of towns, but then they tended to retire outside the town, sometimes miles away.[4] Oxford, for example, contained two houses of secular canons within the town walls in 1100, both of which were soon absorbed by the new Augustinian houses of Oseney and St Frideswide's. According to Postles, these then turned away from the population, except as urban landowners.[5] The presence of Augustinian Canons as the chapter of Carlisle Cathedral presumably did not fulfil all the citizens' spiritual needs: both Franciscans and Dominicans settled there in 1233 and there is no hint that they were considered redundant.[6] Longère's study of medieval preaching makes no reference to popular preaching by canons regular.[7] While parish clergy may have complained of mendicants infringing their rights of confession and preaching in the thirteenth and fourteenth centuries, similar complaints against monks or canons seem to have been limited to the twelfth century.[8]

This does not mean, however, that Augustinians entirely abandoned pastoral care of the laity in the thirteenth century. In 1297, the bishop of Lincoln commissioned the Augustinian subprior and sacrist of Dunstable to hear confessions and grant absolution in their appropriated parish of Dunstable.[9] At Oxford, the canons may not have been as isolationist as Postles has suggested, for St Frideswide's Priory also served as a parish church from the 1220s to 1298,[10] while the canons of Oseney received a papal privilege in 1147 allowing them to serve parish churches appropriated to them by presenting one of their canons to the bishop, to

---

[3] J. Leclerq et al., *The Spirituality of the Middle Ages* (London, 1968), 137–41, and J. Burton, *Monastic and Religious Orders in Britain* (Cambridge, 1994), 43–62, tend to assume pastoral care of the laity; Fizzard, *Plympton*, is sceptical of this as the default assumption.

[4] Postles, 'Austin Canons'.   [5] Ibid., 5–6.   [6] *MRH*, 214, 222.

[7] J. Longère, *La Prédication Médiévale* (Paris, 1983).

[8] Dickinson, *Austin Canons*, 214–22; Constable, *Monastic Tithes*, 172–82.

[9] *Reg. Sutton* V, 207.

[10] Dodd, 'Churches in Norman Oxford'. A vicarage was ordained for the parish of St Frideswide's around 1225 with a secular vicar living with the canons: *Rot. Hugonis* I, 182. A parish congregation continued to worship in the abbey church: Blair, 'St Frideswide's', 255–58. It was united with the parish of St Edward in 1298 for several reasons, including that the canons and the vicar celebrated in very close proximity so that their singing clashed: *Reg. Sutton* VI, 106–7.

be instituted if found suitable.[11] Mayr-Harting argues that the Augustinians of Bridlington also served some of their parishes in person.[12] Moreover, many existing secular collegiate churches were in poor condition in the twelfth century; bringing them under the Rule of St Augustine may have revitalised not only their spiritual commitment but also their relations with the laity.[13]

Before the coming of the friars, the clergy who were called upon to travel around and preach included monks and canons. Alexander of Ashby OSA apparently addressed lay congregations on preaching tours in the first decades of the thirteenth century.[14] One manuscript that gives tantalising evidence of such public preaching by a monk or canon is an English glossed Gospel book from the early thirteenth century.[15] A thirteenth-century scribe filled in the blank pages following the Gospel of Luke with a few sermons.[16] The homiletic nature of the texts bear no resemblance to the *sermo modernus*, the new type of sermon being developed in early thirteenth-century Paris.[17] This suggests either an early date of composition of the text or a later author untouched by that new idiom (and therefore unlikely to be a friar). The first five sermons, for Christmas, Easter, Rogation Sunday, Pentecost and at the beginning of Lent, are clearly intended for preaching to religious, as they are addressed to *fratres karissimi*.[18] But the sermon for the beginning of Lent takes as its text Matthew 6:1–6, on practising piety for the love of God and not to look good in front of others; its terms suggest visibility to the laity rather than competitive holiness within the cloister.[19] This is followed by another sermon to *fratres karissimi*, though without a rubric, comparing priests to the prophets of old in that they are obligated to preach upon peril to their own souls. 'We are exhorted to be prepared to teach common people. He who knows the scriptures ought to preach the scriptures. To the common person, who does not know what is most generally known, let him [the preacher] say that they (*sic*) should turn away from evil and do good, et cetera.'[20] Later in the sermon, the auditors are instructed to remind people during Lent to observe the Lenten fast and abstain from

---

[11] The phrase 'episcopi curam animarum committant' suggests parochial service, not merely celebration at the altar. Salter, ed., *Oseney Cartulary* III, 371–72.

[12] Mayr-Harting, *Religion*, 169–74. [13] Dickinson, *Austin Canons*, 241–54.

[14] Reeves, *Religious Education*, 84–85.

[15] Baltimore, Walters Museum, MS. W.15, ff. 205r–209v; on other aspects of this manuscript, see C. R. Cheney, *English Bishops' Chanceries, 1100–1250* (Manchester, 1950), 124–28.

[16] The script is a Northern Textualis that would be appropriate for thirteenth-century England, but it is difficult to date more precisely. Derolez, *Gothic Manuscript Books*, 72–101.

[17] On the *sermo modernus*, see Chapter 5. [18] Ff. 205r–208v. [19] Ff. 208r–v.

[20] 'Hortamur nos paratos esse ad docendas plebes. Qui scit scripturas predicet scripturas. Qui vero nescit hoc quod notissimum est plebi; dicat ut declinent a malo et faciant bonum, & cetera', f. 208v.

carnal relations, purge themselves of vices, adorn themselves with virtues, persist in almsgiving and prayer and in that state receive the sacrament with all faithful Christians at Easter. The final sermon in the group seems much more appropriate for a lay audience. It includes instructions for making one's Lenten confession and seems to be a model for fulfilling the previous sermon's charge of preaching to the laity.[21] Another sermon on confession in a similar hand at the beginning of the manuscript would be equally appropriate for this purpose; it is followed by notes on hearing confessions.[22] Taken together, the sermons and confessor's notes suggest a house of monks or canons in which the brothers left the cloister around the beginning of Lent to visit multiple parishes, preach to lay congregations, encourage them to confess and perhaps hear some of those confessions themselves.

At other times, laypeople received pastoral care in conventual churches. Monks and canons regular often kept themselves isolated by walls or screens within their conventual churches but did not exclude the laity altogether.[23] Dunster was one of many instances where a monastic nave served also as the parish church, of which the monastery was the rector, and at least by the mid-fourteenth century the parochial and conventual daily masses and festival processions were partially integrated.[24] The nave of St Werburgh's Benedictine Abbey in Chester served as a parish church until the mid-fourteenth century.[25] Before 1226, Pershore Abbey moved the parishioners of its appropriated church of St Michael, along with their baptistry, into the abbey's nave, probably to save itself the cost of maintaining the parish church building.[26] In 1290, the bishop of Lincoln granted an indulgence to encourage laypeople to attend Sunday mass in a chapel in Peterborough Abbey.[27] He did not stipulate whether the celebrant would be a monk or a secular chaplain but, in other cases, monks and canons can be clearly seen providing pastoral care directly to the laity.

The *Libellus de diversis ordinibus*, an anonymous French treatise from the mid-twelfth century, mentions monks and canons preaching to the laity, singing masses and hearing lay confessions – all three aspects of Pecham's

---

[21] Ff. 209r–v. The phrase 'fratres karissimi' does appear towards the end, but it seems out of place. A slight variation in the hand suggests that this final passage may have been an addendum.

[22] Ff. 2r–v. [23] Binski, *Becket's Crown*, 172–74.

[24] K. L. French, 'Competing for Space: Medieval Religious Conflict in the Monastic-Parochial Church at Dunster', *Journal of Medieval and Early Modern Studies* 27 (1997), 215–44. On such churches in general, see M. Heale, 'Monastic-Parochial Churches in Late Medieval England', in Burgess and Duffy, eds, *Parish*, 54–77.

[25] J. Laughton, *Life in a Late Medieval City: Chester, 1275–1520* (Oxford, 2008), 68.

[26] Major, *Acta*, 92. [27] *Reg. Sutton* III, 15.

definition of the care of souls – in the monastic church.[28] Abbot Samson
of Bury St Edmunds (d. 1211), according to the chronicle of his chaplain
Jocelin of Brakelond, preached to the laity in English and had a pulpit
erected in the abbey church to that end. How often he occupied it is
unclear but, elsewhere in his work, Jocelin implies that preaching to the
people on feast days was expected of an abbot in that house.[29] The record
of miracles of St Gilbert at Sempringham tells us of other lay experiences
in a monastic church in the early thirteenth century. In one case of healing at the shrine, a madwoman was restored to her right mind; upon her
recovery she sought and was granted confession and communion from a
Gilbertine canon.[30] Laypeople might live in a monastic precinct and thus
belong to no parish but fall under the spiritual responsibility of the religious. In 1256 some lay servants of the Abbey of Cokersand, nine miles
south-west of Lancaster, were receiving 'ecclesiastical sacraments' (those
normally offered only at one's own parish, such as baptism and physical reception of the Eucharist) at the abbey church, presumably from its
Premonstratensian canons.[31] At least in the later Middle Ages, the tenants
and servants of Bolton Priory (OSA) in Yorkshire, who lived in extra-
parochial space, attended services in the nave of the canons' church, which
was preserved for parochial use at the Dissolution.[32]

Cell churches, small outposts of larger monasteries, sometimes served
as chapels or parish churches for local laity as well. One might not expect
Cistercians to have served parish churches personally in the thirteenth
century, so it is somewhat surprising to read a report from c. 1220 that
'There is neither patron nor parson of the church of Weston, but the
monks of Merevale cause it to be served three days a week by one of their
monks, and they pay two shillings as its synodal dues, since they occupied
the whole ground of the parish in all their parish churches.'[33] Weston
is in Leicestershire, Lincoln Diocese; the Cistercian Abbey of Merevale,
though just six miles distant, was in Warwickshire and in the Diocese

[28] The context suggests singing masses for the laity, though whether this meant for a congregation
or for the souls of the departed is unclear. M. Chibnall, 'Monks and Pastoral Work: A Problem
in Anglo-Norman History', *Journal of Ecclesiastical History* 18 (1967), 165–72, at 167; G. Constable,
ed., and B. Smith, trans., *Libellus de Diversis Ordinibus et Professionibus qui sunt in Aecclesia* (Oxford,
1972), 26–27.
[29] Butler, *Jocelin of Brakelond*, 40, 12.
[30] R. Foreville and G. Keir, ed. and trans., *The Book of St Gilbert* (Oxford, 1987), 332–35. It is not
clear whether communion here meant physically receiving the host or merely gazing upon it.
See Chapter 6 below for this distinction.
[31] W. O. Roper, ed., *Materials for the History of the Church of Lancaster*, vol. I (Manchester, 1892), 52–54.
[32] A. H. Thompson, *Historical and Architectural Description of the Priory of St Mary, Bolton-in-Wharfedale*
(Leeds, 1928), 112.
[33] *Rot. Hugonis* I, 249.

of Coventry and Lichfield.[34] As the monks held the whole manor, they apparently sent over one of their number as a regularly visiting over-seer, doubling as parish priest and saving the cost of a vicar.[35] Distinction must be made, however, between serving at the altar only and serving the parish in such matters as confessions, preaching, baptism, the churching of women and visiting the sick. Many cases are known of secular chap-lains paid by religious houses to tend to the laity in these respects. In the case of Weston, the text may indicate that it was communion alone that was offered, either leaving the parishioners in a partial pastoral vacuum or obliging them to resort to the priests of neighbouring parishes.[36] Perhaps similarly, a chapel in the parish of Wainfleet, Lincolnshire, built as a cell of Bury St Edmunds for the monks overseeing property there, doubled as a chapel-of-ease used by the laity, though it is impossible to say whether a secular chaplain was provided.[37]

Other arrangements could lead to more explicit responsibility for pas-toral care.[38] Theologians and canonists in the twelfth century had dis-tinguished between power to administer sacraments (*potestas sacerdotis*) and the delegated responsibility to exercise it (*executio potestatis*): a monk or canon who was a priest had the first by ordination but the second required an assigned pastorate, whether over other religious or over laity.[39] Thirteenth-century bishops did sanction canonical pastorates of some parish churches. If a house of canons sent some of its members to serve at a parish church appropriated to them, whether temporarily or per-manently, they would have been treading on no one's established rights in the ecclesiastical hierarchy, making it less likely that they would leave records. When recorded, however, the geography of pastoral care can be clearly delineated. Some illustrative cases can be given here.[40]

---

[34] Weston is listed clearly as a parish in the *matriculus*, but appears neither in other thirteenth-century Lincoln registers nor in *RACCL* nor in the episcopal *acta*: it may have been merged into another parish. The editors of *Domesday Book* describe it as part of Sheepy Magna, another parish in the same deanery according to the *matriculus*, and it is to this that measurement has been made. A. Williams and G. H. Martin, ed. and trans., *Domesday Book*, vol. 2 (London, 2003), 642. On Merevale, see *VCH* Warwick II, 75–78. It is not listed in the valuation roll of the archdeaconry on the dorse of the roll carrying the *matriculus* (*Rot. Hugonis* I, 273–79), but it may have been included in 'Sepeheye integra' (p. 279) with Sheepy Magna and Sheepy Parva.

[35] *VCH* Warwick II, 75.   [36] Constable, *Monastic Tithes*, 172–82.

[37] Smith, *Acta*, 60.   [38] *Reg. Romeyn* I, no. 245.

[39] M. Peuchmard, 'Le prêtre ministre de la parole dans la théologie du XIIe siècle', *Recherches de Théologie Ancienne et Médiévale* 29 (1962), 52–76; M. Peuchmard, 'Mission canonique et prédication: Le prêtre ministre de la parole dans la querelle entre Mendiants et Séculiers au XIIIe siècle', *Recherches de Théologie Ancienne et Médiévale* 30 (1963), 122–44, 251–76; Dickinson, *Austin Canons*, 216.

[40] See also Moorman, *Church Life*, 48–51.

The Augustinian priory of Thurgarton in Nottinghamshire (Diocese of York) was granted rights in eight parish churches in the later twelfth century.[41] All but one were within about ten miles of Thurgarton. The priory also obtained a papal privilege in 1209 allowing it to present a canon to any of its churches, provided that the church was vacant, the presentation was made to the bishop and three or at least two other canons accompanied the Augustinian vicar.[42] It would be too great a drain on personnel to serve more than one or two churches at a time under these terms.[43] Though the record is far from complete, we can see secular vicars serving in some of the churches. Of Granby, Tithby and Hoveringham, all within eight miles of Thurgarton, the archbishops' registers tell us nothing.[44] Archbishop Wickwane placed a limit on parochial service at a visitation of the priory in 1280, when he ordered that canons serving churches outside the priory be rotated fortnightly.[45] This may reflect indiscipline among canons serving parish churches but it clearly indicates that it was happening. Parochial service by the canons seems to have been interrupted in February 1293, when Archbishop le Romeyn inhibited them from exiting the priory because they were members of a cloistered order though, since this contradicted Innocent's bull of 1209, it may have been an element in the litigation between priory and archbishop in 1308–11.[46] Innocent III's requirement that several canons of Thurgarton must be present at any church they served was not unique. Lateran III (1179) had ordered that any cell or parish church served by religious must have at least two brothers to maintain liturgical life and to safeguard morals.[47] Dickinson argues that this was frequently ignored but where it was followed it would have provided the laity with a more elaborate and well executed liturgy.[48]

The abbey of Premonstratensian Canons at Langley in Norfolk (Norwich Diocese) received from Innocent III several parish churches, including the nearby church of St Michael's, Langley.[49] Their foundation appears to have used the parish church while their convent church was being built in the later twelfth century. St Michael's was a donative benefice, meaning that the canons appointed the priest directly rather

[41] *EEA 20*, 98–100, dated to 1164 × 22 Nov. 1181.
[42] Cheney and Cheney, eds, *Letters of Innocent*, no. 855; PL CCXVI, 113.
[43] Knowles suggests that Thurgarton had around thirty canons in 1291: *MRH*, 176.
[44] *EEA 20*, 98n; *Reg. Wickwane*, 83, 147; *Reg. Romeyn* I, 254, 306; II, 66.   [45] *Reg. Wickwane*, 146–47.
[46] *Reg. Romeyn* I, 308; W. Brown and A. H. Thompson, eds, *The Register of William Greenfield, Lord Archbishop of York 1306–1315* V (Surtees Society, 1938), 214–15.
[47] *DEC*, 217.   [48] Dickinson, *Austin Canons*, 221, 228ff.
[49] Cheney and Cheney, ed., *Letters of Innocent III*, no. 1125 and pp. 279–80.

than through the bishop. As a result, the church disappears from episcopal registers and we cannot tell whether it was served by canons but doing so would have saved the cost of a chaplain, with minimal interference in the communal life of the abbey.[50] Langley also owned Thurton parish church, three miles away, to which it sometimes presented canons as vicars in the following century.[51] Burscough Priory, an Augustinian house, received in 1285 an episcopal indulgence to present one of their canons to serve the neighbouring church of Ormskirk, with an explicit indication that the canon-vicar must be a priest who would serve the cure. Every known vicar from 1330 to the Reformation was a canon of Burscough: those before 1330 are not recorded but the canons presumably began saving the cost of a secular vicar at the earliest opportunity.[52] The Augustinians of Worksop Priory presented one of their number as vicar of their appropriated parish church of Worksop in 1276.[53]

Plympton, an Augustinian priory in the suburbs of Plymouth, counted St Kew (Cornwall) among its appropriated churches. There were competing claims regarding who had given the church to the priory and under what terms but lay parishioners in 1302 argued that the priory was obliged to keep two of its canons at St Kew to offer divine service and supply hospitality and alms to the poor for the soul of the donor (allegedly King Edgar). These duties, the parishioners complained, had been neglected for the past fifteen years and there had been no services at the church.[54] The priory had presented a secular vicar to the bishop in 1283; either he soon left or the accusation of neglect was a mere smokescreen for someone whose real motive was harassment of the priory.[55] If the church had been left vacant, perhaps preaching and confession had been supplied by priests of neighbouring parishes or by Franciscans from Bodmin, about ten miles away. But the presence of hospitality (a traditional monastic responsibility) and almsgiving (a traditional expectation of parish clergy) in the complaint reminds us that the care of souls was

---

[50] Colvin, *White Canons*, 272–73; P. B. Pobst, ed., *The Register of William Bateman, Bishop of Norwich 1344–1355*, vol. II (C&YS 90, 2000), 145–46.

[51] P. B. Pobst, ed., *The Register of William Bateman, Bishop of Norwich 1344–1355*, vol. I (C&YS 84, 1995), nos. 387, 706.

[52] A. N. Webb, ed., *An Edition of the Cartulary of Burscough Priory* (Manchester: Chetham Society, 1970), nos. 195–200; *VCH* Lancs. II, 148–50.

[53] *Reg. Giffard*, 263. There was a secular chaplain in 1267: ibid., 73, 78–80.

[54] Fizzard, *Plympton*, 155–61.

[55] *Reg. Quivil*, 354, 372; Fizzard, *Plympton*, 160–61; J. MacLean, *The Parochial and Family History of the Deanery of Trigg Minor, in the County of Cornwall*, vol. II (London, 1873), 269–71; W. Picken, 'The "Landouchou" Charter', in W. G. Hoskins and H. Finberg, eds, *The Westward Expansion of Wessex* (Leicester, 1960), 36–44.

not purely non-material. In his 1250 address to the pope and cardinals, Grosseteste wrote,

> The work of pastoral care consists not only in administration of the sacraments and saying the canonical hours and celebration of masses … but also in the true teaching of the truth of life, in terrifying condemnation of vices, in tough and masterful cutting-off and inflexible castigation of vices when that is needed … It consists also in feeding the hungry, in giving drink to the thirsty, in covering the naked, in receiving the stranger, in visitation of the sick and imprisoned and especially of one's own parishioners, whose goods are the temporalities of the church.[56]

If a parish were not served, parishioners might conceivably attend a nearby church but their poor had no claim upon its funds.

Religious houses had several further parts to play in the care of the laity's souls. Many advowsons and rectories were in the hands of religious houses. The loss of many cartularies makes it difficult to find precise figures for any time before the *Valor Ecclesiasticus* of 1535, but it is clear enough that there was an uneven geographical distribution of monastic appropriations and advowsons, the effects of which for pastoral care are not yet fully understood.[57] In addition to presenting rectors and vicars, monastic patrons might appoint chaplains to assist in the parish church or serve at outlying chapels.[58] Particularly in the case of vicarages and rectories with cure of souls attached, the choice they made would have substantial repercussions for pastoral care in each such parish for years to come. However, the considerations for abbeys and priories choosing their appointees included a complex calculus of alliances and exchanges of favours.[59] This may explain why bishops visiting religious houses sometimes complained that priests appointed by the monks or canons were unsuitable and ordered their replacement.[60]

Religious houses were also places of pilgrimage. While saints' shrines were occasionally found in parish churches, they were more often located in convents and monastic or secular cathedrals. Housing a shrine or relics does not neatly fit into the categories of preaching, sacrament or confession, though it could coincide with them, as we see from the example of Sempringham. And, as at Sempringham, visiting a shrine might involve direct interaction with the religious of the house: illustrations in

---

[56] Gieben, 'Grosseteste at the Curia', 358–59.   [57] Robinson, *Augustinian Settlement*, 172–272.

[58] *Rot. Hugonis* I, 179–80; cf. II, 18–19; Fizzard, *Plympton*, 251.

[59] Fizzard, *Plympton*, 179–210; Geddes, 'Lanthony', 110–15; R. H. Snape, *English Monastic Finances in the Later Middle Ages* (Cambridge, 1926), 71–95; Smith, *Acta*, 344; Butler, *Jocelin of Brakelond*, 44; R. Donaldson, 'Sponsors, Patrons, and Presentations to Benefices … during the Later Middle Ages', *Archaeologia Aeliana* 4th ser. 38 (1960), 169–77.

[60] *Reg. Wickwane*, 147.

a mid-thirteenth-century *vita* of St Edward the Confessor show monks supervising visitors to his shrine at Westminster Abbey.[61] Clergy were not indifferent either to pilgrims as a stream of revenue to be managed. When churches compiled dossiers of miracles at their shrines or *vitae* full of miracles, it was partly with an eye to seeking canonisation of a new saint under the procedures introduced in the early thirteenth century or to confirming and advertising the sacred power of a recognised saint, in both cases attracting pilgrims and their donations.[62] Yet these accounts also testify to the popularity of pilgrimage and the perceived needs (spiritual, mental, emotional, medical and economic) that drove laypeople to seek divine intervention through the intercessions of saints whom they could approach through relics. We should not import a distinction of ghost and machine into in a world where the boundary between material and etherial was understood as highly permeable. Like other material monastic activities of dispensing hospitality and receiving pious donations in the name of God or of a saint, housing a saint's shrine provided for the laity a range of material and spiritual benefits.[63]

Abbeys and priories offered to both men and women a form of old-age insurance known as a corrody. The terms of corrodies were highly variable but, in general, in exchange for a sum of money or a grant of land, the donor would be provided with bed and board until death. The corrodian's housing could be in an ordinary house owned by the monastery but in some cases it was in the monastery itself, either in the almonry (where hospitality was extended to travellers) or in the monks' infirmary. It is not always clear what the level of interaction with the monks or canons would be but anyone investing in a corrody would eventually need the last rites of final confession, final communion and extreme unction (anointing), possibly given by monastic priests.[64]

The libraries of canonical houses, like their monastic counterparts, contained many pastoral works, for the canons heard one another's confessions and preached within their communities. The Premonstratensian abbey at Bradsole (Kent) in the late thirteenth century owned, among other *pastoralia*, a copy of Richard of Wethringsett's *Summa Qui bene presunt*, written to instruct parish priests, as well as Peñaforte's *Summa de casibus penitentiae* and the *Summa confessorum* of Thomas of Chobham.[65]

---

[61] Cambridge University Library, MS. Ee.3.59, ff. 30r, 33r.

[62] Farmer, ed., 'Canonization of St Hugh'.

[63] Robinson, *Augustinian Settlement*, 255–59; R. C. Finucane, *Miracles and Pilgrims* (New York, 1995).

[64] Geddes, 'Lanthony', 354–55; B. Harvey, *Living and Dying in England, 1100–1540: The Monastic Experience* (Oxford, 1993), 179–209.

[65] D. N. Bell, ed., *The Libraries of the Cistercians, Gilbertines and Premonstratensians* (London, 1992), 163 (no. 27b), 166 (nos. 52–53). For other examples, see Reeves, *Religious Education*, 84–88.

Friars had some access to monastic libraries and so simply maintaining the library contributed indirectly to pastoral care.[66] How much access parish clergy had to them is not clear but, unless books were physically removed from the library, it is hard to see why anyone would have bothered to record a casual visit.[67] Augustinians and other regulars also produced *pastoralia* that friars and seculars could use. The Primer, which would in later centuries become a book of devotions for the laity, sometimes in the vernacular, developed among the Augustinian Canons before moving outward to the secular clergy in the twelfth and thirteenth centuries.[68] Cistercians compiled collections of *exempla* for preaching which were then appropriated by the friars.[69] The tract on confession attributed to Guy of Southwick OSA was written at the behest of the bishop of Hereford, who presumably saw to its circulation in his diocese.[70] Alexander of Ashby OSA wrote two collections of sermons for use by secular priests, together with a treatise on how to write and deliver a sermon.[71] At the turn of the fourteenth century, an Augustinian wrote the *Northern Homily Cycle* and a Gilbertine produced the catechetical text *Handlyng Synne*.[72]

Monasteries of all kinds, both male and female, were above all powerhouses of prayer. Asceticism was not only for the sanctification of its practitioners but also to make their intercessions more effective.[73] We cannot know what extra-liturgical prayers a monk, nun, or recluse may have offered but the people they left behind when they entered the cloister or anchorhold were presumably not entirely forgotten.[74] The cycle of saints' days might prompt supplications for the laypeople who claimed that day's saint as their patron. A monastery was typically founded an aristocratic, knightly or gentry family who, in return for endowing the community, implicitly or explicitly expected the religious living there to pray for the salvation of their souls and those of their families forever.[75] A few grants included clauses that the abbey would forfeit the benefaction if it neglected these prayers.[76] Prominent lay benefactors could

[66] Jones, 'Monastic Libraries'.   [67] Shinners, 'Parish Libraries', 213.
[68] E. Bishop, 'Introduction', in *The Prymer, or Lay Folks' Prayer Book* (London, 1897), xxxi–xxxiv.
[69] J.-C. Schmitt, 'Recueils Franciscains d'«Exempla»', *Bibliothèque de l'École des Chartes* 135 (1977), 1–22; C. Bremond, J. le Goff and J.-C. Schmitt, *L'«Exemplum»* (Turnhout, 1982), 59.
[70] Wilmart, ed., 'Guy de Southwick'.   [71] Reeves, *Religious Education*, 84–85.
[72] T. Heffernan, 'The Authorship of the "Northern Homily Cycle"', *Traditio* 41 (1985), 289–309; F. Kemmler, *Exempla in Context: A Historical and Critical Study of Robert Mannyng of Brunne's 'Handlyng Synne'* (Tübingen, 1984).
[73] License, *Hermits*, 158–67; *Handlying Synne*, ll. 10,327–516.
[74] Carlin and Crouch, eds, *Lost Letters*, no. 79.
[75] B. Thompson, 'Monasteries and Their Patrons at Foundation and Dissolution', *TRHS* 6th s. 4 (1991), 103–25.
[76] London, ed., *Canonsleigh Cartulary*, no. 135.

be buried in monastic churches, typically accompanied by a substantial bequest, with the clear expectation that their souls would be remembered in the monks' or canons' prayers.[77] Some monasteries contained endowed chantries with hired secular chaplains, but overall almost any monastic house was itself a chantry chapel on a grand scale, one that could continue to receive benefactions from later donors and pray for them together with its founders.[78]

Canonically speaking, only men could exercise the *cura animarum*. Yet there were also women in particular roles sanctioned by the church who could interact with laypeople, especially women and children, in ways we would call pastoral. Nuns had few opportunities to leave the cloister but some of the laity could come to them. Aristocratic children of both sexes were often entrusted to nuns for their raising and education. Boys generally left at a younger age than girls, and some girls took the veil and stayed, but others re-entered the secular world with years of experience of the nuns' spirituality and practice during a formative period of their lives.[79] High-status laywomen could also receive permission to stay at a nunnery, joining in the sisters' religious life for a time and receiving their spiritual counsel without taking vows.[80] The *Ancrene Wisse* testifies to another kind of female pastor: the anchoress, a hermit who, rather than escaping to a remote place, lived in a hermitage built on to or near the parish church. The *Wisse* advises the anchoress that she must not preach, nor (except for the most mature) rebuke or advise men but that she may counsel women.[81]

When monks or regular canons did dispense pastoral care to the laity, what were its features? While monastic and canonical orders produced fewer famous theologians in the thirteenth century than in the twelfth, it does not follow that a monk or canon engaged in pastoral work was poorly qualified. The library of the Premonstratensians at Bradsole, as we have seen, included recent pastoral works in the thirteenth century but, while Wethringsett's *summa* was aimed at parish priests of good education, Peñaforte's and Chobham's required considerably more erudition. We may assume that at least some canons there could digest these works or there would have been little point in having them. Like friars and unlike parish priests, monks and canons submitted to formal novitiates in which both their education and their spiritual lives were developed and they were exposed to frequent preaching throughout their lives. If monks and

---

[77] B. Golding, 'Burials and Benefactions: An Aspect of Monastic Patronage', in M. W. Ormrod, ed., *England in the Thirteenth Century* (Grantham, Lincolnshire, 1985), 64–75.

[78] Robinson, *Augustinian Settlement*, 280–82; Brooke and Postan, eds, *Carte Nativorum*, no. 521.

[79] N. Orme, *From Childhood to Chivalry* (London, 1984), 62–65.

[80] *LAM*, 36–39; Reeves, *Religious Education*, 138.   [81] Millet, trans., *Ancrene Wisse*, 29.

canons were preaching publicly in the later thirteenth century, they may, like some parish clergy, have been influenced by the new preaching style known as the *sermo modernus*.[82] Frequent confession and the receipt of counsel from experienced elders offered the monk or canon experience that would equip him for the confessional and other means of spiritual direction. As the scholarly canon regular Ivo of Chartres (d. 1115) had opined, 'no one is more rightly promoted to the care of another man's life than one who has first become guardian of his own life.'[83] Ralph de Ireton OSA, bishop of Carlisle, instituted a fellow Augustinian Canon to a parochial vicarage around 1280, specifically noting that the new vicar's experience in receiving and administering the discipline of the Rule was good preparation for his new pastoral charge.[84]

Monks, canons regular and even female religious thus did tend to the souls of the laity but in ways that did not always parallel the *cura animarum* of parish priests or mendicant friars. While their direct pastoral care in England in general was apparently dwarfed by that of secular parish clergy and friars, they also occupied particular niches, such as custodians of major shrines, that neither of these groups could comfortably fill. For those with special connections to them, including their immediate neighbours, their presence could be substantial. Their pastoral practices were specific to circumstance and locality rather than generally diffused. As Part III will show in greater detail, such geographical specificity was not confined to monks. Local variation in pastoral care was common across England, determined not only by intangibles now lost to us (such as priests' personalities) but also by such varied factors as proximity to a town, ecclesiastical bureaucracy and physical landscape.

The training of a parish priest was neither as systematic nor as thorough as that of a friar, monk or canon. The monastic and mendicant orders, which had specific entrance requirements, also recruited some of the better-qualified and more diligent clergy who might otherwise have become or remained parish priests. Although some parish clergy perceived the friars as a threat, we should not be too quick to assume that fear of lost prestige and income always had the upper hand. It is more common to find protests in England from the older religious orders than from parish priests. The leadership of the mendicant orders often showed sensitivity to maintaining good relations: they specifically forbade their members to portray monks, canons and parish clergy in a bad light and even prohibited the use of certain papal privileges at the parish clergy's expense.[85] Local contexts were defined by delicate balances and concords,

---

[82] See pp. 106–12 below.   [83] Dickinson, *Austin Canons*, 217.
[84] *EEA 30*, 172.   [85] See further below, especially Chapter 7.

some of which have been enshrined in surviving documents, while others became customary and can only be guessed at. In practice, pastoral care became a co-operative venture among the different orders of clergy. The next three chapters will show how this operated in preaching, liturgy and confession.

PART II

The Processes of Pastoral Care

Chapter 5

PREACHING AND CATECHESIS

Now, to believe some things implicitly, and some explicitly: that is what is necessary of faith for salvation, for it can suffice for the faith of the simple. As to those things that ought to be believed explicitly, they are manifested not only in preaching, but also in the use and custom of the Church. This is the case with the Unity and Trinity, which they are able to know from the act of signing itself, for they sign themselves [with the cross] in the name of the Father and of the Son and of the Holy Spirit. This is the case with the birth, passion, resurrection, and remission of sins, which they are able to know from the solemnities itself that the Church celebrates, and from the actions of priests. Therefore, no-one is excused from awareness and notice of these things; nor is he excused by ignorance, for he cannot be so ignorant except by negligence and contempt. – But certainly, they are held to believe *implicitly* those other articles that are not thus manifested. I say *to believe implicitly*, as they ought to believe universally *in general* all that Holy Mother Church teaches: that is, they ought to dissent *in particular* from none of them, nor disbelieve in any of the articles.

So wrote the Franciscan Bonaventure of Bagnoreggio in his commentary on Peter Lombard's *Sentences* in the early 1250s. In preceding passages he had argued, as had many before him, that the Apostles' Creed contained all articles of faith necessary for salvation.[1] The doctrines and Gospel stories mentioned in the passage above all appear in that Creed, and his emphasis here is on simple folk who perhaps had limited exposure to adequate preaching. The structure of liturgy helped to teach the faith: *lex orandi, lex credendi.* Commenting a few years earlier on the same passage of Lombard's *Sentences*, but considering preaching more specifically, the Oxford Dominican Richard Fishacre had written,

For salvation, it is necessary to have a developed faith in the first article [of the Apostles' Creed, *I believe in God*], explicitly and distinctly. But whether that alone might have sufficed for ancient [pre-Christian Jewish] simple folk ... I dare not assert, nor the contrary, whether it should seem that this would have sufficed

---

[1] Bonaventure, *Opera* III, 544, 534–39; Reeves, *Religious Education*, 1–26.

for the mercy of God. But now, more is expected of simple folk of these times, since more articles [of the Creed] are preached distinctly to them. Thus, firstly, a distinct and developed faith in the first article seems to be sufficient for simple folk, though without contempt for the other articles, if they are able to hear them.[2]

Writing around 1270, the Franciscan Roger Bacon argued that

The things that are most helpful to grasp for human salvation are the vices and virtues, the glory of heaven and the punishment of purgatory and hell. Not only religious and theologians but also all clergy and laity and even poor old women know much about such things ... On account of the custom of the teaching of the church, all Christians have a great knowledge of those things that pertain to salvation ... [I]t is the duty of parish priests (*prelatorum*) to expound to the people the articles of faith and morals ... And therefore it is obvious that preaching depends not upon the study of theology but upon the teaching of the church which is known to anyone, and upon knowledge of vices and virtues, punishment and glory, and of other salvific things, knowledge of which is written in the heart by ritual through the practice of the church.[3]

These friars thus set modest requirements for the complexity of faith required for the salvation of the laity.[4] They hoped for more extensive preaching but were realistic about its limited availability. How limited was it?

Preaching to the laity was a well-established tradition in England by 1200; vernacular homilies had been written and delivered for centuries. One prolific homilist, the abbot Aelfric (d. ca. 1010), expected that bishops and priests should preach regularly, explaining the meaning of the Gospel each Sunday and feast-day and the Creed and *Paternoster* often.[5] The loss of manuscripts makes it impossible to tell how widely homilies such as Aelfric's circulated. Catechesis of the kind he described might create no written evidence in the first place.[6] Aelfric's mention of bishops reminds us that the friars were neither the first nor the only itinerant preachers. When a bishop made visitations, he or an official preached to the gathered clergy and laity of multiple parishes.[7] We have already met monks and canons, too, who preached to the laity in the late twelfth and early thirteenth centuries.[8] As Aelfric suggested, a visiting preacher's message might relate to the day's liturgical readings but could also be generally

---

[2] Richard Fishacre, *In tertium librum sententiarum*, Teil 2: Dist. 23–40, ed. Klaus Rodler (Munich, 2003), 45; Biller, 'Intellectuals'.
[3] J. S. Brewer, ed., *Fr. Rogeri Bacon Opera Quaedam Hactenus Inedita* (RS 15: London, 1859), 427–28.
[4] Tanner and Watson, 'Least of the Laity'; Arnold, *Belief and Unbelief*.
[5] *C&S* I, 205, 208–9.   [6] Pelle, 'Homiletic Eschatology', 16–43.
[7] Millet, 'Pastoral Context'.   [8] See above, pp. 83–84.

catechetical or hortatory. The preaching book of an early fourteenth-century English bishop ended with a long '*sermo*' on the seven sins which, though not a sermon in the restricted sense, might have served as a generic discourse.[9] The same book includes two crusade sermons, reminding us that crusade preaching by senior ecclesiastics travelling on a circuit was merely the best-documented form of such routine preaching.[10] It is not clear who the intended preachers of the late twelfth-century Trinity and Lambeth Homilies were, but Millet has shown that they exhibit considerable familiarity with contemporary developments in Parisian theology and preaching.[11] Whoever the bishops, priests, canons or monks were who used these to teach laypeople, they were participating in a venerable English tradition of preaching that long predated the career of Peter the Chanter and his circle. When he came to preach, the thirteenth-century English friar or parish priest was thus building upon a centuries-old foundation of catechesis of which Bonaventure claimed that no one could be 'ignorant except by negligence and contempt' and which, as Bacon asserted, was well known to 'all clergy and laity and even poor old women'.

PAROCHIAL PREACHING AND TEACHING

Moorman argued that a sermon by a parish priest in thirteenth-century England 'was a rare event' because he did not find the traces he thought it would have left.[12] Robertson countered that the evidence pointed in the other direction and that contemporaries seldom mentioned parish preaching because it was common and unremarkable.[13] Subsequent work has generally favoured Robertson's view but it is worth pausing to evaluate the surviving evidence for parochial preaching. For example, homiliaries or sermon books seldom appear in parish book lists.[14] But this does not mean that they were not there. Such lists recorded only the property of the parish, not the personal property of the priest. Some examples of preaching books that were the personal property of parish clergy in the thirteenth century still survive.[15]

---

[9] Bodleian Library, MS. Lat.th.e.24.   [10] Cole, *Preaching of the Crusades*.
[11] Millet, 'Discontinuity'.   [12] Moorman, *Church Life*, 77.
[13] D. W. Robertson Jr., 'Frequency of Preaching in Thirteenth-Century England', *Speculum* 24 (1949), 376–88.
[14] *Reg. St Osmund* I, 294; Sparrow-Simpson, '1249 Visitations', 31; Sparrow-Simpson, *1297 Visitations*, 18, 25; Feltoe and Minns, eds, *Vetus Liber*, 30, 65.
[15] Reeves, 'Secular Clergy in Dominican Schools'.

Diocesan statutes and other texts provided parish clergy with catechetical outlines and sometimes with the content to expound each point. The statutes of Salisbury, Canterbury and Durham enjoined:

Since the ecclesiastical sacraments ought to be handled and dispensed through our ministry, knowledge and profession of the Catholic faith is necessary for us; since without faith it is impossible to please God; and just as the body without the spirit is dead, faith without works is dead. Therefore, we command that you hold the right faith in good living, very often instructing your parishioners in the articles of faith, without which no-one is saved. So that you may do this more effectively and well, we strictly enjoin the archdeacons that in their chapters [meetings of clergy in the archdeaconry] they shall expound, soundly and with simple words, the exposition of the Catholic faith promulgated in the General Council.[16] And let the priests, as God may inspire them, instruct their parishioners and soundly impress upon them that exposition, frequently and in their local dialect.[17]

The next chapter in the statutes required the priest to instruct the children of his parish regularly, speaking to one or two at a time, in the Apostles' Creed, Lord's Prayer and *Ave Maria*.[18] The statutes also required priests to ensure that parishioners knew the words of baptism, in case of emergency. Priests were to admonish parishioners to have their children confirmed by the bishop and to come to confession at least once each year. Matrimony was to be commended, and the proper words for the vows were to be taught. Priests were to instruct parishioners to call for last rites in time of need and (in the Salisbury version) to encourage them to donate in their wills to the building of the new cathedral. Clergy were also to banish dances, parties and games from churches and churchyards.[19] The chapters on baptism and the mass were homiletic in nature and would have provided the priest with the material for teaching.[20]

In the 1220s, Richard of Wethringsett's summa *Qui bene presunt*, building on the writings of his teacher William de Montibus, instructed the priest to preach regularly on the Creed, Lord's Prayer, seven gifts of the Holy Spirit, seven cardinal virtues, seven deadly sins, seven sacraments, two commandments of love (of God and neighbour), Ten Commandments, rewards of heaven, punishment in hell, common errors and sins and duties corresponding to their station in life. The *summa* provided preaching material for all of these.[21] Grosseteste's *Templum Dei* described the Apostles' Creed, Lord's Prayer and *Ave Maria* – the same texts the Salisbury statutes indicated for teaching to children – as being necessary for

---

[16] That is, Lateran IV, c. 1.   [17] *C&S* II, 61.   [18] See also the statutes of Lincoln: *C&S* II, 269.
[19] *C&S* II, 69, 71, 73, 86–88, 90–91, 93.   [20] *C&S* II, 67–68, 77–79.
[21] Goering, *William de Montibus*, 86–91; Reeves, *Religious Education*, 67–74.

the laity to know, but also expected the priest to have 'a homilary book of Gregory [the Great], or of some other saint, that he may know how to expound the Gospel to the people' and categorised preaching freely to share divine wisdom as a priestly part of the virtue of prudence.[22] Bishop Stavensby of Coventry and Lichfield attached a tract to his diocesan statutes, beginning 'Let this be said by priests to all parishioners each Sunday or other feast-day: there are seven criminal sins which you ought to flee …', with a few hundred words of homiletic commentary on each sin.[23] His mid-century successor Roger de Weseham provided a short exposition of the twelve articles of the Apostles' Creed, reminding priests also to teach about the seven sacraments, seven gifts of the Spirit, seven virtues, Lord's Prayer, eight beatitudes, Decalogue and seven sins.[24] The statutes of Lincoln, Worcester, Norwich and Winchester required priests to know and preach the Decalogue and seven sins; the Worcester statutes provided a homiletic chapter on each of the seven.[25] The statutes of Wells, York, Carlisle and Exeter required the archdeacons, in the course of their visitations, to enquire whether the priest regularly preached on the Decalogue, seven sins, seven sacraments and whether he had a basic understanding of the contents of the Apostles', Nicene and Athanasian creeds.[26] In 1281, the Province of Canterbury received an official catechetical programme in the guise of Archbishop Pecham's canon *De informatione simplicium sacerdotum* (*Ignorantia sacerdotum*). Pecham listed articles of the creeds, the Ten Commandments, the two commandments of love, the seven works of mercy, the seven deadly sins, the seven cardinal virtues and the seven sacraments, though he provided only minimal commentary on each point. These were to be taught in every parish at least once a quarter.[27]

There were some vernacular texts that would enable the preacher to cover the catechetical material by simply reading them out, but not as many as we might expect. Sermon cycles and collections in English survive from the period to ca. 1200 (*Ormulum*, Lambeth and Trinity Homilies) and from ca. 1300 on (*Northern Homily Cycle*) but not from the thirteenth century. With a few notable exceptions, such as *Ancrene Wisse* and the *South English Legendary*, English was not in general use for pastoral texts in the thirteenth century.[28] The reason for this discontinuity are not fully understood. A status-conscious literary bias against the

[22] Grosseteste, *Templum*, 49–50.   [23] *C&S* II, 214–20.   [24] Cheney, *Synodalia*, 149–52.
[25] *C&S* II, 268, 304, 306–12, 345, 403.   [26] *C&S* II, 610, 1017.   [27] *C&S* II, 900–905.
[28] K. Breen, *Imagining an English Reading Public, 1150–1400* (Cambridge, 2010). T. J. Heffernan and P. J. Horner identified only nine English-language homilies or sermons dateable to the thirteenth century, and five of those are translations of sermons by Maurice de Sully: *A Manual of the Writings in Middle English 1050–1500*, vol. XI (New Haven, CT, 2005), 3998, 4043–48.

English vernacular was doubtless a large part of it. But, if the purpose of a written text was oral presentation to the laity anyway, it is hard to see why this literary bias would lead to a curtailment of vernacular homilies at precisely the same time that the emphasis on parochial pastoral care was bringing attention to the need for simple, practical texts for parish priests. French had higher prestige and was syntactically easier to translate into English than Latin was; pastoral, devotional and catechectical works composed in French, or translated from Latin into French, circulated in thirteenth-century England.[29] Knowledge of French had spread from noble and knightly families to the gentry and in some cases can be seen among upper burghers and peasantry, so it should have been familiar to many parish priests.[30] Yet not enough sermons or pastoral texts appeared in French either before ca. 1300 to fill the gap, and the fact that some French texts were translated into English in the early fourteenth century suggests that French did not offer ideal ease of use in the thirteenth century.[31]

Whatever the reason, we are left with a source-base for thirteenth-century English preaching that is mostly in Latin with a modest share of French and a handful of preachable English texts. No Latin sermon to the common people could have been preached precisely as written, for all translation is also interpretation. This also returns us to the problem of the Latin literacy of the parish clergy: even if a priest had a Latin homilary, it might have done him little good. Furthermore, of the few surviving sermon texts from thirteenth-century England where the author can be identified, the authors were friars, bishops, monks, scholars or secular or regular canons. There are no identifiable sermons at all composed by ordinary parish clergy. Yet d'Avray observed that the sermons of the friars often assume a pre-existing base of religious knowledge on the part of lay listeners.[32] The parish clergy must have been the source of much of this catechesis.

Not every priest had a handbook of sermons in any language and not every bishop provided handy content for catechesis. As William de Montibus pointed out, simply preaching 'Do good, and it will be well with

---

[29] Reeves, *Religious Education*, 130–59; T. Hunt, ed., and J. Bliss, trans., *'Cher Alme': Texts of Anglo-Norman Piety* (Tempe, AZ, 2010); H. Deeming, 'French Devotional Texts in Thirteenth-Century Preachers' Anthologies', in J. Wogan-Browne, ed., *Language and Culture in Medieval Britain: The French of England, c. 1100–c. 1500* (York, 2009), 254–65; C. M. Waters, *Translating Clergie: Status, Education, and Salvation in Thirteenth-Century Vernacular Texts* (Philadelphia, 2016).

[30] Bartlett, *Norman and Angevin Kings*, 486–90; Mayr-Harting, *Religion*, 102; M. Richter, *Sprache und Gesellschaft im Mittelalter* (Stuttgart, 1979), 206–15.

[31] I. Short, 'On Bilingualism in Anglo-Norman England', *Romance Philology* 33 (1980), 467–79.

[32] d'Avray, *Preaching*, 82–90; but cf. Reeves, *Religious Education*, 89–129, who demonstrates that many mendicant sermons also imparted catechesis.

you' or 'Avoid evil and do good' was no better than telling a traveller 'Stay on the right road' or a sick person 'Avoid illness': the preacher needed practical content.[33] The Council of Oxford (1222) required priests to expound the word of God to their parishioners as God inspired them but some may not have felt adequately inspired.[34] Grosseteste counselled any cleric who felt unable to preach to review during the week the Gospel text for the next Sunday so he could at least explain it to his parishioners in English, the following year to do the same with the Epistle readings and the third year with the lives of the saints. If he did not understand the Latin well enough, he should consult another priest in the neigh-bourhood. He concluded: 'You have your missal and your breviary with which to work.'[35] In other words, the lack of written preaching texts was no excuse for shirking regular preaching. The vicar of Colebrook (Devon) in 1301 seems to have been doing much as Grosseteste advised: although there was no homilary listed among the parish's books, and he did not teach much on the Creed, Decalogue or seven sins, he did preach in his own way, and on Sundays expounded the Gospels according to his ability.[36] In the same visitation, the vicars of Staverton, St Mary Church, Dawlish, Sidbury and Culmstock, and the chaplain of Dawlish, none of which reported homilaries among the parish books, were all reported to teach the parishioners well in spiritual things.[37] Almost any sacred book – not just the Gospel book, epistolary, breviary and legenda indicated by Grosseteste but also other liturgical books, diocesan statutes, confessor's manuals and assorted other *pastoralia* – could be a source for the parish priest to use in preaching and catechesis.[38] As Bonaventure noted in the quote that opens this chapter, laypeople learned doctrine by participating in the liturgy but that implies that the liturgy was being explained to them at least at a basic level, and liturgical books themselves provided relevant material. The statutes of Chichester required priests to preach regularly on the Trinity, incarnation, nativity, passion, resurrection and ascension of Christ, the general resurrection of the dead and that all coitus outside marriage is sinful.[39] The last two points related respectively to the services of burial and matrimony, while all the others corresponded to points in the church year. Each would be reflected in the liturgies proper to those events, days and seasons.

Preaching aimed not only to inform but also to form. Peter the Chanter insisted that good works should precede doctrine and that preaching should reflect this priority.[40] His colleague Alain de Lille defined

[33] Goering, *William de Montibus*, 305–6.   [34] *C&S* II, 110.
[35] Gieben, 'Grosseteste on Preaching', 111–12.   [36] Whitley, 'Visitations', 451.
[37] Ibid., 454–62.   [38] Shinners, 'Parish Libraries'.
[39] *C&S* II, 455.   [40] *Verbum Adbreviatum*, 34–35.

preaching as 'open and public instruction in morals and faith, serving to form men'.[41] Moral instruction could come verbally and English episcopal statutes are full of directions to exhort the laity to moral living; but it could also be given by the priest's own behaviour. This idea dates at least to the time of Gregory the Great and we find it throughout English statutes and other texts.[42] In this way, even a priest of modest literacy could 'preach' well by living a celibate, sober and peaceable life.

FRIARS AS PREACHERS

Like parish priests, friars could 'preach' by example.[43] Around 1236, Grosseteste wrote the following to Alexander Stavensby, former teacher of Dominic and his first friars, now bishop of Coventry and Lichfield:

For Your Prudence knows how useful the presence and co-inhabitation of Friars Minor are to the people with whom they live; since likewise by the word of preaching and by the example of holy and heavenly manner of life, and the continual devotion of constant prayer, they both bring peace tirelessly and enlighten the land, and they make up on this part for the greater part of the shortcomings of parsons ... the behaviour of the said Friars Minor is the illumination of the people with whom they live, unto the knowledge of truth and the direction, drawing, goading and pushing [of the people] into the way of peace.[44]

When Grosseteste emphasised preaching by example here, it was in part because, unlike the Order of Friars Preachers, the Franciscans arrived in England at a time when their own ministry of preaching was still developing.[45] This was related to their somewhat controversial evolution from a predominantly lay movement into an educated clerical order.[46] The *Regula Bullata*, the Franciscan Rule of 1223, spelt out the limits of preaching in Chapter 9:

The friars may not preach in the diocese of any bishop if he has forbidden them from doing so. And let no friar dare to preach publicly unless he has been examined and approved by the Minister General of this brotherhood, and the office of preaching has been granted him. I [Francis] also warn and exhort those friars that in the preaching they do, their eloquence should be considered and

---

[41] PL CCXX, 111.   [42] PL LXXIX, 100, 153, 154, 158; *C&S* II, 62, 710.

[43] Tugwell, *Early Dominicans*, 16–19.

[44] Luard, ed., *Grosseteste Epistolae*, 120–22; cf. F. A. C. Mantello and J. Goering, trans., *The Letters of Robert Grosseteste, Bishop of Lincoln* (Toronto, 2009), 149.

[45] M. W. Blastic, 'Preaching in the Early Franciscan Movement', in T. Johnson, ed., *Franciscans and Preaching: Every Miracle from the Beginning of the World Came about through Words* (Leiden, 2012), 15–40.

[46] See now Şenocak, *Poor and the Perfect*.

modest, for the usefulness and edification of the people, announcing to them the vices and virtues, punishment and glory, with brevity of speech; since the words of the Lord on earth were brief.[47]

Following the earlier distinction that Innocent III had made for the Humiliati, Honorius III limited lay Franciscans to moral exhortation and did not permit them to preach doctrine.[48] However, preaching on the vices and virtues, the torments of hell and the joys of heaven offered considerable latitude for exhorting lay listeners to a holier life. Even as the order grew more educated and clerical and its preaching remit was extended to include doctrine, these themes remained important, for they were enshrined in the order's Rule; we find this passage, or paraphrases of it, either quoted in Franciscan preaching books or reflected in their content.[49]

The first sentence of the *Regula Bullata*'s chapter on preaching raises the question of permission to preach. Not every friar, regardless of his order, was a public preacher, except by example. Each order developed internal procedures of examination and authorisation.[50] Once licensed by their orders, friars could be invited to preach by parish priests.[51] Pecham's *Ignorantia sacerdotum* ordered the parish priest to see to it that the catechetical items were all taught, whether by himself or through another.[52] The friars would be obvious candidates for guest preachers. Other bishops ordered their parish clergy to admit friars to preach or otherwise indicated official support.[53] However, the *Regula Bullata* did not specifically require the bishop's permission, only that he should not forbid the friars to preach. The Dominicans had been given a papal privilege in 1217 that gave them a universal right of preaching, with no further permission needed or denials recognised, though it encouraged them to consult with local bishops.[54] The orders of friars continued to receive papal privileges

---

[47] *Reg. Bull.* IX.

[48] M. Lauwers, 'Praedicatio – Exhortatio: l'Église, la Réforme et les Laïcs (XIᵉ-XIIIᵉ siècles)', in R. M. Dessì and M. Lauwers, eds, *La Parole du Prédicateur, Vᵉ–XVᵉ siècle* (Nice, France, 1997), 187–232.

[49] E.g. Little, ed., *Liber Exemplorum*; Welter, *Speculum Laicorum*; Wenzel, *Verses in Sermons*, 10 (for the *Monoloquium* of John of Wales); S. Gieben, 'Preaching in the Franciscan Order (Thirteenth Century)', in E. B. King et al., eds, *Monks, Nuns, and Friars in Medieval Society* (Sewanee, TN, 1989), 1–27, at 24); *FM*, 32–33; National Library of Scotland, MS. Advocates 18.7.21, ff. 137r–139v.

[50] Roest, *Franciscan Education*, 272–79, 283–85; Mulchahey, *First the Bow*, 184–93; *Const. Ratisbonenses*, 115–16; D. Gutiérrez, *The Augustinians in the Middle Ages, 1256–1356* (Villanova, PA, 1984), 186–90; Roth, *Austin Friars* II, 61.

[51] *Reg. Stapledon*, 111.   [52] *C&S* II, 901.

[53] *C&S* II, 265, 386, 595–96, 995. Further statutes requiring parish priests to admit friars to hear confessions may have assumed that preaching was permitted as well.

[54] Vicaire, *Dominic*, 222–23, 240–43, 418ff.

granting them rights to preach at will, including the 1254 bull *Etsi ani-marum*, which allowed Franciscan and Dominican friars to enter parish pulpits with or without the parish priest's permission.[55] Later legislation introduced some common-sense restrictions, such as not setting up to preach at a time when the local priest was also preaching.[56]

As this suggests, the borrowed parish pulpit was not the friars' only venue for preaching. They had their own churches, some of which could accommodate very large congregations. Around the end of the century, the London Dominican priory had a nave measuring 120 × 66 feet, nearly 8,000 square feet. While the nave included aisles, the columns were particularly slender, to allow more congregants to view the preacher.[57] A nave of this size could hold perhaps a thousand auditors. Early in the next century the London Franciscans surpassed this with a church measuring three hundred feet long (including the chancel) and eighty-nine feet wide.[58] Friars were also known for preaching outdoors. This could be occasioned by a gathering too large to fit in a single building, as may have happened at Grosseteste's visitations of his diocese, when he preached to the clergy of each deanery (notionally about ten parishes) while an accompanying friar preached to the gathered laypeople.[59] Streets and squares in towns and villages also offered a large venue, with the added benefit that people did not have to be convinced to come into the church for a sermon. London rectors complained in 1309 that the friars were not only funding their large churches by siphoning off lay donations that used to support their poor parish priests but that friars who were preaching in public spaces might be unlicensed.[60]

THE SERMO MODERNUS

Both medieval and modern commentators on later medieval preaching have observed that it fell along a spectrum, with two extremes and a middle ground.[61] One end of the spectrum was simple, unadorned instruction, with little complexity and no pretence of art. At the other end lay the *sermo modernus*, a highly sophisticated structure based on principles of classical rhetoric, first appearing in the later twelfth century and becoming

[55] Little, *Studies*, 110–12.   [56] Lawrence, *The Friars*, 152–65.
[57] *EEFP*, 136.   [58] Kingsford, *Friars of London*, 38–39.
[59] *C&S* II, 265.   [60] *C&S* II, 1256–57.
[61] Thomas of Chobham, *Summa de Arte*, 273–74; Th.-M. Charland OP, *Artes Praedicandi* (Paris and Ottawa, 1936), 325–403, at 356; *Magistri Alexandri de Hales: Quaestiones Disputatae 'Antequam esset frater'* (Quaracchi, 1960), I 518; J. W. Blench, *Preaching in England in the Late Fifteenth and Sixteenth Centuries: A Study of English Sermons 1450–c. 1600* (New York, 1964), 113; H. Caplan, *Of Eloquence: Studies in Ancient and Mediaeval Rhetoric* (Ithaca, NY, 1970), 76–78.

more complex thereafter. The basic catechesis we have considered above would have been at the humble end. The middle ground was occupied by the traditional homily, which took the listeners through a whole biblical text, typically the Gospel reading appointed for the day.[62] Such humble to middling preaching may represent much of what parishioners, especially rural ones, heard in their lifetimes. But the bulk of surviving manuscript evidence represents the *sermo modernus* that was being developed and diffused among learned preachers, especially under the influence of Paris.[63] Unlike the homily, the *sermo modernus* did not go through the whole passage: it began with a very short extract (thema) from the day's lectionary and divided it into several sections of one or a few words each.[64] Each of these sections was developed in a division of the sermon to make a catechetical or moral point. A variety of works co-evolved with educated preaching, designed to help the preacher find the information he needed to expand upon his text or theme.[65] The undeniable utility of these new technologies of communication meant that even an otherwise conservative preacher would gladly turn to them in preparing sermons.[66] The friars were the primary but not the sole agents through whom such sermons and ideas about preaching were disseminated.[67] They not only composed new sermons themselves; they also received and re-used sermons by others, such as the manuscript of the sermons of Philip the Chancellor of Paris owned by the Canterbury Franciscans.[68] So, it must be emphasised, did some educated secular clergy; but their numbers, locations and activities are much harder for us to trace. In part because so many *sermones moderni* survive – tens of thousands – the literature on them is vast and it is possible to read a great deal about medieval preaching without ever reading a surviving sermon. This does not bring us close to the experience of the medieval parishioner. We shall examine here one sample sermon that would have required additional content in practice and then consider the types of content that could have been added and what sources a preacher had for them.[69]

---

[62] For examples of such homiles, see S. Irvine, ed., *Old English Homilies from MS Bodley 343* (Early English Text Society, Original Series no. 302: Oxford, 1993) and A. B. Thompson, ed., *The Northern Homily Cycle* (Kalamazoo, MI, 2008).
[63] Bériou, *L'Avènement*; Rouse and Rouse, *Preachers*.
[64] S. Wenzel, ed. and trans., *The Art of Preaching: Five Medieval Texts and Translations* (Washington, DC, 2013), 24–39, 108–21.
[65] Rouse and Rouse, *Preachers*, 3–42.
[66] J. G. Tuthill, 'The School Sermon Exported: The Case of Pelagius Parvus', *Viator* 22 (1991), 169–88.
[67] d'Avray, *Preaching*; Roest, *Franciscan Education*, 279–91; Mulchahey, *First the Bow*, 400–479.
[68] R. M. Thomson, *Catalogue of the Manuscripts of Lincoln Cathedral Library* (Cambridge, 1989), 26.
[69] Fuller sermons are examined in detail in Wenzel, *Artes Praedicandi* and Akae, *Sermon Collection*.

Cambridge, St John's College MS. 255/S19 is a sermon manuscript, apparently of the second half of the thirteenth century, bearing marks of English Franciscan provenance, such as notes in English and a preponderance of English or Franciscan saints.[70] The authors of its sermons have not been identified, but we may safely assume that it was used: at a mere 5 × 3 1/2 inches, it is certainly a *vademecum*, a compact book made for travelling, the sort that friars particularly favoured for sermons and breviaries to take on preaching tours. It also has a table of contents and marginal notations to help the preacher keep track of his place while preaching. It is a fairly complete sermon collection for the year, comprising two *temporale* cycles (the ordinary Sundays, feasts and fasts of the year) and one *sanctorale* (set of sermons for saints' days).[71] What follows is a single sermon from the first *temporale* cycle.[72] It is not quite an outline: even shorter forms, little diagrams called *distinctiones*, exist in many preaching manuscripts and could have provided the structure to largely extemporaneous sermons.[73] It is, however, a well-articulated skeleton, leaving the preacher a great deal of discretion in what content to include, at what intellectual level and in what quantity. The text is as follows:

Volo mundare. Mt' 8. Benedictus salvator sicut omnium est creator inesse primo sic omnium se ostendit reformatorem inesse secunda et ideo in verbis premissis erga peccatorem convertendum.	I want to clean [you]. Matthew 8. As the blessed Saviour is firstly the creator of all things that exist, so, secondly, he shows himself to be their reformer, and thus in the foregoing words towards the sinner to be converted.
Primo manifestat affectum ibi volo. Secundo subiungit effectum. ibi mundare.	Firstly, he displays the desire, here I want; secondly, he connects the result, here to clean.
¶ Dicit igitur pro primo. volo ¶ Circa quid est advertendum quod voluntas beneplaciti dei circa animam humanam requirit pro preteritis commissis penitentiam pro presentibus oblatis abstinentiam	Therefore, he says I want first. Regarding this, it should be noted that the will of the pleasure of God regarding the human soul requires penance for things committed in the past; for things offered in the present, abstinence; and for things

[70] The hand of the first part of the manuscript, from which this example comes, is a Gothic Northern Textualis Textus Quadratus script with thirteenth-century features, but it is not narrowly dateable. Derolez, *Gothic Manuscript Books*, 72–97.

[71] M. R. James, *A Descriptive Catalogue of the Manuscripts in the Library of St John's College, Cambridge* (Cambridge, 1913), 291; J. B. Schneyer, ed., *Repertorium der lateinischen Sermones des Mittelalters für die Zeit von 1150–1350* (Münster, in 9 vols, 1964–) VII, 202–12.

[72] This sermon appears on pp. 6–7 of the manuscript.

[73] For examples and discussion, see O'Carroll, *Studies*, 175–91.

et pro futuris offerendis vel custodiam premuniti<o>nam circumspectationem.

¶ Pro primo dei pe[ter] .3. *Non tardat dominus promissi sed pacienter agit propter vos nolens aliquos perire sed omnes ad penitentiam converti*[74] ¶ Pro 2° thessalonicanses 4 *Hec est voluntas dei sanctificatio vestra ut abstineatis vos a fornicatione* et cetera.[75] ¶ Pro 3° dicit apostolus ad colossenses 1 *Non cessamus pro vobis orantes ut impleamini agnicione voluntatis eius ut ambuletis digne deo per omnia placentes et in bono opera fructificantes*[76] videlicet ad precavenda futura

¶ Sedque dominus voluit quid placeret in opere. quod latuit in affecione. ideo subiungit in themate *mundare.* ¶ Circa quod est advertendum quod per tria consuevit dominus nostrum procurare mundiciam. videlicet per lavacrum regeneracionis in baptismate. per profluvium lacrimarum in sacramento penitentie. et per collacionem elemosinarum quantum ad opera misericordie.

¶ Pro primo dicit dominus in ezechiel 26 *Effundam super vos aquam mundam et mundabimini.*[77] ¶ Pro 2° dicit Psalmista *Lavabo per singulas noctes* id est per singulas culpas *lectum meum* id est conscienciam meam *lacrimis meis stratum meum rigabo*[78] et infra *Asperges me domine hysopo er mundabor* et cetera.[79] ¶ Pro 3° Dic' salvator Luc' xi *Date elemosinam et ecce omnia munda sunt vobis.*[80]

to be offered in the future, protection, preparation and caution.

Firstly, God [says in] Peter 3: *The Lord does not delay his promises, but acts patiently towards you, not wishing anyone to perish but that all should convert to penance.* Secondly, Thessalonians 4: *This is the will of God: your sanctification, that you should restrain yourselves from fornication* etc. Thirdly, the Apostle says to the Colossians, 1: *We do not cease to pray for you, that you may be filled with the knowledge of his will, that you may walk, worthy of God, pleasing in all things and bearing fruit in good works,* namely, in future things to be guarded against.

But the Lord wanted what would please him in work that lay hidden in the desire; therefore, he added *to clean* in the thema. With respect to this, it should be noted that our Lord is accustomed to administer cleanness by three means, namely: through the font of regeneration in baptism; through the flowing forth of tears in the sacrament of penance; and through the contribution of alms insofar as it is a work of mercy.

Firstly, the Lord says in Ezekiel 26: *I will pour out clean water upon you and make you clean.* Secondly, the Psalmist says: *Every night* (that is, in every fault) *I will wash my bed* (that is, my conscience); *with my tears will I water my couch* and, later, *You shall sprinkle me with hyssop and I will be cleansed* et cetera. Thirdly, the Saviour said in Luke 11: *Give alms: and behold, all things are clean to you.*

Not all features of a full *sermo modernus* are evident in this example. Like other sermons in this manuscript, it does not contain the optional

---

[74] II Peter 3:9.   [75] I Thess. 4:3–4a.   [76] Cf. Col. 1:9–10.
[77] Actually Ezekiel 36:25.   [78] Ps. 6:7.   [79] Ps. 50 (Vulg.):9.   [80] Lk. 11:41b.

introduction called the *antethema* or *prothema* found in many sermons, where the thema was introduced, the audience exhorted to listen well, the preacher's humility emphasised and a short prayer offered for preacher and audience alike, before the re-introduction of the thema.[81] It is merely the outline of a sermon, and would last about three minutes if preached as it stands here. It also lacks any kind of conclusion. Yet the features that this sermon does display were typical of a *sermo modernus*.

The thema was drawn from the day's appointed Gospel reading, in which Jesus cleansed a leper, but the story is not told here. In a *sermo modernus*, some decontextualisation of the thema was common.[82] In the second collection in this manuscript, for instance, the sermon for Palm Sunday is on the text *Behold your king comes to you, meek* and, instead of there being a sermon on the triumphal entry of Jesus into Jerusalem, there is merely a note referring the reader to the sermon for the first Sunday in Advent, since it uses the same scriptural thema.[83] That sermon spoke of the three comings of Christ (in the incarnation; in the resurrection; in the believer's heart), making it sufficient for either occasion. Decontextualisation from the biblical passage may not have been as complete in practice as it appears on the page, however. Notes before some sermons in an English Dominican collection remind the preacher to tell the Gospel story before beginning the sermon, which may have been common practice.[84] In this Franciscan collection, too, the thema is not chosen without regard for the feast itself; other Advent sermons are on the appropriate themata 'Come, Lord Jesus' and 'Prepare the way of the Lord'.[85]

After introducing the thema, the preacher divides it into 'members' (here *volo* and *mundare*); a longer text might be divided into three or more members.[86] Each member will be developed in a major part of the sermon, a 'principal'. Each principal is subdivided, here into three sections apiece, each one in turn confirmed by an appeal to authority. In this sermon, the Bible is quoted in every case but patristic and other authorities were often used.[87] Finding biblical passages with the verbal parallelism seen here was made possible by the Dominicans' creation of the textual Bible concordance earlier in the century.[88] The first principal

---

[81] O'Carroll, *Studies*, 26; Wenzel, *Artes Praedicandi*, 55–62; Akae, *Sermon Collection*, 124–27.

[82] On selection of a *thema*, see Wenzel, *Artes Praedicandi*, 50–55; Akae, *Sermon Collection*, 124–25.

[83] Cambridge, St John's College, MS. 255/S19, p. 179; the sermon is on pp. 53–58. Matthew 21:5b; Zecharaiah 9:9b.

[84] O'Carroll, *Studies*, 26.   [85] Cambridge, St John's College, MS. 255/S19, pp. 65–79.

[86] For the exceedingly technical details of *sermo modernus* composition, see Wenzel, *Artes Praedicandi* and Akae, *Sermon Collection*.

[87] O'Carroll, *Studies*, 398–405.   [88] Ibid., 31–32.

concerns the benevolent will of God for the past, present and future: God *wills* for no one to perish for past sins, *willing* instead their present sanctification, while Paul prays that they may know the *will* of God that in the future they may please God in fruitful works. The second principal is shown to flow logically from the first, not once but twice: in the initial *divisio*, in which the author had promised to address how God's *affectus* (desire) for good works has its *effectus* (result) in cleansing the Christian, and again in the transition between the principals, where he proposed to show how one leads to the other. Here too, there is a logical and chronological progression. The liturgical washing of baptism comes first, followed by confession (with a two-fold washing: the penitent washes himself with tears of contrition, after which God washes the penitent of sin), and finally almsgiving, which the passage from Luke quoted here described as a means of cleansing oneself inwardly, and which was one means of doing penance after confession. This sermon turns out to be artificial, not in the sense of 'strained' as it might at first appear, but rather as a work of artifice, a reflection upon what the words *volo mundare* would mean for the individual Christian who needed to repent, beginning with the benevolence of God, working through the sacraments and ending with an exhortation to pious action in the world. Decontextualised from the story of the leper, it was recontextualised to the listener's moral life and salvation, and even to the liturgical season. Since Advent was treated as a lesser Lent, especially in dioceses where laypeople physically received the Eucharist at Christmas as well as at Easter, it was a particularly appropriate time for a sermon encouraging confession and penance.[89]

When a preacher came to deliver a sermon such as this one, he would want additional material to illustrate and support his points. The first sermon cycle in this manuscript consists entirely of skeletal sermons such as our example, while the second contains fuller treatments that provided the preacher with everything he needed. There existed many textual aids, source books made specifically for the preacher who wanted to put flesh on the bones of a sermon. These might be consulted in a library while writing a full sermon text, but they could be read there to commit ideas to memory.[90] There are also *vademecum* miscellanies apparently compiled for the friar going on a preaching tour.[91] These source books display the same range of material that can be found in fuller sermon texts but the

---

[89] *C&S II*, 72–73, 236–37, 593, 639, 705.

[90] J. Berlioz, 'La mémoire du prédicateur. Recherches sur la mémorisation des récits exemplaires (XIIIe–XVe siècles)', in *Temps, mémoire, tradition au Moyen Age* (Aix-en-Provence, 1983), 157–83.

[91] E.g. British Library, Royal MS. 7.D.i; Bodleian Library Laud Misc. MS. 2 (Campbell, 'Franciscan Preaching in Thirteenth-Century England', 18–25). A later example (dated 1372) is National Library of Scotland, Advocates MS. 18.7.21.

experienced preacher who wanted more freedom to shape his message might well have preferred the skeletal sermon and be free to choose his illustrations and expositions.

EXEMPLA, MORALISATIONS AND EMOTIONAL APPEAL

One common way to support a point in a sermon was by using *exempla*. Both in the Middle Ages and in modern medieval scholarship, the term *exemplum* is used in both a broader and a narrower sense. The narrower sense is the narrative *exemplum*, a moral tale, while the broader sense includes non-narrative forms. Each of these has several different types, though the boundaries among them are indistinct.[92] Narrative and non-narrative *exempla* alike were used not only to illustrate a point but also to give it rhetorical and emotional force.[93] Alain de Lille wrote that the preacher 'should make use of examples to prove what he says, because teaching by means of examples is a familiar method'.[94] Alexander of Ashby commented that *exempla* could be a two-edged sword for confirming the preacher's message: he ought to expound 'some sweet allegory and narrate some humorous *exemplum*, that the profoundness of the allegory may delight the educated and the levity of the *exemplum* might edify the simple, so that each of them may have something to take away'.[95]

Narrative *exempla* included saints' lives, miracle tales, historical stories and fables. Stories from a saint's life would naturally occur in a sermon for that saint's feast-day. In the sermon of John of Wales OFM (d. 1285) for the feast of Martin of Tours, there are two *exempla*, both drawn from legends of that saint.[96] But hagiographical *exempla* are also often found wherever they could drive home the preacher's point. Legends of saints also furnished miracle tales. There was much overlapping between hagiographical collections such as the *Vitae Patrum*, the *South English Legendary* and the *Golden Legend* on the one hand and explicitly sermon-oriented *exempla* sourcebooks such as the *Dialogus Miraculorum* of Caesarius of Heisterbach (c. 1220) and the English Franciscan manuals *Speculum Laicorum* (1279 × 1292) and *Fasciculus Morum* (c. 1300). Historical tales from both the Christian and the pagan past were also a rich source of material often encountered in *exempla* collections. John of Wales, an enormously prolific and

---

[92] Akae, *Sermon Collection*, 151–72; O'Carroll, *Studies*, 191–201.

[93] L. Scanlon, *Narrative, Authority and Power: The Medieval Exemplum and the Chaucerian Tradition* (Cambridge, 1994), 30, 35.

[94] Alan of Lille, *The Art of Preaching*, trans. G. R. Evans (Kalamazoo, MI, 1981), 22.

[95] F. Morenzoni, ed., 'Aux origines des «Artes praedicandi». Le «De artificioso modo predicandi» d'Alexandre d'Ashby', *Studi Medievali* 3rd ser. 32 (1991), 887–935, at 905.

[96] Paris, Bibliothèque Nationale, MS. 14947, ff. 187rb–188va.

influential compiler, specialised in stories and moral *dicta* from classical antiquity.[97]

Fables or other fabricated stories had to be used with care to prevent confusion with stories of the supernatural that were presented as historically true. Thomas of Chobham insisted that the preacher distinguish between 'parables', which may not have happened but must be plausible, and 'exposition of deeds ... in histories', which must be true stories.[98] In the twelfth century, 'Walter of England' created his Christianised version of Aesop's Fables so that those using these *exempla*, metaphors and similitudes might more effectively persuade various sorts of people to live better lives.[99] Odo of Cheriton, an English secular clerk, wrote his compilations of *Fabulae* and *Parabolae* in the second quarter of the thirteenth century, some years after writing sermon cycles that made use of such stories as *exempla*.[100] These stories were used in turn by other authors of *exempla* collections and sermons, such as *Speculum Laicorum* and some sermons in an English Dominican collection.[101]

Non-narrative *exempla* or *similitudines* were also important parts of the preacher's repertoire. William de Montibus explained the purpose of his *Similitudinarium*:

For explaining an argument in any kind of discourse (*sermone*), I have collected similitudes from wherever they were given by God, knowing that examples and similitudes prove propositions brought forth in public and clarify authorities and reasonings.[102]

Moralisations from nature drew upon encyclopaedic works such as bestiaries, many of which had explicitly religious aims: some even contain moral verses by William de Montibus.[103] The phoenix reborn from the ashes of its immolation and the 'pelican in her piety' (resurrecting her young with her blood from self-inflicted wounds) were both obvious Christological images; they appear in this guise in the Aberdeen Bestiary (English, ca. 1200) and were commonplace in sermons and books of sermon material.[104] Moralisations from nature overlapped with moralisations from everyday experience. One sermon in the St John's

[97] Swanson, *John of Wales.*   [98] Thomas of Chobham, *Summa de Arte*, 272.
[99] A. E. Wright, ed., *The Fables of 'Walter of England'* (Toronto, 1997), 20–21.
[100] Sharpe, *Handlist*, 403–5; A. C. Friend, 'Master Odo of Cheriton', *Speculum* 23 (1948), 641–58.
[101] Welter, *Speculum Laicorum*, xxiii–xxxiii; O'Carroll, *Studies*, 192–93.
[102] Goering, *William de Montibus*, 313. For other 'mixed' collections and the types of material they contained, see *FM* and Rouse and Rouse, *Preachers.*
[103] C. Van Duzer and I. Dines, 'The Only Mappamundi in a Bestiary Context: Cambridge, MS Fitzwilliam 254', *Imago Mundi* 58 (2006), 7–22, at 17.
[104] Aberdeen University Library, MS. 24, ff. 34v–35v; O'Carroll, *Studies*, 347, 349; *FM*, 209; Reeves, *Religious Education*, 73.

manuscript explained that confession of sins is like plucking an iron from the fire: the iron is hot enough to injure at first but it cools down over time.[105]

The emotional content of narrative *exempla* was intended not only to hold the listener's attention but also to move the emotions. The mendicants' penitential preaching was designed to induce contrition: sorrow over sin and the intention to amend one's life, including confession to a priest and undertaking the penance he would enjoin.[106] Humbert of Romans OP wrote, 'Fruit is sowed in preaching and harvested in confession.'[107] Anthony of Padua OFM counselled that 'The preacher's wise words should ... produce sorrow for past sins and for meriting the pains of hell.'[108] The textual relics of the mendicants' preaching in England show the same tendency.[109] The contents of the Dominican sermon collection in MS. Laud Misc. 511 confirm that penitential preaching was considered particularly appropriate in Lent but took place at other times as well.[110] It is no surprise, then, that the friars' penitential sermons were often followed by hearing confessions.[111]

PREACHER AND STYLE

Tempting as it is to assume that parish priests only used homilies and friars always preached *sermones moderni*, we have no solid reason for such a conclusion and reason to doubt it. Several surviving manuscripts of *sermones moderni* show signs of having been owned by pastorally active and well-educated parish priests.[112] Meanwhile, some friars worried that the rhetoric of the *sermo modernus* had become so stylised that a preacher might focus too much on showing his sophistication and too little on communicating his message.[113] There is also evidence that the friars preached and taught in less formal ways. They created and used texts that

---

[105] Cambridge, St John's College, MS. 255/S19, p. 551.

[106] K. L. Jansen, 'Mary Magdalen and the Mendicants', *Journal of Medieval History* 21 (1995), 1–25; Rivi, *Francis* 55–99; Roest, *Franciscan Education*, 316.

[107] Humbert, *Opera* II, 479; cf. 31. Cf. also words of Pierre de Rheims OP, quoted in d'Avray, *Preaching*, 50.

[108] Anthony of Padua, *Sermones*, 106.

[109] Little and Douie, 'Sermons of Jordan of Saxony'; *FM, passim*; Welter, *Speculum Laicorum, passim*; O'Carroll, *Studies*, esp. 180, 183, 189.

[110] O'Carroll, *Studies*, 149–56; Wenzel, *Sermon Collections*, 246.   [111] d'Avray, *Preaching*, 51.

[112] Reeves, 'Secular Clergy in Dominican Schools'; Reeves, *Religious Education*, 74–82.

[113] O'Carroll, *Studies*, 28; *C&S* II, 901; T. Johnson, 'Preaching Precedes Theology: Roger Bacon on the Failure of Mendicant Education', *Franciscan Studies* 68 (2010), 83–95; T. Johnson, 'Roger Bacon's Critique of Franciscan Preaching', in F. J. Felten, A. Kehnel and S. Weinfurter, eds, *Institution und Charisma: Festschrift für Gert Melville* (Vienna, 2009), 541–48.

were more systematic and topical in nature, such as the *Summa iuniorum* of Simon of Hinton OP. This text covers the twelve articles of the Creed, the seven petitions of the *Paternoster*, the Ten Commandments, the seven sacraments, the seven virtues, the gifts of the Holy Spirit and the eight beatitudes.[114] Simon's *Summa* could be used as a handbook for catechesis; his table of contents is very similar to Pecham's preaching syllabus *Ignorantia sacerdotum* and Wethringsett's *Qui bene presunt*. Wethringsett wrote for the parish priest, and we may assume that *Qui bene presunt* was used as a 'crypto-preaching aid' for teaching the laity.[115] Yet a friar too could have used it, or Hinton's *summa*, or any other appropriately edifying text, to catechise laypeople without using the *sermo modernus* style, following instead the structure of the text in front of him. If a friar was invited to help a parish priest comply with *Ignorantia sacerdotum*, this would have been the most straightforward way to accomplish it. A mendicant preacher also could have used *Fasciculus Morum* – which embedded *exempla*, moralisations, verse tags, patristic *sententiae* and biblical quotations and glosses in an orderly running commentary structured on the seven sins – as an unmediated source for homiletic presentations.[116]

There is other evidence of informal spiritual discussion between mendicants and individuals or small groups which was neither preaching nor confession in the narrow sense. The legislation of the Franciscan, Dominican, Carmelite and Austin Friars all made specific prescriptions to permit a friar to speak with a woman for legitimate reasons without leading to scandal or libidinous thoughts, words and deeds.[117] The constitutions of the Austins give the most detail. A friar could speak to a woman in the convent church through the locked chancel gate; the possibility of discussing spiritual matters with a group of women is also envisaged with certain safeguards. Conferences with laymen are not mentioned only because there was no such perceived risk and presumably they occurred the more freely for it. John of Wales was even more explicit. He opened his *Communiloquium*, a collection of *exempla* and other preachable material, by stating that good preaching is often not enough: intimate discussion, *in collacione familiare et mutua*, allows for more potent exhortation. John quoted from the Homilies on the Gospels by Gregory the Great: 'The voice of speaking together stirs up the torpid heart more than the reading of a sermon: it strikes listeners with the hand of deep concern to

---

[114] Carroll-Clark, 'Practical Summa'.   [115] d'Avray, *Preaching*, 90n.   [116] *FM*.
[117] Franciscans: Bihl, 'Statuta', 70, 84. Dominicans: Denifle, 'Constitutiones', 208. Carmelites: Saggi, ed., 'Londoniensis', 217, 222; Saggi, ed., 'Burdigalensis', 140, 145. Austins: *Const. Ratisbonenses*, 46–47, 155.

awaken them."[118] John added that the preacher should share the word of life not only in private conversations but also *in mensa* – table-talk.[119]

CONCLUSION

The effectiveness of medieval preaching is hard to measure, but it is even harder to escape the conclusion that its cumulative effects were substantial. We can look at this in two thematic ways (marriage and crusades) across Europe, and more generally at the longer-term development of preaching in later medieval England.

According to d'Avray, marriage and marital religious symbolism did not feature heavily in popular sermons until around 1200 and early medieval marriages were not so tightly regulated by the church. But the twelfth century saw the development of theological parallels between earthly marriage and the union of Christ and the church, the union of the Son to human nature in the incarnation, and the union of God to the faithful soul, and these begin to appear in sermons around the turn of the thirteenth century. As all of these unions were indissoluble and sacred, it followed that earthly marriage should be as well. Accordingly, during the twelfth and thirteenth centuries there was a considerable tightening of the church's juridical control over sex and marriage, including clerical celibacy and the Fourth Lateran Council's initiatives to make annulments harder to obtain by reducing the forbidden degrees of consanguinity, publishing the banns of marriage, and making a wedding a public event. The church in thirteenth-century England used canon law to enforce these new strictures – the records of medieval church courts are filled with citations for fornication and adultery – but it also employed preaching for, if too few people were convinced of the church's position, they could turn a blind eye to one another's quasi-marriages and promiscuities. Church courts that depended on public *fama* for evidence would have no way to proceed. Many bishops instructed their parish priests to commend matrimony, to ensure that people knew what forms of words would legitimately contract it and to teach that all sex outside marriage was a sin, all of which could be accomplished by preaching.[120] At the same time, writers of *sermones moderni* often selected the thema *There was a marriage at Cana* (John 2:1) from the Gospel reading for the second Sunday after Epiphany and used that as a springboard to teach this more elevated view

---

[118] R. Etaix, ed., *Gregorius Magnus: Homiliae in Evangelia* (CCSL 141: Turnhout, 1999), 173–74 (= PL LXXVI, 1169).

[119] British Library, Harley MS. 632, f. 36r–v (prologue to *Communiloquium*).

[120] *C&S* II, 1403 (adultery), 1405 (banns), 1422 (fornication), 1429 (marriage).

of marriage. The frequency and insistence of this preaching, rather than any one individual sermon on an individual day, helped to transform the social expectations and social realities of marriage in the thirteenth and fourteenth centuries. By no means was the project perfected during that time but, as d'Avray argues, the cumulative effect of marriage preaching, as a mass medium in a culture before print, was very considerable.[121]

Considered as military expeditions, the crusades to the Holy Land in the thirteenth century began with an abuse (the sack of Constantinople in 1204) and ended with a crushing defeat (the fall of Acre in 1291). But they also represented a major success in public relations, which was largely effected by preaching. To gather the largest possible audience for a crusade sermon, church officials offered indulgences for attendance or threatened excommunication for absence.[122] The preachers were frequently friars, pressed into service by bishops. The friars, with their experience of public speaking, seem to have been adept at 'working the crowd'; the chronicler Thomas Wykes' account of people rushing to 'take the cross' (commit themselves to going on crusade) has a strong element of crowd behaviour to it.[123] In one *exemplum* in the Franciscan collection *Speculum Laicorum*, a man confessed on his deathbed to the bishop of Ely, who encouraged him to take the cross, going on crusade in person, should he recover, but bequeathing a share of his goods to pay another's passage if he should die. The man died soon after but at his burial he appeared to his brother in a vision, assuring him that he had been freed from purgatory and had gone directly to heaven.[124] Since the friars were engaged not only in encouraging people to take the cross but also in persuading many to 'redeem' their vow – to fund someone else to travel in their stead – an *exemplum* underlining the efficacy of the crusader's plenary indulgence, undiminished by the vow being redeemed, would have been quite useful.[125] A crusade sermon by the thirteenth-century English Franciscan John Russel includes a note to the preacher that many will not wish to take the cross and go to the Holy Land; they should be encouraged 'to take the cross and give the cross, that is, cross-signed money according to their ability, that you may obtain the merit of the cross'.[126] The lay response to such mendicant preaching made the crusades financially possible.[127]

---

[121] d'Avray, *Marriage Sermons*; d'Avray, *Symbolism and Society*; Akae, *Sermon Collection*, 119.

[122] Maier, *Preaching the Crusades*, 35, 50, 54, 73, 102, 106; *Chron. Maj.* III, 312.

[123] *Annales Monastici* IV, 217–18.

[124] Welter, *Speculum Laicorum*, 34, no. 149; see also nos. 148, 151–52, 324–25.

[125] Cole, *Preaching of the Crusades*, 83, 106, 162.

[126] 'Accipe crucem et da crucem id est pecuniam cruce signatam secundam tuam facultatem ut meritum crucis optineas'. Bodleian Library, MS. Lat.th.e.24, f. 2r. 'Pecuniam cruce signatam' may be a play on the cross on the English penny at this date.

[127] Maier, *Preaching the Crusades*, 61–62.

The manifest success of preaching in changing beliefs and practices of marriage and in raising support for the crusades may serve as a proxy for the general effectiveness of thirteenth-century preaching across Latin Christendom. But we may also look more specifically at England. The century from 1350 to 1450 has long been considered 'the golden age of English preaching between the Conquest and the Renaissance'.[128] It is certainly the golden age of the *recording of sermons* in England and of the *recording in English* of sermons. Wenzel, the most recent author to repeat this comment, does so in a study that is of surviving written sermon texts, not of the lost but living moment of preaching. The written sermons and preachable texts surviving from thirteenth-century England are fewer and not yet adequately studied yet they reveal a vibrant silver age of preaching.[129] This need not derogate from the achievements of sermon writers or preachers in post-plague England. But their flourishing was made possible by the legacy they inherited from their predecessors. These men in turn did not invent preaching either but all the evidence points to a rapid and intensive development of the art of Christian teaching across the Latin Church in the two centuries after 1150, a trend as observable in England as anywhere else, that was a vital part of the cultural and religious transformations of the thirteenth century.

---

[128] Wenzel, *Sermon Collections*, xv.

[129] On the massive loss of thirteenth-century sermon manuscripts, see d'Avray, *Medieval Marriage*, 40–58.

Chapter 6

SACRAMENTAL AND LITURGICAL PASTORAL CARE

The passages from Bonaventure and Fishacre that opened the preceding chapter asserted that laypeople were expected to know, at a minimum, those articles of faith that were reflected in the church's liturgy and must be willing to accept additional articles if they should have the opportunity to hear them. The implicit assumption was that preaching might not be universally available but that liturgical practice was and that laypeople should have had at least a basic understanding of what it meant. We have seen that the frequency of preaching is uncertain and debated and in the next chapter we shall find that the same is true of the frequency of confession. By contrast, the regularity of liturgical and sacramental practice is not in much doubt. Even if particular churches were devoid of clergy from time to time, or particular clerics neglected their duties, on the whole the clergy spent much of their time concerned with the daily round of ritual that was their primary responsibility.[1] Among friars and other conventual or collegiate bodies, communal discipline ensured performance of ritual practice. Furthermore, while preaching aids and confessors' manuals could be used loosely, in the liturgy the priest was expected to stick to the script.

This might seem to make liturgical and sacramental pastoral care more accessible to the historian. Even if clergy performed their liturgical and sacramental offices according to the letter, however, what that meant to the laity is difficult to know. When modern churchgoers are polled about why they go to church, they give a variety of answers and rank the spiritual, communal and experiential factors differently.[2] The Gallup and Pew research companies were not around to survey parishioners in the Middle Ages; and while the observations of peasants of Languedoc were recorded by inquisitors, and some Lollards would later commit their

---

[1] C&S II, 1078–80 (=Epist. Pecham III, 948–49).
[2] F. Newport, 'Just Why Do Americans Attend Church?,' Gallup News Service, 6 April 2007: www .gallup.com/poll/27124/just-why-americans-attend-church.aspx.

beliefs to writing, the thoughts of thirteenth-century English laypeople have not come down to us.[3] Our sources are overwhelmingly normative. The manuals for preachers and confessors discussed in Chapters 5 and 7 make explicit reference to how the priest should engage and respond to listeners and penitents in ways that allow for, and thus describe, a variety of lay responses. But missals and breviaries, being more formulaic, are less enlightening.

The liturgy itself was also heterogeneous, especially at the parish level. Most English dioceses elected, at various points in and after the thirteenth century, to follow the Use of Salisbury (also known as Sarum Rite), the liturgical codification developed at Salisbury Cathedral around the beginning of the thirteenth century. Some other dioceses, including York, Hereford and (until about 1415) London, maintained their own diocesan uses.[4] Yet the Use of Salisbury in the thirteenth century remained not only in flux but highly variant at any one time, to judge from the few surviving missals and breviaries. There were doubtless many other locally peculiar characteristics manifested in books that no longer exist. Such variation would have taxed not only the liturgical theorist but also the liturgical practitioner. One can imagine the parish priest's consternation when, every time the parish replaced a serive book, he spent the next year encountering unfamiliar texts, rubrics and notations. This must have been particularly acute when, in a practice that bishops regularly denounced but parish book lists just as regularly evidence, a parish acquired a second-hand book of monastic provenance, which could be quite different. Finally, few parish churches had the resources of personnel, books, expertise and furnishings comparable to the cathedrals for which the liturgies were initially designed. Their liturgical practices would have been simplified in ways that their books themselves might not reflect. For example, a small church or chapel would have provided little room to move about or to accomodate liturgical assistants, so the whole service might have been led by the priest alone from the altar.[5] In a larger parish church with more clergy, such as an old minster, the possibilities for imitating cathedral worship were much greater. In sum,

[3] E. Le Roy Ladurie, *Montaillou*, trans. B. Bray (New York, 1980); A. Hudson, *The Premature Reformation* (Oxford, 1988).

[4] N. Morgan, 'The Introduction of the Sarum Calendar into the Dioceses of England in the Thirteenth Century', in M. Prestwich, R. Britnell and R. Frame, eds, *Thirteenth Century England VIII: Proceedings of the Durham Conference, 1999* (Woodbridge, 2001), 179–206.

[5] P. S. Barnwell, 'The Laity, the Clergy and the Divine Presence: The Use of Space in Smaller Churches of the Eleventh and Twelfth Centuries', *Journal of the British Archaeological Association* 157 (2004), 41–60.

surviving service books provide at best only an approximation of parochial liturgy.[6]

Nor were all sacraments liturgically scripted. There was no standard rite for confession. Marriage was supposed to be contracted in church, but while a couple pledging themselves to one another in their own words in a tavern or a house were disobeying church authorities and subject to sanctions, they were still legitimately married.[7] Baptism was ideally performed in church and required a correct verbal formula but, as we have seen, bishops strictly ordered priests to teach their flocks the words in their native language so that a layperson could perform an emergency baptism for a sickly or dying newborn.[8] Extreme unction – the anointing of the dying – was a sacrament that followed a liturgical formula.[9] A layperson might expect to witness this ritual numerous times around the deathbeds of family and friends, probably including one or more of his or her own children, before finally receiving it himself or herself. At such an emotional time, the rite was liable to make an impression on bystanders, but its place was in the home, or the hospital, or wherever someone had fallen, injured too badly to move, not the church building itself.

Other sacraments were less likely to be a part of the laity's regular religious experience. Confirmation was said to strengthen the believer to resist the devil but was not considered necessary for salvation nor a prerequisite for sacramental confession or receiving the host during mass. It could only be performed by bishops and there are signs both that laypeople were lax about taking their children to be confirmed when the bishop was passing through and that not all bishops were assiduous in performing the brief rite: St Hugh of Lincoln was described as unusually devoted because he never failed to get off his horse.[10] Ordination was a sacramental liturgy necessary for supplying clergy but there is no reason to believe that many laypeople were expected to attend. Furthermore, many of the liturgies regularly attended by the laity were non-sacramental, such as Rogationtide processions, the Office of the Dead, the purification of women after childbirth and the daily office services found in the breviary.

---

[6] Shinners, 'Parish Libraries'; R. Pfaff, 'Prescription and Reality in Rubrics of Sarum Rite Service Books', art. XII in Pfaff, *Liturgical Calendars, Saints, and Services in Medieval England* (Aldershot, 1988); N. Morgan, 'The Sanctorals of Early Sarum Missals and Breviaries, c. 1250–c. 1350', in G. Brown and L. Voigts, eds, *The Study of Medieval Manuscripts of England* (Tempe, AZ, 2010), 143–62; S. Reames, 'Unexpected Texts for Saints in Some Sarum Breviary Manuscripts', in ibid., 163–84.

[7] d'Avray, *Marriage Sermons*; d'Avray, *Symbolism and Society*.

[8] *C&S* II, 1405, *s.v.* 'Baptism', and see above, p. 100.

[9] *C&S* II, 1445, *s.v.* 'Unction, Extreme'.

[10] *C&S* II, 1414, *s.v.* 'Confirmation'; Adam of Eynsham, *Vita* I, 127–28; Gerald, *Opera* VII, 94–96.

Capturing and understanding how these liturgies worked and what they meant to the people who attended them can be difficult.

With these caveats in mind, the bulk of this chapter focuses on the performance and understanding of the parish mass. Despite the interpretive challenges, this material provides us with the best sources for understanding the lay experience of the sacraments. The procedure of the thirteenth-century English parish mass can be outlined, not only because some missals survive, but also thanks to the survival of the *Lay Folk's Mass Book*, a thirteenth-century English translation of a lost twelfth-century French text.[11] The *Mass Book* was both prescriptive and descriptive: it told the lay reader what to do during the mass but also indicated what he or she could expect to see the clergy and other laypeople doing around them. Its survival in four different English versions suggests that its six extant manuscripts are all that remain of a much larger circulation, its textual transmissions complex but now beyond reconstruction. The multiple forms of the book, especially when cross-referenced with the surviving missals, give some sense both of the kind of variations that existed in practice and of the more uniform elements.

To appreciate the pastoral effect of the mass, we first have to follow its proceedings, which differed from its modern analogues, the Tridentine Mass and the high-church Anglican Eucharist. The Sarum Missal begins with blessings of salt and water and the aspersion of the altar, the clergy and (where there was one) the choir.[12] This ritual was to be followed on Sundays and feast days by a procession, which in a parish church presumably went from the chancel or apse to the nave and back, going around by the side aisles if the church had them.[13] These opening rites nominally preceded vesting for mass, which had attendant rituals of its own; as a simplification, it may have been done already vested.[14]

After the celebrant and attendants re-entered the chancel, the celebrant confessed to another priest if one was present, and to the whole congregation. The Use of Salisbury was originally intended for use *in choro* and this

---

[11] Legg, *Sarum Missal*; *LFMB*. Legg's edition is based on the Crawford Missal (ca. 1260), now in the John Rylands Library, which appears to have been for parish use. I have not used F. C. Dickinson, ed., *Missale ad usum Insignis et Praeclare Ecclesiae Sarum* (Burntisland, Fife, 1861–83) because the date of its rubrics is not clear, nor A. J. Collins, ed., *Manuale ad usum Percelebris Ecclesie Sarisburiensis* (London, 1960), based on sixteenth-century printings which may not reflect thirteenth-century practice. Sandon, ed., *Use of Salisbury*, is laid out for actual use and shows more clearly the sequence of events. It has been used in this respect only.
[12] Legg, *Sarum Missal*, 10–12; Sandon, ed., *Use of Salisbury*, 1–3.
[13] E.g. Legg, *Sarum Missal*, 13.   [14] Sandon, *Use of Salisbury*, 1–11; *LFMB*, lxii, 3, 6.

exchange was to be between the celebrant and the (clerical) choir; but the *Lay Folk's Mass Book* directed the reader to confess back to the priest, as he sees other lay congregants do, 'in loude or stille' (aloud or silently).[15] After responsorial prayers and the blessing and lighting of incense, the *Kyrie* and *Gloria in excelsis* followed, the latter omitted in Advent and Lent. Several collects were then sung, followed by the Epistle reading. In theory, the subdeacon would intone the reading, but in practice, it may have been spoken if the *Epistolarium* (the book with the Epistle readings) were not musically punctuated, or if the person doing the reading could not sing; and another cleric may have done the task if there were no subdeacon or if he were insufficiently literate. During the reading, the vested chalice was brought in by the acolyte and set on the altar, though again this may have been done ahead of time, especially if there were not enough clergy or assistants to do such tasks during the service. After the Epistle, the Gradual, Alleluia and Sequence were sung (or said) from the altar steps, these texts being contained in the books called the *Graduale* and *Troparium*. All of this may be considered standard.[16] However, the thirteenth-century Crawford Missal skips directly from the lighting of incense to the Gospel, not only shortening and simplifying the liturgy but also rendering several liturgical books unnecessary.[17] The *Lay Folk's Mass Book* made no mention of what the priest might do, only that the congregant should say the *Paternoster* between the Gloria and the Gospel: if the Epistle were eliminated, its primary effect would be time for fewer repetitions.[18]

The Gospel was then read or sung.[19] We might expect a sermon at this point, though it is mentioned neither here nor anywhere else in the Crawford Missal nor in the *Lay Folk's Mass Book*. This omission might seem to indicate that a sermon was atypical, but it is probably because the sermon was not a required part of the liturgy and its familiar position after the Gospel may not have become standard yet. The Nicene Creed directly followed the Gospel in the *Lay Folk's Mass Book* although it is omitted from the ordinary of the mass in the Crawford Missal. The laity probably joined in reciting the Creed in Latin or English. The English laity had been expected to know and understand the *Paternoster* and Creed as long ago as the laws of Cnut (ca. 1020).[20] Two recensions of the *Lay Folk's Mass Book* provide English verse versions, intended for recitation or teaching;

---

[15] *LFMB*, 6; Legg, *Sarum Missal*, 216; Sandon, *Use of Salisbury*, 12.

[16] For earlier and later examples, see M. Rule, ed., *The Missal of St Augustine's Abbey, Canterbury* (Cambridge, 1896), 5–41; Sandon, *Use of Salisbury*, 12–21.

[17] Compare Sandon, *Use of Salisbury*, 13–21, with the rubric in Legg, *Sarum Missal*, 218: 'Diaconus . . . procedit ad legendum evangelium'.

[18] *LFMB*, 16.   [19] Legg, *Sarum Missal*, 218.   [20] *C&S* I, 482–84.

Clanchy argues that lay ability to recite the Creed and *Paternoster* in Latin was widespread before 1200.[21] If the church owned an Offertory book, that text would follow. At this point the chalice and paten were placed on the altar.[22] After washing his hands, the priest asked the congregation for their prayers; he Crawford Missal expects that they could respond with an appropriate Latin sentence.[23]

The *Sursum corda* introduced the proper preface, changing with the season, festival or intent of the mass.[24] This was followed by the apex of the ritual, the canon or consecration prayers, which included both spoken and silent prayers by the priest. The *Lay Folk's Mass Book* prescribed lay prayers during this time, co-ordinated with, but not directly reflecting, the priest's prayers.[25] After the consecration, Christ was understood to be truly present. As the statutes of Lichfield explained,

> Nothing is more holy than the sacrament of the altar; unless the Lord had left this to us . . . we would not be able to answer those who asked, 'Where is your god?'; now, however, we are able to say, 'Our God is here; . . . daily here he is seen on earth, when he is lifted up by the hands of priests.'[26]

As this statute (and those of most dioceses) indicated, the completion of the consecration was indicated to the whole congregation by the priest lifting the host above his head so the whole congregation could see.[27] While genuflection at the moment of consecration was apparently known in England at the beginning of the century, the elevation was not. This practice is first noted in Paris in the late twelfth century and seems to have been introduced to England in the immediate aftermath of the interdict through the statutes of the Parisian-trained Archbishop Langton and Bishop Richard Poore.[28] Further statutes enjoin and bear witness to the elevation and acts of reverence throughout the century. As Bishop Quinel of Exeter wrote in his 1287 diocesan statutes,

> Since truly through these words: 'This is my body', and not through any other words, the bread is transubstantiated into the body, let the priest not raise the host before he has said this completely, lest the created thing be venerated in place of the Creator by the people.[29] For the host is to be raised so high that it may be gazed upon by faithful bystanders; through this, moreover, the devotion of the faithful is excited and the merit of faith receives increase. Let parishioners

---

[21] Clanchy, *Memory to Written Record*, 239–42; *LFMB*, 20–22; *C&S* II, 304, 423, 516–17, 609–10. See in general Reeves, *Religious Education*.

[22] Legg, *Sarum Missal*, 218.   [23] Ibid., 218–19.   [24] Ibid., 211–15.

[25] *LFMB*, 26–38.   [26] *C&S* II, 210.

[27] *C&S* II, 33, 79, 143, 268, 299–300, 345, 372, 404, 424, 517, 593, 641, 704, 894, 990; Kennedy, 'Consecration and Elevation'.

[28] Binski, *Becket's Crown*, 153–54.   [29] Cf. Romans 1:25.

be diligently exhorted that, at the elevation of the body of Christ, they should not only reverently bow but also bend the knee and adore their Creator with all devotion and reverence; to which, let them be excited at first through the ringing of the bell, and at the elevation let the greater bell be struck thrice.[30]

Quinel assumed that bowing already took place at the time of the elevation and was to be encouraged through teaching and exhortation, through a stronger physical manifestation of devotion and through an auditory addition to the visual spectacle, the ringing of bells.[31] At some point, extra candles were lit, not only for added visibility, but also to express veneration, as with candles before statues of saints.[32] The spectacle of the mass, created through word, music, gesture, posture, embroidery, ornament, architecture and other symbolic objects and acts, undergirded the claim that the holy was being made manifest.[33]

As Christ was now understood to be fully present and thus fully able to intercede, the priest and people addressed petitions through Christ (in the form of the host) to God the Father. Priestly prayers were offered for the dead and the living, that they might join with the Apostles and martyrs and all the saints in heaven.[34] During this time the *Lay Folk's Mass Book* counselled, 'sondry men prayes sere, / Ilk mon on his best manere' – let each pray as well as he knows how.[35] The statutes of Chichester Diocese (1292) mentioned spoken prayers and other devotions (*orationibus et aliis devotionibus*) during the mass, indicating that not all lay devotions were verbal.[36] Prayers continued with the *Paternoster*, spoken audibly by the priest; the last line was to be spoken by the congregation in Latin as a response. The *Lay Folk's Mass Book* considered that only 'lewed men' did not know this.[37] The priest prayed for deliverance from all evils, present and future and for peace.[38] The priest then broke the host in quarters, a gesture known as the Fraction.[39] The Peace was spoken back and forth between the priest and the congregation and, the ceremony of sacrifice complete, the *Agnus Dei* was sung.[40] Another expression of peace followed: the *Lay Folk's Mass Book* indicated that the priest would kiss a paxboard but does not suggest that he passed it on to the rest of the congregation, as would later be customary; the Crawford Missal ambiguously

---

[30] *C&S* II, 990. *LFMB*, 38, also assumes the sacring bell is commonplace.
[31] *C&S* II, 210–11, 299, 593, 894, 990, 1006.   [32] *C&S* II, 592–93; *RACCL* III, 721.
[33] Rubin, *Corpus Christi*, 55–64.   [34] Legg, *Sarum Missal*, 221–24.
[35] *LFMB*, 38.   [36] *C&S* II, 1117.   [37] *LFMB*, 46.   [38] Legg, *Sarum Missal*, 224–25.
[39] The theological meanings of these fractions, which revolved around prayer for the living and the dead (especially friends and household members), are discussed in Bossy, 'Mass as Social Institution'.
[40] Legg, *Sarum Missal*, 225. The responsorial Peace is not in *LFMB*.

reads *Hic detur pax*, here the peace is given.[41] The precise nature of the gesture is unclear and probably varied.

After the peace, the celebrant consumed the elements on behalf of the whole congregation, followed by careful ablutions.[42] There were several minutes of prayer in between the elevations and the consumption, giving parishioners time to pray in devotion to the host or to use the host as a locus of God's presence to make their prayers and intercessions heard in a close and immediate way.[43] The service being over, the deacon or assisting priest announced, *Ite, Missa est:* 'Go forth, it is finished'.[44] The congregation afterward consumed non-eucharistic blessed bread, broken and shared among them.[45]

THE LAY EXPERIENCE OF THE MASS

The *Lay Folk's Mass Book* proclaimed, 'Þo worthyest þing, most of god-nesse, / In al þis world, [hit] is þo messe.'[46] Here the divine presence was manifested to the laity in a manner that was visible and, at least once a year, tangible and ingestible. While transubstantiation as such was a rela-tively new doctrine in the thirteenth century, it was only the latest refine-ment of much older ideas about the presence and power of God in the mass.[47] Both documentary and architectural evidence shows that the new, higher eucharistic theology of the schools was already affecting English parishioners' experience of the mass in the twelfth century; this developed steadily across the thirteenth and early fourteenth centuries.[48] The feast of Corpus Christi originated on the Continent in the thirteenth century and spread quickly within England after its arrival early in the fourteenth. This was the enthusiastic reception of an outlet for well-established devo-tion to the consecrated host, implying widespread popular belief in the doctrine of the real presence in the thirteenth century. Richard Poore enjoined strongly upon his priests that

You ought to instruct the laity as often as they communicate that in no way are they to doubt the truth of the body and blood of Christ. For without a doubt they receive under the species of bread that which hung for us upon the cross; they receive from the chalice what flowed from the side of Christ.[49]

---

[41] *LFMB*, 48; Legg, *Sarum Missal*, 227. For later medieval practice, see Duffy, *Stripping of the Altars*, in index *s.v.* 'pax'.

[42] Legg, *Sarum Missal*, 226–28.   [43] Rubin, *Corpus Christi*, 155.

[44] Legg, *Sarum Missal*, 229.   [45] Ibid., 455.   [46] *LFMB*, 2. All citations are to text B.

[47] J. Goering, 'The Invention of Transubstantiation', *Traditio* 46 (1991), 147–70.

[48] Cragoe, 'Written in Stone', esp. 130–84; Macy, *Theologies of the Eucharist*, esp. 86–105; *C&S* II, 33; Kennedy, 'Consecration and Elevation'; Binski, *Becket's Crown*, 153–55; Rubin, *Corpus Christi*.

[49] *C&S* II, 77–78.

The church hierarchy nurtured these beliefs and regulated associated devotions. *Exempla* collections used in preaching include a variety of eucharistic miracles, such as those in which doubters see the consecrated host bleed or appear in form of the Christ child and others in which people misused it in various ways and were punished.[50] As Goering has argued,

> The twelfth- and thirteenth-century developments of eucharistic devotion seem to have originated largely in popular piety. This popular interest in the eucharist was taken up by the theologians of the period, discussed in the schools and academic milieux, and eventually channelled back to the people in authoritative, ecclesiastically sanctioned forms.[51]

This process can be seen in English episcopal statutes, which insist that the consecrated host kept at all times in the chancel should be in a locked pyx, lest laypeople steal it for unapproved superstitious purposes – a testament to lay belief that it held innate supernatural power.[52]

COMMUNION AND COMMUNITY

The mass was held to reconcile Christians to one another as well as to God.[53] The expression of peace in the mass came between the moments of consecration and the consumption of the elements, when Christ was understood to be present. People were encouraged to pray during the mass – especially between the consecration and fraction or consumption – for friends and kin, both living and dead.[54] Thus at the highest devotional point, when the congregants were to focus on the consecrated host as Body of Christ, their minds were also directed towards the Body of Christ in its Pauline sense, the body of fellow believers, praying especially for the welfare of those closest to them. Particularly in a rural parish, many of those for whom prayers were offered would probably be in the same parish, even if they were not themselves present at the mass, or if they were buried in the churchyard just outside. This aspect of the communality of the mass could have carried over into private or sparsely attended masses as well. Grosseteste recommended that laypeople should attend mass each day, physically if possible, mentally if not.[55] Such mental attendance would be prompted by church bells, which reminded all within earshot that liturgies were offered in behalf of the whole community while they themselves went about their daily business.[56]

---

[50] Jones, trans., *Friars' Tales*, 32–35, 157–58.   [51] Goering, 'Popularization', 145.
[52] Binski, *Becket's Crown*, 155; *C&S* II, 1435, *s.v.* 'Pix'.   [53] Macy, *Theologies of the Eucharist*, 118–32.
[54] Bossy, 'Mass as Social Institution', esp. 38–47; *LFMB*, 48–54.
[55] Grosseteste, *Templum*, 44.   [56] *C&S* II, 894.

The communal nature of ritual has long been the study not only of liturgists but also of sociologists and anthropologists. This can provide useful tools and terminology, though it has not provided a reliable and universally applicable theory of what ritual means to practitioners, or even where the boundaries of 'ritual' lie.[57] The mass was not a uniform observance and participants understood it in multiple ways, as have historians.[58] Bossy seems to be of two minds. He has argued, 'If we take the late medieval mass on its own terms, not as a service of instruction or a liturgical fossil but as a contemporary and evolving social ritual, we may agree that it involved a good deal of participation',[59] yet elsewhere he has described the mass in the later Middle Ages as 'a relatively non-participatory rite'.[60] This discrepancy might be resolved by defining the 'rite' as what the clergy did and describing the participatory elements of the laity, such as their devotions, as the 'social ritual' happening concurrently in the nave. Thirteenth-century English laity doubtless made some distinction between the priest's action and theirs but they were taught to understand the 'social ritual' under a theological gloss of the community as Body of Christ that may not be conveyed by the bare words 'social ritual': *corporate* ritual would be a more appropriate expression. Interaction between priest and people – which seems to be what Bossy means by participation – is not the only valid measure of communal participation. Interior devotion may be considered passive participation and exterior devotion as active. Summerson's assessment that 'the laity were encouraged to attend [liturgies] so that they could associate themselves with that worship, not so that they should be instructed or otherwise involved'[61] skirts the problem by turning the question towards precisely how those laypeople associated themselves and what mutual association meant to them.

Durkheim's *The Elementary Forms of Religious Life* of 1912 argued that collective rituals produce in their practitioners an effervescence of emotion which arises out of, conditions, reinforces and constitutes the experience of existence as a social being rather than an insular individual. Insofar as collective ritual articulates fundamental stories – mythos – it harmonises the subjectivities of its participants with one another and with their culture's understanding of the world. Recent developments in neuroscience have underscored the idea that ritual experiences create

---

[57] C. Bell, *Ritual Belief, Ritual Practice* (Oxford, 1992).   [58] Rubin, *Corpus Christi*, 288.

[59] Bossy, 'Mass as Social Institution', 36. See also H. M. Carey, 'Devout Literate Laypeople and the Pursuit of the Mixed Life in Later Medieval England', *Journal of Religious History* 14 (1987), 361–81, at 364; Duffy, *Stripping of the Altars*, 109–16.

[60] J. Bossy, 'Christian Life in the Later Middle Ages: Prayers', *TRHS* 6th s. 1, 1991, 137–48, at 148.

[61] Summerson and Harrison, *Lanercost*, 21.

enduring neural pathways, which may be expected to shape the individual's thought and action.[62] Applied to the medieval mass, this would mean that, as people assemble, focus their attention on a common object – perhaps the rood or other representations, but especially the consecrated host, illuminated with candles or by a window deliberately positioned to spotlight it[63] – and take and change bodily postures together and engage in contagious emotional outpourings, a certain communal identity may be imparted to those assembled. Atkins has identified four ways in which corporate ritual creates enduring neural pathways:

Through natural sharing, observation and modelling ... Through formal teaching ... Through the sharing of rituals that are associated with the life of the group ... Through hearing and repeating the corporate 'songs and sayings' of the various communities ... [In sum,] by participation rather than by formal instruction.[64]

All of these seem to have been characteristic of thirteenth-century liturgical pastoral care: kneeling or standing when others did, hearing sermons, attending not only the mass but also weddings, funerals and baptisms, and repeating the *Paternoster* and other prayers.

If ritual attempted to express what the church wanted the local community to be, it also exposed to the community what it already was. Medieval society was hierarchical, so we must not imagine that any sense of *fraternité* meant *égalité*. If 'the celebration was more than just an occasion or object for personal devotion; it was also a focus for community in communion',[65] and if that communion repeatedly reinforced the community and its values (hierarchy and all), it seems difficult to accept Rubin's contention that '*communitas* is dissolved as soon as the sweat evaporates off the brow of the ritual performer.'[66] Insofar as the point of the mass was the creation and re-creation of the Body of Christ as an emotionally bonded community, this is to pose the question of ritual efficacy: did the ritual work? Or in the language of sacramental theology: did the sacrament signify what it effected and effect what it signified?

According to Quack and Töbelmann's interpretation of Bell and Durkheim, ritualisation obscures its true intentions, 'the production, re-production and, sometimes, reconfiguration of power relations'. For the

[62] C. J. Throop and C. D. Laughlin, 'Ritual, Collective Effervescence and the Categories: Toward a Neo-Durkheinian Model of the Nature of Human Consciousness, Feeling and Understanding', *Journal of Ritual Studies* 16.1 (2002), 40–63.

[63] Cragoe, 'Written in Stone', 149–51.   [64] P. Atkins, *Memory and Liturgy* (Aldershot, 2004), 69–70.

[65] Swanson, *Religion and Devotion*, 138.

[66] Rubin, *Corpus Christi*, 2; see also A. Barnes' review of *Corpus Christi* in *Journal of Ritual Studies* 8.1 (1994), 136–38.

ritual to succeed, participants must share an adequately common culture of understanding of the ritual's meaning, which medieval parishioners apparently had.[67] Let us mark, however, this interpretation's troubling implication that thirteenth-century people (and, according to Bell, ritual participants universally) were too blind to understand their rituals' 'true intentions', requiring modern social theorists to discover the interpretative key, like hidden gnosis or a chronological orientalism. It seems absurd that medieval laypeople would not recognise 'the production, reproduction and, sometimes, reconfiguration of power relations' going on in the mass. The rising eucharistic theology of the twelfth and thirteenth centuries coincided with rising Gregorian ideals of the priesthood and its separation from the lay estate. Laity and lower clergy were probably aware of the growing emphasis on clerical celibacy that was part of this development but Macy argues that nowhere was it more clearly proclaimed than in the mass, by the power of which 'a new society was slowly being invented … with two clearly separated realms', clerical and lay.[68] The priest alone consecrated the elements and, except for a few times a year, he alone consumed them, in and on behalf of the whole parish. Physical changes to parish churches also altered the dynamics of the community. Over the high to late Middle Ages, chancel rebuildings, which were typically the responsibility of the rector, moved the main altar and its rites progressively further from the congregation, while the development of rood screens rendered it progressively harder to see.[69] While a consecrated host was to be kept in the church for devotional prayer and taking to visit the sick, only the priest had direct access to it. How parishioners felt about this monopoly doubtless depended on how they felt about the local man who wielded it.[70]

Status differences were also evident among the laity. Rebuilding and decoration of the nave was incumbent upon the parish at large but was predominantly paid for by the wealthier parishioners. The expenditure of their funds, proclaiming their status in the communal space, was visible in both the active construction and the finished product, particularly if it bore heraldic motifs.[71] Pecking orders and favoured spots may have existed throughout the nave as a point of social competition, based not

[67] J. Quack and P. Töbelmann, 'Questioning "Ritual Efficacy"', *Journal of Ritual Studies* 24.1 (2010), 13–28; Reeves, *Religious Education*, 168–76.
[68] G. Macy, *Treasures from the Storeroom* (Collegeville, MN, 1999), 182.
[69] Royal Commission on the Historical Monuments of England, *Churches of South-East Wiltshire* (London, 1987), *passim*.
[70] On this problem, see Chapter 2.
[71] Cragoe, 'Custom of the English Church'. For a full analysis of financing church building after the thirteenth century, see Byng, *Church Building*.

only on proximity to the altar but also on being on the south (right) side of the nave rather than the left and being within the area from which the host was visible at the elevation.[72] During the mass, the lay patron of a parish church, often the lord of the manor, was allowed a special seat closer to the high altar, which proclaimed his status even when he was absent.[73] The practice of burying knights and other lay dignitaries inside the parish church, complete with effigies or brasses, first appears in the thirteenth century, allowing leading families to demarcate their space and status indefinitely.[74] By the later thirteenth century, we find evidence that family neighbourhoods were commonly recognised in town and village alike.[75] The socio-spatial hierarchy within the nave presumably corresponded to the hierarchy of family neighbourhoods outside it. When Richard Gough sat down to write his parochial history of Myddle (Shrops.) in 1701, he told it as the story of the family and lands associated with each pew in the nave.[76] This was a unique way to organise a written parish history but the pattern of thought it represents might have been very familiar to the thirteenth-century family taking up their accustomed place and seeing on display the 'web of connections that organized and explained his or her life and relations with others ... [in which] no two people had precisely the same connections ... [V]illage society generated the raw material of performance and ritual, [and] village existence was profoundly formed by ritual'.[77]

The Great Chain of Being, the hierarchy of all things celestial and terrestrial, was apparently taken as a truism.[78] In the parish church, there was a hierarchy of rector, vicar and chaplains, of priest, deacon, subdeacon, acolyte and clerks. To constitute and reinforce the social Body of Christ in any parish or town was inseparable from enacting power relations. It strains credulity to imagine that medieval laypeople could not recognise this. Certainly, people aspired to higher rank and status and this produced competition among individuals and families; so much is certainly visible in later Corpus Christi processions, which articulated hierarchy more clearly than gathering in the nave did because of their

[72] C. P. Graves, 'Social Space in the English Medieval Parish Church', *Economy and Society* 18.3 (1989), 297–322.

[73] *C&S* II, 275, 297, 433, 1007–8.

[74] J. Scholfield and A. Vince, *Medieval Towns: The Archaeology of British Towns in their European Setting* (London, 2003), 185.

[75] Olson, *Mute Gospel*, 110–18.

[76] R. Gough, *The History of Myddle*, ed. D. Hey (Harmondsworth, 1981).

[77] Olson, *Mute Gospel*, 81.

[78] E.g. the hierarchy of Pseudo-Dionysius frames the penitential theology of Grosseteste's confessors' manual: Wenzel, 'Deus est'.

linear arrangement.[79] Even within the Pauline metaphor of the inter-
dependent members of the body, people disagreed 'as to their appropriate hierarchical position as to who was the stomach, who the head,
for how long, and why'.[80] However, while the members might disagree
about which part of the body they represented and might even resent
those above and despise those below, that is a far cry from rejecting
the idea of being part of the parochial *corpus* altogether. Together with
the 'Toronto School', Hatcher and Bailey argue that rural conflict in
general, and Marxist class-based conflict in particular, have been greatly
overstated.[81] Once power relations and social cohesion are viewed as two
sides of the same coin, *communitas*, far from being extinguished along with
the altar candles, begins to look like a much more durable good – and
one that, in any case, only needed to last until it was renewed at mass
next Sunday. The rhythm of regular repetition over decades, informed
by the sort of preaching and instruction envisaged in English episcopal
statutes, would have impressed it deeply into the collective consciousness
of the parish community. Parochial identities could be both displayed
and reinforced over against other parishes: Grosseteste remarked to his
archdeacons that, when multiple parishes made an annual visitation to
a mother church, they bore their parish banners before them and fights
leading to bloodshed arose over which banner, and thus which parish,
had precedence.[82] Rough competition among parishes could also arise
when Rogationtide 'beating of the bounds' processions met while perambulating and demarcating their parish boundaries.[83] While such fights
might not look like good Christian behaviour, they certainly testify to a
level of voluntary lay adherence to a parochial identity, which they also
served to reinforce. But the main ritual stimulus to parochial solidarity
was not found in isolated acts of inter-parochial rivalry: it was found in
the quotidian, in the daily and weekly celebration of the mass with one's
neighbours. The mass as the symbolic focus of community as well as hierarchy, so clearly seen in the fourteenth century, was not some newborn
creation inexplicably grown to full maturity in just a few years.

Yet, when the community was a locus of internal conflict, the mass
brought that into sharp relief. Occupying one's allotted place in the
nave could teach each person his or her standing relative to the neighbours without necessarily teaching him or her to like it – or them. Here

[79] M. James, 'Ritual, Drama and Social Body in the Late-Medieval English Town', *Past and Present*
98 (1983), 3–29.
[80] Rubin, *Corpus Christi*, 270–71.
[81] Dyer, *Everyday Life*, 6–10; J. Hatcher and M. Bailey, *Modelling the Middle Ages: The History and
Theory of England's Economic Development* (Oxford, 2001), 99–106; Raftis, *Economic Development*.
[82] Luard, ed., *Grosseteste Epistolae*, 75 (=*C&S* II, 205).   [83] Duffy, *Stripping of the Altars*, 136–38.

resentment of a fellow parishioner could take concrete form.[84] The passing of the peace ideally represented reconciliation but a snub at that point in the liturgy, or a refusal to come to mass with one's neighbours at all, would be a particularly pointed and public manifestation of community's limits. When the bishop of Winchester forbade giving the peace to priests' concubines, he apparently considered it a harsh sanction.[85] If the mass were to resolve conflict through reconciliation at a conscious rather than a subconscious level, then exposing that conflict was a necessary first step. The mass did not function alone. Local courts were routinely used to settle disputes and indeed had social rituals of their own, though the fact that cases were sometimes settled out of court indicates that arbitration and compromise played an important part in maintaining the social fabric.[86] Moreover, the losing party in a suit (and their friends) might not believe that justice had been truly served and could seek extrajudicial vengeance. Some bishops' statutes expected the priest to act as peacemaker in the parish without specifying the means or venue for doing so, though confession was an obvious opportunity.[87] The mass was another. The priest who had ordered a penitent to make restitution to his neighbour on Ash Wednesday but doubted that he had done so could refuse to give that parishioner the host at Easter, as it signified impenitence. If two parties at enmity were preparing for physical reception of communion, they were expected to effect a reconciliation in the nave if they had not already done so.[88] Preaching could also be directed towards forgiveness, humility and reconciliation. But the mass' crucial role in reconciliation and community-building was neither accidental nor a function that just any ritual could have accomplished equally well. It expressed the metaphorical Body of Christ in the congregation, recounting the story of the Last Supper, with the priest taking the role of Jesus and the congregants that of the Apostles, including Judas, the quintessential cautionary tale of the unreconciled. The mass also pointed to the literal body of Christ with its mortal wounds, manifested in the broken host and the blood-red wine and represented graphically – indeed, ever more graphically over the course of the Middle Ages – in the rood facing the parishioners.[89]

For the church taught that the mass offered not only sacrament and spectacle but also sacrifice. Bossy suggests three different anthropological interpretations of the social implications of sacrifice that can reasonably

---

[84] For later examples, see Duffy, *Stripping of the Altars*, 126–27.   [85] *C&S* II, 180.
[86] Bailey, ed., *English Manor*, 173; Olson, *Mute Gospel*, 52–91; E. Powell, 'Arbitration and the Law in England in the Late Middle Ages', *TRHS* 33 (1983), 49–67.
[87] See Chapter 7.   [88] Hyams, *Rancor*, 195.   [89] Ross, *Grief of God*, 41–66.

be applied to the medieval mass, all of which agree that sacrifice binds people together. The one that appears most consonant with the medieval mass is that of René Girard, according to whom sacrifice is

a judicial act. It represents the separation between men in so far as sacrificial murder symbolizes the mutual murder which is the extreme expression of conflicts subsisting within a population; it binds them together in so far as ritual murder takes the place of actual murder and hence enables the population to live in peace.[90]

The Peace was passed only after the Fraction, the breaking of the host representing and re-enacting the sacrificial breaking of Christ's body, implying that the sacramental Body of Christ took on, and ideally took away, the brokenness of the communal Body of Christ. For the thirteenth-century laity, to whom transubstantiation was regularly taught, attendance at, and mutual (if interior) participation in, that sacrificial event itself – understood not just as a symbolic reminder but as genuine re-creation and re-enactment of Christ's sacrifice – could become emotionally and spiritually charged. Only this can account for the intensity of eucharistic devotion, individual and corporate, that was to characterise the later Middle Ages. We find it already in the early thirteenth century, as in Matthew Paris' account of Edmund of Abingdon:

At the altar he was greatly given to tears, and conducted himself in the service of the altar as if he discerned the Lord's passion being visibly enacted in the flesh. In fact he celebrated the divine sacraments with such great reverence that his ministration itself enhanced the faith and influenced the conduct of those who witnessed it.[91]

The parish church building was intended to be a worthy setting for such a spectacle. We should picture it as imperfect: visitation records routinely report leaky roofs, broken windows and crumbling mortar. At least one bishop ordered parishioners to enlarge their nave since, on festival days, some parishioners who wished to attend divine service were unable to get in.[92] City churches could also be cramped into uncomfortable shapes by the buildings around them. As for the human environment inside, bishops' statutes complain of drowsing and idle chatter.[93] Nonetheless, even a humble church was often the largest building in the parish, perhaps the only one built of stone, and in many cases the most highly decorated.[94] The statuary, glass, embroideries and wall paintings of churches served not only to glorify God and the saints, to set apart the building, to

[90] Bossy, 'Mass as Social Institution', 50–51.   [91] Lawrence, *St Edmund*, 127.
[92] *Reg. Stapledon*, 286.   [93] *C&S* II, 31, 299.
[94] Reeves, *Religious Education*, 160–65, 170–72.

contribute to the spectacle and to educate the illiterate but also to sur-
round parishioners with edifying images.[95] In dark Norman churches, the
small windows were sometimes positioned to throw light on the altar or
the rood, drawing the congregants' eyes towards such devotional foci.[96]
Although little direct evidence survives identifying the patrons of devotional art in parish churches, the apparently increasing popularity of roods
in thirteenth-century naves – for which the laity were becoming responsible – suggests congregational participation in creating the settings for
their own devotions.[97] The distancing of the high altar from the nave
was countered by the creation of subsidiary altars in the nave itself, either
flanking the chancel arch or against the pillars, presumably created at the
behest of, and at the expense of, the parishioners. These were mostly used
for chantry or votive masses rather than the general parish mass, and by
hiring the priest to say the mass, the laity asserted growing control over
the liturgy.[98]

The congregation at the mass was not a Platonically ideal community,
but a real one made up of real people, warts and all. The mass, the building
and its furnishings and decorations were designed to accommodate this
fact. Each Sunday, each feast-day, parishioners gathered to participate in a
ritual of reconciliation with God and with one another, a ritual that was
certainly guided by the ecclesiastical hierarchy, but one that the parishioners also conspired through means as diverse as patronage and prayer
and needlework to make very much their own.

THE MENDICANTS

While the friars had intended from their early days to make the singing of
the praises of God part of their purpose, the care of the souls of the laity

[95] The vestments, hangings and ornaments of thirteen parish churches and chapels in the 1220s are
detailed in *Reg. St Osmund* I, 275–314.
[96] Morris, *Landscape*, 297–300.
[97] C. D. Cragoe, 'Belief and Patronage in the English Parish before 1300: Some Evidence from
Roods', *Architectural History* 48 (2005), 21–48; Cragoe, 'Custom of the English Church'; Binski,
Becket's Crown, 149, 176–77; R. Marks, 'From Langford to South Cerney: The Rood in Anglo-
Norman England', *Journal of the British Archaeological Association* 165 (2012), 172–210; R. Marks,
Image and Devotion in Late Medieval England (Stroud, 2004). For post-1300, see Byng, *Church Build-
ing*; Graves, *Form and Fabric*; French, *People of the Parish*, 141–207; K. French, 'Parochial Fund-
Raising in Late-Medieval Somerset', in K. French, G. Gibbs and B. Kümin, eds, *The Parish in
English Life, 1400–1600* (Manchester, 1997), 115–32, and E. Duffy, 'The Parish, Piety, and Patronage
in Late-Medieval East Anglia: The Evidence of Rood Screens', 133–62, in ibid.
[98] Marks, *Image and Devotion*, 89, 137–38; Cragoe, 'Custom of the English Church'. On the growth of
lay donors' authority to determine spiritual activities, see B. Thompson, '*Habendum et Tenendum*:
Lay and Ecclesiastial Attitudes to to the Property of the Church', in C. Harper-Bill, ed., *Religious
Belief and Ecclesiastical Careers in Late Medieval England* (Woodbridge, 1991), 197–238.

through administering liturgical sacraments was not in the original plan. Emphasising study and preaching, both Minorites and Preachers developed streamlined liturgies.[99] Thomas Docking OFM wondered whether preaching or baptism gave more grace and decided for preaching.[100] Humbert of Romans OP argued that the laity were more edified by preaching than by the offices, for they understood the former but not the latter.[101]

However, the mendicants did take their liturgies seriously and laypeople did sometimes attend them.[102] The founders of both orders had encouraged eucharistic devotion.[103] Screens in Dominican churches were to have shuttered windows to allow laypeople in the nave to view the host at its elevation in the mass, when the shutters would be opened.[104] The Dominican Compline service, which culminated in a procession with the singing of the *Salve Regina* and the aspersion of the congregation with holy water, was designed to accommodate lay attendance. Its success as a public service was probably enhanced by the fact that laypeople were more free to come to an evening office.[105] The friars seem to have used the brief liturgy not to get people out of the door faster but to make a longer sermon a prominent part of the service.[106] The potential impact of changing lay expectations for what a service should be like, which they would then take back to their parish churches, must not be underestimated. If a mendicant church developed a clientele of regular worshippers, the result for the worshipper would be similar to having access to two denominations. In an age of predominantly foot traffic, a mendicant church might develop a sort of quasi-parochial district overlapping the parish boundaries.

In mendicant liturgy, as in preaching, we see the geography of pastoral care in action. There was also a chronology. The first mendicants worshipped in parish churches, not yet having churches of their own. When they did begin to build it was initially on a small scale appropriate to their vows of poverty. The early Franciscans at Cambridge had a chapel erected that was so small, according to Friar Thomas, that a single carpenter erected the fifteen pairs of roof-timbers in a single day.[107] Moreover, it took time after arriving in a town to arrange the resources to

[99] Denifle, 'Constitutiones', 194; O'Carroll, *Studies*, 122, 357–58; Harper, *Forms and Orders*, 20–21, 31. Some Franciscans wished to abbreviate their liturgy even further, but Pecham prevented it: Douie, *Pecham*, 41; Pecham, *Tractatus Tres*, 49–51.

[100] J. Leclerq, 'Le Magistère du Prédicateur au XIIIe siècle', *Archives d'Histoire Doctrinale et Littéraire du Moyen Âge* 21 (1946), 105–47, at 109–11.

[101] Humbert, *Opera* II, 432–33.   [102] *EEFP*, 120.

[103] Brooke, *Coming of the Friars*, 117–19, 180–81.   [104] *EEFP*, 144.

[105] *EEFP*, 219–22.   [106] Goering, 'Popularization', 116–17.

[107] *De Adventu*, 28. Only lashed poles could be erected so quickly, indicating a thatched roof.

build a sizeable church: Matthew Paris wrote of them beginning by setting up portable altars.[108] From mid-century onwards, the rules requiring small, humble chapels were increasingly bent, as both orders sought to accommodate increasing lay congregations. By the century's end, as we have seen, some mendicant churches had become grand affairs capable of holding many hundreds for both services and sermons.[109]

Preaching seems to have been closely connected to its liturgical context, which lent it its emotional power.[110] Preaching in the mass about the mass itself would play especially well on this synergy. *Exempla* regarding the Eucharist, particularly miraculous tales, might effectively penetrate the lay conscience and mendicants seem to have been the primary promoters and users of *exempla* in thirteenth-century England.[111] Eucharistic *exempla* in English and related collections are not wanting.[112] By the later thirteenth century, theological discussion of the Eucharist had passed largely into the hands of mendicant theologians.[113] Later, one of Wyclif's complaints about the friars was that they had spread belief in transubstantiation among the English people.[114] In practice, parish priests were just as important a vector for this belief but, especially for those whose priests were neglectful in this regard, being taught about transubstantiation in a mendicant church might then have affected subsequent experience of the mass in a man or woman's own parish church.

Physical reception of the host by the laity in mendicant churches does not seem to have been regular practice. The nine Easter Sunday sermons in the Dominican manuscript MS. Laud Misc. 511 all indicate reception of the host during the service in which the sermon is being preached but this reflects Dominican Easter preaching in parish churches, not lay reception in Dominican ones.[115] In 1255, the Dominican Master-General Humbert of Romans reiterated strictures against giving the host to the laity (except in cases of necessity) or even admitting parishioners to liturgies or sermons on Sundays or feast days when they should be attending their own parish churches instead.[116] Humbert was being conciliatory to parish

---

[108] *Chron. Maj.* III, 332–33; *EEFP*, 66.   [109] *EEFP*, 136; Kingsford, *Friars of London*, 38–39.

[110] Rubin, *Corpus Christi*, 95.   [111] Rubin, *Corpus Christi*, 108–14.

[112] Welter, *Speculum Laicorum*, 33–36; Little, ed., *Liber Exemplorum*, 6–14; *FM*, 412–15; Herbert, ed., *Catalogue of Romances*, 477–503, nos. 9, 14, 22–32, 34, 50, 72, 80, 262, 297, 303.

[113] Rubin, *Corpus Christi*, 66–68; D. Burr, 'Eucharistic Presence and Conversion in late Thirteenth-Century Franciscan Thought', *Transactions of the American Philosophical Society* 74.3 (1984); Bonaventure, *Opera* IV, 201–43; Bacon, *Opera*, 144–48, 187–88, 400–401.

[114] C. J. Fraser, 'The Religious Instruction of the Laity in Late Medieval England with Particular Reference to the Sacrament of the Eucharist' (unpublished DPhil thesis, Oxford University, 1995), 267.

[115] O'Carroll, *Studies*, 213–54; O'Carroll, 'Preaching for Easter Sunday from MS Laud Misc. 511', *Medieval Sermon Studies* 45 (2001), 75–88.

[116] *Annales Monastici* I, 434–35.

clergy: this was despite the bull *Nec insolitum est* given to the religious orders by Alexander IV on 30 December 1254, allowing them to receive parishioners to sermons and liturgies at those times.[117] In 1269 the Franciscan order similarly forbade its members from giving the Eucharist to laypeople at Easter without their parish priest's permission.[118] Continuing lay demand is indicated by the bishop of Lincoln's letter of 1293 forbidding the Boston Carmelites to admit laypeople on Easter Day.[119] Trouble arose when several parishioners communicated in a Dominican church on Easter Sunday in 1309, though this was an exceptional case because one of them was excommunicate at the time.[120] Perhaps more indicative is the fact that, when the rectors of London churches presented the Council of Lambeth of 1309 with a litany of complaints against the friars for encroaching on their pastoral prerogatives of preaching, confession and burial, not a word was said about laypeople playing truant from their parish churches to attend mendicant liturgies, much less receiving the host there.[121] The weight of the London rectors' complaints (which also included friars preaching and hearing confession) fell instead on two other forms of liturgical pastoral care: visitation of the sick and last rites. Bishops' statutes suggest that not all parish priests were diligent in visiting the sick.[122] Friars helped to fill this gap and would have been sought out if a secular priest were unavailable.[123] Visiting the sick also included bearing the consecrated host to the patient and might involve administering extreme unction.[124] While it is impossible to measure the impact of friars in this area, their availability would have drawn them into action from time to time, especially in cases of accident and emergency.

But it may also be that friars, being recognised as expert confessors – as we shall see in our next chapter – were particularly sought out by laypeople as their end drew near, for a highly trained confessor might deal properly with a mortal sin that a more careless priest could have passed over and that could be the difference between salvation and damnation. A last confession was no time to take chances. Whatever the reason, the London rectors complained that Franciscans and Dominicans were attending far more than a reasonable share of deathbeds and receiving in turn many bequests that would otherwise have formed a large part of the income of the parish clergy. To make matters worse, a small but perhaps

[117] van Luijk, ed., *Bullarium*, 96–97.
[118] Ehrle, 'Generalconstitutionen des Franziskanerordens', 40.
[119] *Reg. Sutton* IV, 127–28.   [120] *EEFP*, 327.
[121] *C&S* II, 1255–63.   [122] Goering, 'Popularization', 100–101.
[123] Ehrle, 'Generalconstitutionen des Franziskanerordens', 40.
[124] Friars provide last rites in some *exempla*: Herbert, ed., *Catalogue of Romances*, 477–503, nos. 25, 45, 47, 58, 62, 73, 78, 245, 291.

growing number of these dead were being buried in mendicant churches. It was expected that the dead buried in any church would have masses celebrated to pray for their souls and it was further understood that the clergy deserved remuneration for their trouble in doing so.[125] In 1279, the bishop of Bangor issued two indulgences for laypeople who visited the house of the Austin friars at Clare to hear preaching, pray for the souls of the dead buried there, especially Richard of Chrishall, and give alms for the building of the house or to pay the friars to pray the Office of the Dead.[126] The individuals whose bodies were laid to rest in mendicant churches were disproportionately the urban elite, whose bequests to the friars – bequests they might have given to their parish churches otherwise – could be substantial.[127]

The most common complaint of the seculars against the friars was not over liturgy or burial, however, but over whether and when friars were allowed to infringe the parish priest's traditional prerogative of hearing the confessions of his own parishioners. Anti-fraternalism in thirteenth-century England was nowhere near as pronounced or pervasive as it would become by 1400 but, in the Latin Church as a whole, this right of confession was repeatedly appealed to popes, who variously upheld, struck down, modified and limited it throughout the thirteenth century and beyond.[128] To appreciate why an event that took perhaps an hour for each penitent, performed as seldom as once per year, was fought over so strenuously, we first need to understand the significance of the sacrament of penance in thirteenth-century Catholic life.

---

[125] Goering, 'Popularization', 108–9.   [126] Harper-Bill, ed., *Clare Cartulary*, nos. 169–70.
[127] *C&S* II, 1255–63.   [128] Lawrence, *The Friars*, 152–65.

Chapter 7

CONFESSION AND PENANCE

The vision of a pious lay society that developed among twelfth- and thirteenth-century clergy was published to the laity in preaching and ritually enacted in sacrament and liturgy. Neither of these means, however, could determine whether individual members of the laity conformed to this vision. This could only be established by annual person-by-person canvassing of all the adult laity of Latin Christendom, enforced with the church's strongest spiritual sanctions and capable of holding the individual accountable to the clergy's standards of beliefs and behaviour. Such a project would have been impossibly ambitious if just such an institution – confession and penance – had not already been established by the church and more or less accepted by the laity.[1]

We do not know how often thirteenth-century English laypeople confessed, though the ordination of a vicarage in 1225 included twenty-two shillings per year in 'confession-pence'; if each penitent gave a customary oblation of one penny, this suggests 264 confessions per year in that parish.[2] The theoretical norm was established in 1215 by Canon 21 of Lateran IV, *Omnis utriusque sexus fidelis*: each layman or laywoman, upon reaching the age of discretion, must make confession of sins at least once a year to his or her own priest, ideally at the beginning of Lent, in preparation for receiving the sacrament of the Eucharist at least once a year, ideally at Easter.[3] The sceptic may doubt that this was rigorously enforced at the parish level: how many priests would risk the ire of their parishioners by refusing one of them Christian burial, the Council's threatened sanction? Yet, while we are limited to prescriptive sources, *Omnis utriusque* built on much older and more stringent standards requiring confession

---

[1] An Anglo-Saxon list of clerical duties from the early eleventh century seeks more to regulate than to enjoin confession, suggesting that it was at least not uncommon: *C&S* I 421. See also Meens, *Penance*; Firey, *Penance*.

[2] *Rot. Hugonis* II, 127; cf. I, 185; III, 40–41, 84–86, 194; *Reg. Bronescombe* I, 212. The Legate Otto forbade collection of confession-pence in 1268, but it was mentioned in vicarage ordinations in 1274 and 1275: *C&S* II, 749–50; *Rot. Gravesend*, 61, 123.

[3] *DEC*, 245.

not once annually but thrice.[4] Some thirteenth-century English bishops continued to direct the laity to confess before receiving the Eucharist at Christmas and Pentecost as well.[5] Pregnant women approaching full term were told to confess because of the hazards of childbirth.[6] Lateran IV forbade a physician to care for a patient for more than two days before sending for a priest because sin could be causing the patient's physical ailments and the latter could not be cured before the former.[7] English diocesan legislation described such visitation of the sick as including hearing the patient's confession and displaying the *viaticum*, the consecrated host.[8] Laypeople were encouraged to confess as soon as possible if they fell into sin.[9] If the English laity managed to evade this penitential dragnet from time to time, the church certainly aimed to minimise the likelihood of total escape.

We also do not know how often they resorted to confessors (friars, household chaplains, monks) other than their parish priests, though we have some indication as to why they might wish to do so. According not only to Lateran IV but also to older canon law, under normal circumstances a priest ought not to hear the confessions of another priest's parishioners; each parishioner ought to confess to his or her *sacerdos proprius*, 'own priest'. Gratian's *Decretum*, already the standard textbook on canon law, allowed only one exception: if one's own priest were 'blind' (incompetent). Other motives, such as personal animosity or embarrassment, did not justify stepping outside the established ecclesiastical structure. Some authorities argued for the efficacy of confession to a fellow layman on the basis of James 5:16, 'Confess your sins to one another'.[10] How often this was practised is unclear and in any case it was only recognised as a way of expunging venial, not mortal, sins. Exceptions could also be made on an emergency basis, such as dying on a battlefield.[11] In practice, dying when the priest was away from the village was a more probable scenario for most English laity: some English diocesan statutes explicitly allowed deacons to hear confessions in that very circumstance.[12]

---

[4] A. Murray, 'Confession before 1215', *TRHS* 6th s. 3 (1993), 51–81, argues that lay confession was rare before Lateran IV; R. Meens, 'The Frequency and Nature of Early Medieval Penance', in Biller and Minnis, *Handling Sin*, 35–61, counters that annual confession was probably common. See also Goering, 'Popularization', 129n110; N. Vincent, 'Some Pardoner's Tales: The Earliest English Indulgences', *TRHS* 6th s. 12 (2002), 23–58; S. Hamilton, *The Practice of Penance, 900–1050* (Woodbridge, 2001), 201–6; and Cornett, 'Form of Confession', 14–16, and works cited there.

[5] Salisbury, Durham, Coventry, Canterbury, Worcester, Exeter. *C&S* II, 72–73, 211, 236, 303–4, 992.

[6] *C&S* II, 35, 89, 444, 706.   [7] *DEC*, 245–46.

[8] *C&S* II, 1419, *s.v.* 'communion of sick and dying'.

[9] E.g. 'Peniteas cito peccator': Goering, *William de Montibus*, 107–38.

[10] Teetaert, *La confession*.   [11] Larson, *Master of Penance*, 212–23.   [12] *C&S* II, 141, 183.

The mendicant orders were just emerging on the eve of Lateran IV. Their primary mission, first for the Dominicans and later for the Franciscans, evolved into pastoral care of the laity, including shriving. Gratian's *Decretum* and *Omnis utriusque*, along with certain papal bulls, reinforced the tradition that each layperson should confess to his or her own parish priest (*proprius sacerdos*), or to another priest *by his licence*. This potentially upset Gratian's compromise between ecclesiastical order and pastoral necessity: what if one's own priest were too ignorant to be trusted, yet he refused to give permission to confess to another priest? As the friars proliferated as alternative confessors, opportunities for this problem to rear its head multiplied.

Some parish clergy and members of the older religious orders perceived the friars as competitors. They used the legal technicality of the *proprius sacerdos* clause as a means to undermine the friars' pastoral mission and thus their *raison d'être*.[13] Archbishop Pecham, himself a Franciscan and a forceful protector of mendicant privileges, was obliged to counter rumours in his own diocese that friars had no power to absolve without license of the parish priest.[14] Around 1255, the English Benedictine chronicler Matthew Paris described the friars as a mixed bag: they were persistent in their preaching, but they weakened the authority of the parish priest; some were laudable, others reprehensible. The latter were guilty of arrogantly teaching the laity that they need not confess to their parish priests at all.[15] Matthew's view on this was clear: *ecce nocumentum* – behold the damage. But he immediately added that some people refused to confess to their own priest on the grounds that he was a drunk or for other hidden reasons and so they confidently fled to passing mendicants for 'the nourishment of consolation and counsel' in confession. This he viewed as praiseworthy: *et ecce refugium*.[16] Stealing sheep was an evil but protecting sheep who had already fled an unworthy pastor was a good. Others doubtless shared this ambivalence. Many cases in which laypeople resorted to mendicant confessors probably fell into the grey area between these extremes.

Successive popes attempted to solve the problem in a long series of bulls that experimented with various compromises, none of which proved entirely satisfactory and there were indeed a few *causes-célèbres*.[17] Historians have sometimes assumed that this must reflect strife between English parish priests and their mendicant counterparts. But, given that discord is

---

[13] Little, *Studies*, 92–157; *Reg. Cantilupo*, 232.
[14] *FM*, 467–69; J. Smith, *The Attitude of John Pecham toward Monastic Houses* (Washington, DC, 1949), 131; *Epist. Pecham* III, 952–53 (cf. 956–57); Little, *Studies*, 113n.
[15] E.g. *Northern Registers*, 102–3.   [16] *Chron. Maj.* V, 528–29.
[17] *EEFP*, 318–28; Little, *Studies*, 92–157.

typically over-represented in historical records, it is surprising how thin the evidence of it from thirteenth-century England is; we should assume that local co-operation was much more common than conflict.[18] The shrill anti-mendicant polemics of William of Saint-Amour and of University of Paris officials have little obvious relevance to English town and countryside.[19] What is clear, however, is that some English laity were keen to be able to choose their own confessors and in most cases the friars were the obvious alternative to the parish priest. The closer one lived to a major town, the more easily one might find a friar; and the larger the town, the more orders of friars were likely to be represented.

The mendicants never formed an entirely independent penitential system for the laity. Even when friars were appointed as diocesan penitentiaries to settle reserved cases on the bishop's behalf, they were being co-opted into the existing secular church structure; and some sins required, as a matter of liturgy, theology and canon law, papal absolution.[20] In 1267, Walter Giffard, archbishop of York, confirmed the Franciscans' right to hear lay confessions but to pronounce absolution of secret sins only. For public sins requiring public penance, the friars, like parish priests, were obliged to denounce offenders to the secular ecclesiastical hierarchy, which had jurisdiction over such offences.[21] Archbishop Winchelsey of Canterbury reminded the friars that they still had to refer reserved cases of public penance and excommunication to the bishops. Thomas Jorz, the Dominican provincial prior, gently replied to Winchelsey that the bishops should not believe everything they heard. If a parishioner told his priest that a friar had absolved him of a reserved sin, the priest may have been too quick to doubt the friar's right to do so; and if, as Pecham noted, bishops commonly delegated to friars the right to settle reserved cases because they trusted their erudition, that multiplied the occasions that might lead to a dispute.[22] Complaints that friars absolved above their jurisdiction continued to be heard, with increasing frequency, in the fourteenth century.[23] But excommunications and cases reserved to the bishop would be relatively few; laypeople probably saw them happen from time to time but most did not personally undergo their rigours and rituals. Pecham actually complained in 1281 that public penance was

[18] *EEFP*, 328; Roest, *Franciscan Education*, 321.   [19] William of Saint-Amour, *De periculis*.

[20] *Reg. Romeyn* I, 246, 251; *Reg. Sutton* III, 13, 39–40, 86, 90, 100; V, 210; VI, 3.

[21] The letter to the Franciscans of York in Giffard's register presumably stands in for similar letters to the other mendicant orders. Raine, ed., *Northern Registers*, 9–10.

[22] *Epist. Pecham* III, 957.

[23] *C&S* II, 1176–77, 1257; *Reg. Winchelsey*, 187–89; *EEFP*, 509–11; Haren, *Sin and Society*, 161–62, 185–89; G. Geltner, *The Making of Medieval Antifraternalism* (Oxford, 2012), 23–37, 59–62; Walsh, *FitzRalph*, 408, 424.

disappearing.[24] Part of the problem may have been the vague borderline of those semi-private, semi-public sins known to one's intimates but not one's neighbours, for divisions between public and private in penitential theory and practice were never clearly defined.[25]

Mendicants' pastoral rights often depended upon privileges granted by bishops, applicable only within their dioceses.[26] Some of these appear in the diocesan case studies below. But there were also relevant papal privileges, which sometimes trumped local jurisdiction and sometimes empowered bishops and parish priests to permit or prohibit friars to hear lay confessions. Innocent IV's *Etsi animarum* (1254), applicable to Franciscans and Dominicans alike, reaffirmed that friars could not hear the confessions of parishioners or preach in their parish church without their parish priest's permission.[27] The friars perceived this as an assault on their privileges, which suggests that, despite the bull's restatement of official policy, they had been shriving parishioners and entering parochial pulpits with episcopal approval over the objections of parish priests.[28] Parish clergy who were unsympathetic, or who feared the diversion of their sometimes meagre revenues to the friars, now had a papal privilege upon which to call. It did them little good: Innocent IV was soon replaced by Alexander IV, who promptly rescinded *Etsi animarum* in favour of the *status quo ante bullam*, but it is helpful as a landmark in the fog.[29] Despite continued objections to the mendicants, papal and episcopal support for the friars in their pastoral ministry remained strong.[30]

The last decades of the century saw dramatic change. The bull *Ad fructus uberes* (1281) removed the friars from any secular ecclesiastical control below the pope; bishops and priests were not permitted to impede the pastoral ministry of Franciscans or Dominicans in any way. The pope satisfied the *proprius sacerdos* clause of *Omnis utriusque* by requiring laity to confess annually to their parish priests even if they had confessed to mendicants, though he did not specifically require them to confess again sins already confessed and absolved.[31] The friars' opponents protested vociferously and continued their obstructions despite the papal privilege.[32] A more lasting balance was finally achieved in 1300 by Boniface VIII in his bull *Super cathedram*. Under its terms, friars could not preach in any place when the local priest was preaching; they could only preach in parish churches by the permission of the priest, though the bishop could

---

[24] *C&S* II, 899–900.   [25] Meens, *Penance*, 118–23ff., Mansfield, *Humiliation*.

[26] *Reg. Romeyn* I, no. 160.   [27] Little, *Studies*, 110–12.   [28] Ibid., 111–12.

[29] Ibid., 112.   [30] *C&S* II, 480, 595–96, 706; but cf. ibid. 415.

[31] Sbaralea, *Bullarium Franciscanum* III, 480; Little, *Studies*, 113; Gratien, *Histoire*, 337–54; Raine, ed., *Northern Registers*, 102–3.

[32] *Epist. Pecham* III, 952–53, 956–57; Little, *Studies*, 113n.

commission a friar to preach and thus overrule the parish priest;[33] confessors must first be approved by their orders and then be presented to the bishop to be licensed to hear confessions in his diocese, their number proportional to the needs of the population; if a bishop categorically refused to license friars as confessors, his refusal was illegitimate and friars might proceed to shrive by apostolic authority; and finally, the friars must hand over one-quarter of all bequests to the parish priest of the deceased.[34]

Each order also had its own internal developments and rules across the course of the century. As we have seen, when the Dominicans arrived in England in 1221, they were already allowed to hear lay confessions and numerous works were soon being written by Dominican scholars to instruct their fellows.[35] The most influential and enduring of these was Raymond of Peñaforte's *Summa de casibus penitentiae*, which reached quasi-official status by mid-century.[36] It remained one of the most important canonical works on the subject, cited often not only by Dominicans but also by other friars and seculars. The beginnings of lay confession to Franciscans are murkier because they originated as a mostly lay order. The confessions of the brethren alone are discussed in the *Regula Bullata* of 1223.[37] The bull *Quoniam abundavit iniquitas*, issued for the Franciscans in 1237, was an almost exact repetition of the bull of that name in favour of the Dominicans in 1221; in each case, the order was commended to bishops for use as preachers and confessors.[38] It is probable that clerical Franciscans were already hearing confessions before 1237, with local rather than papal permission. According to Friar Thomas, Alexander of Hales spent three days in 1224 hearing lay parishioners' confessions in response to his Easter sermon.[39] In 1235, Matthew Paris specifically accused the Minorites of hearing lay confessions and enjoining penances in England, to the prejudice of parish priests. He alleged that the pope rebuked them for this insolence and, while Matthew was hardly impartial, it may indeed have been the case that some Franciscans anticipated *Quoniam abundavit*, acted prematurely and were reprimanded.[40] The support of English bishops after 1237 is easier to trace, as for example when

[33] The Dominican Prior-General Humbert of Romans had urged such co-operation with parish clergy in a letter of 1258: *Annales Monastici* I, 435.
[34] Sbaralea, *Bullarium Franciscanum* IV, 498–500; *DEC*, 365–69; Little, *Studies*, 114–16; Gratien, *Histoire*, 354–59; Little, *Papers*, 230–43.
[35] Right to hear confessions: Mulchahey, *First the Bow*, 53. On instructional literature, see Mulchahey, *First the Bow*, 193–217; Boyle, *Pastoral Care*, Chapters II and III; Teetaert, *La confession*; O. Langholm, *The Merchant in the Confessional* (Leiden, 2003), 32–65, 122–37; P. Michaud-Quantin, 'Deux formulaires pour la confession du milieu du XIII⁰ siècle', *Recherches de Théologie Ancienne et Médiévale* 31 (1964), 43–62.
[36] *EEFP*, 335; Raimundus, *Summa.*   [37] *Reg. Bull.*, IX.
[38] Şenocak, *Poor and the Perfect*, 64–65.   [39] *De Adventu*, 28.   [40] *Chron. Maj.* III, 332–34.

Grosseteste brought two Franciscans and two Dominicans on his diocesan visitations, probably starting around this time, to preach to the laity and hear their confessions.[41] The first statutes of Winchester (1224) permitted and encouraged confession to Dominicans; the second statutes (1247?) added the Franciscans to this provision.[42] Episcopal support for foundations may also indicate support for pastoral activity but, as friars were sometimes already active in an area before settling there, the lack of a convent might not reflect a lack of support or activity.[43]

In 1243, Innocent IV had granted some of the Austins the right to hear the confession of anyone who came to them. This privilege passed to the whole order at the union of 1256. The same bull also guaranteed the right to preach publicly. The hearing of confessions required the licence of the bishop and parish rector. Richard of Swinfield, bishop of Hereford, had an *inspeximus* of the bull entered in his episcopal register in 1283, apparently in defence of the privilege; Ralph Walpole, bishop of Norwich, also confirmed it in 1291.[44] This suggests both that both bishops supported the order in its pastoral goals and that there had been some opposition among their parish clergy. The timing of Swinfield's *inspeximus* may reflect uncertainty whether the Austins' right to hear confessions was freed from the secular ecclesiastical structure by *Ad fructus uberes* of 1281, which had given those privileges to the Dominicans and Franciscans, a bull also recorded in Swinfield's register in 1282.[45] John le Romeyn, archbishop of York 1285–96, Conservator of Privileges for the Austins in England, delegated authority to act as Conservator to his *officialis* so that neither travel nor business would prevent the defence of their rights.[46]

In 1262, Urban IV granted the Carmelites the right to hear the confessions of any faithful who came to them, provided that the local secular prelates gave licence. As this bull was copied in 1273 into the register of Archbishop Giffard of York, who elsewhere referred to Carmelites but no other mendicant order as 'beloved' (*dilecti*), at least one English diocesan apparently supported their cause.[47] Another was Richard Gravesend, bishop of London, who founded the Carmelite friary at Maldon (Essex) in 1293.[48] When adjudicating a dispute between that friary and the local parish church in 1300, he declared that the friars might hear the

---

[41] *C&S* II, 261–65.   [42] *C&S* II, 133, 415.   [43] See above in Chapter 3.

[44] *Reg. Swinfield*, 80–81; Harper-Bill, ed., *Clare Cartulary*, no. 166; see also Roth, *Austin Friars* II, 42n. It is ambiguous whether permission was required for preaching, but in a bull of 1254, another of the future constituents was granted both privileges, again requiring episcopal or parochial permission: van Luijk, *Bullarium*, 96–97.

[45] *Reg. Swinfield*, 34–35.   [46] *Reg. Romeyn* I, no. 86 (July 1291).

[47] *Reg. Giffard*, 304; for *dilecti*, see ibid., 298.

[48] *MRH* 235; A. Simpson, *The Carmelite Friary at Maldon Essex* (Maldon, 1986), 46.

confessions of the laity but only by permission of the parish priest.[49] Urban's bull and Gravesend's settlement agreed with the Constitutions of London (1281), the earliest surviving for the order, which provide that 'no friar may, without the licence of the prior-general or -provincial and the [secular] prelate, hear the confessions of outsiders ... and so let him be diligently examined and found sufficiently suitable'. Regarding the circumstances of confession, it established that 'confessions should be heard in our houses in visible places, and in confessions outside our house let one friar be able to see another.'[50] As with other mendicant constitutions, these probably incorporate material from lost earlier constitutions of the order.

Archbishop Pecham was perhaps unaware of these bulls when he reacted to his observation of Austins and Carmelites shriving clergy and laity at his visitation of Oxford. The local diocesan, Richard Gravesend, bishop of Lincoln (nephew to bishop Gravesend of London) had presumably given them permission. In 1280, Pecham ordered the archdeacon of Oxford to stop them until they should prove their right to do so.[51] One can only assume that both orders quickly presented the relevant bulls. When *Super cathedram* curtailed mendicant pastoral privileges in 1300, John Dalderby, bishop of Lincoln, limited the number of Dominicans he licensed to hear confessions in his diocese on the grounds that he needed to leave space for requests from Austins and Carmelites as well.[52] While the historiography of the thirteenth-century mendicant movement has largely focused on the Preachers and Minorites, it is clear that the Austins and Carmelites bore a significant and increasing share of the care of souls by the last quarter of the century.

CONTRITION

Since at least the time of Anselm of Canterbury, the sacrament of penance had been discussed in three parts: contrition, confession and satisfaction (serving one's assigned penance).[53] Most theological and pastoral writings on penance in the thirteenth century, from simple instructions for simple curates to sophisticated treatises, followed this division, so it is only sensible to do so here. The division is somewhat neater in theory than in practice, however. A penitent might be persuaded to true contrition by

---

[49] 'Nullum etiam parochianum dicte ecclesie ad confessionem admittant nisi qui eis confiteri voluerit et prius a suo curato licentiatus fuerit et dimissus'. British Library, Cotton Charter V.33.
[50] Saggi, ed., 'Londoniensis', 222. The Constitutions of 1294 show no substantive changes: Saggi, ed., 'Burdigalensis', 144–45.
[51] *Epist. Pecham* I, 99–100.   [52] Roth, *Austin Friars* II, 82.
[53] Anciaux, *Pénitence*, 63. Cf. C&S II, 220.

the priest during the confession; the priest was told to mitigate satisfactions to some degree on the basis of the penitent's sincerity of regret.

Contrition was considered indispensable for remission of sins. Typical indulgences state that they were only valid if the recipient were *contritus et confessus*. The Dominican *Speculum iuniorum* defined contrition as 'sorrow adopted for sins, with the intent to confess and make satisfaction'.[54] Grosseteste considered a confession 'sufficient when it has been true, whole, clear, uncovered, bitter, and ashamed'.[55] Blushing and tears, indicating shame and sorrow, were widely considered the outward signs of inner contrition.

Before the twelfth century, penitential manuals gave primary place to satisfaction and penances prescribed by canon law filled their pages. The sinner was absolved only after the assigned penances (often lengthy and harsh) had been completed, although they also clearly accepted that contrition was necessary for those penances to be truly salvific.[56] The apparent emphasis on making legal satisfaction led generations of scholars to view early medieval penance as an essentially exterior and juridical act; but the importance of contrition in the process of confession goes at least as far back as the Carolingian era.[57] Although in the early twelfth century there were new departures in how the relationship between contrition and satisfaction was discussed, this now appears to relate more to the development of the classroom as a new nexus of intellectual life rather than to a sea-change in attitudes that pitted rigourist canonists against contritionist theologians.[58]

One of these new expressions, a tract destined to be influential, was the anonymous *De vera et falsa penitentia*, written in the twelfth century but quickly misattributed to St Augustine of Hippo. The 'discovery' that the greatest of the church fathers had written in terms congruent to those of early twelfth-century theologians must have been very convenient indeed. According to *De vera et falsa*, in passages promoted further by the canonist Gratian in his treatise *De penitentia*, God forgives sins when

[54] J. Goering, 'Pastoral Texts and Traditions: The Anonymous *Speculum Iuniorum*', in Gunn and Innes-Parker, *Texts and Traditions*, 89–99. I am grateful to Joe Goering for providing me with a copy of his annotated typescript of the work as it appears in Bodleian Library, MS. Bodley 655, fols 1–141, a copy written at Oseney Abbey, Oxford, in 1302–3. He is preparing a critical edition. 'Contricio est dolor pro peccatis assumptus cum proposito confitendi et satisfaciendi'. MS. Bodley 655 fol. 92v; cf. fols 92r, 93v; cf. also Raimundus, *Summa*, 803–4; *C&S* II, 220–21.
[55] Wenzel, 'Deus est', 247. On the development and variety of such lists, many of which were longer, see B. Millet, '*Ancrene Wisse* and the Conditions of Confession', *English Studies* 3 (1999), 193–214.
[56] E.g. Robert of Flamborough, *Liber*. R. E. McLaughlin, 'Truth, Tradition, and History: The Historiography of High/Late Medieval and Early Modern Penance', in Firey, *Penance*, 19–72, at 46.
[57] Meens, *Penance*; Wagner, '*Cum aliquis*'.
[58] J. Goering, 'The Scholastic Turn (1100–1500): Penitential Theology and Law in the Schools', in Firey, *Penance*, 219–38; Meens, *Penance*, 190–213.

one becomes truly contrite and ashamed, though it is understood that
true contrition necessarily implies the intention to confess, undertake
penances and avoid sin thenceforth; and that shame and sorrow, which
were part of the debt one owed to God, were most acutely experienced
during the act of oral confession itself.[59] For Peter Lombard and Gerald of
Wales, 'confession of sin has shame, and the blushing itself is a heavy punishment (*erubescentia est gravis poena*); and so we are commanded to confess
sins, that we should suffer this blushing as a punishment: indeed, this too
is a part of the divine judgement.'[60] Godfrey of Salisbury OFM, when
he observed no contrition in a penitent, would weep openly himself to
induce it.[61] Shame could be pastorally problematic if the sinner were too
ashamed to confess. One manual has the priest advise the abashed penitent that it is better to blush today before one man than at the day of
judgement before all men, angels and demons together.[62]

Around 1215, Thomas of Chobham, an English student of Peter the
Chanter at Paris, wrote in his confessors' *summa*,

Since any sacrament ought to have a sign and a material, in this sacrament that
material is the remission of sins itself which God gives to man. The sign is the
contrition of the heart, since, just as when a stone is pulverised, it is annihilated,
likewise when a heart is crushed, sin is annihilated. Therefore, in confession,
blushing itself is the sign of interior contrition; and in satisfaction, devotion itself
is the sign of remission … That all sin is remitted by contrition alone is plain
through the Psalmist saying, 'I said, "I will confess my transgressions unto the
Lord", and You forgave the iniquity of my sin.'[63]

A rubric in the *Tractatus metricus de septem sacramentis* of William de Montibus argues that 'contrition is the greatest part of satisfaction' (*contritio
est maxima pars satisfactionis*).[64] Variations on this tag proliferated. For the
Benedictine Matthew Paris, 'Blushing, and anxiety of shame, and the
humility of confessing, are the greatest part of penance (*maxima pars est
poenitentiae*)'.[65] In a passage on venial sins, Richard Fishacre OP gave it as

---

[59] Larson, *Master of Penance*, 35–99, esp. 45–47; Lombard, *Sentences* 4, 94–105; Payer, *Sex and Confession*, 12–44; S. Hamilton, 'Penance in the Age of Gregorian Reform', *Studies in Church History* 40, 47–73; Little, *Religious Poverty*, 188–90; Carroll-Clark, 'Practical Summa', 140.

[60] Lombard, *Sentences 4*, 105; Gerald, *Opera* II, 51; cf. gloss on Matthew 3:6 in Walters Museum MS. W. 15 f. 12r.

[61] Little, *De Adventu*, 63.

[62] Quoting here from Rider, ed., '*Sciendum*', 167–68. On the longer history of this advice, see Pelle, 'Homiletic Eschatology'. Similar advice appears in a short text on confession in Walters Museum MS. W. 15 f. 2v. See also Firey, 'Blushing'; Barr, *Care of Women*, 113–16.

[63] Thomas of Chobham, *Summa Confessorum*, 8; Ps. 31:5.

[64] Goering, *William de Montibus*, 173. The rubric may be the copyist's, not William's, but the MS. is not later than mid-thirteenth century.

[65] *Chron. Maj.* III, 401.

his opinion that 'blushing in confession, since it is painful, makes satisfaction' (*Erubescencia enim confessionis, quia penalis, satisficiat*).[66] Writing around 1250, the Dominican author of *Speculum iuniorum* noted that 'blushing in confession is the greater part of satisfaction', and elsewhere wrote 'shame in confession is the greatest part of satisfaction'.[67] In 1287, Peter Quinel, bishop of Exeter, wrote in his diocesan statutes,

Let [the confessor] not have wandering eyes, but eyes bowed down to the ground, not looking at the face of the confessing one, except so that he may evaluate the contrition and blushing of the penitent's heart, which is the greatest part of penance (*que est maxima pars penitentie*).[68]

While not using the clause, the author of *Fasciculus Morum* argued,

If then, as I have said, your confession is bitter, it has such power that, even if you had sinned more than any person alive and the devil were to write down all your sins against you in his book of condemnation, they would all be deleted and your name would be written with the just.[69]

In his bull *Inter cunctas* of 1304, while adjudicating between friars and seculars over confession, Benedict XI denied that it was necessary (as some seculars claimed) to re-confess to one's parish priest any sins already confessed to a friar but he considered it salubrious nonetheless, on the grounds that repeating one's confession was a fresh opportunity for blushing over one's sins, and *erubescentiam ... magna est penitentie pars*.[70]

This view raised two theological problems that became standard discussions in treatises on penance. Each problem arises from the need to clarify the relationship between the internal court of conscience and the external court of satisfying canon law.[71] First, God's forgiveness of guilt (*culpa*) might not equate to remission of penalty (*poena*), so how much should a priest mitigate penances based on the penitent's contrition?[72] This will be explored below in the section on satisfaction, the third part

[66] R.J. Long, 'The Moral and Spiritual Theology of Richard Fishacre', *Archivum Fratrum Praedicatorum* 60 (1990), 5–141, at 139–40.
[67] 'Erubescentia in confessione est maior pars satisfactionis' and 'tamen pudor in confessione, sit magna pars satisfaccionis'. MS. Bodley 655 ff. 94r, 98r.
[68] *C&S* II, 992.
[69] *FM*, 478–81. This is Wenzel's translation; the first line more literally appears as 'If, then, your confession will have been as it has been said ...', referring back to 'bitter contrition' in a previous paragraph.
[70] *Corpus Iuris Canonici: Extravagantes Communes*, printed Paris 1507 by Thielman Kerver, Liber V f. 51v; quoted also in complaints of London rectors to the Council of Lambeth, 1309: *C&S* II, 1257.
[71] J. Goering, 'The Internal Forum and the Literature of Penance and Confession', *Traditio* 53 (2004), 175–227.
[72] Jarosz, 'Sacramental Penance'.

of penance. But the more serious question was: if it is interior contrition itself that remits sins, are confession to a priest and works of satisfaction necessary at all? Almost all medieval authorities agreed that they were, especially for mortal sins – though God would give value to the merit of the deed if a truly penitent sinner died before he had the opportunity to confess or undertake satisfaction.[73] The significance of contrition was seldom allowed to eclipse entirely the priestly power of the keys, Jesus' commission empowering the Apostles (and, it was inferred, their successors) to bind and loose people from their sins. While many authors agreed that contrition and a variety of meritorious acts delete venial sins even without confession to a priest, they also came to argue that it was safer to confess venial sins to a priest as well, for he held the keys.[74]

CONFESSION

With confessions as with sermons, the historian's access to the living event comes almost exclusively through instructional texts for the priest. A priest who revealed what had been said to him in a confession faced severe discipline – he would be defrocked and banished to a strict monastery – and recording what went on in a particular confession could violate the seal of secrecy.[75] While some *exempla* purport to describe confessions, they were crafted to serve the rhetorical needs of the preacher. Even if they were accurate depictions of real events, those events were not a representative sample of reality. Nonetheless, manuals for priests, whether written by theologians or by canonists, suggested to their readers what could happen, what a priest might expect to find, what sins might be confessed to him, and how he ought to respond. Both genres usually offered practical advice to the confessor, from which the historian can glean some idea of what priest and penitent did and said in general terms.

The confessional booth was unknown to the thirteenth century. Confession generally took place within the parish church, unless on a battlefield or in childbed, sickbed or deathbed.[76] Bishops directed their parish

---

[73] Bodleian Library, MS. Laud Misc. 471, apparently a parish priest's *pastoralia* book, includes at f. 126r a brief formulary specifically for hearing the confessions of the dying.

[74] Mokry, 'Henry of Wodestone's *Summa de sacramentis*', 100–104, 216–18; brief discussion in John of Wales OFM, *Summa de penitentia*, British Library MS. 10.A.IX, fól. 20r; Victorine school, Anciaux, *Pénitence*; Jarosz, 'Sacramental Penance'; Teetaert, *La confession*, 296–300, 354–56; Raimundus, *Summa*, 816–17.

[75] Punishment: Bodleian Library, MS. Bodley 655, f. 99v. The exception was when priests and bishops spoke or corresponded behind the seal. *Reg. Quivil*, 314; Murray, 'Confession as a Historical Source'.

[76] Murray, 'Confession as a Historical Source', 289; *C&S* II, 144.

clergy to hear women's confessions in plain sight but out of earshot to avoid both real and suspected malfeasance by the priest.[77] Some added that women's confessions should not take place behind a curtain, which suggests that penitents sought privacy, and it is possible that some men confessed behind a curtain or screen.[78] The Dominican *Speculum iuniorum* advised that a male penitent should sit humbly at the priest's feet, while a female penitent should sit at an angle (*ex transverso*) so the priest would not be looking at her face.[79] The two could begin with prayer: the priest alone might pray, he might pray with the penitent, and he might even ask the penitent to pray for him.[80]

Then followed an enquiry into the penitent's faith. In older penitentials, the requirements were only the most fundamental beliefs, such as the Trinity and the resurrection of the flesh before the final judgement.[81] By the time of Chobham's *Summa*, the question was not whether the penitent was simply a Christian but rather 'whether he holds the correct faith', and the penitent was to be quizzed on the Apostles' Creed and the Lord's Prayer, being taught them if ignorant – though on the individual articles of the Creed, he was to be questioned *sine subtilitate*.[82] Peñaforte's *Summa* and the *Speculum iuniorum* expected quizzing on the Lord's Prayer, Creed and *Ave Maria*.[83] Such major treatises on penance were beyond the resources of many parish clergy, but diocesan statutes from across England encourage similar questioning, as do a variety of short confessors' manuals.[84] Around 1320, William of Pagula observed that a priest might not have time to question each penitent individually, but instead could give a sermon at the beginning of Lent covering the vital points.[85] A sermon for the third Sunday after Epiphany (thus just before Lent) in a late-thirteenth-century English collection may have had the same idea when it charged that the priest should teach his people, if they did not

[77] E.g. *C&S* II, 72.
[78] *C&S* II, 188, 637. William Lyndwood explained that this particularly referred to the veil hung between altar and congregation during Lent but could also mean any other covered place (*Provinciale* V.16.14).
[79] Bodleian Library, MS. Bodley 655, f. 98v.
[80] Rider, 'Sciendum', 165. See also examples in J. T. McNeill and H. M. Gamer, ed. and trans., *Medieval Handbooks of Penance* (New York, 1938).
[81] E.g. the eleventh-century *Corrector et medicus* of Burchard of Worms: PL CXL, 950.
[82] Thomas of Chobham, *Summa Confessorum*, 242–44; cf. J. Goering, ed., *William de Montibus*, 128.
[83] Raimundus, *Summa*, 830–31; Bodleian Library, MS. Bodley 655, f, 98r.
[84] *C&S* II, 73, 134, 172, 269, 305, 346, 405, 424, 519, 648, 713. Manuals: Rider, 'Lay Religion'; Rider, 'Sciendum', 166–67; Bodleian Library, MS. Laud Misc. 471 (apparently owned by a parish priest), f. 126v.
[85] Pantin, *Fourteenth Century*, 192n.

know them, the articles of faith, Decalogue, mortal sins, 'counsels of the Gospel', sacraments of the church and circumstances of sin.[86]

As the confession proceeded, the confessor was to help the penitent search his or her conscience. Many confessors' manuals had schemata intended to give the confessor a thorough programme of investigation. A table, such as those found in Grosseteste's *Templum Dei*, or the pithy verses of William de Montibus' *Peniteas cito peccator*, could be committed to memory or consulted very rapidly in the living moment of confession; the priest who spent time hunting for a particular passage in a book risked losing the emotional momentum that contrition implied. Models included sins against faith, hope and love; by thought, word and deed; the seven deadly sins and the seven cardinal virtues; the Ten Commandments; by misusing the five senses; and other standard systems of medieval moral analysis.[87] Such questioning was needed because the penitent may not have given much thought to preparing for confession or may have been unaware (or unconvinced) that certain actions or thoughts were sinful.[88] Some manuals counselled the priest to let the penitent shape the confession at first, before inquiring further about specific sins and circumstances, but cautioned priests not to ask questions (especially about sexual or unusual sins) in a manner that gave the penitent new and exciting ideas.[89]

Confessors' manuals insisted that an ideal confession should be complete, covering all of one's sins. *Handlyng Synne* (c. 1303) unabashedly recommended terrifying penitents into a full confession.[90] John of Wales OFM contrasted the penitential forum with human courts: while concealing crimes may lead to acquittal in a human court, only full disclosure can bring mercy in the heavenly court; while, according to the Law of God, the testimony of two or three witnesses is required for credence in an earthly court, the testimony of one's own mouth is the only accuser needed in the court of penance. A thorough 'accounting' is thus to be encouraged 'before the vicar and dispensator of [the penitent's] church

---

[86] Cambridge, St John's Coll., MS. S 19, p. 89. Priests were required in some dioceses to teach on these same or similar topics several times a year: see above, pp. 97–101.

[87] E.g. Grosseteste, *Templum*; Goering, *William de Montibus*, 122–26, 202–9; Goering and Payer, ed., 'Summa Penitentie', 17–20.

[88] Murray, 'Counselling', 74. Some argued that the priest should not interrogate but only listen, but this was a minority view: Mansfield, *Humiliation*, 72–73; P. Michaud-Quantin, *Sommes de casuistique et manuels de confession au moyen âge* (Louvain, 1962), 23–24; Raimundus, *Summa*, 827.

[89] Payer, *Sex and Confession*, 60–62, 137–44; *C&S* II, 73; Raimundus, *Summa*, 819–20, 827–35; Goering and Payer, ed., 'Summa penitentie', 14–16, 28.

[90] R. Hasenfratz, 'Terror and Pastoral Care in *Handlyng Synne*', in Gunn and Innes-Parker, *Texts and Traditions*, 132–48.

in full and true confession'.[91] In doing so, the penitent was not to divide a confession among multiple priests, for example by confessing some sins to a friar and others to the parish priest.[92] However, this did not exclude confessing several times a year to a friar but to one's own parish priest during Lent.[93] This practice was promoted by the diocesan statutes of Winchester (ca. 1247):

Because of the religion of the Friars Preachers and Minors and the profit to souls, we decree that it is permitted to the faithful to go to them to receive penance whenever they wish, except in Lent, and even then if licence has been sought from [their] own priest and the accustomed oblations have been given to [their] own church.[94]

This mixed practice was also assumed under the terms of *Ad fructus uberes*, which required the laity to confess annually to their parish priests but otherwise allowed them to confess as often as they liked to friars.[95] This would allow the laity whatever benefit they found in confessing to friars while reassuring their parish priests, who had the right to withhold Easter communion from a parishioner whom they did not believe to have confessed. One perceived benefit may have been that a friar not pressed to hear a whole parish's confessions in Lent could afford to take more time. Even when papal bulls allowed parish clergy a monopoly, Lateran IV's *Omnis utriusque* specifically allowed the *proprius sacerdos* to give parishioners leave to confess to another priest and there is no reason to believe that every parish priest was too proud to welcome assistance at a busy time of year. This could allow him, too, to give more time to penitents who needed it. Parishioners could also confess outside Lent to their parish priests. If following the thrice-annual schedule given in some dioceses, their Advent confessions might be the longest: Pentecost to Christmas is more than half the year, while Christmas to Ash Wednesday varies from six to eleven weeks, leaving less time for sins to accrue.

If a parishioner seldom confessed, however, or had been a particularly industrious sinner, or was unusually scrupulous, a complete confession would have taken a great deal of time. If many parishioners made annual confession around the beginning of Lent, a priest would have to prioritise in his questions to get them all done.[96] Biller argues that those 'grainier sins which hurt or upset neighbours or members of one's family' were

[91] 'Computacione vel enumeracione ... ante vicarium et dispensatorem ecclesie sue in plena et in vera confessione': British Library, Royal MS. 10.A.ix, fols 22v–23r.
[92] *DEC* 245; Raimundus, *Summa*, 819–21; Bodleian Library, MS. Bodley 655 ff. 94v, 96v, 97r. Gratian had also discouraged this: Larson, *Master of Penance*, 208. See also above, pp. 141–47.
[93] Bodleian Library, MS. Bodley 655 fol. 94v, 96v; Raimundus, *Summa*, 819–20.
[94] *C&S* II, 415.   [95] *Reg. Swinfield*, 34–35.
[96] P. Marshall, *The Catholic Priesthood and the English Reformation* (Oxford, 1994), 12–13.

considered of utmost importance for confession was an important tool for orchestrating social harmony.[97] Payer counters that manuals give a great deal of space to sexual sins, which suggests that confessors spent a lot of time dealing with them.[98] (The distinction disappears for sex acts that were also social sins, such as adultery; and Cels argues that, while confessors' manuals naturally discuss the deadly sin of wrath, they do not, as we might have expected, pay much attention to personal reconciliation.)[99] But the amount of time a confessor spent dealing with a particular kind of sin, whether social, sexual, both or neither, did not have to reflect the number of pages on the topic in his manual. Some sins might receive more extensive treatment not because they were more common but because they were more complex, either morally or in canon law, while a different subject – perhaps exhorting chronic truants to come to mass more often – might be discussed briefly precisely because it was so commonplace that a priest already knew the script. Either way, canon law required the priest to search out mortal sins, which had to be absolved before receiving the Eucharist, and other sins reserved to episcopal or papal jurisdiction, such as striking a cleric.[100]

How far was confession a means of social control over the laity? Foucault and Tentler probably over-emphasised its role in this respect.[101] Since both authors included in their analyses the Continent and the later Middle Ages – places and times where confession was part of the mechanism of inquisition and repression of heresy – their analyses of control were shaped by those sources as well as their by respective theoretical bents. Whether or not their analyses hold true for later medieval Europe, they seem inapplicable to the decidedly non-inquisitorial England of the thirteenth century. Yet the English clergy were fallible men and some doubtless enjoyed or even abused the power that confession gave them. The option of going to another confessor, even if seldom exercised, would be powerful leverage against a domineering, incompetent or lazy rector or vicar, or one who might be personally aggrieved by a sin to be confessed. But checks and balances of this sort were also viewed as disruptive by at least some secular clergy and we should not assume that this must reflect bad faith or jealousy on their part.[102] French secular clergy

---

[97] Biller, 'Introduction', in Biller and Minnis, *Handling Sin*; see also Hyams, *Rancor*, 43–59; Swanson, *Religion and Devotion*, 61–63; Pounds, *English Parish*, 303–4.

[98] Payer, *Sex and Confession*, 3–4.

[99] Cels, 'Interrogating Anger'. See above for reconciliation in the context of the mass, pp. 127–35.

[100] *C&S* II, 222–24; Bodleian Library, MS. Laud Misc. 471, f. 127r–v.

[101] M. Foucault, *History of Sexuality, Vol. 1*, trans. R. Hurley (New York, 1978), esp. 58–63; T. N. Tentler, *Sin and Confession on the Eve of the Reformation* (Princeton, 1977); Tentler, 'Social Control'.

[102] Moorman, *Church Life*; Lawrence, *The Friars*, 152–65.

complained to Pope Martin IV that his *Ad fructus uberes* gave such complete prerogative to the friars that the seculars could not render account for their charges before God; Archbishop le Romeyn of York similarly argued that shepherds must know their flocks in order to care for them properly, something which parish clergy could not accomplish if their parishioners resorted to friars for confession.[103] Archbishop FitzRalph of Armagh would make these same arguments in the 1350s and seems to have been converted from the friars' friend to their nemesis in part because of this very question.[104] This was a genuine structural problem that went beyond ignorance of the laity's besetting sins. If a parishioner claimed that he or she had confessed to a friar, we know of no system by which a priest could verify the claim. Even when parishioners confessed to him, the parish priest had to take a great deal on faith: that they were truly contrite, had confessed all and not just some of their sins and had completed their penances or fulfilled the terms of indulgences in lieu thereof.[105] An inability to confirm whether parishioners had confessed at all, and thus whether they should be permitted to receive the host at Easter, would have undercut attempts to use confession as social control. Indeed, Tanner and Watson have argued that the medieval church, '[a]ware that overreach would publicly reinforce its limits ... recognised the wide gulf between what was expected and what was enforced ... This patience paid off' over the long run.[106]

It is natural to suppose that the itinerant friar would give less attention to matters pertaining to the local community than the deeply connected parish priest would.[107] But this may reflect practice more than theory. A newly arrived parish priest might know his charges no better than a visiting friar. At least with regard to the deadly sins of wrath and envy – which could be both causes and effects of interpersonal sin, potentially leading to lasting feuds – friars as preachers and confessors seem to have given it its due attention.[108] Mendicant peacemaking and arbitration were certainly important in fractious thirteenth-century Italian cities.[109] Nor were friars always strangers; they could spend much of their lives near the places of their origins, particularly if they had less common language skills such as Welsh or Cornish. Even if English friars were successful at defusing social

---

[103] G. Post, 'A Petition Relating to the Bull *Ad fructus uberes* and the Opposition of the French Secular Clergy in 1282', *Speculum* 11 (1936), 231–37; Raine, ed., *Northern Registers*, 102–3.

[104] Walsh, *FitzRalph*, 318–76.   [105] Swanson, *Indulgences*, 11.

[106] Tanner and Watson, 'Least of the Laity'.   [107] Haren, *Sin and Society*, 187.

[108] *FM*, 116–311; M. Cels, 'God's Wrath against the Wrathful in Medieval Mendicant Preaching', *Canadian Journal of History* 43.2 (2008), 217–26; M. Cels, 'Reconciling Mendicant and Secular Confessors in Late Medieval England', *JMH* 38 (2012), 225–43; Cels, 'Interrogating Anger'.

[109] A. Thompson, *Revival Preachers and Politics in Thirteenth-Century Italy: The Great Devotion of 1233* (Oxford, 1992), 136–78.

tensions and reducing cycles of vengeance, however, this is not the same as understanding the social context in which an initial sin had led to anger in the first place. The parish priest was more likely to know the personalities and social contours involved and the circumstances according to which an action's relative virtue or viciousness needed to be measured. From the second quarter of the fourteenth century onwards, we find complaints that friars did not adequately order penitents to make restitution to victims.[110] But these may have been misplaced and in any case should not be read back into the thirteenth century without independent warrant. The Dominican *Speculum iuniorum* ordered sinful profits to be returned as restitution, not given as alms.[111] A friar may have failed to order restitution because of a lack of local knowledge; he may have ordered it but moved on before he had the chance to make sure that it was paid. In the eyes of critics among the secular clergy, the result would be the same but this does not prove that he had been careless.

Some laypeople apparently desired more careful guidance than their priests could give. The *forma confessionis*, a genre of works aimed at helping not the priest but rather the penitent preparing for confession, assisted the literate with penance much as the *Lay Folks' Mass Book* did with the Eucharist. Examples in Middle English proliferate only in the fourteenth century, though one survives from *ca.* 1200 as do numerous Anglo-Saxon texts from the eleventh century. Several Anglo-Norman versions exist from the latter half of the thirteenth century, however, and while most of the surviving manuscripts indicate cloistered provenance, others point to lay ownership and the texts probably circulated widely in now lost copies.[112] England had by far the largest output of such texts in the later Middle Ages, which suggests that the promotion of regular and thorough confession from the thirteenth century onwards had been more successful there than elsewhere.

The complexity of life made ethical judgements delicate. Over the course of the twelfth century, clergy were given increasingly detailed and sophisticated instruction in how to question penitents about the circumstances of the sin and the sinner alike and how to temper penances accordingly. This idea was widely disseminated in England in the

---

[110] Haren, 'Confession in the *Memoriale presbiterorum*'; Walsh, *FitzRalph*, 364.
[111] Bodleian Library, MS. Bodley 655, ff. 100r, 108v (the model presumably being Zacchaeus: Luke 19:8).
[112] Middle English: Cornett, 'Form of Confession', 76–78, 543–54, 684–93. Earlier English: 340–68. Thirteenth-century Anglo-Norman, monastic or clerical provenance: ibid., 496–509, nos. C1, C5, C6.1, C6.2, C7.2; C11 and C12 undetermined, but probably clerical from Latin texts in MSS. Private (presumably secular) ownership: C7.1; perhaps C8.

thirteenth century, not only through confessors' manuals but also through diocesan legislation.[113] Often these appear in mnemonic verses:

> Quis, quid, ubi, quibus auxiliis, cur, quomodo, quando.
> Quilibet observet anime medicamina dando.
> (Who, what, where, with what help, and why and how and when –
> Check these when you try to give medicine to a soul.)[114]

Upon judging one rector's learning to be deficient, Grosseteste ordered that he 'should come at Michaelmas to be fully examined regarding the Ten Commandments, the seven sacraments and the seven sins *with circumstances*'.[115] The assumption in older historiography that pre-twelfth-century penitentials insisted on following the canons rigidly, while thirteenth-century confessors' manuals ignored the old canons and gave free rein to the confessor to assign penances as he saw fit, is now seen as a trick of the evidential light. Older penitentials routinely indicated that penances ought to be modified on a case-by-case basis, while later confessors' manuals, such as the *Memoriale presbiterorum*, do not necessarily show an abandonment of canonical penances. The twelfth and thirteenth centuries represented, in penance as in other fields, a period of debate as theologians sought to harmonise diverse traditions.[116] The priest also had to reckon with demand: if people saw him as too harsh, they were less likely to be completely open about their sins.[117] But we must also ask what documents parish priests had to hand, and it seems that they were more likely to have copies of works that did not provide lists of penances, even as a starting-point for modification, such as Grosseteste's *Templum Dei* or the various tracts issued together with diocesan statutes. In one such short manual disseminated to diocesan clergy, Alexander Stavensby, bishop of Coventry and Lichfield, simply wrote, 'Since penances are given according to judgement (*arbitrarie sunt*), we shall not define for you any certain penances that you ought to enjoin.' His statement was not unique but it was one of the clearest.[118]

---

[113] E.g. *C&S* II, 71, 220–27.

[114] Quoted here from *FM*, 478–79; cf. Raimundus, *Summa*, 828, and National Library of Scotland, MS. Advocates 18.7.21, fol. 103r, both of which read:

> Quis, quid, ubi, per quos, quotiens, cur, quomodo, quando:
> Quilibet observet anime medicamina dando.

These come originally from Cicero and were applied to penance by Peter the Chanter: Baldwin, *Masters* I, 56.

[115] Hoskin, *Grosseteste*, no. 1438 (=*Rot. Grosseteste*, 416–17).

[116] P. Payer, 'The Humanism of the Penitentials and the Continuity of the Penitential Tradition', *Mediaeval Studies* 46 (1984), 340–54.

[117] Tentler, 'Social Control', 113.   [118] *C&S* II, 224; Payer, *Sex and Confession*, 36–44.

It also would have defined a geography of pastoral care, since the tract bore episcopal *imprimatur* within his diocese but not beyond it.

In addition to assigning appropriate penances, the priest was to counsel the penitent on how to avoid sins in the future.[119] Schemata could include clear direction on such matters. William de Montibus, following common medical principles, noted that contraries cure contraries: the glutton must practice sobriety, the lustful must castrate himself (figuratively, one presumes) and so on.[120] The *Speculum iuniorum* advised the priest to enjoin penance in opposition to the sin, such as works of humility for the proud and works of gentleness for the wrathful and so on through the seven sins, giving the Dominican reader great leeway for his discretion, wisdom, creativity and assessment of the sinner's contrition.[121] A table in Grosseteste's *Templum Dei* correlates the seven vices that are counterparts of the seven cardinal virtues, the seven petitions of the *Paternoster*, seven beatitudes and seven 'medicines', attitudes that must be assumed to conquer the vices and achieve the virtues and beatitudes. Thus someone lacking the virtue of temperance has the vice of intemperance; he should pray 'deliver us from evil' and practice abstinence, helping him to become poor in spirit and thus fit to receive the kingdom of heaven. By applying this schema in hearing a confession, the confessor would not only have a system for enquiring after different sorts of sin: he would also be able to guide the penitent towards the corresponding virtue and give practical direction on how to carry it out. Beneath this diagnostic tool, Grosseteste wrote, 'In this table consists the whole care of the pastoral office.'[122]

Penitents ran the full spectrum of personality, status and condition, as manuals tended to point out. To modern eyes, the most obviously underrepresented concern in many manuals is women as penitents rather than as objects of men's lust. Confessors' manuals were written exclusively by men, for male use, growing out of centuries of the male monastic tradition, with male concerns foregrounded.[123] Hearing women's confessions posed a number of problems to the confessor. He could only assign an

---

[119] Murray, 'Counselling'.   [120] Goering, *William de Montibus*, 173.

[121] Bodleian Library, MS. Bodley 655, fol. 106v; cf. Goering and Payer, ed., 'Summa Penitentie', 39, where the author explains that such flexibility only serves for venial sins; mortal sins require canonical penance.

[122] Grosseteste, *Templum*, 38.

[123] J. Murray, 'Gendered Souls in Sexed Bodies: The Male Construction of Female Sexuality in Some Medieval Confessors' Manuals', in Biller and Minnis, *Handling Sin*, 79–93; J. Murray, 'The Absent Penitent: The Cure of Women's Souls and Confessors' Manuals in Thirteenth-Century England', in L. Smith and J. H. M. Taylor, eds, *Women, the Book and the Godly* (Woodbridge, 1995), 13–25; Payer, *Sex and Confession*, 8–9. For manuals that did attend to female penitents, see Rider, 'Lay Religion', at 332.

unfaithful wife penances that she could keep secret from her husband: assigning obvious penances would be a serious *de facto* violation of the seal of secrecy and might place her in danger of violence.[124] He had to balance privacy with visibility, and private talk, especially if sexual sins were concerned, could challenge the chastity of the priest's imagination as well as his body.[125] The safest course of action for the priest might be to keep the confession as short as possible. *Ancrene Wisse*, a guide for anchoresses written around the late 1220s, advised its readers to confess all of their common sins to any priest except for sexual thoughts. These they should confess only in vague terms to a younger priest. Only if speaking to a known and trusted confessor should a woman pour out such sins in full; but when she does so, she must choose shocking and vulgar language to expose the filth of it.[126] Such problems doubtless affected this most personal and individual experience of pastoral care for women in a way that was not altogether helpful.[127]

The friars' pastoral mission prevented them from avoiding women as monks did. Each order developed its own regulations. Concern about over-familiarity with women appears in the Franciscan Rule both in general discussion and in the context of confession: 'Let no friar, whether for hearing a confession or for any other reason, stand or sit next to a woman, except where he and his *socius* can see one another. And let all friars beware of the lengthy talks of women.'[128] While the latter sentence may have been intended as a separate precept to avoid gossips, it was probably read as an injunction to keep women's confessions short, possibly putting female penitents' souls at risk. Even a sympathetic and highly self-disciplined Franciscan could be limited by the judgement of a more prudish *socius*: the next sentence in the constitutions enjoins *socii* to report infractions of this rule.[129] The Franciscan *Fasciculus Morum* advised that the only safety from lust was to flee.[130] The Dominican constitutions of 1228 considered speaking 'alone with a woman neither for confession nor about useful or honourable matters ... without licence and great necessity' a 'grave' sin (as opposed to 'lighter', 'graver' or 'gravest'), on par with riding a horse or breaking a fast, to be penanced by three days on bread and water.[131] The comparative mildness of the threat, together with the specific exception for confession, contrasts with the Franciscan constitutions, and a parallel contrast may have been discernible in practice.

---

[124] E.g. Goering, *William de Montibus*, 172; *C&S* II, 32, 71, 639. [125] See above, p. 152.
[126] Millet, trans., *Ancrene Wisse*, 129–31. [127] Barr, *Care of Women*.
[128] *Reg. Bull.* XI; Monti, ed., *Bonaventure's Writings*, 169–70; Bihl, 'Statuta', 70, 84.
[129] Bihl, 'Statuta', 70; Monti, ed., *Bonaventure's Writings*, 99.
[130] *FM*, 657–59. [131] Denifle, 'Constitutiones', 208.

The Carmelite constitutions of 1281 and 1294 required a friar speaking with a woman to have a *socius* nearby where the latter could both see and hear them, though this seems to refer to normal conversation, not confessions specifically. The statutes regarding lay confessions outside the convent required mutual visibility in all cases and said nothing in particular about confessions of women; the *socius* may have had to sit near enough that he too would be able to hear a woman's confession.[132] The Austins' constitutions of 1290 made similar provisions for speaking with a woman though, in the case of a friar's close relatives, the *socius* could retreat from earshot. An Austin could not be left alone in the church to shrive or counsel a woman unless separated by the locked gate between nave and choir. If a friar is hearing the confession of a sick woman in her bedroom or some other small room, his *socius*, so far as possible, should stay at the door so that he can see but not hear. When hearing confessions while travelling, each of the *socii* should be able to see the other when shriving women. Any friar contravening this would be penanced by three days on bread and water, as the Dominican regulations also ordered, but he would also be forbidden to hear confessions (and to preach, if a licensed preacher) for one year.[133] An Austin also committed a 'grave' sin (as opposed to light, graver or gravest) if he routinely went to a place where he could fix his eyes on women, or if he spoke with a woman for purposes other than confession, except briefly to ask or answer a question.[134]

Yet neither parish priests nor friars were monks. Parish priests spent their whole lives in mixed lay communities; friars circulated outside the convent. While confession provided dangerous opportunities, practice in maintaining continence would be quotidian. Most clergy doubtless came from ordinary families, with mothers, sisters, grandmothers, aunts, female cousins and so on. If a priest were from the higher social ranks, he grew up in a household with single female servants with whom he presumably had opportunities just as tempting as the confessional. A priest or friar who had been raised by a widow, or one who was dispensed for illegitimacy, may have come of age in a matriarchal household. If a priest were a widower, or had a past or present concubine, he had sexual and marital experience (and, if present, an outlet for desires).[135] Women were fully a part of his world.

---

[132] Saggi, ed., 'Londoniensis', 217, 222; Saggi, ed., 'Burdigalensis', 140, 145.
[133] *Const. Ratisbonenses*, 46–47.   [134] Ibid., 155.
[135] P. Cullum, '"Give Me Chastity": Masculinity and Attitudes to Chastity and Celibacy in the Middle Ages', *Gender and History* 3 (2013), 621–36.

SATISFACTION

The *Speculum iuniorum*, like many texts, prescribed hidden penances for hidden sins and public penances for public sins.[136] However, this distinction was never quite clear in theory and even less so in practice, for even private penance could have publicly visible aspects. There also existed 'solemn penance', which was, more or less, the public penance and reconciliation of the excommunicated.[137]

Private penance consisted of fasting, almsgiving and prayers. Canonical penitentials offered 'commutations' by which one sort of penance could be converted into another: for instance, if a person had not the health to allow fasting, recitation of psalms could suffice.[138] Following this logic, indulgences of the thirteenth century used days of fasting as their currency; one was excused from a set number of days by making monetary offerings or by praying at certain times and places (such as at a particular saint's shrine, which might require a pilgrimage there). Indulgences developed and expanded over the high and later Middle Ages, with practice always leading the way and theology struggling to keep up; clerics were loath to deny the efficacy or justice of such a widespread practice.[139]

The effects of private penance, even if only an annual affair, should not be underestimated. Burgess has argued that the sacrament of penance was more formative for laypeople's minds than the mass.[140] A parishioner in the habit of annual confession might well remember the shame of repeatedly owning up to a certain sin and then having to undertake penances that put strains on stomach, purse or time and thus discouraged recidivism. In addition, one of the seminal works from which medieval confessors' manuals derived was Gregory the Great's *Regulae pastoralis liber*, according to which

> some active behavioural response was required for the proper reception of the Eucharist ... For if you are serious about behavioural change, Gregory thought, you will work incrementally by small steps to modify actually revisable behaviour as evidence of your earnest desire for change.[141]

As a safeguard against penitents' failure to work out private penances, which were not easily monitored by the priest, some confessors' manuals reminded the priest to warn the penitent that any penance not done in this life would need to be worked off in purgatory; some added that this

---

[136] Bodliean Library, MS. Bodley 655, f. 100r.
[137] All three categories had fluid boundaries in the thirteenth century. Mansfield, *Humiliation*; Firey, 'Blushing'; Wagner, '*Cum aliquis*'.
[138] Robert of Flamborough, *Liber*, 275–76.   [139] Swanson, *Indulgences*, 10–16.
[140] Burgess, 'A Fond Thing Vainly Invented'.
[141] T. C. Oden, *Care of Souls in the Classic Tradition* (Philadelphia, PA, 1984), 51–52.

would involve incomparably more suffering.[142] Robert of Flamborough put it thus:

I wish to admonish you, priest, that if through gross ignorance or negligence or on account of some grace or favour or consideration of the person[143] ... you punish the penitent less than the authentic penances require canonically (provided that he requested and was prepared to undertake the full canonical penance), that same person, I argue, will be saved, and even freed from purgatory, I say, the penance enjoined by you on him being completed; you, however, will be in danger ... however much you are able, you should induce repentance so that he may undertake canonical and authentic penance ... Say to [the penitent]: 'Brother, it is right that you shall be punished either in this life or in purgatory. Moreover, the pain of purgatory is incomparably more grave than anything in this life. Behold: your soul is in your hands; therefore, choose for yourself whether you are to be punished sufficiently in this life by canonical or authentic penances, or to look forward to those of purgatory.'[144]

Flamborough was a more cautious voice than many, however, and was directly criticised for his reliance on the old penances, which were increasingly seen as too harsh for the softer men and women of his day.[145] Bonaventure argued that relaxations of penance by the priest not only reduced the penance one paid in this life, in the *foro ecclesiae* (judgement of the church), but also relaxed what the penitent owed to God in the *foro Dei*, the deficit being made up by the merit Christ gave to the church of which the penitent was a member, operated through the sacerdotal power of the keys.[146] *Fasciculus Morum* quoted an *exemplum* from the *Vitae patrum* in which a penitent monk asked his abbot to give him three years' penance; the abbot insisted on only three days, for God would accept that in light of his thorough contrition.[147] Raymond of Peñaforte demurred, arguing that purely arbitrary penances were the easy way out for the priest: referring to the penitential canons and restricting one's *arbitrium* (judgement) to modifications of them was intellectually more demanding for the priest but safer for the penitent.[148] Peter Lombard had staked out a middle position: if an undiscerning priest gave inadequate penances, God would accept them as paid in full if the penitent's contrition were sufficient but would add punishment insofar as contrition was insufficient.[149]

[142] Burgess, 'A Fond Thing Vainly Invented'; Payer, *Sex and Confession*, 67–69; Welter, *Speculum Laicorum*, 98; Carroll-Clark, 'Practical Summa', 142–43.
[143] Cf. Acts 10:34.   [144] Robert of Flamborough, *Liber*, 276–77.
[145] Baldwin, *Masters*, 55.   [146] Bonaventure, *Opera* IV, 533.
[147] *FM*, 643.   [148] Raimundus, *Summa*, 842–43; Bodleian Library, MS. Bodley 655, 106v.
[149] Lombard, *Sentences 4*, 123–24. As Lombard notes, this is the same standard given for those who die unable to complete their penances. Cf. Carroll-Clark, 'Practical Summa', 144.

Public penance has a longer history than private, dating to the patristic era, when notorious sinners were excommunicated and, after completing a period of penance measured in days or years, were liturgically reconciled by the bishop, often during Holy Week. Jerome, in a much-quoted passage, wrote that post-baptismal sin was a shipwreck but one could stay afloat by grabbing on to a plank from the flotsam, and that plank was penance.[150] In the patristic and early medieval periods, the sacrament of penance, like baptism, could be undertaken once only; in essence, this solemn penance was the only sort available. This gradually changed, however: laypeople, in imitation of monks regularly confessing to their abbots, began repeatedly confessing their sins to their priests.[151] Even as late as the early thirteenth century, Flamborough considered private penance repeatable but not really sacramental, while solemn penance was sacramental but not repeatable; but his was a minority view.[152] It was now possible to slip off that plank into the water but return to grasp it again as often as was needed.

Sins requiring public penance had to be referred to the bishop or his delegated penitentiary. In 1290, the penitentiary of Bishop Sutton of Lincoln absolved

Richard son of Henry of Empingham from the sentence of excommunication which he had incurred by assaulting a clerk in Empingham church. Richard was to appear in Empingham church as a penitent and receive five beatings on the hands on five successive Sundays, and on three of them he was to make offerings and kneel before the altar from the end of the Gospel until after the elevation of the host.[153]

This was a fairly typical instance of public penance. Other punishments could include going on pilgrimage or ritual humiliation, such as walking in procession in one's underclothes bearing a candle. Although Archbishop Pecham lamented in 1281 that solemn public penance was falling into disuse, Sutton was certainly using it in Lincoln Diocese.[154]

Public penance also shaded into public justice. If a layperson had been convicted in a secular court for a crime that was also a sin, then the sin was already public knowledge. If the crime had harmed another person, the court, in addition to sentencing the guilty party to a penalty, would

[150] Jerome, Epist. 84, *Corpus Scriptorum Ecclesiasticorum Latinorum* 55.6, p. 128. Cited, for instance, in *C&S* I, 1062; *C&S* II, 67, 898, 986, etc.; Raimundus, *Summa*, 77.
[151] T. O'Loughlin, 'Penitentials and Pastoral Care', in G. R. Evans, ed., *A History of Pastoral Care* (London, 2000), 93–111.
[152] Robert of Flamborough, *Liber*, 84, 271–73.
[153] *Reg. Sutton* III, 40–41, quoting editor's synopsis.
[154] *C&S* II, 899–900; R. Hill, 'Public Penance: Some Problems of a Thirteenth-Century Bishop', *History* n.s. 36 (1951), 213–26.

have ordered restitution to the plaintiff. Public knowledge would make it difficult to hide the sin from the parish priest or to neglect restitution. Perhaps penitents who had paid a secular penalty balked at the double jeopardy of paying an ecclesiastical one as well but the reverse was sometimes true. Ecclesiastical courts had primary cognisance of fornication and adultery but these show up in the rolls of manorial courts too. Formally, a villein's chattels belonged to his or her lord. When a villein was convicted of sexual sin in an ecclesiastical court and opted to pay a cash fine in lieu of penance, the money handed over to the church was legally the lord's. The villein would then be fined again in the manorial court as well, less for the sin itself than for the alienation of the lord's property.[155] In opting to commute penance to a cash fine, the villein was choosing to accept punishment in two courts and presumably thought it a price worth paying.

Public penance, no less than secular justice, had a role in defusing social tensions by the perception that the guilty were being punished. If someone's sins were publicly known and had public repercussions, then public admission of guilt and visible undertaking of shameful or painful penance could aid in reconciliation as well as assuring a victim's friends and family that they did not need to take revenge to save face.[156] Parish priests could use social pressure to induce confession.[157] If laypeople believed that 'the sin of one redounds upon everyone', they might also believe that the penance of the guilty averted divine wrath from the whole community.[158] Public or private satisfaction could mean paying a tangible debt to society through restitution, almsgiving and indulgences. Restitution of ill-gotten gains, while not itself a satisfaction, was considered necessary for absolution. In his analysis of the confessors' manual *Memoriale presbiterorum* (1335 × 1345), Haren notes that more than one-third of the work is given over to discussing restitution.[159] When a sin was such that the aggrieved party could not be repaid, indulgences were an option for divesting oneself of unjust gains. Although indulgences had their abuses, proceeds from their sale could go to help needy individuals, especially victims of accidents, and to maintain bridges, roads and hospitals. Here

---

[155] Punishments for *leyrwite* and *childwite* also appear in manorial court rolls without reference to church courts or fines paid there, simply as an event for which the lord could fine servile tenants. L. R. Poos and L. Bonfield, eds, *Select Cases in Manorial Courts, 1250–1550: Property and Family Law* (Selden Society no. 114, 1997), clxxxi–iv; J. A. Raftis, *Tenure and Mobility: Studies in the Social History of the Mediaeval English Village* (Toronto, 1964), 38; Bailey, ed., *English Manor*, 193.
[156] Hyams, *Rancor*, 199–200.
[157] J. Berlioz, '«Quand dire c'est faire dire»: Exempla et confession chez Étienne de Bourbon', in *Faire croire: Modalités de la Diffusion et de la Réception des Messages Religieux du XIIe au XVe siècle*, ed. École Français de Rome (Rome, 1981), 299–335, at 301–2.
[158] *Verbum Abbreviatum*, 471.   [159] Haren, 'Confession in the *Memoriale presbiterorum*', 121.

it might actually be more effective than the manor court in which the perpetrator paid a fine to the lord rather than to the community. Penance could result in tangible manifestations of the penitent's 'paying back' of his or her neighbours.[160] This was a vital aspect of the parish priest's role in maintaining and repairing the social fabric, a task explicitly assigned to him in numerous diocesan statutes.[161]

Some historians have accused the friars of undermining the parish priests in this part of their task by assigning penances that were too light; but, at least for thirteenth-century England, there is no clear evidence that this was so.[162] It is true that some mendicant authors promoted the importance of contrition at the relative expense of satisfaction, and that they helped to develop and spread the doctrine of purgatory, which formalised the manner in which satisfactions unfulfilled in this life could be worked off in the hereafter.[163] But for this to be a real point of contention, we would have to know that thirteenth-century parish clergy were, as a class, steadfastly maintaining the standards of heavier penances. Bishops' statutes and confessors' manuals for the parish clergy do not present this picture. The *Summa* of Master Serlo, presumably a secular priest, was arch-conservative in promoting unmitigated canonical satisfactions but comparison with other thirteenth-century English writings on penance highlights how out of step it was. Its existence in a single manuscript suggests further its lack of popularity.[164] While Grosseteste and Flamborough implied that the priest should not moderate the rigour of canonical penances any more than necessary, others (seculars included) argued that satisfaction was entirely at the priest's discretion, with the exception of excommunication and other reserved cases.[165] As we have seen, some seculars seemed genuinely troubled by their parishioners choosing mendicant confessors. But there is no indication that the level of penance imposed was an important factor in the parish clergy's resentment.[166]

[160] Haines, *Ecclesia Anglicana*, 183–87; Smith, *Acta*, 13, 96, 257; *Reg. Sutton* III, xxxvi–xxxvii.

[161] J. Hughes, 'The Administration of Confession in the Diocese of York in the Fourteenth Century', in D. M. Smith, ed., *Studies in Clergy and Ministry in Medieval England* (York, 1991), 87–163; *C&S* II, 64, 231, 460, 607, 720, 1029–30.

[162] Lawrence, *The Friars*, 152–65, cites evidence this this effect, but it is all either Continental or well after 1300; Hinnebusch made the claim in *EEFP* 323–24, specifically with regard to England before ca. 1320, but the evidence he cited does not bear this out.

[163] *FM* 643; Raimundus, *Summa*, 860; Swanson, *Religion and Devotion*, 36–38, 196; Burgess, 'A Fond Thing Vainly Invented'; J. le Goff, *The Birth of Purgatory*, trans. A Goldhammer (London, 1984).

[164] J. Goering, ed., 'The *Summa de penitentia* of Master Serlo', *Mediaeval Studies* 38 (1976), 1–53; J. Goering, 'The *Summa* of Master Serlo and Thirteenth-Century Penitential Literature', *Mediaeval Studies* 40 (1978), 290–311.

[165] Wenzel, 'Deus est', 292–93; *C&S* II, 220–26.

[166] E.g. it is conspicuously absent from the London rectors' complaints of 1309: *C&S* II, 1255–63.

Paradoxically, it may be that the attention given to heavier penances and public penance in manuals written by fourteenth-century English parish priests was made possible by the friars. A parish priest always had to contend with the reality that some of his parishioners were not particularly devout or contrite, and that assigning heavy penances would discourage parishioners from confessing some or even any of their sins in the future. If the friars significantly helped the parish priests in creating a more devout and contrite culture over the course of the thirteenth century, perhaps parish priests in the later Middle Ages could afford to be more demanding.

PART III

The Landscape of Pastoral Care

Chapter 8

TOWARDS A GEOGRAPHY
OF PASTORAL CARE

The church was one of medieval Europe's most centralised and bureaucratic institutions, but the appearance of standardisation this implies is
at least partly an illusion. Even the parish, the basic constituent unit of
the church, was by no means homogenous. One may be tempted to
speak of the development of 'the parish' as an institution in society and
canon law, the natural end-point of the evolution of the local church,
but it would be just as proper to speak of *each* parish as an independent institution in a constant state of flux, both convergent with and
divergent from other parishes. It stands to reason that a local community
will develop its own ways of doing things, which will change over time.
Although most internal parochial records date from later centuries and
thus the internal dynamics of thirteenth-century parishes can be difficult to observe, we can do more than speculate about parochial diversity.
There are two ways to approach the problem: by analogy and from the
outside.

The analogue is the manor. According to Raftis, manors exhibited 'complex differences in tenurial structures and service obligations even between contiguous manors belonging to the same lord'.[1]
Schofield emphasises the 'diversity of experience, across time and
between regions ... It is in that diversity that the multiplicity of experiences of peasants and their communities is located and it is from that
diversity that multiple explanations and historical anomalies begin to look
like different but still reasonable explanations.'[2] Olson notes that

the full range of local variations ... has not been fully disclosed, nor have the
causes of such variation. Comparative studies of peasant communities have been
few, even though the work done to date has established that a basis for such
comparison exists. Such an omission is perhaps all the more surprising in view
of the growing recognition among historians of the intense localism of medieval

---

[1] Raftis, *Economic Development*, 6.
[2] P. Schofield, *Peasant and Community in Medieval England, 1200–1500* (New York, 2003), 7–8.

society . . . [T]he individuality of villages as well as villagers remains properly to be explored.[3]

The lord of the manor and the rector of the parish both ostensibly governed the people in their respective spheres of authority but each institution was also a self-organising lay community adapting its forms to its context.[4] Indeed, the rise of churchwardens in later centuries may reflect eclecticism giving way to a newly dominant paradigm. In addition to managing quotidian features of parish life, such as whose turn it was to bake the host, lay parishioners were, as we have seen, usually responsible for maintaining or rebuilding the nave, a very substantial undertaking. Whether costs and designs were agreed upon by common consent, determined by the patron or decided by an *ad hoc* committee, the parish was required to organise itself in ways that both reflected and shaped its local social dynamics.[5] Since parochial life was so thoroughly intertwined with all other aspects of local life, divergent characteristics of manorial and agricultural life themselves constituted divergent characteristics of parochial life.[6]

Parishes' internal developments as seen by external authorities appear in such sources as cartularies and bishops' registers. Even in the thirteenth century, parishes occasionally appeared and disappeared, birthing new parishes or absorbing old ones; their patronage, which included the right to nominate the parish priest, changed hands among kings, bishops, lay lords and monasteries; parishes formerly served by a rector found themselves with a vicar and an absentee or institutional rector; their meeting-places moved into and out of local monastic churches and cathedrals; dependent chapels were built and abandoned; boundaries were drawn, contested, redrawn; disputes led to *ad hoc* settlements. One characteristic of a 'typical' parish should probably be that it was atypical in one or more respects.[7]

As Christopher Brooke reflected:

Historians still feel a deep urge, an inescapable urge, to generalise; they feel it their duty, even in circumstances which are hardly congenial to generalisation . . . [But] in church history its place must commonly be perpheral . . . It is often

---

[3] S. Olson, *A Chronicle of All That Happens: Voices from the Village Court in Medieval England* (Toronto, 1996), 2; cf. Harvey, ed., *Records of Cuxham*, 35.
[4] See Chapter 2 above.   [5] Byng, *Church Building*.
[6] Mason, 'A Truth Universally Acknowledged'; see also Chapter 2 above.
[7] E.g. Burgess and Duffy, eds, *The Parish*. Robert Swanson comments in that volume (p. 148) that 'the "standard parish" did not exist'. See also Pounds, *English Parish*.

in diversity, in the range of possibilities open to men [of the past], that one finds a truer key to understanding.[8]

Taking Brooke's words seriously presents us with a dilemma. The first option, as Swanson has acknowledged, is that in order to write a survey of later medieval English religion, one must accept that 'almost every positive statement made could be qualified virtually out of existence.'[9] Universal sources, such as canon law or Parisian sermons, were not implemented in the same way or to the same degree in every place, while the sources that tell us the most about what was actually going on tend to be much more local, and more diverse, in nature. The foregoing chapters have sought to establish general benchmarks in pastoral care, always with one eye on 'the range of possibilities'. Without establishing some norms, we could not recognise what was distinctive when we saw it; without exploring diversity, we could not determine how normative they were. But we would still be trading in too many generalities if we went no further.

The alternative, if we take existing literature as a guide, is to limit oneself to a local or regional case study. Local history-writing is a venerable tradition in England, with roots that stretch back to gentleman-antiquaries of the seventeenth century writing histories of their counties and parishes and beyond them to monastic chroniclers. Local case studies remain an important part of medieval scholarship, offering a precision that eludes broader treatments.[10] They can also ignore evidence that does not appear to have affected, or reflected, the lives of people in that specific place and time, in favour of sources that more clearly do, such as charters, bishops' registers, archaeological evidence, and (for the later Middle Ages) churchwardens' accounts. There is no need to qualify statements out of existence, or to acknowledge, as Swanson has done elsewhere, that 'the very nature of the evidence means that the overall generalisations have to be constructed from pieces which were never intended to fit together.'[11]

But local studies often achieve accuracy at the expense of wider applicability. Arnold has cautioned that the 'traditional Anglo-American suspicion of French historiographical abstraction and "theory"' (an

---

[8] Brooke, *Collected Essays*, 45, 172.

[9] Swanson, *Church and Society*, viii; see also Duffy, *Stripping of the Altars*, 4.

[10] Ecclesiastical examples include Dohar, *Black Death*; Logan, *University Education*; Owen, *Church and Society*; Shaw, *Creation of a Community*; French, *People of the Parish*; J. Hughes, *Pastors and Visionaries: Religious and Secular Life in Late Medieval Yorkshire* (Woodbridge, 1988). To these one might add local studies of village life by such historians as J. A. Raftis, S. Olson and P. D. A. Harvey.

[11] R. N. Swanson, *Catholic England: Faith, Religion, and Observance before the Reformation* (Manchester, 1993), 40.

instinctive suspicion that, it must be acknowledged, underlies this present book) might 'eschew any kind of structural analysis of the past [and] can end up presenting no more than a pedantic insistence on endless specificity [in which each] tale tells us only about that particular time and place'.[12] To be fair, few local studies go so far: there is often a call for further comparative work to discover what was peculiar and what was part of broader social structures and cultural trends. Investigating how the bishops and clergy of Hereford responded to the Black Death, Dohar expressed a hope 'that this excursion into local history will prompt other such analyses of regional churches in order to find piecemeal what seems so elusive and imposing on the grander scale'.[13] More than twenty years later, we still await any comparable (or comparative) study of pastoral responses to the plague in another English diocese. It is not yet possible to determine whether Dohar's findings were characteristic of England or were unique to Hereford. This is an inherent limitation of the local case study, the counterpart of Swanson's trade-off.

In his DPhil thesis of 1985, Townley studied pastoral provision in Hereford and Worcester dioceses in the thirteenth century. He saw similar trends in parochial patronage, clerical recruitment and the place of secular clergy in local society across the neighbouring dioceses, despite differences in 'settlement, landownership, monastic influence and general economic development'. He concluded:

it would appear that by the later thirteenth century, the success of the Church's reform programme – and the nature and scope of the problems which remained – were not primarily conditioned by purely local circumstances, social, economic or political. To this extent some aspects of the situation described above, despite the localized nature of the evidence, may perhaps have a more general application outside the region.[14]

His study, concerning only certain aspects of the secular clergy, does not necessarily indicate that pastoral care as a whole showed no geographical variations across these dioceses. Worcester's three sets of diocesan statutes during the thirteenth century present a marked contrast to Hereford, to which no statutes have been certainly attributed. However, not all authors of local studies indicate either a call for further comparative work, as Dohar did, or an appropriately tentative tone like Townley's.[15]

---

[12] Arnold, *Belief and Unbelief*, 12–13.   [13] Dohar, *Black Death*, xi.

[14] S. C. Townley, 'Patronage, Pastoral Provision and the Secular Clergy in the Dioceses of Worcester and Hereford during the Thirteenth Century' (unpubl. DPhil thesis, Oxford, 1985), 341–42.

[15] A. R. DeWindt and E. B. DeWindt commented, 'We cannot enter the private places of parishioners' minds, so to assume that the people of Ramsey were not unlike people in other parishes

Some simply present their local conclusions and leave it to the reader to guess whether, and to what extent, their features were peculiar or general.

In the remainder of this book, we shall be pursuing a third way that aims to resolve the dilemma through local case studies from across England held in comparative tension with one another. It is the first attempt to compare church life in thirteenth-century England at all levels: between the provinces of Canterbury and York, among multiple dioceses, among multiple regions within each diocese and among multiple parishes within each region. Previous studies have focused only on larger or smaller scales and seldom is any attempt made to compare dioceses within a province or realm.[16] Arnold has recently commented that Brentano's *Two Churches*, 'which looked in detail at the institutional and social structures of the Church in thirteenth-century England and Italy, remains pretty much the only truly comparative study, yet surely invites further, similar investigations'; Forrest concurs that *Two Churches* 'is a good example of what can be gained from looking at two regions in some detail. However, future work might proceed best if "Church" is disaggregated and narrower questions asked of several or many regions.'[17] The comparative case studies here, which allow us to measure local exceptionalism, aim to do just that, asking the 'narrower question' of pastoral care. In order to highlight both internal and external differences, each diocesan chapter includes both a chronological survey of diocesan direction of the care of souls and a comparative geographical survey of various regions and parishes within it. It is hoped that this solution will be similarly applied to other regions and centuries but also that this will serve as a matrix into which other local studies of the thirteenth-century English church, both existing and yet to be written, can be fitted to make a whole that is greater than the sum of its parts. Only such close scrutiny and comparison will allow us to construct a more genuine understanding of lived religion in the Middle Ages.

GEOGRAPHY AND PASTORAL CARE

In order to consider geography as an aspect of the history of pastoral care, we must also consider pastoral care as an aspect of historical geography. At

---

with better, more abundant and varied records is tempting but presumptuous.' *Ramsey: The Lives of an English Fenland Town, 1200–1600* (Washington, DC, 2006), 30.

[16] Mason, 'A Truth Universally Acknowledged'; Brown, *Popular Piety*; Brentano, *Two Churches*.

[17] J. Arnold, 'Histories and Historiographies of Medieval Christianity', in Arnold, *Medieval Christianity*, 23–41, at 38; I. Forrest, 'Continuity and Change in the Institutional Church', in ibid., 185–200, at 193.

first glance, this might seem a fruitless enterprise. Studies of the geography of medieval England are usually preoccupied with such questions as soil types, crop cultivation, hedgerows, road networks and settlement and landholding patterns, not sermons or masses. The closest that landscape studies seem to get to our subject are patterns of monastic settlement or parish church architecture.[18] Yet even these apparently unpromising features had implications for the care of souls, since they reflected and shaped the local dynamics within which the church operated.[19] Some regions of the country, particularly the Midlands, were typified by 'Champion' or 'Champagne' countryside, with highly nucleated settlements, commonly pictured as a village nestled around its parish church and churchyard.[20] Other areas favoured small hamlets and farmsteads scattered across the landscape. Even where settlements were nucleated, the parish church was situated away from the settlement more often than we might expect.[21] Parishes varied in shape and size. Urban ones were normally compact, though some city churches also served large extramural districts.[22] There were also substantial differences in average parish size on different soil types, as less fertile areas needed more land to support a parish. The average rural parish size was around four square miles in southern England, but this grew to ten square miles in Wales and Yorkshire, and 18.5 square miles in Cheshire, Lancashire, Cumbria, Northumberland and Durham.[23] Nor are all miles created equal. The almost exclusive use of hilltop sites for parish churches in eastern Devon must have been inconvenient even for healthy parishioners, let alone the sick, the weak, the old and the pregnant.[24]

The historical causes and social effects of such variations are not always understood.[25] At least one effect, however, should be obvious, though it is seldom remarked upon: it was simply harder to get to church (and, by extension, receive pastoral care) in some places than in others. The parish priest faced the same challenges in getting to his more distant parishioners to provide extreme unction to the dying, to hear the confessions of invalids or to baptise a sickly newborn. Urban parishes seldom had this problem but often had others. Spatial limitations could

---

[18] E.g. Morris, *Landscape*; G. J. White, *The Medieval English Landscape, 1000–1540* (London, 2012), 143–82; and *VCH*.
[19] Brown, *Popular Piety*, 67–91.
[20] C. Dyer et al., 'Lowland Vales', in J. Thirsk, ed., *The English Rural Landscape* (Oxford, 2000), 78–96, at 81; S. Rippon, *Beyond the Medieval Village* (Oxford, 2008).
[21] Morris, *Landscape*, 240–74; J. Blair, *The Church in Anglo-Saxon Society* (Oxford, 2005).
[22] Pounds, *English Parish*, 115–52. [23] Morris, *Landscape*, 233.
[24] S. Rippon, *Making Sense of an Historic Landscape* (Oxford, 2012), 66–69.
[25] S. Rippon, *Beyond the Medieval Village* (Oxford, 2008), 196–200, 250–68.

cramp church buildings into awkward configurations and leave inadequate space for burials, while urban parishes were more likely than rural
ones to be economically unsustainable.[26] Our evidence cannot tell us
whether church attendance was higher in urban parishes because of easy
access, nor whether it was lower in parishes with a church located away
from the village, nor whether, within dispersed settlement regions, those
living close to the church became more pious than those who lived at
the far end of the parish. But thirteenth-century bishops acknowledged
that geographical access to pastoral care was a real challenge. It was also,
it seems, a growing one. As the population growth of the twelfth and
thirteenth centuries led to assarts – settlements in previously uninhabited
areas – an increasing number of parishioners must have perceived their
churches as out of reach. Parishes could have detached portions, often land
reclaimed from waste before or during the period of parish formation,
as may be seen in the Halvergate Marshes in East Anglia.[27] Thirteenth-
century assarts were not confined to one corner of the country, nor to
monastic estates, nor to a particular type of landscape, but were found
across England on a variety of types of land.[28] As Bailey has shown, the
'marginal' land thus settled was not always economically poor; sometimes
it was productive but access was difficult.[29]

Bishops' response by the thirteenth century, when most parish boundaries were already established, was to authorise the building of chapels-
of-ease.[30] These were daughter churches of the parish church which did
not have full parochial status (lacking a baptismal font and graveyard) but
gave the laity of distant parts of the parish access to a chaplain and his
pastoral services. The chaplain's support was generally the responsibility of the vicar or rector, or the chapel might be directly endowed with
land.[31] Yet chapels-of-ease were not always feasible. Upland areas of some
parishes were used only for seasonal grazing and so were unlikely to have
a chapel. Furthermore, building and maintaining the nave was generally
the laity's responsibility, above and beyond their tithes. Where marginal
land was economically poor, those living there might be both physically
distant from their parish church and unable to afford a chapel-of-ease.[32]

[26] Sekules, *Form and Fabric*; Pounds, *English Parish*, 113–49.
[27] T. Williamson, *The Norfolk Broads: A Landscape History* (Manchester, 1997), 43–45.
[28] J. Thirsk, ed., *The English Rural Landscape* (Oxford, 2000), *passim*; Hallam, *Agrarian History*,
139–271.
[29] Bailey, *Marginal Economy*.   [30] Pounds, *English Parish*, 91–94.
[31] E.g. *EEA* 7, nos. 216, 227, 330. Sometimes the chaplain would be called a perpetual vicar, even if
his church did not have full parochial status: nos. 214, 235. N. Orme, 'The Other Parish Churches:
Chapels in Late-Medieval England', in Burgess and Duffy, eds, *The Parish*, 78–94.
[32] *Reg. Bronescombe*, 292.

We have seen that each order of friars had a distinctive pattern of settlement in Britain, but that does not indicate the extent of each house's local influence.[33] While friars were most often found in towns and suburbs, they went beyond the immediate settlement in their pastoral work and in their quest for alms. Each order assigned a specific territory to each house though, unfortunately, no records of their boundaries survive from thirteenth-century England.[34] A minimum distance is suggested by the Dominicans of Auxerre. When a new Dominican house was founded some distance away and the boundaries of the surrounding houses had to be redrawn, the Preachers of Auxerre were limited to four leagues in one direction and six in another, which suggests that they had previously surpassed these limits and without restriction would have continued to do so.[35] In 1274, it was reported at the village of Snaith in Yorkshire that Franciscans and Dominicans came and preached often (*sepe*).[36] The Dominicans probably came from Pontefract, fifteen miles west, while the nearest Franciscan house at that time was at York, over twenty miles to the north. In our diocesan case studies, we shall find friars active up to forty miles from their convents, typically along well-travelled roads.[37] Mendicant pastoral districts probably followed existing ecclesiastical boundaries. At certain times in the thirteenth century when friars needed to be licensed by bishops to preach and shrive, their pastoral boundaries would naturally coincide with diocesan boundaries. Such boundaries must have been very important in areas with many friaries, such as East Anglia, while having little significance in Wales, where friaries were so thinly spread that each one was probably assigned a district much larger than it could cover. The more licensed preachers and confessors a given friary had, the more thoroughly it could extend its influence. The number of friars in a given convent is occasionally known, the number of licensed pastors in only a few instances.[38]

What was the significance of living in the hinterland of a mendicant house? We can establish a working hypothesis by combining the observations of Smalley and Haskins. Smalley proposed, in her article 'Ecclesiastical Attitudes to Novelty, 1100–1250' that over that period the connotations of *novus* moved from negative to positive, from 'newfangled' to 'progressive'. This change in attitude was driven along because the sheer 'pace of events imposed it. Unprecedented phenomena [including the

[33] See Chapter 3.
[34] For an example from 1388, see Harper-Bill, ed., *Clare Cartulary*, nos. 175–76.
[35] M.-D. Chapotin, *Les Dominicains d'Auxerre* (Paris, 1892), 47–49.
[36] *Reg. Giffard*, no. 918.   [37] See below, pp. 207, 240–41, 244, 256–57.
[38] Moorman, *Church Life*, 408–10; Little, *Papers*, 230–43.

mendicants] sprang up like mushrooms' and needed to be explained and defended.[39] Haskins described the high Middle Ages as a period in which 'ideas and information spread only slowly, and against great resistance, from one district to another; custom determined everything, and the type differed little from age to age', while ideas flowed chiefly between 'stations of high tension ... communicating with other stations of the same type with comparatively little reference to distance ... [These] consisted mainly of monasteries and cathedrals, courts, towns, and universities.'[40] Taken together, these arguments would imply that areas with constant exposure to new pastoral ideas and practices from early in the century will have been more deeply affected by them than areas with less or later exposure – those further from houses of friars, situated in more remote areas, and with less active supervision by their archdeacons and bishops.

We must not stretch this line of reasoning too far. The local church was hardly stagnant in the centuries before 1200.[41] Nor did church structures have a monopoly on the transmission of ideas; *pace* Haskins, common laypeople were perfectly capable of spreading *rumor* and *fama*, and by implication ideas in general, on their own.[42] The glimpses that we get, however, do suggest that the parish clergy and people tended towards a conservatism that may be vaguely described as pre-Scholastic (occasionally even pre-Gregorian) and that they were more comfortable following custom rather than new ideas without outside intervention.[43] For our purposes, that intervention took place not only through the preaching and shriving of the friars but also through the diocesan *magisterium*: textual dissemination of statutes and other *pastoralia* and the enforcement of visitations, synods and courts.[44] Where we see plenty of evidence of new influences on pastoral care, such as the presence of friars or activist bishops, we should expect the theory to be translated into practice to some degree and, where such influences were lacking, unless there is evidence to the contrary, we may assume that established practice tended to prevail, as Gerald of Wales found in the stubbornly unreformed clergy of his archdeaconry.[45] Thus, by studying the geographical dissemination of

[39] B. Smalley, 'Ecclesiastical Attitudes to Novelty, 1100–1250', *Studies in Church History* 12 (1975), 113–31.
[40] C. H. Haskins, 'The Spread of Ideas in the Middle Ages', *Speculum* 1 (1926), 19–30, at 20–21.
[41] See Chapter 1 above.
[42] M. Billoré and M. Soria, eds, *La Rumeur au Moyen Âge: Du mépries à la manipulation (Vᵉ–XVᵉ siècle)* (Rennes, 2011); Olson, *Mute Gospel*, 9.
[43] For the example of clerical marriage, see Thibodeaux, *Manly Priest*, 141.
[44] Biller, 'Intellectuals'.   [45] Bartlett, *Gerald*, 27–57.

ideas and practices, through both personnel and texts, and by exploring the local social contexts in which the church operated, we may describe a landscape of pastoral care in thirteenth-century England, as the laity knew it, in a much more variegated manner than has been attempted hitherto.

Chapter 9

THE PROVINCES OF CANTERBURY
AND YORK

In certain ways, there was such an institution as 'the medieval English church'. The church in England dealt with one king; it experienced one interdict; it received papal legates as a whole; it served an increasingly cohesive nation. Yet we must draw finer distinctions and refer to ecclesiastical as well as political boundaries to describe it properly. Wales was an integrated part neither of the English political kingdom nor of the English cultural nation. Certain Welsh churchmen, most notably Gerald of Wales, attempted unsuccessfully to have the pope establish it as an independent ecclesiastical province with its own archbishop, but until the twentieth century, the Welsh dioceses remained in the Province of Canterbury. Canterbury Province covered the greater part of England, including fourteen English dioceses as well as the four Welsh ones. The archbishop of York, however, who governed his own great diocese as well as overseeing the English dioceses of Durham and Carlisle and the Scottish diocese of Whithorn, was not normally subject to his colleague at Canterbury in matters internal to the Province of York. Pastoral initiatives based on the decrees of the Fourth Lateran Council, and on the ideology of Peter the Chanter and his followers that animated the Council's pastoral concern, nonetheless came to the Northern Province, as for example by copying statutes from southern dioceses.

THE PROVINCE OF CANTERBURY

Canterbury Province developed a high degree of bureaucratic complexity over the course of the thirteenth century.[1] Throughout the thirteenth century, a series of provincial and legatine councils promulgated legislation for Canterbury Province which, together with archiepiscopal administration, impinged upon local conditions, especially through diocesan legislation and administration. But as Gibbs and Lang showed,

[1] For fuller treatments, see Churchill, *Canterbury Administration*; *EEA* 2 and 3; Major, *Acta*; Cheney, *Becket to Langton*.

181

the diffusion of papally led reforms to diocesan and parochial realities required the co-operation of local ordinaries to effect real change.[2] This was also the case with provincial ecclesiastical reform.

In the twelfth century, the surviving evidence 'suggests that the archbishop was not very active in his suffragans' dioceses *sede plena* as a matter of course. The suffragans' inferiors were more inclined to have recourse to him *sede vacante* or in the absence of their own bishop.'[3] After the death of Archbishop Hubert Walter in July 1205, metropolitan jurisdiction was weakened by two successive quashed elections, the dispute over Langton's appointment, the papal interdict and the subsequent presence of papal legates.[4] The legate Pandulf resigned in July 1221 and Archbishop Langton returned from Rome a month later; finally holding the reins, he called a provincial council to meet at Oxford the next year.[5]

Of the sixty canons issued for Canterbury Province in 1222, a quarter dealt directly with pastoral care.[6] Priests were prohibited from celebrating two masses in a day, except on Christmas and Easter.[7] The origins of this canon are unclear but, if medieval church attendance peaked at these festivals, this would allow the priest of a church too small for its congregation to offer mass twice, enabling more to attend. Each church was required to have appropriate books, utensils and vestments for liturgical celebration, though these are not listed.[8] Every parish that could afford it was to have two or three priests so that divine service and visitation of the sick can continue if one priest is absent or ill.[9] Parish clergy were commanded to preach and to visit the sick.[10] Clergy were to be admitted to vicarages only if they pledged to reside and to be ordained to the priesthood soon.[11] Perpetual vicarages were to be established, with a minimum stipend of five marks or four marks for poorer parts of Wales.[12] Designated priests were to hear clerical confessions in each deanery.[13] Injunctions were laid down for archdeacons concerning the manner of visiting and inspecting parish churches,[14] while rural deans were forbidden to pass judgements in cases of matrimonial law.[15] It does not appear that Langton went on visitations of his province to determine how effective his injunctions had been.[16]

Langton died in July 1228. The next man to hold the see for any duration was Edmund of Abingdon, from 1233 to 1240.[17] Edmund, a

---

[2] Gibbs and Lang, *Bishops and Reform.*   [3] *EEA* 2, xxxv.   [4] *Fasti* Monastic, 5–6.
[5] Powicke, *Langton,* 151, and see above, p. 36.
[6] *C&S* II, 106–25, cited below by 'Oxford (1222)' and canon.
[7] Oxford (1222), 11.   [8] Oxford (1222), 16.   [9] Oxford (1222), 22.
[10] Oxford (1222), 15.   [11] Oxford (1222), 19; cf. also 20.   [12] Oxford (1222), 21; cf. also 43.
[13] Oxford (1222), 24.   [14] Oxford (1222), 27–29; on the history of visitations, see Frere, *Visitation.*
[15] Oxford (1222), 25.   [16] Frere, *Visitation,* 81.   [17] *Fasti* Monastic, 6–7.

quiet scholar by nature, accepted the pallium reluctantly and showed little enthusiasm for business.[18] He was frequently tied up in crises in church and state but he had inherited many of Langton's most talented administrators.[19] He attempted to visit his province in 1237 but was heavily opposed.[20] He issued no known provincial or diocesan legislation himself but his archiepiscopate was marked by the legatine visit and council of the Cardinal Otto. While the presence of a legate undermined the archbishop's authority, it also gave Edmund and his suffragans the opportunity to confer with him. This they clearly did, for the canons issued in Otto's Council of London of 1237 show awareness of English conditions.[21] The council was attended by prelates of, and was binding for, both English provinces.

The council that met at St Paul's Cathedral that November focused on improving the care of souls from the ground up.[22] Otto invited Grosseteste to preach the opening sermon, a fair indication of his priorities.[23] The reading of papal bulls encouraging the veneration of Francis and Dominic elevated the moral authority of their orders.[24] The sequence of canons begins with an order that churches be consecrated.[25] The seven sacraments were next listed and their importance to the *cura animarum* stressed; accordingly, those undertaking the care of souls and priestly orders were to be examined on these in particular, while archdeacons were ordered to teach about baptism, penance, the mass and matrimony in ruridecanal chapters.[26] Otto noted that two days, Holy Saturday and the Saturday before Pentecost, were prescribed by canon law for baptisms but he had heard that some people 'in these parts', under diabolical suggestion, feared danger if children were baptised on these days. He ordered parish priests to preach frequently against this, noting that if the pope himself (not to mention the rest of the world) performed baptism on these days, there was surely nothing to fear. It is not clear if he intended these to be the only days of the year on which baptisms were performed, except for emergencies – he added an order to give parishioners frequent instruction on the words for baptism in emergencies – or whether he was indicating a more general desire that at least some baptisms, if possible, should occur on these two days.[27] Parish clergy were also forbidden to extort money in exchange for baptism and other sacraments.[28]

---

[18] Lawrence, *St Edmund*, 39.   [19] Ibid., 50–89.   [20] Frere, *Visitation*, 81.
[21] Lawrence, *St Edmund*, 78–79; *C&S* II, 238–39.
[22] *C&S* II, 237–59; canons, cited below by 'Otto (1237)' and canon number, begin on 245.
[23] *C&S* II, 238.   [24] *C&S* II, 238, 243.   [25] Otto (1237), prologue and 1.
[26] Otto (1237), 2.   [27] Otto (1237), 3.   [28] Otto (1237), 4.

The supervision of parish priests was regulated in the appointment of confessors for the clergy and the screening of candidates for ordination.[29] Only priests, or deacons about to be ordained priests, could be made vicars, and upon institution a vicar was to renounce any other benefice with care of souls and reside in his parish.[30] Abuses in archidiaconal visitations were reined in and the visitors were directed to enquire about vessels, vestments, the conduct of the liturgy and attention to spiritualities in general. Otto reiterated that archdeacons were to attend ruridecanal chapters frequently, instructing priests and others about the words of the canon of the mass and of baptism.[31] He reminded bishops that they should perambulate their dioceses to correct and reform, consecrate churches and preach.[32] As we shall see in the chapters on Exeter and Lincoln, some bishops went personally on visitations of their dioceses.[33] Most of the remaining canons dealt with improving ecclesiastical administration.

Edmund was succeeded by Boniface of Savoy, uncle to the queen. Boniface, though elected in February 1241, was unable to return to England until April 1244 and was not consecrated until 1245 nor enthroned until 1249.[34] His first move upon his return was towards eliminating the see's considerable debts.[35] Despite his royal connexions, he surprised Henry III by managing to check the king's growing encroachments upon ecclesiastical liberties, including illegal financial exactions and two attempts to thwart papal authority in the elections of bishops.[36] He spent the later 1240s abroad again, attending the First Council of Lyons in 1245 and serving the papacy.[37] Returning to England in 1250, Boniface attempted a formal visitation of his province but met with heavy resistance, a confrontation leading to excommunications and suits and counter-suits before the papal curia. Boniface believed the church to have a strictly hierarchical structure. Thus, exercising such direct supervision of his suffragans seemed to him analogous to a bishop visiting his own diocese or a papal legate visiting England. His suffragans, however, openly suspected him of engaging in the visitations to raise money. They viewed their dioceses as customarily exempt from the meddling of archbishops, except during a vacancy in the see or a disputed election, and they believed themselves obliged to stand firm against allowing precedents prejudicial to their own and their successors' customary independence. In the end, Boniface won. He was required to make certain

---

[29] Otto (1237), 5, 6. See further Chapter 2 above.   [30] Otto (1237), 10, 13.
[31] Otto (1237), 20.   [32] Otto (1237), 22.   [33] See also Moorman, *Church Life*, 185–96.
[34] *Fasti* Monastic, 7.   [35] *C&S* II, 445–47; Lawrence, *St Edmund*, 39.
[36] Williams, 'Boniface', 91–103; *C&S* II, 568–85, 659–92.
[37] C. H. Knowles, 'Savoy, Boniface of (1206/7–1270)', *ODNB*; Williams, 'Boniface', 117–40.

concessions but he established the metropolitan's prerogative to intervene in suffragan dioceses *sede plena* and seems to have given encouragement by example to bishops to conduct more regular visitations within their own dioceses.[38] Adam Marsh OFM accompanied Boniface on some of his visitations and gave it as his opinion that the 'heaven-sent reform of the pastoral care ... depends so much upon this primacy of the lord archbishop.' While Marsh also grumbled at the frequency with which he himself was called upon to assist the archbishop, his presence also suggests that he, like Grosseteste, had considerable influence upon Boniface.[39]

Another centralising enterprise was the creation in 1251 of the Court of Arches to deal more efficiently with the archbishop's judicial role. This was an appellate court for cases already decided by diocesan courts. The metropolitan's right to hear appeals, and to delegate officials to hear them on his behalf, was already established, but the creation of a sitting court relieved him of the burden of business, enabled a specialist bureaucracy to emerge, and contributed to the sense that suffragans were answerable to their archbishop in quotidian as well as extraordinary circumstances.[40] He rationalised his administration in a variety of other ways and recruited an exceptionally large and talented staff.[41]

Boniface's fortunes fell in the 1260s. The baronial revolt left him caught between the pope and king on the one hand and the barons and some English bishops on the other. As a result, he spent more than half of the decade in exile, in the full knowledge that his careful work in England was being undone. Even when he was in England, the presence of Ottobuono, papal legate *a latere* sent to re-establish peace and discipline, rendered him a cipher within his own province. He left England in 1268 to live out his last years in his native Savoy. Despite these setbacks, he had set important precedents for Canterbury's provincial administration, as a result of which his successors would be able to pursue more extensive supervision of the province.[42]

Before Boniface left the country, Cardinal Ottobuono held a legatine council at London in 1268, legislating for both English provinces and as well as those of Ireland and Scotland.[43] The canons issued there included several matters of pastoral import. Many were reiterations of Otto's material, such as that regarding the times of baptism,[44] requiring

[38] *Chron. Maj.* V, 119–20, and VI, 228–29; Frere, *Visitation*, 81–83; *LAM*, 92–93; Churchill, *Canterbury Administration*, 289–91; Williams, 'Boniface', 141–91.
[39] *Chron. Maj.* V 382; *LAM*, 434–35; Williams, 'Boniface', 114–16.
[40] F. D. Logan, ed., *The Medieval Court of Arches* (C&YS 95, 2005); Williams, 'Boniface', 192–221.
[41] Williams, 'Boniface', 354–88.   [42] Williams, 'Boniface', 415–56; *C&S* II, 693–94, 725–92.
[43] *C&S* II, 725–92, cited below as 'Ottobuono (1268)' with canon number.
[44] Ottobuono (1268), 1, which states that Otto's canon was not being observed.

vicars to be ordained and resident[45] and preventing abuses in the visitation of churches,[46] but some new points were added. The formula for pronouncing the absolution of a penitent was standardised, and obstructing prisoners' access to a priest for confession was prohibited.[47] Also forbidden was the impeding of the solemnisation of matrimony.[48] Bishops were exhorted to spend more time in their dioceses.[49] Attempts were made to reduce indirect simony and pluralism's attendant problem of absenteeism.[50] To ensure that his decrees were followed, he ordered that every bishop, religious house and secular cathedral chapter keep a copy of his canons and that they be read out in diocesan synods every year.[51]

Robert Kilwardby, the English Dominican Provincial Prior from 1261, was appointed to Canterbury by the pope in autumn 1272 and was enthroned a year later; he was elevated to the Cardinal-Bishopric of Porto in 1278.[52] Several provincial councils met during his archiepiscopate but none issued canons.[53] Tactful provincial visitations enabled him to supervise administration (and thus indirectly the care of souls) in his suffragan dioceses.[54] His records, along with a considerable stash of the see's valuables, went with him to Porto and were never recovered, making it difficult to trace provincial government in detail.[55]

Because Kilwardby resigned his see into the hands of Nicholas III, that pope was able directly to appoint the Franciscan John Pecham, at that time lector at the papal *curia*. Pecham was enthroned in October 1279.[56] Pecham, like Langton, was a pastoral theologian and vigorous reformer. He held a council of his suffragans at Reading in 1279 at which he renewed some of Ottobuono's canons. The statutes of Otto and Ottobuono requiring baptism to be done on the vigils of Easter and Pentecost were still not being followed, so Pecham conceded that only babies born within the octaves preceding Easter and Pentecost should be kept for baptism on those Saturdays and then only if it could be done without danger. Pecham recognised that the laity could not always be expected to remember the formula of baptism perfectly and so would be reluctant to keep their infant unbaptised in case an emergency occurred and the priest could not be found in time. Therefore, Pecham allowed parents of children born in the rest of the year to choose whether to wait for one of these dates or have their infant baptised sooner.[57]

---

[45] Ottobuono (1268), 9.   [46] Ottobuono (1268), 18.   [47] Ottobuono (1268), 2.
[48] Ottobuono (1268), 13.   [49] Ottobuono (1268), 21.   [50] Ottobuono (1268), 29, 30, 33.
[51] Ottobuono (1268), 36.   [52] *Fasti* Monastic, 7; Trivet, *Annales*, 278–79.
[53] *C&S* II, 802–17, 820–26.   [54] S. Tugwell, 'Kilwardby, Robert (*c.*1215–1279)', *ODNB*.
[55] Smith, *Guide*, 1; F. M. Powicke, *The Thirteenth Century* (Oxford, 1953), 471n; Douie, *Pecham*, 54, 65–66.
[56] *Fasti* Monastic, 7; Douie, *Pecham*, 47–52.   [57] *C&S* II, 836.

Pecham held a more celebrated provincial council at Lambeth in October 1281, at which he promulgated a lengthy series of statutes aimed at improving the care of souls.[58] The pastorally oriented decrees cover the sacraments and preaching. After his prologue, Pecham dealt first with the Eucharist, insisting that the consecrated host be treated with due reverence, including the manner in which it was kept as reserved sacrament. He also ordered that a bell be rung at the elevation in daily masses so that the people, who did not always go to daily mass, might hear it and genuflect; he noted that many bishops had granted indulgences to those who did so. Priests were to inform their parishioners that they receive the body and blood of Christ together under the form of bread alone, and that the unconsecrated wine they were given was only to wash down the host: Pecham forbade anyone but the celebrant to consume the consecrated wine in parish churches.[59] In his canon on baptism he made no mention of restricted times.[60] His discussion of penance concerns only serious sins, excommunication and public penance, insisting that canonical penances be assigned for such serious sins as incest and voluntary homicide.[61] Perhaps the canon of greatest significance was his catechetical syllabus *De informatione simplicium sacerdotum*, which provided an extensive list of the major points of thirteenth-century catechesis and required parish priests to give clear instruction on each heading at least once a quarter.[62]

Pecham was a complex character. Though a theologian, like Edmund and Kilwardby, his attitude towards his suffragans was just as autocratic and stubborn as Boniface's, producing similar results of entrenched local opposition to what was seen as unjustified outside meddling.[63] Most famously, he excommunicated the saintly Thomas Cantilupe, bishop of Hereford, for his resistance to visitation.[64] While Pecham's activism probably pushed through some reforms, it may also have created a counterproductive atmosphere of nonconformity among aggrieved churchmen in his province. Pecham died in December 1292 and was succeeded by Robert Winchelsey, a Paris and Oxford alumnus and archdeacon of Essex from 1288.[65] Winchelsey was heavily involved in defending ecclesiastical liberties against the financial and other encroachments of Edward I, yet he also found time for visitations of the nearer parts of his province.[66] Some of his visitation business may be reflected in his

---

[58] *C&S* II, 886–918; canons from 892. [59] *C&S* II, 894–95. [60] *C&S* II, 896–97.
[61] *C&S* II, 898–900; also 905–7. [62] *C&S* II, 900–901, and see above, pp. 100–101.
[63] Douie, *Pecham*, 143–234; Churchill, *Canterbury Administration*, 291–92, 295–304.
[64] R. C. Finucane, 'Cantilupe, Thomas de (c. 1220–1282)', *ODNB*. [65] *Fasti St Paul's*, 14.
[66] J. H. Denton, 'Winchelsey, Robert (c.1240–1313)', *ODNB*; Churchill, *Canterbury Administration*, 305–7; *Reg. Pecham*, xvi–xx.

'so-called statutes', but it is not possible to disentangle when or whether these were promulgated.[67] He died in 1313.[68]

The Province of York in 1200 comprised four dioceses: York, Durham, Carlisle and the Scottish diocese of Whithorn and Galloway. In the thirteenth century, York Province had ties to the Scottish Church that, while different from its ties to Canterbury, remained significant. Indeed, until 1192, York had claimed – albeit with little effect – primacy over the whole Scottish Church, which did not have its own primate until 1472.[69] In the thirteenth century, although the claim of York's primacy had been surrendered, the border was fluid and frequently crossed. During the twelfth century, southern Scotland had become part of the Norman world. Landholding and relationships among the baronial classes and monastic houses across the still-forming border tied the realms together, much as it did between England and Normandy.[70]

Despite the archbishop of Canterbury's nominal seniority over the archbishop of York, his writ as metropolitan did not run in the Northern Province. When Hubert Walter held a provincial synod at York in 1195, he did so in his capacity as papal legate, not by right of his archbishopric of Canterbury.[71] The Canterbury provincial councils and statutes discussed above had no direct effect in these dioceses under separate jurisdiction, though some had indirect effect by inspiring northern bishops to follow certain paths in their administration or to include certain regulations in their diocesan statutes. In contrast to Canterbury Province, the Northern Province issued not one known set of provincial statutes in the thirteenth century and indeed had fewer provincial convocations, though it did participate in pan-English councils. Of these, only the legatine councils of Otto (1237) and Ottobuono (1268) issued canons but both series of canons were equally binding in York.[72]

Because of its small size, relationships between the archbishop of York and his suffragans did not require the administrative machinery that evolved in Canterbury Province.[73] Furthermore, the archbishops of York must have looked upon the bishops and priors of Durham as overmighty

---

[67] *C&S* II, 1382–93.   [68] *Fasti* Monastic, 8.

[69] *EEA 20*, liv–lviii; *EEA 27*, lxxxvi–xci, cxxxviii–cxxxix.

[70] M. L. Holford and K. J. Stringer, *Border Liberties and Loyalties: North-East England, c. 1200–c. 1400* (Edinburgh, 2010); K. J. Stringer, 'Aspects of the Norman Diaspora in Northern England and Southern Scotland', in A. Jotischky and K. J. Stringer, eds, *Norman Expansion: Connections, Continuities and Contrasts* (Farnham, 2013), 9–48.

[71] *C&S* I, 1042.   [72] For these canons, see above, pp. 183–86.   [73] Rodes, *Administration*, 108–9.

subjects, holding a great deal of wealth and power (including a degree of secular authority unique among English bishops), contesting every modicum of jurisdictional authority in a manner that the bishops of Carlisle and Whithorn obsequiously avoided.[74] The exercise of the archbishop's metropolitan jurisdiction over the latter two sees took the form of personal meetings (leaving few direct records) rather than provincial assemblies. In 1284, for example, the archbishop, preparing to go abroad, summoned the bishop of Carlisle to meet with him to discuss many matters, the nature of which he did not record for our benefit.[75] Professions of obedience from new bishops of Carlisle and Whithorn – but not those of Durham – included a pledge to make an annual pilgrimage to York, which, in addition to symbolising submission, doubtless offered regular opportunities for the suffragans to meet with the archbishop or his officials.[76] Chiefly because of Durham's intransigence, attempts at larger assemblies could be abortive. In the 1280s and 1290s, Archbishop le Romeyn called a series of provincial convocations to discuss aids to the king, and while the leading clergy of Carlisle and York attended (Whithorn being exempt, as it owed fealty to the kings of Scots), Antony Bek, bishop of Durham, deigned neither to attend nor even to send any clergy, proctors or excuses.[77] Unable to hold effective provincial councils, the archbishops of York did not issue any provincial canons either, though Otto's and Ottobuono's legatine canons were still the letter of the law. There must have been much more interaction among the bishops than we will find in the documentary record, so the paucity of mentions need not indicate a loose hand on the province's tiller: Brentano argued that we have no record of metropolitan visitations of Carlisle in the 1280s and 1290s because it was so subservient to York that the archbishops judged such measures superfluous.[78] By contrast, the archbishops' attempts to visit Durham – even *sede vacante* – were utter failures.[79]

All the same, it is clear from a variety of sources that canons and principles of Lateran IV were implemented in the dioceses of York, Durham and Carlisle, just in as the southern dioceses.[80] Yet divergences also persisted. An unusually high proportion of churches in York Diocese with absentee or monastic rectors were served by curates, not vicars, even in the fifteenth century, when vicarages had been the norm elsewhere for centuries.[81] This may correspond to the terms of the York I diocesan

[74] Brentano, *York Jurisdiction.*   [75] *Reg. Wickwane*, 314.
[76] Brentano, *York Jurisdiction*, 8.   [77] *Reg. Romeyn* II, 93–95; *C&S* II, 1093–96.
[78] Brentano, *York Jurisdiction*, 86.   [79] Thompson, *English Clergy*, 1–2.
[80] H. Birkett, 'The Pastoral Application of the Lateran IV Reforms in the Northern Province, 1215–1348', *Northern History* 43 (2006), 199–219.
[81] Thompson, *English Clergy*, 116.

statutes (1241 × 1255). These required rectors to present suitable priests for their churches, to be paid at the customary rate, and monasteries to present vicars to vicarages established in their churches or which the archbishop might care to establish in the future, but nowhere specifically required that a vicarage be established in every church with a monastic or absentee rector.[82] Langton's Council of Oxford of 1222 had reiterated Lateran IV's decree that every church without a resident rector must have a vicar in an established vicarage but this was binding on the southern province only; Poore's Salisbury statutes (1217 × 1219) had ruled similarly and he carried this provision north when he became bishop of Durham in 1228.[83] The statutes of Carlisle and York II (1259), borrowed nearly verbatim from Wells, required rectors who did not have vicars to be resident so their churches did not go unserved, but in practice chaplains may have been considered adequate. Monastic rectors were not mentioned at all in this regard and churches which were appropriated to prebends or dignities of collegiate churches were specifically exempted.[84] The establishment of stable vicarages, apparently so important in Canterbury Province, entered its northern neighbour only indirectly and imperfectly.

Such differences between the two provinces only begin to account for the variety of the English church. Although the dominant trend across the century was towards greater centralisation, this played out in disparate ways. Two bishops might both regulate parochial life strictly but one might do so by empowering and trusting his archdeacons while another preferred to intervene personally. The same could be said of archbishops with their suffragans. Beyond bishops' and archbishops' preferred modes of leadership, ecclesiastical structures were diverse. Within the Diocese of York, one archdeacon (Richmond) held a unique quasi-episcopal authority within his archdeaconry, so that archbishops had to trust him to use his delegated authority well whether they liked it or not.[85] Other districts, rather than having traditional exemptions from visitation, were particularly subservient. Prior to 1238, the bishop of Rochester, an ancient but small diocese, was not elected by his cathedral chapter, being appointed instead by his archbishop, to whom he doubtless remained highly deferential.[86] In some dioceses, peculiar parishes were under the direct supervision of their bishop, with no archdeacon to act as intermediary.

The chapters that follow will uncover differences of these and many other kinds, comparing and contrasting their effects on pastoral care and

[82] *C&S* II, 487–88, 492.   [83] *C&S* II, 110, 96, 58.   [84] *C&S* II, 610, 658.

[85] J. Raine, ed., *Wills and Inventories from the Registry of the Archdeaconry of Richmond* (Surtees Society 26, 1853), xx.

[86] *Fasti Monastic*, 75.

lived religion at all levels: between provinces, among dioceses, among archdeaconries and quasi-archdeaconries, between town and village, and from parish to parish. By no means will this survey be exhaustive. That is not its purpose. The aim is to recover some indication of the great diversity that practitioners and recipients of pastoral care in thirteenth-century England recognised and to consider the effects both of pastoral care itself and of its variability upon the people and culture of England. We shall begin with England's largest diocese, Lincoln. Its great size presented its bishops with significant administrative challenges, leading them to create extensive records. Its geographical extent also provided ample opportunity for regional variations in pastoral care, while its abundant documentation allows us to discover them.

Chapter 10

THE DIOCESE OF LINCOLN

Lincoln was the largest diocese in England, covering eight and a half counties from the Humber to the Thames, including most of the East Midlands as well as sizeable portions of East Anglia (Fenlands near The Wash) and the south-east. It comprised more than nineteen hundred parishes, more than 20 per cent of all those in England and Wales; it had eight archdeaconries, while the average for the rest of England and Wales was 2.7.[1] The diocese presents us with a true embarrassment of documentary riches for several reasons. Most obviously, there was simply more to document. But the diocese's size would also make administration unwieldy if it were not reduced to order in writing. This doubtless explains the fact that Hugh of Wells, bishop of Lincoln 1209–35, systematised the record-keeping process. His episcopal register, the earliest known to have been kept in England, has survived, along with those of most of his successors, giving the historian a continuity of documentation paralleled only in York in this century.[2] Oxford University also lay within the diocese, supplying the historian with its records as well.[3]

Despite – perhaps because of – the wealth of documentation, works that survey Lincoln Diocese are few and tend to be very specific.[4] Its size also guaranteed that it ranged across landscapes dissimilar in their social, economic, geological and agricultural characteristics: Owen observed that at the diocese's founding in the late eleventh century, 'the Bishop himself must have been the only unifying element in the diocese.'[5] While more comprehensive examinations will be given of the dioceses of Exeter and Carlisle, only limited geographical coverage can be attempted here. Each successive bishop's contributions and other general changes will be

---

[1] Southern, *Grosseteste*, 235–36; archdeaconries calculated from *Fasti* volumes.
[2] Smith, *Guide*.   [3] *BRUO*, xv–xliii.
[4] There is no general history of the medieval diocese more recent than E. Venables and G. Perry, *Lincoln* (London, 1897). See, however, Owen, *Church and Society*; M. Bowker, *The Secular Clergy in the Diocese of Lincoln, 1495–1520* (Cambridge, 1968); Logan, *University Education*; and introductions to ecclesiastical volumes published by the Lincoln Record Society.
[5] Owen, *Church and Society*, 20; D. Stocker, *The East Midlands* (London, 2006).

reviewed in the first part of this chapter but there will be no attempt to discuss, for instance, every mendicant house established. The second part will examine the northernmost archdeaconries, Lincoln and Stow, while the third will focus on the archdeaconry of Oxford in the south-west of the diocese. The other five archdeaconries (Huntingdon, Northampton, Leicester, Buckingham and Bedford) must receive only incidental mention.

BISHOPS AND PASTORAL LEADERSHIP

In 1200, Hugh of Avalon (Hugh I), a Carthusian monk and future saint, had been bishop for fourteen years and was coming to the close of his life. Hugh was a close disciple not only of Gregory the Great but also of Peter the Chanter. In practice, these influences led him to an emphasis on the role of the sacraments and encouraging clerical residence and lay participation in church life. Hugh himself confessed weekly and maintained a system of diocesan penitentiaries to hear the confessions of the clergy, anticipating the mandate of Lateran IV.[6] Adam of Eynsham and Gerald of Wales, his principal biographers, both wrote of his devotion in giving confirmation to children.[7] Around 1192 he founded a fraternity to which he granted special religious privileges,[8] and he directed his archdeacons to enjoin parish priests to encourage renewed lay participation in processions at Pentecost.[9] While both measures aimed at increasing income for rebuilding the cathedral, they did so in ways designed to promote devotion. According to Mayr-Harting, he held the 'exceptionally rigorous stance' that canons of Lincoln Cathedral 'should treat their positions as ones of pastoral care and should actually reside at Lincoln'.[10] This could directly benefit pastoral care in prebendal benefices in or near Lincoln, such as All Saints in Hungate, but one does wonder whether a policy encouraging residence at more distant prebendal parishes such as Aylesbury (Oxfordshire), rather than the cathedral, might not have been more beneficial. Nonetheless, keeping a cadre of capable administrators at Lincoln would be a distinct improvement upon allowing prebends

---

[6] H. Mayr-Harting, 'Hugh of Lincoln [St Hugh of Lincoln, Hugh of Avalon]', *ODNB*.

[7] Adam of Eynsham, *Vita* I, 127–28; Gerald, *Opera* VII, 94–96. Gerald also recorded Hugh's devotion in visiting the sick (ibid., 107), which may have involved anointing, shriving, and other sacramental functions.

[8] *EEA* 4, 97. This damaged document is also printed in *RACCL* II, 381, where it is misattributed to Hugh of Wells, Bishop of Lincoln 1209–35, and associated with the end of the papal interdict in 1213–14.

[9] *RACCL* I, 298, *EEA* 4, 92.

[10] Mayr-Harting, 'Hugh of Lincoln'. Adam Marsh OFM would later take the same view: *LAM*, 184–91.

to be treated as sinecures. A monk himself, Hugh permitted appropriation of parish churches to monastic houses; he often, though not always, ordained perpetual vicarages in them.[11] In allowing some vicars to be non-resident, serving through chaplains, he followed accepted practice, though the tide was turning against it elsewhere.[12] Adam of Eynsham recorded that Hugh was diligent in instituting men of knowledge and character to the parish churches in the diocese, a comment which suggests examination of candidates.[13] Many of Hugh of Avalon's administrators continued to serve under his successor, William of Blois (1203–6); some of his *acta* also mirror those of his predecessor.[14] William had been a Master of Arts at Paris and had served in the household of the bishop of Durham in the 1180s before serving at Lincoln successively as subdean and precentor.[15] He seems to have effected no new departures in pastoral care before his death in 1206.

William was succeeded in 1209 by Hugh of Wells (Hugh II), a highly placed royal clerk. Hugh had also served as archdeacon of Wells from 1204 and as a household clerk to successive bishops of Bath and Wells; his younger brother Jocelin was elected bishop there in 1206. No stranger to Lincoln, he had been royal custodian of the diocese during the vacancy between Hugh of Avalon and William of Blois and had been a canon of the cathedral since 1203. Hugh II remained abroad during the interdict, returning to his see in 1213. He lingered abroad after attending the Fourth Lateran Council and returned to royal service from time to time, but devoted most of his attention to his diocese.[16] Though no theologian, Hugh II was an energetic and diligent bishop who kept close watch on the care of souls at the parochial level. From the historian's perspective, his most outstanding feature was his extensive and systematic keeping of records, probably a legacy of his time in royal administration. In addition to the first known rolls of institutions of vicars and rectors anywhere in England, he commissioned, in the mid-1220s, the *Registrum Antiquissimum*, a compilation of some 874 charters and documents relevant to the diocese and cathedral.[17] He appears to have had a *matriculus*, a detailed parish-by-parish survey, compiled for each archdeaconry, though only that for Leicester survives.[18] Likewise, the existence of a charter roll for

---

[11] E.g. *EEA* 4, 39, 50; but it was left to his successor Hugh of Wells (Hugh II) to ordain vicarages in some others, e.g. ibid., 48, 49 (= *Rot. Hugonis* I, 205).

[12] D. M. Smith, 'Hugh's Administration of Lincoln Diocese', in H. Mayr-Harting, ed., *St Hugh of Lincoln* (Oxford, 1987), 19–47, at 38–39. See also above, pp. 41–42.

[13] Adam of Eynsham, *Vita* II, 96.   [14] *EEA* 4, xxvii–xxviii, 256, 258.

[15] *EEA* 4, xxiii; *Fasti* Lincoln, 3, 13, 22.

[16] *Fasti* Wells, 33; *Fasti* Lincoln, 129; D. M. Smith, 'Wells, Hugh of (d. 1235)', *ODNB*.

[17] Now printed with 2,106 additional documents as *RACCL* I–X.

[18] *Rot. Hugonis* I, 238–72.

the archdeaconry of Northampton suggests that similar rolls were compiled for the other archdeaconries.[19] Hugh of Wells continued Hugh of Avalon's emphasis on residence of cathedral canons by augmenting the income of canons resident at Lincoln, a move which could make more of them available for diocesan administration.[20] In obedience to the mandate of Lateran IV, Hugh ordained or confirmed hundreds of perpetual vicarages, and we can see him explicitly citing the Council of Oxford regarding the minimum annual stipend of five marks. The effect on pastoral care would include greater security for the parish priest, enabling him to build more solid relationships with the community for which he was responsible. Perhaps this made the priesthood a more attractive career and thus aided recruitment. Hugh's ordinations also indicated which parishes needed to be served by several clergy.[21] The careful stipulations of whether the rector or the vicar was to bear the cost of procurations (the fee paid in lieu of hospitality for the archdeacon or bishop making a formal visitation) suggest that Hugh kept his archdeacons in the field, keeping an eye on the parish clergy.[22] A charter from 1218 × 1230 indicates that archidiaconal visitation of parishes was an annual event in the archdeaconry of Bedford,[23] as it probably was elsewhere in the diocese. The efficient administration of the large diocese made possible by such records and bureaucracy must have served Hugh and his successors well.

Hugh II was also diligent in ensuring that the clergy charged with the care of souls were continent, sufficiently educated, resident in their parishes and sufficiently ordained. His institution rolls record fifteen cases of suspected or convicted incontinence or clerical marriage.[24] The real figure must have been much higher, for clergy appeared in these rolls only when being instituted as rectors or vicars; only occasionally were the reasons for deposing a cleric given in the record of his replacement's institution. However, we can learn Hugh's policy from these records. A first offence was penanced,[25] while recidivism resulted in deprivation of the benefice. This was threatened in numerous instances[26] but is only recorded to have happened twice.[27] The threat of deprivation was also used to encourage presentees to obtain sufficient education. Hugh rejected one presentee on grounds of illiteracy, probably in 1217 × 1218.[28]

---

[19] *Rot. Hugonis* II, 183–272.   [20] Smith, *Acta*, 135, 379.   [21] E.g. *Rot. Hugonis* I, 178.

[22] A. Gibbons, ed., *Liber Antiquus de Ordinationibus Vicariarum* (Lincoln, 1888); *Rot. Hugonis* I, 177–210; *DEC*, 249–50; *Reg. Ant, passim*; Smith, *Acta*, 188; *C&S* II, 112–13.

[23] R. Ransford, ed., *Early Charters of the Augustinian Canons of Waltham Abbey* (Woodbridge, 1989), 45–46.

[24] *Rot. Hugonis* I, 79, 87–88, 96–97, 148; II, 23, 72; III, 34, 39, 103, 109–10, 117–18.

[25] E.g. ibid. III, 34, 39, 109, 110, 117.   [26] E.g. ibid. I, 79, 97; cf. 96.   [27] Ibid. II, 23, 72.

[28] Date as judged from its position in the institution roll. *Rot. Hugonis* I, 101.

Other candidates had periods of study enjoined upon them, generally one or two years.[29] 'It is ordered that he frequent the schools and learn' (*Iniunctum est quod scolas frequentet et addiscat*) is the usual form in the rolls but abundant variations demonstrate that each man was examined individually and his particular deficiencies remedied. For instance, fourteen men were ordered to learn to sing[30] and another was instituted on the condition 'that he should study in the schools continually, until he knows how to govern a parish'.[31] Frequently, Hugh ordered presentees in minor orders to study before he would ordain them subdeacons.[32] Either he or the relevant archdeacon would examine clergy, both at ordinations and at other times, giving force to threats of deprivation.[33] Some clergy were ordered to provide their parishes with suitable chaplains while they were away at the schools or until they were qualified for pastoral office.[34] Simon de Koleby, presented to the vicarage of Nocton (archdeaconry of Lincoln), though already a master, was given leave to absent himself for study whenever he wanted so long as he provided a suitable priest in the meantime: Hugh presumably expected him to come and go, applying his learning to his cure when present.[35] He also ordered six presentees to provide suitable priests who could hear confessions and preach in English, which the presentees presumably could not.[36]

Scores of other presentees were simply ordered to reside and serve personally. Full personal service of a church as vicar or rector could only be done by a priest, and most presentees to benefices were not yet priests. These were also commanded to present themselves for ordination at the first opportunity. Master Osbert of Wycombe, presented to the vicarage of South Stoke (archdeaconry of Oxford), was instituted

with the obligation that he shall come to the next ordination, to be promoted to the order of subdeacon, and thus successively order by order, until he is ordained priest, so that from that time he may serve the church personally in the priestly office, according to the bishop's command.[37]

Such a large diocese must have required frequent ordinations, perhaps at all four canonically sanctioned seasons (Ember Days) in a normal year. This is suggested by Hugh's injunction that if Rochester Cathedral Priory should present clerks to the vicarage of Haddenham and its dependent chapels, they must be ordained to the priesthood within a year.[38] In the

[29] On clerical education, see Chapter 2 above.
[30] *Rot. Hugonis* I, 22–24, 49–50, 80–81; II, 12, 34, 119, 151, 314; III, 188, 191.
[31] Ibid. III, 114.   [32] Ibid. II, 12–14; III, 32, 34.
[33] Ibid. I, 161, 216–17; II, 29 (*bis*); 142, 157, 170–71, 282–83, 286; etc.
[34] Ibid. I, 49–50, 161.   [35] Ibid. III, 170.   [36] Ibid. I, 33, 48, 108; II, 18; III, 192.
[37] Ibid. II, 1; cf. ibid. I, 156.   [38] Smith, *Acta*, 346.

earlier records, Hugh's registrar used *clericus* to designate minor orders through subdeacon and possibly deacon: almost all institutions recorded before 1220 describe the presentee as either *clericus* or *cappellanus* (*presbiter* and *sacerdos* are almost never used).[39] Later institutions in the rolls distinguish subdeacons and deacons from lower *clerici*. As this document is from September 1231, *clericus* here indicates that one in the order of acolyte or below could still become priest within a year, suggesting that three or four ordinations in a year was considered the normal frequency at this time. If Hugh held ordinations with this frequency, a parish would spend the minimum amount of time canonically possible without a priest. Hugh's injunctions were not empty words: on at least two occasions he deprived men for failing to receive orders, reside and obtain sufficient education.[40]

While Hugh II issued no diocesan statutes and produced no known *pastoralia*, his episcopate was marked by diligence combined with careful consideration of the necessity of providing qualified and dutiful clergy to the parishes of his diocese. Though diocesan records do not mention it, the friars also arrived in the diocese under Hugh: the Franciscans settled at Oxford, Leicester, Lincoln, Northampton and Stamford, while the Dominicans established themselves at Oxford and Northampton.[41] Hugh's administration is a reminder that the more famous saintly theologian-bishops, such as Robert Grosseteste, Alexander Stavensby, Richard Poore and Thomas Cantilupe, should not be regarded as the only 'good' bishops. Even the most curial of bishops could be remarkably effective administrators.[42] Indeed, if we consider the volume of extant documents, it appears that bishops whose chief talent was administration rather than theology or personal holiness were the ones who performed the most effective service for the reform of pastoral care in the thirteenth century. This may be an illusion in part, since of course the bishops whose administrations produced the most documents are the ones easiest to see in action. Bishops and archbishops whose diplomatic remains today are thinner, such as Edmund of Abingdon, cannot be dismissed as ciphers just for that fact. If all were known, perhaps the main protagonists would appear to be not the bishops at all but relatively lowly administrators such as registrars, archdeacons' officials, rural deans and *ad hoc* deputies.[43] Hugh II's record as bishop of Lincoln strongly suggests that he had been a highly effective archdeacon and episcopal clerk at Wells before his election as bishop, which we probably would not know if he had not been raised to

---

[39] *Rot. Hugonis* I, 1–176. [40] Ibid. II, 270–71; Smith, *Acta*, 286, 437. [41] *MRH*, 222–23, 213–14.
[42] A. Reeves, 'Lusignans, Curiales, and Assorted Non-Saints: Must a Good Bishop be a Good Man?' Paper delivered at the International Conference on Medieval Studies (Kalamazoo, Michigan), May 2015.
[43] Burger, *Diocesan Governance*.

the episcopate. But the larger point remains despite these caveats: Hugh II was a prelate of a type, the 'holy bureaucrat' who ran a remarkably tight ship.[44] He established offices, documents and procedures that would allow his more famous successor to implement his visions of pastoral care far more effectively than he otherwise could have done.

That successor, elected and confirmed shortly after Hugh of Wells' death in 1235, was Robert Grosseteste, who had been not only teacher to the Oxford Franciscans but also part of the diocesan administration as archdeacon of Leicester from 1229 to 1232.[45] Although the roll of presentations to Leicester benefices during his archidiaconate has no distinguishing features – as he was busy teaching at Oxford, he may have deputised administration to an official – his episcopate would be marked by an uncompromising insistence on the primacy of the care of souls above all other considerations.[46] Grosseteste's approach to pastoral care is a substantial subfield of its own; here we must select a few key emphases.[47] Upon his consecration, despite already being in his mid-sixties, Grosseteste embarked upon a process of visiting his entire diocese, deanery by deanery, to preach to the clergy, confirm children and correct abuses.[48] He seems to have covered much of the diocese within the first few years of his episcopate but he did not stop there: Matthew Paris records further visitations under the years 1246 and 1251[49] and there is no reason to doubt that other regular visitations took place. Grosseteste, like most medieval bishops, moved around his diocese frequently, giving ample opportunity for official and unofficial visitation.[50] Deaneries near his episcopal manors would have been the easiest to inspect regularly. In this process, which he acknowledged was unprecedented, he discovered several problems that his predecessors had not eradicated: games took place in cemeteries; in some parishes, it was customary for the laity to withhold oblations at Easter unless the Eucharist was given to them; merchants had set themselves up in the church and churchyard of All Saints, Northampton; clandestine marriages were occurring. He directed his archdeacons to deal with these abuses.[51]

If those committing such abuses hoped for a mild old man in their new bishop, they were soon undeceived. As Southern described him,

---

[44] A. Davis, *The Holy Bureaucrat: Eudes Rigaud and Religious Reform in Thirteenth-Century Normandy* (Ithaca, NY, 2006).

[45] *Fasti Lincoln*, 34. He had retained his prebend of St Margaret's church, Leicester, as the stalls of archdeacons were not affixed to particular prebendal churches at this time: *Fasti Lincoln*, 77.

[46] *Rot. Hugonis* II, 308–20.

[47] See most recently Hoskin, *Grosseteste*, particularly the introduction and bibliography.

[48] Southern, *Grosseteste*, 257–60; *C&S* II, 261–65.   [49] *Chron. Maj.* IV, 579–80; V, 256–57.

[50] *Rot. Grosseteste*, x–xii.   [51] *C&S* II, 201–5.

Grosseteste believed that there was precisely one right way to do everything; that almost any argument should be backed up by citing the Bible with overwhelming force; and that successful reform could be expected urgently.[52] At the same time, he was more of a pastor and theologian than a systematic administrator. Hoskin's careful analysis of the rolls of institutions during his episcopate shows that they were not nearly as well kept as those of Hugh II. She ascribes this not to inefficiency but to a different vision of ecclesiastical administration. Where Hugh had centralised responsibility, Grosseteste devolved it to his archdeacons and took great pains to recruit men of great ability and commitment to that office.[53] Grosseteste held that the salvation of souls was at stake and that, at the last judgement, he would be called to account for any single soul in his diocese that was lost, so he (and his diocesan administrators) could never rest content.[54] Uncompromising activist reform of clerical and lay behaviour was the hallmark of his eighteen years as bishop.

Grosseteste issued, probably in 1239, the only known statutes for Lincoln Diocese in the thirteenth century.[55] Most of the general abuses mentioned in his mandates to his archdeacons are rehearsed here, along with others that he had presumably discovered in the meantime through his diocesan officials and his visitations. Grosseteste's statutes thus offer some indications of problems his predecessors had not solved. We have heard, the bishop wrote, that some priests have their deacons hear confessions: this must cease.[56] He had heard that some priests extort money from the laity for sacraments, including confession, or impose fines as penances: this also must cease.[57] Several vicarages ordained by Hugh of Wells sanctioned 'oblations' at confession as part of the vicar's support.[58] While these were supposed to be free offerings, avaricious clergy could, and sometimes did, demand such payments as theirs by right and refuse services otherwise, as was the case with Easter oblations mentioned by Grosseteste.[59] Aside from these strictures, surprisingly little attention is given in the statutes to confession, a major concern of Grosseteste's: he wrote three works on the subject before he became bishop and three more during his episcopate.[60] Grosseteste's statutes, considered as a prescriptive and proscriptive document on pastoral care and church life, show a programme different from that of Richard Poore's longer and more thorough

---

[52] Southern, *Grosseteste*.   [53] Hoskin, *Grosseteste*, xxvi–liv.

[54] Southern, *Grosseteste*, 243–57. For an instance of vetting candidates for the archdeaconry of Oxford, see *LAM*, 98–99.

[55] *C&S* II, 265–78, cited below as 'Lincoln' with chapter number; see also Cheney, *Synodalia*, 110–41.

[56] Lincoln, 29.   [57] Lincoln, 27.

[58] *Rot. Hugonis* II, 127, 185; III, 40–41, 56, 84–86, 194.   [59] *C&S* II, 205; Lincoln, 22.

[60] Goering, 'When and Where', 29.

Salisbury statutes and their derivatives.[61] While, like most other sets of statutes, the Lincoln statutes include proscriptions of clerical drunkenness and incontinence and some instructions for pastoral care and clerical knowledge, this shorter document is not conceived as an instructional tract in its own right. He opened his first statute by commending the Decalogue as necessary for the health of souls, yet did not list or expound the Commandments as Pecham later would in his provincial statutes.[62] While Poore's statutes included a general exposition of the seven sacraments and further homiletic material on several of them individually, Grosseteste merely told priests that they should know about them (especially confession) and teach the laity about them (especially the form of baptism for emergencies): he provided no exposition, nor even a list.[63]

This was because Grosseteste expected priests to have other *pastoralia*. In *Templum Dei*, he considered 'a book of canonical penances, so that he may know how to discern between one disease and another, that is between sins, and enjoin penances' to be essential reading for the parish priest, along with 'the book of the homilies of Gregory or another saint, so that he may know how to expound the Gospel to the people'.[64] Very few parish churches are known to have owned such books, though parish book lists would exclude texts that were the personal property of the priest.[65] Many of the thirteenth-century manuscripts of his statutes include other *pastoralia*. In particular, Grosseteste's confessor's manual *Quoniam cogitatio* appears with the statutes in some early manuscripts.[66] *Quoniam cogitatio* may have been designed to accompany the Lincoln statutes, just as Stavensby appended two pastoral tracts to his Lichfield statutes around this time.[67] Grosseteste's statutes and *Quoniam cogitatio*, while not as abstruse as his academic writings, lack the simple genius of Richard Poore's language. As a result of previous bishops' emphases on

---

[61] Salisbury I/Durham I/Canterbury I and II; Exeter I; Chichester I; London II (all in *C&S* II). Each included more extensive theological glossing than Grosseteste's Lincoln statutes.

[62] *C&S* II, 902–3.   [63] Lincoln, 1.   [64] Grosseteste, *Templum*, 50.

[65] One 'dictionary of penance' and four homiliaries are listed in the following visitation records: Sparrow-Simpson, *1297 Visitations*, 18, 25; Sparrow-Simpson, '1249 Visitations', 31; *Reg. St Osmund* I, 294.

[66] These include Richard of Wethringsett's *Qui bene presunt* and works of William de Montibus, discussed below: Cheney, *Synodalia*, 111–16.

[67] *C&S* II, 207–26. Leonard Boyle suggested that *Templum Dei* had been so appended, but Joe Goering suggests the *Quoniam cogitatio*, which the manuscript evidence supports more strongly (personal communication with the latter, August 2004). Moreover, *Quoniam cogitatio* is based around the Decalogue and seven sins, which Grosseteste in his statutes ordered priests to know: *C&S* II, 268. I have used Cambridge, Peterhouse College Library, MS. 255 Part III fols 23r–30r for *Quoniam cogitatio*, where it is immediately followed by the statutes in the same thirteenth-century hand.

education and the proliferation of schools, the parish clergy of Lincoln Diocese in 1239 may have been somewhat more literate than those of Salisbury twenty years earlier, when Poore issued his statutes; but Grosseteste may have aimed too high, leaving laity in parishes with only moderately literate priests largely untouched by his textual endeavours.

Liturgical books, however, would certainly be at the disposal of parish priests, and Grosseteste hoped that Lincoln Diocese's clergy would learn theology from them. In addition to enjoining devotion in liturgical prayer, the bishop encouraged clergy to attend to the prayers and lessons so as to be able to teach others (i.e. the laity) what they had learned.[68] He gave similar advice in a sermon to parish clergy: those who know not how to preach are not thereby excused. They should spend each week working through the Gospel text for the next Sunday so that they can at least explain its general meaning to their parishioners; in the second year, they should do the same with the Epistle readings; and, in the third, the lives of the saints. Those who do not know enough Latin should seek the help of a neighbouring priest.[69]

Grosseteste continued Hugh of Wells' programme of examining clerical education, with more regular threats of deprivation.[70] As can also be seen in Hugh's institution rolls, presentees closely related to the patron presenting them were disproportionately likely to have such strictures laid upon them: for instance, Thomas of Mablethorpe, presented by his father Haco of Mablethorpe to the rectory of Mablethorpe St Peter (archdeaconry of Lincoln), was obliged 'to be examined each year, and unless he makes impressive progress, he is to be entirely deprived of the foresaid church'.[71] The presentee of two portions of Sproxton (archdeaconry of Lincoln), who was expected to serve personally, was ordered 'to come at the feast of St Michael, to be fully examined regarding the Ten Commandments, the seven sacraments, and the seven sins with circumstances'.[72] This corresponds to the first three items in Grosseteste's statute listing what parish priests should know, which suggests that the statutes themselves were used as the basis for examination.[73]

On his visitations of his diocese, Grosseteste brought the four friars he kept in his household, two Franciscans and two Dominicans, to preach to the people and hear their confessions. In this way he showed to the people his equal respect for both orders and showed to the parish clergy that the friars had his sanction, lest any try to prevent their preaching

---

[68] Lincoln, 6, 7.   [69] Gieben, 'Grosseteste on Preaching', 112.
[70] Hoskin, *Grosseteste*, lv–lviii, lxvi–lxx.
[71] Ibid., no. 218 (=*Rot. Grosseteste*, 60). For an example from Hugh of Wells, see *Rot. Hugonis* I, 19–20.
[72] Hoskin, *Grosseteste*, no. 1438 (=*Rot. Grosseteste*, 416–17).
[73] *C&S* II, 268; Hoskin, *Grosseteste*, no. 1438n.

in the future.[74] In addition, this levelled the terrain in the geography of pastoral care, for no corner of his diocese that he visited would go untouched by the friars during these perambulations. However, we do not see many new mendicant houses being founded under Grosseteste: it appears that they had already reached a temporary ceiling under Hugh of Wells. The Franciscans, already spread throughout the diocese in their six convents, settled at Bedford by 1238 and Grimsby by about 1240, but these dates are merely first mentions and one or both houses may have been founded earlier.[75] The Carmelites and Austins entered the diocese in 1256 and 1258, respectively, during the short and poorly documented episcopate of Grosseteste's successor, Henry de Lexington (1253–58), who had been cathedral dean under Grosseteste.[76]

Master Richard Gravesend, dean of the cathedral, was elected bishop of Lincoln in September 1258 and consecrated in November.[77] Almost immediately, he was sent abroad on royal business for over a year, leaving Robert Marsh, brother of the Oxford Franciscan Adam Marsh, as his vicegerent.[78] Gravesend spent several other periods abroad in the 1260s on various kinds of business but when in England seems to have stayed in his diocese most of the time.[79] His register also clearly shows that a vicegerent was appointed for each major absence, carrying on business as usual, at least as regards institutions. Although his ordination lists are lost, the editors of his rolls have reconstructed his ordination dates, often showing four or even five ordinations in a year at rotating locations around the diocese.[80] This would ensure a minimal time without a sacerdotal presence in parishes presented with clerks. He improved pastoral provision in some large rural parishes by establishing chapels-of-ease in outlying settlements.[81] On the basis of Gravesend's itinerary, his register's editors also have suggested that he attempted to visit his diocese on a triennial basis; however, there is no trace of inquiry along Grossetestian lines.[82] Nonetheless, the fact that Grosseteste had chosen Gravesend to accompany him on his trip the papal curia in 1250 and the nature of Gravesend's correspondence with Adam Marsh indicate that he shared their vision

---

[74] He also directed his archdeacons to act against rectors and vicars who impeded friars from preaching to their parishioners and hearing their confessions: *C&S* II, 480. In the same mandate, he ordered his archdeacons to induce the laity to attend the sermons of either order of friars and to confess to them.

[75] *MRH*, 222.

[76] *Fasti* Lincoln, 4, 10; *Rot. Grosseteste*, 509–18; Egan, 'Carmelite Houses', 79; *MRH*, 240.

[77] *Fasti* Lincoln, 4.

[78] *Rot. Gravesend*, vii. Robert had also served as official and vicar-general when Grosseteste was abroad: *LAM*, 94–95.

[79] *Rot. Gravesend*, ix–xv.   [80] Ibid., xv–xvi.

[81] R. M. Haines, 'Gravesend, Richard of', *ODNB*.   [82] *Rot. Gravesend*, xvi–xvii.

of pastoral care as the final cause that ought to animate all ecclesiastical business.[83] Another mendicant order, the Friars of the Sack, entered Lincoln Diocese during Gravesend's episcopate, settling at Oxford, Lincoln, Northampton, Leicester and Stamford between 1261 an 1274, giving the diocese five of England's sixteen convents. What they added to pastoral care before their suppression in 1274 cannot now be ascertained, but as their numbers were never great and they settled in sizeable towns already occupied by other orders, their influence must have been a minor local uniqueness confined to the urban environment. Only the Leicester house closed before 1300, however, indicating strong continuing support from the laity.[84]

In 1280, Oliver Sutton, an Oxford theologian and canonist, became the third successive dean of Lincoln Cathedral to be elevated to the bishop's throne. Sutton had been a student and friend of Adam Marsh at Oxford and shared that friar's vision and high ideals for the care of souls.[85] The records of Sutton's episcopate show him faithfully and efficiently administering the diocese and improving the quality of pastoral care by enforcing residence,[86] ordination,[87] literacy[88] and good behaviour. He made extensive use of the officers of diocesan government, such as his archdeacons,[89] and commissioned qualified clergy *ad hoc* for administrative tasks.[90] His ordination lists for the 1290s, the earliest to survive for the diocese, show an average of four ordinations a year.[91] The lists also record which diocesan officials examined the candidates. Of some interest are the ordinations of friars, which show that Sutton conferred orders on Franciscans 201 times, Dominicans 121 times, Carmelites 114 times and Austins 88 times during this decade.[92] This offers a rough comparison of the relative strength of each order in the diocese. The proximity of the Dominicans to the Carmelites rather than to the Franciscans is striking, though it may indicate merely that Dominicans recruited more men already in higher orders.

Sutton supported the Dominicans, defending their right to hear the confessions of the laity in opposition to the claims of the canons of Dunstable, with whom they had been engaged in litigation for forty years.[93]

[83] *LAM*, xxviii–xxix.   [84] *MRH*, 274.

[85] *Reg. Sutton* I, v; ibid., III, xiv; *LAM*, 75; R. Hill, 'Sutton [Lexinton], Oliver', *ODNB*; R. Hill, *Oliver Sutton, Dean of Lincoln, later Bishop of Lincoln* (Lincoln, 1982), 12.

[86] E.g. *Reg. Sutton* III, 10, 82; IV 49–50.   [87] E.g. ibid. IV, 80.

[88] E.g. ibid. III, liii, lxxvii, 43, 48, 66–67, 104, 184; IV, 73–74.   [89] Ibid. III, xxx.

[90] Ibid. III–VI, *passim*.   [91] Ibid. VII.

[92] Ibid. VII, 124–25. These are the figures for total ordinations, not total individuals: a single friar ordained to successive orders would thus be counted several times.

[93] Ibid. VI, 162. This intervention took place in 1299. For the rivalry see *EEFP*, 79–81; *Chron. Maj.* V, 742.

However, documents expressing support for Franciscans appear more often in his register.[94] For example, he appointed Franciscans as penitentiaries four times in the 1290s.[95] Although thirteenth-century English Dominicans have left behind more compelling sources suggesting knowledge of canon law on penance, these appointments by such a careful canonist as Sutton clearly indicate that the Franciscans were not second-class in this respect. His friendship with Adam Marsh may have led to a special affection for the order.[96]

Sutton's successor John Dalderby, bishop of Lincoln from 1300 to 1320, is beyond the scope of this book, but documents from the first year of his episcopate shed unique light on the question of how many friars were pastorally active. In 1300, Boniface VIII's bull *Super cathedram* required friars to be licensed by bishops to hear confessions in their dioceses, and Dalderby's register includes not only the names of those so licensed but also the full number of friars put forward on these occasions, only about one-third of whom he licensed.[97] The number proposed is more important for our purposes, for it approximates the number of friars each order considered qualified to hear confessions at the end of the century. The records for 1 July to 12 October 1300 show that seventy-three Franciscans and eighty-eight Dominicans were proposed; but these came from only four of the nine Franciscan friaries and four of the six Dominican friaries, so we may estimate that somewhere around 150 Franciscans and 125 Dominicans were active confessors in Lincoln Diocese on the eve of *Super cathedram*. As confession was a more complex and tightly regulated task than preaching, which was not restricted under *Super cathedram*, the number of potentially active preaching friars from these two orders can be set higher still. Even this takes no account of the Carmelites and Austins, which the figures from Sutton's ordinations suggest were not far behind the Dominicans in the diocese. At a guess – and we can do no more – this indicates that over 300 Franciscan and Dominican friars in the diocese were qualified to preach to the laity, and around 140 Carmelites and Austins, which would give one preaching friar to every four to five parishes in the diocese. Coverage of the countryside would be intermittent according to the preaching seasons, the necessity of travelling in pairs could reduce the dispersal of preachers, and only careful co-ordination of itineraries among the four orders could have reduced overlapping; but such a number of preachers, and the smaller but not inconsiderable number of confessors, would have been a very substantial presence in all but

---

[94] E.g. *Reg. Sutton* III, 22, 195.   [95] Ibid. III, 13, 39–40, 86, 90, 100; V, 210; VI, 3.
[96] Ibid. III, xiv; *LAM*, 185–97.
[97] Sbaralea, *Bullarium Franciscanum* IV, 498–500; Little, *Papers*, 230–43.

the remotest corners of the diocese.[98] It is small wonder that Dalderby, who was no enemy of the friars, satisfied himself with licensing a smaller number of confessors, especially if the reforms of his predecessors had improved the quality parish clergy.

THE ARCHDEACONRIES OF LINCOLN AND STOW

The cathedral city was situated in western Lincolnshire, the northernmost county in the diocese. The north-west quarter of the county, immediately north of Lincoln, constituted the archdeaconry of Stow, while the archdeaconry of Lincoln covered the remainder of the county. The cathedral was far from the geographical centre of the diocese, though there is little sign that this had ever been an important criterion in choosing cathedral cities. Bishops in any case typically moved around their dioceses with their administrators in tow from one episcopal manor to another and sometimes even avoided their cathedrals due to tensions between them and their cathedral clergy.[99] Nevertheless, there were particular opportunities and advantages that that were more available to those in closer proximity to the cathedral city.

While it did not rival Oxford, Lincoln was a centre of clerical education. The cathedral library held Peter Lombard's *Sentences* and Peter Comestor's *Historia Scholastica*, among many other texts ranging from patristic to contemporary.[100] Even if not open for public consultation, the library had an indirect effect on pastoral care, since the school (which presumably had access to the library) was an official institution of the cathedral under the direction of its chancellor. Hugh I had installed the Lincoln native and Paris scholar and master William de Montibus as chancellor in 1194.[101] Like his erstwhile colleague Peter the Chanter, William gave high priority to matters of pastoral care and put this programme into action in the Lincoln cathedral school.[102] Many of William's writings were aimed at elementary applied theology students.[103] Several works of his concern the sacrament of penance, such as the versified *Peniteas cito peccator*, indicating that he expected the hearing of confessions to be an important

[98] Liturgically, the friars' seasons for missionary travel were Advent, Lent and Eastertide, but it is likely that they also took advantage of good weather in the summer. O'Carroll, *Studies*, 213–14; d'Avray, *Preaching*, 56, 210.

[99] Hoskin, *Grosseteste*, 425–33; Moorman, *Church Life*, 185–96.

[100] Gerald, *Opera* VII, 165–71. The *Sentences* (p. 169) were bequeathed by Bishop Robert de Chesney, who died in 1166 (*Fasti* Lincoln, 2), less than a decade after the work was finished; the *Historia* (p. 168) was given by a canon named Sampson, who died around 1190 (*Fasti* Lincoln, 144).

[101] Goering, *William de Montibus*; Mayr-Harting, *Religion*, 199–200.

[102] On William's teaching, see Goering, *William de Montibus*, 42–57, and above, pp. 30, 100.

[103] MacKinnon, 'William de Montibus'; Goering, *William de Montibus*, 58–83, 98–99.

part of pastoral care and instructed parish clergy accordingly.[104] He had also written on the still new list of the seven sacraments before returning to Lincoln and presumably taught it there.[105] Many of his writings reflect thoughtful and effective pedagogy in their use of mnemonic devices such as verse, numbering and alphabetisation. While William's teaching would have been *gratis*, no provision is known to have been made to support poor scholars at Lincoln. Clergy who already lived in Lincolnshire had easier access to William's teaching at the cathedral school while those elsewhere might find it easier and cheaper to study at schools closer to home. William's cunningly communicated, up-to-date pastoral theology would therefore be felt the most by the laity within Lincoln's catchment area.[106] As chancellor, he was also responsible for preaching to the laity on set occasions and some of his extant sermons explicitly address lay audiences.[107] He continued to teach at Lincoln until shortly before his death in 1213.[108]

Several of William's students can be identified. The best known is Gerald of Wales, archdeacon of Brecon.[109] When war prevented Gerald from studying at Paris in 1196–99, he chose studying under William at Lincoln as the best alternative in England.[110] It was presumably William's influence that inspired Gerald to write his *Gemma Ecclesiastica*, a *pastoralium* aimed at equipping parish clergy, though it was so cumbersome that few could have found it useful.[111] Another student, less well known, was Samuel Presbiter, whose notes were preserved at Bury St Edmunds together with several other minor theological works that he wrote.[112] To these two we may add Richard of Wethringsett. Richard wrote the very popular pastoral manual *Qui bene presunt*, which often quoted William's works and mimicked his techniques: so heavy was its debt to William that several manuscripts ascribe authorship to him.[113] He is almost

---

[104] Ibid., 107–38. [105] Ibid., 472–96.
[106] 'The provenance of the mss. [of William's works], where known, suggests that his influence was largely in the eastern part of England'. MacKinnon, 'William de Montibus', 35n.
[107] Goering, *William de Montibus*, 19–20, 527–66.
[108] *Fasti Lincoln*, 16–17; Goering, *William de Montibus*, 25–26.
[109] For others, see Goering, *William de Montibus*, 44–47. [110] Gerald, *Opera* I, 93.
[111] Dating is difficult, but it postdates the beginning of Gerald's study in Lincoln: Bartlett, *Gerald*, 146–47, 218. Gerald quotes William's *Versarius* (Goering, *William de Montibus*, 393). Gerald gave a copy to the cathedral library (Gerald, *Opera* VII, 168); presumably this was the copy read by William himself (Bartlett, *Gerald*, 146–47).
[112] Samuel Presbiter, *Notes*; Goering, *William de Montibus*, 504–14; Sharpe, *Handlist*, 600–601.
[113] Goering, 'Qui bene presunt'. I am grateful to Goering for sharing with me his working catalogue of approximately sixty-five manuscript copies of *Qui bene presunt*, from which this information comes. He is currently preparing an edition, which will show more precisely Richard's indebtedness to William.

certainly the same man as Master Richard Weathershed, William's successor as chancellor of Lincoln from 1220 until his election as archbishop of Canterbury just before his death in 1229.[114] If this association is correct, Lincoln once again had a chancellor of strong pastoral commitment. As Goering dates the *Qui bene presunt* to 1215 × 1220, its content probably reflects Richard's teaching at Lincoln, where he would have made this work available to local clergy and as chancellor would have preached to the laity. Schools at Lincoln carried on under Grosseteste: Adam Marsh commended the Oxford scholar Master William of Grimele for the mastership of the schools there.[115] Other pastoral scholarship was taking place at the Lincoln convents of the Franciscans and Dominicans, who had arrived ca. 1230 and 1237, respectively.[116] While secular scholars could have attended their lectures, the presence of the cathedral school better directed to their needs probably precluded much commixture. Lincoln's location at the intersection of two Roman roads, Fosse Way and Ermine Street, would have made it particularly easy for friars to travel into the countryside, especially to those parishes near the roads, which ran to the north, south and south-west. This would have made for a region of particularly dense mendicant rural influence running from north to south along the western side of Lincolnshire.

The same roads that bore friars out of the cathedral city could carry pilgrims into it. Bishop Hugh I was canonised in 1220, giving Lincoln Cathedral its first significant saint's cult and primary relics. Hugh II arranged the financial support of the wardens of the altar of his predecessor. News of miracles and canonisation made the cathedral a site of pilgrimage, the translation of the late bishop's relics providing both a focus for devotion and an event for publicity. Hugh's canonization records inform us about those who experienced healing at the shrine between 1200 and 1219. Of the thirty people whose cures were recorded, a majority (nineteen) were women; six of these were women who had been mentally or emotionally disturbed but were restored to their right minds. Unfortunately, women were less likely to have toponyms recorded, so we can trace the origins of petitioners in only a handful of the total cases. Several supplicants were of local origin, including a matron of Lincoln; a boy and a man from the Lincoln suburb of Wigford; and a man from Ancaster, Lincolnshire, eighteen miles south of the cathedral city. Lincoln was only a few miles from York Diocese, so pilgrims could easily have come not only from another diocese but from another province. Matilda

---

[114] Goering, 'Qui bene presunt'; *Fasti* Lincoln, 17.
[115] *LAM*, 166–67.   [116] *MRH*, 222, 214.

of Beverley, who was cured of severely swollen limbs, presumably came directly from her namesake town, forty-four miles to the north and in the Diocese of York.[117]

Work commenced on the 'Angel Choir' of the cathedral in 1255 to provide a magnificent home for the shrine of St Hugh and adequate space for pilgrims.[118] Two years later, Bishop Henry of Lexington issued an indulgence of twenty days' enjoined penance to encourage people to come to the cathedral, hear the sermons of its canons and pray the *Paternoster* and *Ave* thrice each.[119] Thereby he established yet another source for preaching to clergy and laity alike, complementing the offerings of the friars and supplementing the homilies of the parish clergy. The indulgences also encouraged pilgrimage at a time when a major building project was just beginning and additional donations were needed. Moreover, miracles were soon witnessed at Grosseteste's grave as well, encouraging the dean and chapter and the bishop to promote his cult as well and seek papal canonisation.[120] The tomb erected over his remains a few years after his death resembles contemporary saint's shrines.[121] Canonisation required posthumous miracles; miracles, for the most part, required supplicants. The more pilgrims who came through the great west doors, the more probable the canonisation would become. While these canonisation attempts eventually failed, supplicants who had not met with success at Hugh's shrine may have turned to Grosseteste's nonetheless. Matthew Paris reported that miracles were being wrought at the tombs of 'St' Remigius, St Hugh and 'St' Robert Grosseteste in 1253 and 1255; in the latter year he wrote mostly about Grosseteste, noting that twenty miracles had occurred at his tomb and that they had been diligently examined by the chapter.[122] While we know nothing of the content of the sermons preached in the cathedral by members of the chapter, some of them must have dealt with the purported saints whose shrines lay in the cathedral, especially on their obits or feast days. Since the indulgences for hearing the sermons were (like all indulgences) only valid for those who were contrite and confessed, some of the preaching may have been penitential and opportunities for confession could have been provided.

[117] *RACCL* III, 830; Farmer, ed., 'Canonization of St Hugh'; D. H. Farmer, 'The Cult and Canonization of St Hugh', in H. Mayr-Harting, ed., *St Hugh of Lincoln* (Oxford, 1987), 75–87, at 83; D. Stocker, 'The Mystery of the Shrines of St Hugh', in ibid., 89–124; P. Kidston, 'Architectural History', in D. Owen, ed., *A History of Lincoln Minster* (Cambridge, 1994), 14–46, at 39–42.
[118] J. W. F. Hill, *Medieval Lincoln* (Cambridge, 1965), 112.   [119] *RACCL* II, 406.
[120] E. W. Kemp, 'The Attempted Canonization of Robert Grosseteste', in D. A. Callus, ed., *Robert Grosseteste, Scholar and Bishop* (Oxford, 1955), 241–46; *RACCL* I, 280d; ibid. II, 607.
[121] D. A. Stocker, 'The Tomb and Shrine of Robert Grosseteste in Lincoln Cathedral', in W. M. Ormrod, ed., *England in the Thirteenth Century* (Grantham, Lincolnshire, 1985), 143–48.
[122] *Chron. Maj.* V, 419, 490–91.

As with other religious provisions made at the cathedral, it is likely that parishioners in the city and outlying areas would come to the canons' sermons, taking advantage of the bishop's indulgence, most readily. The approach to the cathedral is quite a climb – Ermine Street south of the cathedral is, in fact, today aptly named Steep Hill – but sparing an hour or two and some perspiration to have twenty days' enjoined penance remitted would be a very attractive proposition, perhaps to the chagrin of local parish priests or friars who found such an easy remission too light. In coming years, however, reissues of this indulgence appear to have made Lincoln an attractive pilgrimage destination from much further afield. A bishop only had the authority to issue an indulgence for the parishioners of his own diocese, but other bishops could declare that it applied to their parishioners as well.[123] It is not surprising that Archbishop Godfrey Ludham of York was apparently the first to do so (1264), for the southern part of his diocese lay very close to Lincoln itself.[124] He thoughtfully added that the auditors of these sermons were expected to strive to follow what they heard. In 1266–67, seven other English bishops extended the indulgence, while three Scottish bishops did so in the 1270s.[125]

If the canons did not offer public masses or hear confessions, visitors may have made their way to the northwest corner of the nave, where they would have found the altar of St Mary Magdalene. This served as the church of the Lincoln parish of that name from the second quarter of the century until a new church was built for them within the cathedral precinct in the 1290s.[126] John de Schalby, a cathedral canon, considered the parishioners disruptive; this seems to have been the most common view that secular collegiate churches and monastic bodies held when they shared a church building with a parish community.[127] In practice, however, pilgrims must often have been disruptive as well, yet cathedrals and monasteries actively competed for visitors to their shrines through indulgences. The difference in approach probably reflects not only the fact that pilgrims brought offerings but also that the monks or canons could more easily regulate entry and exclusion of pilgrims while parishioners might claim the right to enter the part of the church that they considered their own.

Just north of Lincoln sat the archdeaconry of Stow, the smallest of the eight archdeaconries, with around a hundred parishes.[128] We know that Bishop Sutton had held multiple visitations of the archdeaconry,

---

[123] Vincent, 'Pardoners' Tales'.   [124] *RACCL* II, 407.
[125] *RACCL* II, 410–20.   [126] *RACCL* III, 1099.
[127] M. Heale, 'Monastic-Parochial Churches in Late Medieval England', in Burgess and Duffy, eds, *Parish*, 54–77; J. W. F. Hill, *Medieval Lincoln* (Cambridge, 1965), 375–76; *Reg. Sutton* IV, 174–76.
[128] Southern, *Grosseteste*, 235.

facilitated by the presence of the favoured episcopal manor of Stow Park, because of a note in his register mentioning the accidental burning of the rolls of his first visitation there.[129] However, a scrap of evidence of visitation by an archdeacon or archdeacon's official has survived, listing the defects of five parish churches and ordering that they be made good by Michaelmas 1287.[130] Its contents – the repair of a window, the rebinding or acquisition of books and the like – are similar to other visitation records, but the form is different. The surviving visitation records of appropriated churches of St Paul's and Salisbury cathedrals and the book of the archdeacons of Ely describe defects of property but, regarding ornaments, vestments and books, they are more concerned with listing what is present than what is lacking.[131] A list of items present would provide a checklist against which to measure losses. This archidiaconal record from Stow, however, lists defects only, which suggests that the visitor travelled with a list of what each church had owned in the past or asked the parishioners whether specific items were missing, making for a more systematic enquiry. We find, for example, the mention of the missing 'processional cross of Limoges work with painted staff' at Highbaldstow.[132] The rough nature of the document, scratched out unevenly on a scrap of parchment, would be appropriate to a draft intended to be copied onto official rolls or to be checked at the archidiaconal chapter meeting on Michaelmas. The cancellation of several items listed suggests that this was used as a working document; perhaps this recorded defects remedied before the deadline. The impression is of systematic and regular visitation in the archdeaconry of Stow.

Since the archdeacon's post was apparently vacant at this time, the visitor of these parishes must have been the official designated by Sutton to carry on such business until a permanent replacement was appointed. The name of this official is not recorded. Internal evidence shows that the scribe expected an archdeacon to be in place by Michaelmas 1287, but this did not happen, so we cannot be sure whether the corrections were enforced. However, this is a corrective to the assumption that absent archdeacons leaving officials to do their work meant poor supervision of pastoral care. Bishop Sutton kept Master Jocelin of Kirmington, archdeacon of Stow from 1291 to 1300, at his side while perambulating the

---

[129] *Reg. Sutton* V, 130.

[130] Lincolnshire Archive Office, Dean and Chapter MS. Dij/64/2, no. 7; Owen, *Church and Society*, 35.

[131] Sparrow-Simpson, '1249 Visitations'; Sparrow-Simpson, *1297 Visitations*; *Reg. St Osmund* I, 275–314; W. H. Rich Jones and W. Macray, eds, *Charters and Documents Illustrating the History of the Cathedral, City, and Diocese of Salisbury* (London, 1891), 369–70; Feltoe and Minns, ed., *Vetus Liber*.

[132] 'Crux processional' de Limon' cum baculo picto'.

diocese, leaving his archidiaconal official, Master Benedict of Ferriby, in charge; and we may assume that the conscientious Sutton considered that supervision of the archdeaconry was still in good hands.[133]

THE ARCHDEACONRY OF OXFORD

The archdeaconry of Oxford, coterminous with Oxfordshire, was of an average size for the diocese, at around 265 parishes.[134] The religious life of the town of Oxford had long been dominated by the churches of Oseney and St Frideswide, originally secular minsters re-founded as Augustinian houses in the early twelfth century. Postles has argued that, following their adoption of the Rule of St Augustine, their role shifted from pastors to urban landlords, but, as we shall see, they did not entirely turn their back on pastoral responsibilities.[135]

Around 1190, Hugh I authorised Oseney to build a chapel at its own expense for the convenience of its household servants, guests and parishioners staying within the abbey precinct.[136] It is likely that this was to move such a congregation out of the abbey church. This chapel, dedicated to St Thomas, was considered a parish church by 1222; the abbot had full jurisdiction over the chaplain, though the archdeacon had normal jurisdiction over the parishioners.[137] Hugh II admonished Oseney to be more careful in its appointments of assisting clerics and Sutton mandated the arrangement of perpetual vicarages in two of its appropriated churches in 1296 in terms suggesting that ministry in them had not been satisfactory.[138] Oseney also held extensive properties in Oxford.[139] Thus far Postles' argument seems to hold true. However, some abbots contributed to pastoral care in other ways. In 1235, Abbot John took his abilities, education and spiritual formation to the Franciscan order.[140] In 1294 Sutton commissioned the abbot to hear confessions and assign penances to laity in the archdeaconry of Oxford.[141] Grosseteste, who was generally reluctant to permit appropriations, allowed the abbey to appropriate the parish church of Fulwell in 1238 × 1239.[142]

There is also thirteenth-century evidence of the involvement of St Frideswide's Priory in pastoral care. Like many religious houses, it was the patron of numerous parish churches, including seven in or just outside Oxford.[143] Hugh II did not admonish them in the same terms as

---

[133] *Fasti* Lincoln, 47; *Reg. Sutton* III, xxvi.   [134] Southern, *Grosseteste*, 235.
[135] Postles, 'Austin Canons'.
[136] *EEA* 4, 147; Salter, ed., *Oseney Cartulary* III, no. 1040.   [137] Ibid., nos. 1041, 1042.
[138] *Rot. Hugonis* I, 179–80; cf. vol. II, 18–19; *Reg. Sutton* V, 134.
[139] Salter, ed., *Oseney Cartulary* I–IV *passim*.   [140] *Annales Monastici* I, 98; IV, 82–83.
[141] *Reg. Sutton* IV, 191.   [142] *RACCL* III, 940.   [143] *VCH* Oxford IV, 373.

Oseney and appears not to have needed to. Of its presentees to him, the high proportion of 69 per cent were already priests, not one of whom was found to need further study.[144] Master Sylvester of Cornwall, presented by the priory to the Oxford vicarage of St Michael at Northgate in 1223, was ordered to be ordained priest and to serve personally.[145] Moreover, St Frideswide's itself served as a parish church from at least the 1220s, and probably earlier. The secular vicar was supported in part by living with the canons.[146] St Frideswide's parish was united with the neighbouring parish of St Edward (also appropriated to the priory) in 1298, the combined parish worshipping in St Edward's church. This was done for several reasons, including the poverty of both parishes, but also because in St Frideswide's church the canons and the vicar had celebrated in such close proximity that their singing clashed.[147] The reasons for moving the parish altar to a separate building were probably similar to those at Oseney but the canons of St Frideswide, like the canons of Lincoln Cathedral, bore with this cohabitation for a century more. Perhaps the canons were simply accustomed to the bustle of pilgrims and supplicants at the shrine of St Frideswide herself, which lay to the north of the choir in a chapel that was enlarged at least twice during the century.[148] The majority of supplicants whose names can be traced came from within forty miles. If providing the locus of a saint's cult is considered as an aspect of liturgical pastoral care, a geographical delineation can here be observed.[149]

In addition to the cathedral school at Lincoln, there was a school in the diocese at Northampton in 1233.[150] Most clergy who needed to study were simply directed to 'the schools', some of which would have consisted merely of a grammar master who hung out his shingle in a provincial town.[151] But the diocese's school *par excellence* was, of course, Oxford.[152] The university quickly emerged as one of the town's leading

---

[144] *Rot. Hugonis* I, 5; II, 10–11, 20–21, 36, 37 (*bis*), 38, 41, 72, 75, 87. This calculation counts twice Martin of Nutley, priest, presented first to the vicarage and then the rectory of Over Winchendon. Analysis of St Frideswide's presentations in *Rot. Grosseteste*/Hoskin, *Grosseteste* give a similar result.

[145] *Rot. Hugonis* II, 10–11.

[146] Dodd, 'Churches in Norman Oxford'; *Rot. Hug.* I, 182; Blair, 'St Frideswide's', 255–58. Blair suggests (pp. 255–56) that canons discharged parochial functions before the vicarage was ordained.

[147] *Reg. Sutton* VI, 106–7.   [148] Blair, 'St Frideswide's', 246–55.

[149] H. Mayr-Harting, 'Functions of a Twelfth-Century Shrine: The Miracles of St Frideswide', in Mayr-Harting and R. I. Moore, eds, *Studies in Medieval History presented to R. H. C. Davis* (London, 1985), 193–206.

[150] *Rot. Hugonis* II, 170–71; H. G. Richardson, 'The Schools of Northampton in the Twelfth Century', *English Historical Review* 56 (1941), 595–605; C. H. Lawrence, 'The University of Oxford and the Chronicle of the Barons' War', *English Historical Review* 95 (1980), 99–113.

[151] R. W. Southern, 'From Schools to University', in Catto, ed., *Oxford Schools*, 1–36, at 2.

[152] Catto, *Oxford Schools, passim.*

institutions: in 1236 the prior of St Frideswide and the archdeacon and university chancellor of Oxford were commissioned as papal judges delegate, which may suggest that they were already seen from Rome as approximate peers.[153] The university supplied a storehouse of talent for diocesan administration: at least six of the archdeaconries were held by Oxford men at some point,[154] and doubtless many of the less well documented administrators, such as archdeacons' officials, bishops' clerks and rural deans, were also educated in the Oxford schools.[155] Bishops Grosseteste, Sutton and (probably) Gravesend, who among them ruled the diocese for nearly six decades, were likewise drawn from Oxford.

A sermon preached at Oxford by Jordan of Saxony OP in 1229 presumes a large number of rectors and perhaps vicars in the audience, though they may have come from far and wide to study and subsequently returned to their distant benefices.[156] If pastoral care around Oxford itself benefited from the university, what were the mechanisms of mediation? One was through public preaching by scholars, as is well-attested at Paris.[157] Alexander Nequam, a secular master at Oxford before he joined the Augustinian Canons at Cirencester, was the author of an influential treatise on preaching, and this suggests that he had exercised that office. Nequam praised his colleague Master Philip of Oxford, probably the author of a Crusade-preaching guide laced with sacramental and pastoral theology, as a fine theological teacher and a pastorally sensitive public preacher.[158] Both of these men predated the friars, who also both studied and preached. Oxford was the first city in England with houses of both Franciscan and Dominican friars. As both orders recruited learned men and put some of them to pastoral work, the friars had the intellectual resources to digest and apply major works on pastoral care, giving to the local laity the first-fruits of scholastic and mendicant pastoral care. From the 1220s and 1230s, therefore, Oxonians appear to have had some of the most theologically advanced, state-of-the-*ars artium* pastoral care on offer anywhere in the British Isles. Since Oxford was a major town which attracted many people for many purposes, even preaching within the town allowed the friars a widespread pastorate proportional to the origins of the travellers who attended their sermons or received other pastoral care from them.[159] Long after the Dominicans and Franciscans established

---

[153] British Library, Add. Ch. 21888.
[154] *Fasti Lincoln*, 25–47; *BRUO* as cited there. The archdeaconries without known Oxford men at the helm were Northampton and Stow.
[155] E.g. *BRUO*, 1625–26.   [156] Little and Douie, 'Sermons of Jordan of Saxony'.
[157] Bériou, *L'Avènement*.
[158] Both men were active in the 1210s. Cole, *Preaching of the Crusades*, 110–11.
[159] J. I. Catto, 'Citizens, Scholars and Masters', in Catto, ed., *Oxford Schools*, 151–92.

a foothold in Oxford, they were joined by the Carmelites (1256),[160] the Friars of the Sack (ca. 1261),[161] and the Austin Friars (1266).[162] The Friars of the Sack had the right to preach to the laity and hear their confessions until the Second Council of Lyons proscribed the order in 1274.[163] The Carmelites and Austins administered pastoral care in Oxford as well.[164]

Parish clergy would also have attended the friars' sermons and absorbed ideas about preaching and theology from them.[165] Some local parish clergy may have received a pastorally oriented education in the friars' schools.[166] Relationships between friars and seculars were occasionally acrimonious but they could also be friendly or even fraternal. The Oxford Franciscan Adam Marsh was not only a confidant of Grosseteste's: he was probably the brother of the Oxford theologian and archdeacon Master Robert Marsh and was also close to Robert's predecessors as archdeacon, John of St Giles and Master Richard Gravesend (later dean and then bishop of Lincoln).[167] Such cordial associations and family relationships between friars and seculars at the higher level may well have had many equivalents among the lower clergy.

Very few parishes in thirteenth-century England were served pastorally by priests with full masters' degrees, though we have recently encountered Master Sylvester of Cornwall serving St Michael Northgate, Oxford, from 1223. Starting in the 1260s, however, there is a sudden surge in the recorded institutions of *magistri* to rectories and vicarages in the archdeaconry of Oxford. With rectories, which are the lion's share of these, it can be difficult to tell whether the presentee spent much time exercising the care of souls: often he simply had a vicar. There are indications of residence in some cases, however. From the early 1260s we find *magistri* being instituted to Oxford parishes, some of which reported incomes too small to support vicars.[168] University scholars, it seems, were taking on pastoral jobs to augment their income while they taught or studied. They may have internalised the Parisian university ethos of preaching and scholarship going hand in hand, perhaps by listening to university sermons, often delivered by mendicant scholars.[169] We do not know whether masters of arts read and digested the latest handbooks on preaching and confession; but at least they could not plead lack of education.

[160] Egan, 'Carmelite Houses', 79. [161] *MRH*, 247 [162] *MRH*, 243.
[163] *DEC*, 326–27. [164] *Epist. Pecham* I, 99–100, dated 28 Feb. 1280.
[165] Moorman, *Church Life*, 79. Jordan of Saxony certainly expected his Oxford sermon to have this effect.
[166] Reeves, 'Secular Clergy in Dominican Schools'; Mulchahey, *First the Bow*, 50–51.
[167] *Fasti* Lincoln, 37; *LAM*, 94–99, 184–91, 198–201, 206–15, 248–51.
[168] Assuming that the minimum value of five marks for a vicarage was observed: *C&S* II, 112.
[169] Bériou, *L'Avènement*; d'Avray, *Preaching*, 187; Mulchahey, *First the Bow*.

The institution rolls of Gravesend and Sutton include in almost every instance the name of the previous incumbent and by what means he vacated his benefice. This allows us to piece together the service of individual churches over a long period, even if imperfectly because the institution rolls for Oxford from 1253–58 and 1280–89 are lost. Nonetheless, we can see that numerous Oxford parishes were held for long periods, and some presumably served, by masters. Master Robert Maynard was vicar of St Mary Magdalene from December 1268. He was certainly a priest by 1274.[170] He had not been replaced before the record breaks off in 1279, so presumably he was still serving at that time, though he had become an Augustinian Canon of Oseney by 1281.[171] Master Hugh of Lincoln became rector of St Aldate in 1271 and held the benefice until his death in 1299.[172] Master Thomas de Stamford resigned the vicarage of St Giles in 1274 after an unknown tenure.[173] Master Robert de Fletham, instituted to St Mary's, Oxford, in 1275, became Doctor of Theology sometime before 1284; he was still rector in 1285.[174] His rectory apparently helped to finance his studies in theology, which may have been repaid at least with the occasional sermon to his parishioners and perhaps much more. One of his predecessors, Peter de Kyllum, is not known to have been a graduate but, when he was presented by the crown to St Mary's in 1248, Adam Marsh commended him to Grosseteste in the strongest terms as being 'fit for the ministry of salvation ... in a place frequented by such a great concourse of people and clergy'.[175] Four years later, Marsh referred to a meeting with Master John le Gracius at Oxford in which the latter refused 'to resign the cure of souls that he has undertaken' while he continued his studies in canon and civil law.[176] Marsh and Grosseteste both considered rectories and even cathedral prebends to have responsibility for the care of souls, even if a vicar served the parish, insofar as they were responsible for supervising the vicar, so we need not construe 'cure of souls' here in the strict canon law sense; and the benefice in question has not been identified. If, however, Marsh did mean 'cure of souls' in the narrower sense of a vicarage or a rectory without a vicarage and Master John was the primary pastor of the church, it was presumably near Oxford. Otherwise, Grosseteste could have deprived him for non-residence.

There are further instances of masters being appointed to serve parish churches. Master William of Winchester was instituted to All Saints',

[170] *Rot. Gravesend*, 221, 250, 252, 225.   [171] *BRUO*, 1250.

[172] *Rot. Gravesend*, 223; *Reg. Sutton* VIII, 202.

[173] *Rot. Gravesend*, 225. The institution rolls are imperfect, but there is no entry for St Giles before this time in Gravesend's episcopate, so Thomas may have served there since before 1259.

[174] *BRUO*, 701.   [175] *LAM*, 26–29, 252–57.   [176] *LAM*, 62–63.

215

Oxford, in 1249; Master Richard de Staunford received the church in 1263; the church was commended to Master William de Dunham in 1269, probably on Richard's death or resignation; and William held it until his death in 1290.[177] When Master William's mortal illness in 1290 rendered him incapable of pastoral work in All Saints' parish, Sutton appointed as his coadjutor the rector of St Michael Northgate. The terms of the appointment suggest that Master William had been seeing to his spiritual charge personally.[178] As All Saints' was not a wealthy parish, all three of these graduate vicars probably served in person.[179]

At St Peter-in-the-East, Master Henry de Stanton, vicar from 1261 to 1274, was a doctor of canon law by 1265 and after his tenure as vicar would become Chancellor of the University. In 1271–72, while still vicar, he also served as an official in the Court of Canterbury.[180] Clearly he was not resident all the time; the archbishop may have issued a dispensation for non-residence to him to be able to make use of his services. This was Oxford's wealthiest benefice and its vicarage was probably sufficient to be treated as a rectory, with Henry taking an income and paying chaplains to do pastoral work. However, provincial canons and Grosseteste's statutes forbade such practices and, in the absence of a long-term dispensation, he probably delivered at least intermittent pastoral service in his vicarage.[181] The rectory was appropriated to Merton College in 1294 after which the vicars were mostly fellows of the College, who would be locally resident.[182] The extramural church of St Cross, just northeast of Oxford, was a dependent chapel of St Peter-in-the-East, and Merton may have kept more funds 'in house' by employing their own fellows as chaplains there as well. Merton also acquired the manor and advowson of the rectory of Cuxham, twelve miles south-east of Oxford, late in the century, and appointed a long succession of former fellows of the college, beginning with the priest Master Adam of Watlyngton (first occ. 1295).[183] There are a few other mentions of masters as rural vicars in the archdeaconry of Oxford but the concentration on the urban and suburban parishes is pronounced.[184] Of the sixteen parish churches in or near Oxford, only five are not recorded to have been held or served by *magistri* in the thirteenth century; and, given the incompleteness of the

---

[177] Hoskin, *Grosseteste*, no. 1150 (=*Rot. Grosseteste*, 493); *Rot. Gravesend*, 216, 221; *Reg. Sutton* VIII, 172.
[178] *Reg. Sutton* III, 1.   [179] *VCH* Oxford IV, 370.   [180] *Rot. Gravesend*, 214–15, 225.
[181] *C&S* II, 112, 249, 273. No papal dispensation appears in *CPL*.   [182] *VCH* Oxford IV, 399.
[183] P. D. A. Harvey, *A Medieval Oxfordshire Village: Cuxham, 1240 to 1400* (Oxford, 1965), 152.
[184] Rural vicarages with masters include Cuddesdon (Hoskin, *Grosseteste*, no. 1148); Bampton (*Rot. Gravesend*, 214, 224; *Reg. Sutton* VIII, 189); Lewknor (*Rot. Gravesend*, 226); and Chipping Norton (ibid., 223).

records, some of those may have been.[185] Further, unbeneficed students in holy orders would be an obvious source of chaplains, liturgical assistants, chantry priests and guest preachers.[186] It is difficult to imagine anywhere else in England that could claim such a concentration of masters and scholars serving parish churches.[187]

It took more than education to make a good pastor and some historians have argued that highly educated clerics were 'hopelessly over-qualified' for parochial service.[188] This must be seen as situational rather than a general rule. Adam Marsh wrote to Grosseteste to caution him against instituting the young scholar Oliver Sutton (later bishop of Lincoln) to a parish benefice, saying that he was entirely unsuited to the task.[189] It is certainly true that many clerics who pursued university studies did so in hopes of attaining a higher office, a cathedral canonry or an archdeaconry or at least a sinecure rectory.[190] They may have been disappointed to find themselves in backwater benefices. But there are plenty of counterexamples, including the two *magistri* whom Marsh strongly recommended for parochial service.[191] Nor were all parish communities the same, as Marsh indicated when supporting a candidate for institution in Oxford.[192] Scholars who were not members of regular orders were still considered parishioners, and even when private college chapels were established, they were expected to attend their Oxford parish churches.[193] Parish churches in Paris saw regular visits by scholars to preach to mixed audiences of clergy and laity, and there is no obvious reason why Oxford would have been different.[194] The surviving Oxford university sermons of 1291–93 have never been studied in depth because the palaeography of the manuscript is exceptionally difficult, but a determined student might find that they too bear witness to mixed audiences.[195] An educated priest who did not much care for a remote vicarage might find in Oxford just the kind of enlightened congregation appropriate to his

[185] Counting as extramural churches St Budoc, St Mary Magdalene and St Clement. Those to whom no master is known to have been presented are St George-in-the-Bailey, St Martin, St Edward (too poor to be served at all in the late thirteenth century), St Frideswide and St Budoc. The vicars of St Thomas outside Oseney Abbey, appointed directly by the abbot, were not enrolled in diocesan records, so it is not counted here.
[186] Little, *Papers*, 64; Bériou, *L'Avènement*.
[187] Cambridge is less well documented, as there are no Ely bishops' registers from the period, but Cambridge had no theology faculty until late in the century: Little, *Papers*, 122–43.
[188] Hoskin, *Grosseteste*, lxx.   [189] *LAM*, 34–37.   [190] See above, pp. 51–52.
[191] *LAM*, 562–63.   [192] *LAM*, 26–29, 252–57.
[193] *Reg. Sutton* III, l–li; IV, 83–85, 94–95, 97, 132–33.
[194] Bériou, *L'Avènement*; and for the next century, C. Burgher, 'Preaching for Members of the University in Latin, for Parishioners in French: Jean Gerson (1363–1429)', in R. Andersson, ed., *Constructing the Medieval Sermon* (Turnhout, 2007), 207–20.
[195] B. Smalley, *Studies in Medieval Thought and Learning* (London, 1981), 183–203.

talents, a congregation in which an uneducated priest would hardly be suitable.

Oxford parish churches were sometimes not served at all for a period of time and the parishioners presumably resorted to other parish churches. When the poor and long vacant church of St Edward was united with the neighbouring parish of St Frideswide in 1298, it was doubtless a recognition of the existing practice of the two parishes, both under the patronage of St Frideswide's Priory, acting as one: for parishioners of St Edward's, the mother church next door would be the obvious place to go. St Budoc's parish was diminished by the growth of the precincts of the Dominicans and the Friars of the Sack. The resultant loss of tithes and parishioners led to its closure in 1265. The church itself became the chapel of the Friars of the Sack and the parish was divided among St Ebbe, St Peter-le-Bailey and St Thomas.[196] The mendicant churches, especially of the Franciscans[197] and Dominicans,[198] could hold large congregations by the later thirteenth century; the temporary or permanent closure of one's own parish church may have encouraged many of the laity to resort to them as parish churches, changing their expectations of the style and form of the liturgy, the level of preaching and the subtlety of moral distinction in hearing confessions. Attending another parish church served by a master could have had similar effects. Between friars, canons, scholars and parsons, churches filled and churches vacant, the laity in thirteenth-century Oxford were offered a shifting hodgepodge of pastoral care quite different from that in the countryside and probably without close parallel anywhere else in England. Even within the town, pastoral care had a topography. The Franciscans and Dominicans living in the southern suburbs and the Carmelites and the Austins to the north may have attracted adherents from their respective neighbourhoods.

The great numbers of friars in Oxford cannot all have been pastorally useful in the town. Many were students at the *studia generalia* but these were hosted by otherwise normal convents with pastorally active friars. The Oxford friars who were proposed for licences to hear confessions in 1300 were more numerous than those from any other convent in the record, twenty-two Franciscans and thirty-eight Dominicans.[199] The number of qualified preachers was doubtless greater still. By 1266 there were five friaries in Oxford and, at busy preaching seasons such as Lent

---

[196] *VCH* Oxford IV, 373.
[197] The size of the Franciscan church is not known: A. R. Martin, *Franciscan Architecture in England* (Manchester, 1937). However, the convent had about the same number of friars as the London convent in the later thirteenth and early fourteenth centuries (*MRH*, 226–27), and the London convent had a large nave: Kingsford, *Friars of London*, 38–39.
[198] *EEFP*, 1–16.   [199] Little, *Papers*, 231.

and Advent, many of their inhabitants, perhaps including lectors and students, went into the countryside.[200] Nonetheless, the laity living in the town and suburbs must have encountered friars and their pastoral care far more often than their country cousins.

By any measure, Lincoln in the thirteenth century was an extraordinary diocese. The extensive records created in the processes of governance and scholarship, and the prominence of many of its leading clergy, make the environs of Lincoln and Oxford attractive as case studies in pastoral care. Yet what makes them attractive now made them atypical then. This chapter has allowed us to glimpse what was possible but not necessarily to grasp what was normal. Determining which of these features was common across England, and which made Lincoln an outlier, can only be approached by comparison to other dioceses pursued in a similar way. This we shall now attempt.

[200] O'Carroll, *Studies*, 213–14; d'Avray, *Preaching*, 56, 210.

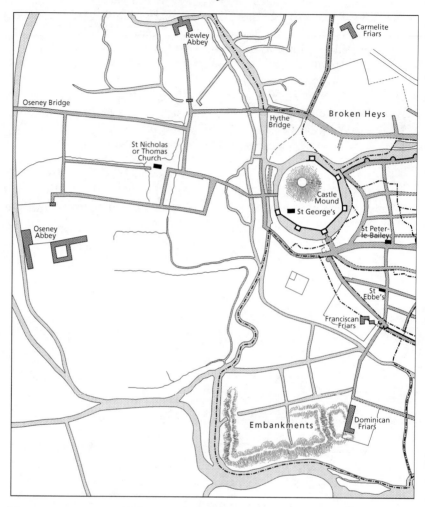

Map 3   Medieval Oxford. *Source:* A. Clark, ed., *Survey of the Antiquities of the City of Oxford, Composed in 1661–6, by Anthony Wood, vol. II: Churches and Religious Houses* (Oxford, 1890), opposite title page.

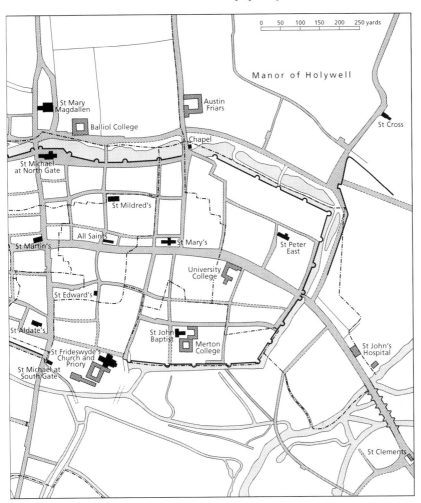

Map 3   (*cont.*)

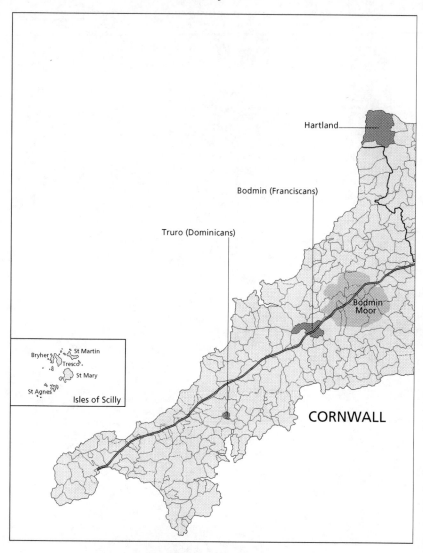

Map 4   The Diocese of Exeter. *Sources:* N. Orme, ed., *Unity and Variety: A History of the Church in Devon and Cornwall* (Exeter, 1991), 52; N. Orme, *The Saints of Cornwall* (Oxford, 2000), 55.

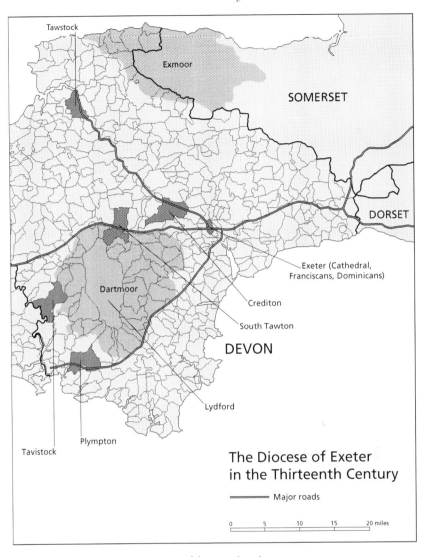

Tawstock

Exmoor

SOMERSET

DORSET

Exeter (Cathedral,
Franciscans, Dominicans)

Crediton

South Tawton

Dartmoor

DEVON

Lydford

Plympton

Tavistock

The Diocese of Exeter
in the Thirteenth Century

Major roads

| 0 | 5 | 10 | 15 | 20 miles |

Map 4   (*cont.*)

223

Chapter 11

THE DIOCESE OF EXETER

DIOCESAN ADMINISTRATION AND THE CARE OF SOULS

Although Exeter's records are fairly rich for the latter half of the century, its earlier thirteenth-century bishops have left nothing akin to the records left by their contemporaries in Lincoln. Bartholomew, bishop 1161–84, was one of the leading pastoral scholars in England in his day, compiling an influential penitential but his successors did not rise to this level of pastoral influence for perhaps a century.[1] The cathedral chapter did not even have a dean until 1225.[2] By itself, this fact may mean little for pastoral care but one such divergence from the main stream of development may reflect others that are not now visible to us. Henry Marshall, bishop 1194–1206, was a political appointee, though not careless in pastoral duties.[3] In most of his appropriations of parishes, he required the appropriator to make suitable provision for a chaplain or vicar.[4] He also consolidated the position of the vicars choral who maintained the cathedral liturgy.[5] Chroniclers mention him with little detail.[6] In 1207, King John commissioned Eugenius, bishop of Armagh, to act in the diocese *sede vacante*, but he had little opportunity to exercise episcopal functions before the interdict.[7] Once the interdict was lifted, Simon of Apulia, dean of York Minster, was elected bishop. His few surviving *acta* tell us nearly nothing with regard to pastoral care.[8] He attended the Fourth Lateran Council, but how far he executed its provisions in his administration is unknown.[9] Presumably he was involved in the division of the city of Exeter into parishes in 1222.[10] Chroniclers noted his death in 1223 with little comment.[11]

---

[1] A. Morey, *Bartholomew of Exeter, Bishop and Canonist* (Cambridge, 1937).
[2] Fasti *Exeter*, xviii.   [3] *EEA 11*, xliv–xlv; *Chron. Maj.* II, 407.   [4] *EEA 12*, 181–216a ff.
[5] Orme, 'Medieval Clergy I', 81.
[6] Having examined *Chron. Maj.*; *Annales Monastici*; Trivet, *Annales*; Matthew Paris, *Historia Anglorum*, ed. F. Madden (Rolls Series 44, 1866–69); and the 'Breve Chronicon Exoniense' in *Ordinale Exon.*, xix–xxiii.
[7] *EEA 11*, xlvi.   [8] *EEA 11*, xlvi–xlvii; *EEA 12*, 217–25.   [9] *C&S* II, 48.
[10] *Ordinale Exon.*, xxi.   [11] Chronicles as in note 6 above.

It is only with William Brewer, bishop 1224–44, that episcopal pastoral administration becomes more visible. Barlow has observed that 'the main qualification of the new bishop ... was that he was a nephew of the royal servant of the same name who had become very powerful in his native shire.'[12] Matthew Paris described him as 'remarkable in morals, lineage and knowledge', though since he gave no further details, these words may be mere filler.[13] Nonetheless, his surviving *acta* are more numerous than those of his two predecessors combined.[14] He reorganised the cathedral chapter and issued the first known statutes for his diocese.[15] By accompanying Peter des Roches, bishop of Winchester, on crusade from 1227 to 1231, he also drew chroniclers' attention.[16] Barlow argued that 'because of his absences his government [of the see] must have been lax and might be regarded as irresponsible.'[17] But a look at des Roches is instructive. Des Roches was on crusade for longer than Brewer was and his close association with the king's court also led to extended absences. Yet he set his diocese in order by appointing diligent administrators and, despite being the quintessential curial bishop, his diocese was effectively run.[18] There is reason to think that Brewer, though less well documented, did likewise.

Brewer set reforms in motion in the first few years of his episcopate, some of them apparently motivated by a desire to organise his affairs before leaving on crusade.[19] His diocesan statutes, probably issued before his departure, provided diocesan clergy with a significant pastoral treatise.[20] The statutes survive in one fragmentary copy. They show strong dependence on Richard Poore's recent Salisbury statutes but are not without independent pastoral attention. For instance, in Poore's statute ordering parish clergy to maintain peace among the laity, he wrote only of their own parishioners; Brewer's statutes expanded this to include peacemaking with people from other parishes.[21] Although the statutes are fragmentary, the borrowings that appear in other sets that show no independent use of Salisbury I enable a conjectural and partial reconstruction of what Brewer borrowed from Poore and how he adapted it. Powicke and Cheney noted some parallels between Salisbury I and Exeter II, issued by Bishop Quinel in 1287 (discussed below), but in no case are there grounds to argue that Quinel had Salisbury I before him as well as Exeter I; the

---

[12] *EEA 11*, xlvii.   [13] *Chron. Maj.* IV, 491.   [14] *EEA 12*, 226–315.

[15] *Fasti* Exeter, xviii; *C&S* II, 227–37; Cheney, *Synodalia*, 76–79.

[16] E.g. *Annales Monastici* I, 70, 73; II, 85, 303; III, 112.

[17] *EEA 11*, liii.   [18] Vincent, *Peter des Roches*.

[19] *EEA 11*, lxxii; K. Giles, 'Two English Bishops in the Holy Land', *Nottingham Medieval Studies* 31 (1987), 46–57.

[20] *EEA 11*, l. The absence of any debt to des Roches' 1224 Winchester Statutes (*C&S* II, 125–37) suggests they were written before Brewer spent several years in des Roches' company on crusade.

[21] *C&S* II, 64, 231; Cheney, *Synodalia*, 78.

Wells statutes (ca. 1258), Quinel's other main source, likewise appear to have borrowed directly from Exeter I but not Salisbury I.[22] Most textual content that is in both Salisbury I on the one hand and Wells or Exeter II on the other was probably also in the intermediary text, Exeter I.[23]

Notably absent from Exeter I are several of Poore's chapters relating to clerical discipline and tithes. The Exeter I fragment follows Poore's order loosely; this omission might mean that the chapters were merely relegated to a later (now lost) part of the text. There is, however, reason to doubt this. Both Wells and Exeter II omit the disciplinary chapters, which suggests that their source text, Exeter I, had omitted them as well. The pastoral material in the Exeter I fragment includes Poore's injunctions on teaching doctrine to the laity, his introductory chapter on the seven sacraments, most of his material on baptism and some of his material on penance. This includes Poore's injunction that laypeople should communicate at Christmas, Easter and Pentecost, preparing each time by confession, to which Brewer added that one may confess to another priest with permission of one's own priest.[24] We also learn from this chapter about the bishop's penitentiary, who dealt with major and notorious sins. The penitent was to be sent to the penitentiary with a letter explaining the case and its circumstances; he or she would then be sent back to his or her priest with a letter of absolution including the assigned penance. Anyone returning without such a letter, the statute ordered, is not to be trusted.[25] If Brewer's treatments of baptism and penance are representative of the rest of his statutes, we may assume that he reproduced much of Poore's homiletic material on the other sacraments as well. By considering Wells and Exeter II, we can suggest that Exeter I also included the following provisions: pregnant women approaching full term should be enjoined to confess; clergy are given the words for 'conditional baptism' for cases when it is uncertain whether someone was properly baptised; matrimony is to be commended; the laity should be enjoined to believe in transubstantiation of bread and wine; priests hearing confessions must not ask the names of others implicated in the penitent's sin.[26] Brewer also introduced the strictures of the Council of Oxford against clerical concubines and its requirements for sufficient liturgical books, vessels and vestments.[27] Whatever else Brewer's statutes contained, we may trust that they put a significant amount of pastoral instruction into the hands of parish clergy.

---

[22] *C&S* II, 586–626.

[23] The exception is where another set of statutes can be seen as the intermediary text, as for instance Salisbury II for Wells; yet this does not indicate that matter was not in Exeter I as well.

[24] *C&S* II, 228, 232–34, 236–37. The addition may have been prompted by the arrival of the friars.

[25] *C&S* II, 235–36.   [26] Ibid., 589–91, 596–97, 991–92.   [27] Ibid., 229–30, 232.

Richard Blund, who had served as cathedral chancellor since 1227 and as Brewer's official from an unknown date, was elected bishop early in 1245 and consecrated in October.[28] His few surviving *acta* include a modification of the competing jurisdictions of the cathedral chapter and the archdeacon of Exeter and the ordination of two vicarages.[29] While his administration is not well documented, his career had supplied him with first-hand knowledge of the diocese, its personnel and its administrative structures. His election had apparently proceeded with minimal royal interference, which may indicate that his demonstrated administrative capacities were the chapter's primary motive for electing him.[30] Matthew Paris, noting his death in 1257, called him 'a man without controversy, commendable in morals and all literature', though Paris may have been calling upon another stock phrase to conceal a lack of information.[31]

Walter Bronescombe, who, like Blund, had been Exeter Cathedral's chancellor, succeeded him in the episcopate. He was consecrated on 10 March 1258, less than three months after Blund's death.[32] Bronescombe's records show a capable ecclesiastical administrator at work. He had been archdeacon of Surrey since 1245 and was probably a Devon man.[33] Though a pluralist himself by papal licence, he did not permit unlicensed pluralism.[34] He declined to admit the notorious pluralist Bogo de Clare (already a canon of Exeter Cathedral) to a rectory in his diocese despite papal licence, perhaps because he 'thought Bogo's pluralism and non-residence beyond reason', an opinion generally shared by historians.[35] Through his archdeacons and other assistants, he had the diocese searched for abuses such as neglect of parochial duties. Their findings included the failure of the abbot of Hartland to supply a vicar and chaplains to the parish church of Hartland and its chapels as well as the closure of the parish church of Dotton by the monks of Dunkeswell who farmed the manor. The latter was discovered and settled at Bronescombe's personal visitation; he ordered the church to be restored, providing a monk or secular to celebrate divine service there.[36]

There are other mentions of episcopal visitation of parishes in the register, one of which refers to a visitation roll.[37] The roll does not survive

[28] *Fasti* Exeter, 5, 14.   [29] *EEA* 12, 320, 321, 327.   [30] Harvey, *Episcopal Appointments*, 71.
[31] *Chron. Maj.* IV, 491.   [32] *Fasti* Exeter, 5–6, 15.
[33] *Fasti* Monastic, 94; *Reg. Bronescombe*, xv.   [34] *Reg. Bronescombe*, xvi–xvii, 674, 1248–50.
[35] Ibid., 966, 1124–25 and n.; *Reg. Sutton* II, 3; *Epist. Pecham* I, 271–72; Thompson, 'Pluralism'; Hartridge, *Vicarages*, 155.
[36] *Reg. Bronescombe*, 1248–50, 335, 213. As one of the abuses corrected at Dotton was the removal of the font, if a monk did serve the church thereafter, he may have baptised and carried out other pastoral duties, though this is uncertain.
[37] Ibid., 127 (cf. 131), 1110; see also xxxiv.

but its existence would indicate systematic supervision of parochial life. Bronescombe also visited parishes to consecrate churches and altars in several extended tours in autumn 1259 and Lent 1269.[38] Other inspections, formal or informal, doubtless took place on these occasions, particularly since if these were declared official visitations, the bishop was entitled to procurations, cash payments due from churches to support the bishop and his household on visitation tours.[39] Bronescombe also ordained sixty-five vicarages in a geographically systematic fashion in August 1269. Though this was done from the bishop's manor, not on the road, he may have gathered information for it on the previous spring during his consecration tour.[40] Though Bronescombe perambulated his diocese, he could not cover it alone, something he clearly felt by 1278 when he wrote to his archdeacons, 'The burden of our office presses upon us with so heavy a weight that our care to remain with due diligence on watch both day and night scarcely suffices to lighten the pressure of so great a burden'.[41] Consequently, he took care in ordering the systems of visitation and administration through deputies. There is other evidence of his diligence in diocesan supervision. He issued the final settlement in a long-running dispute between the dean and chapter of the cathedral on the one hand, and the archdeacon of Exeter on the other, regarding jurisdiction over churches in the cathedral city and its suburbs and churches appropriated to the chapter. Oversight and discipline would have been difficult in these churches while it had remained unclear who had the right to exercise it. Cleaning house late in 1277 before the impending visitation of Archbishop Kilwardby, he ordered that the procurations of archdeacons and their assistants be kept within the limits laid down by Lateran IV, implying that they had been over-zealous collectors. He also ordered his archdeacons in February 1278 to search out parish clergy who were not sufficiently ordained, failing in their duties or unlicensed absentees or pluralists.[42]

Like many other bishops, Bronescombe was called away from his diocese frequently by the demands of royal service or ecclesiastical business. Preparing to leave his diocese in the first year of his episcopate, he issued letters empowering certain dignitaries of his cathedral, together with the dean of Wells, to carry out specific duties in the bishop's absence, including issuing letters dimissory to ordinands and admitting men to benefices worth up to ten marks.[43] He made similar provisions in 1273 '[s]o that the benefices which shall fall vacant while we are travelling overseas may

---

[38] Ibid., 138–205 *passim*, 731.   [39] On procurations, see Rodes, *Administration*, 137–38.
[40] *Reg. Bronescombe*, 734–43, 745–98. Several more were ordained in August 1270: ibid., 809, 813–16.
[41] Ibid., 1248–50, Robinson's translation.   [42] Ibid., 818–19, 1242, 1248–50.   [43] Ibid., 46.

not be deprived of pastoral care'. On this occasion he attended the Second Council of Lyons, which sat from May to July 1274.[44] Bronescombe was soon invoking that Council's thirteenth canon, which reaffirmed that clergy with care of souls who took too long to be ordained priests could be deprived.[45] This had already been a concern of his: barely a month after his consecration, he wrote to his archdeacons to cite all insufficiently ordained rectors and vicars to come to the cathedral two months hence to be ordained. He issued similar injunctions at least twice more.[46]

In December 1276, Bronescombe had collated Master Peter Quinel,[47] an Exeter man and archdeacon of St Davids, to a prebend in Exeter Cathedral.[48] Upon Bronescombe's death on 22 July 1280, Quinel was elected his successor and consecrated on 10 November. Once again the diocese spent little time without a consecrated bishop and received one with local knowledge and connections, to which (rather than any apparent royal interference) he owed his election.[49] He governed the see for the next eleven years. Quinel's register survives only in part, mostly confined to the years 1281–84, but this probably gives a representative sample of his activity. Licences for non-residence for study survive for the longer period from September 1281 to January 1288.[50] During this time Quinel granted twenty-nine licences to twenty-seven men, totalling forty-eight years of study.[51] Philip of Exeter, archdeacon of Barnstaple, was licensed to study theology for two years from September 1281, unless recalled sooner. This could benefit parish clergy whom he might teach in archidiaconal chapters and help him clarify theological matters in cases he heard in his consistory. However, Quinel did recall him earlier and had to admonish him because he did not respond with due haste; perhaps Philip's official, Master Ralph, rector of Hemyock, had been found wanting.[52] Quinel licensed Laurence, vicar of South Tawton, in March 1283 to come to Exeter to study because 'he desires to be more fully informed in Sacred Scripture', provided that he returned to his church at least once every fortnight, at important feasts and during the whole of Lent and Advent.[53] South Tawton is on the northern fringe of Dartmoor, seventeen miles west of Exeter by a direct road.[54] Laurence's parishioners may have found

[44] Ibid., 954, 976–82.   [45] Ibid., 1092 (cf. 1134); *DEC* 321–22.
[46] *Reg. Bronescombe*, xxx; 23, 30, 986, 1248–51; cf. 1200.
[47] Or 'Quinil'; often incorrectly 'Quivil' in older literature, hence *Reg. Quivil.*
[48] *Reg. Bronescombe*, 1211; Denton, 'Quinil'; *Fasti Wales*, 54; *Fasti Exeter*, 61.
[49] *Fasti Exeter*, 6; Harvey, *Episcopal Appointments*, 71. Quinel had, for example, made donations to Canonsleigh Priory in Devon in 1264, where his brother was a canon: London, ed., *Canonsleigh Cartulary*, nos. 192–93.
[50] *Reg. Quivil*, 327, 375.   [51] Ibid., 313–82ff.   [52] Ibid., 327.   [53] Ibid., 375.
[54] Now the A30, this is the road on Map 4 that runs directly west from Exeter.

their care of souls temporarily impeded in some respects, such as visitation of the sick and regular liturgical functions – no provision seems to have been made for a chaplain, though this may suggest that he had one already – but his sermons and confessions ought to have improved.

Quinel continued Bronescombe's policies of enforcing residence and sufficient ordination, ordaining vicarages and visiting parishes, and he similarly delegated authority to induct presentees to parish churches in his absence.[55] But Denton's statement that he 'continued the work of previous bishops rather than making significant new departures' is puzzling.[56] Significant departures were certainly made in Quinel's statutes of 1287 (Exeter II), which, when taken together with the appended treatise on confession, were the longest statutes known to have been issued by any English bishop in the thirteenth century, exceeding ninety pages in print.[57] Although Quinel's work was heavily indebted to the Wells statutes of ca 1258 and drew on numerous other sets, including the Exeter I statutes discussed above, much original work was done in bringing in further points of canon law, including the more recent provincial councils.[58]

Quinel's statutes begin with the trope of Christ as the physician of the soul and the sacraments as the medicines for the wounds of sin.[59] The first chapter is on the sacraments in general and the next seven chapters address the sacraments individually.[60] The longest of these concerns the legally complex subject of matrimony.[61] Only slightly shorter is the chapter on penance, which includes the thrice-yearly requirement of confession, as well as instructions from the statutes of Wells and Exeter I, such as hearing women's confessions in a visible place and not asking the names of others involved in a sin being confessed.[62] The office of bishop's penitentiary, mentioned here, had been envisioned in Brewer's statutes, but the office may have lapsed, as we see Quinel handling a case in person in 1283; it had been re-established with the newly endowed joint office of penitentiary and cathedral subdean in 1284.[63] Establishing or re-establishing a dedicated official in the diocesan administration would make penance for reserved cases – sins that could be absolved by the bishop or his deputy alone – more efficient. Local penitentiaries who heard clerical confessions

---

[55] *Reg. Quivil*, 316, 337–38, 363, 365–67, 369–72, 381. His absences seem to have been few: Denton, 'Quinil'.

[56] Denton, 'Quinil'.

[57] *C&S* II: discussion, 982–84; statutes (cited as 'Exeter II' with editorial chapter number), 984–1059; *summula*, 1059–77.

[58] *C&S* II, 984. [59] Exeter II, prologue. [60] Exeter II, 1–8. [61] Exeter II, 7.

[62] Exeter II, 5; cf. *C&S* II, 73 (Salisbury I, 40), which we may assume was included in Exeter I.

[63] *C&S* II, 235–36; *Reg. Quivil*, 314, 324–25; *Fasti* Exeter, 79; Edwards, *Secular Cathedrals*, 154–55.

were also encouraged to seek the judgement of the bishop's penitentiary in cases of doubt. These local penitentiaries, moreover, were to be
selected on the basis of knowledge and merit. Thus, serious or complex
penitential cases were to be referred up a hierarchy of specialists, enabling
greater standardisation of the penances assigned. If part of clerical education in hearing confessions was having one's own confession heard,
this system formed a hierarchy dedicated to penance which could diffuse
such specialist knowledge to practising priests in the most concrete of
forms.

Quinel also provided direct literary instruction in the art of shriving,
by appending a *summula* on confession to his statutes. This work, originally written by Walter Cantilupe, bishop of Worcester, to accompany
his own statutes of 1240, occupies fifteen pages in the modern edition;
combined with the chapter on confession in the statutes (another four
pages), Exeter's parish priests had more instructional material put into
their hands by their bishop in this form than any other English diocesan clergy of whom we know.[64] Perhaps reflecting his experience as an
archdeacon, Quinel added:

Let this tractate be had in each church or separate parish under penalty of one
mark due to the archdeacon of the place, or less or more according to the ability of the ignorant priests [to pay], which we commit to the judgement of the
archdeacon, in peril of his soul, reserving to ourselves the power of punishing
the archdeacon if he should be found negligent.[65]

Four questions can be said to concern any attempt to reconstruct the
realities of pastoral care using prescriptive texts: dissemination, comprehension, interpretation and implementation. In addition to the encouragement for textual dissemination given by Quinel's cautionary clause,
we have the records of the visitations of parish churches fourteen years
later, in 1301, which will be discussed further at the end of this chapter. Of
the fifteen parishes whose records were printed by Hingeston-Randolph,
at least five had copies of the statutes, and this may have included the
summula.[66] This is far from universal dissemination but it gives us concrete evidence of textual circulation. Since the visitations were apparently
made using the detailed directions for them given in Quinel's statutes,

[64] J. Goering and D. Taylor, 'The Summulae of Bishops Walter de Cantilupe and Peter Quinel',
Speculum 67 (1992), 576–94; *C&S* II, 1059–77.

[65] *C&S* II, 1077; cf. Exeter II, 20 *in fine*.

[66] Whitley, 'Visitations', 451–63; J. L. Shaw, 'The Parishes of Devonshire and Cornwall, 1301–1333, as
seen in the Exeter Visitations' (unpubl. BA thesis, Univ. of Wisconsin, 1899). There may have been
more copies: the record for Winkleigh seems incomplete, and that of Upottery records nothing
except that the antiphoner needed correction.

we may surmise that the vicars or rectors lacking these texts were fined, learned their costly lesson and acquired copies quickly.[67]

Comprehension raises the question of literacy. Quinel required his archdeacons to search out insufficiently lettered parish clergy and denounce them to him so that, if found incompetent, they might be summarily suspended.[68] Parish clergy were to be examined as to whether they knew the Decalogue and seven sins well enough to expound them diligently to the laity, as well as whether they had sufficient knowledge of how to confer the sacraments and at least a simple understanding of the articles of faith in the Athanasian, Apostles' and Nicene Creeds, in which they were also to instruct the laity. This list is similar but not identical to that given in Pecham's *Ignorantia sacerdotum* six years earlier: Pecham had not required the Athanasian Creed and had merged the Nicene and Apostles' Creeds into a list of fourteen points. Pecham also listed the two commandments of the Gospel (love of God and of neighbour), the seven works of mercy and the seven cardinal virtues as required preaching topics, none of which appears in Quinel's statute. Priests who had Quinel's statutes but not Pecham's canons would only have been following part of Pecham's preaching syllabus. Quinel referred the reader to the attached *summula* for instruction on the Decalogue and the seven sins and to his foregoing chapters on the sacraments, while the penultimate chapter of the *summula* expounds the articles of faith.[69] These supplied the priest with some of the catechetical material he might need: to obey the statutes, he could preach directly from the statutes. Quinel further required clergy entering the diocese, before they could minister, to be examined on their orders, literacy, behaviour and manners, by himself or the relevant archdeacon.[70] This presumably parallels his ordination examinations. Although clergy were not to be ordained without title, such as a vicarage, nonetheless they were forbidden to undertake the care of souls in the first year after ordination, unless required to by virtue of a vicarage or rectory.[71] This suggests that unbeneficed chaplains had to serve an apprenticeship directly under their vicar or rector before being entrusted with a chapel or with the whole parish in the senior priest's absence. Finally, Quinel attempted to revive the practice of churches supporting a young clerk as holy-water bearer, enabling him to pursue studies in the schools.[72]

As for interpretation and implementation, Quinel ordered that each parish priest should not only have a written copy of the statutes (which

---

[67] Exeter II, 40.   [68] *C&S* II, 609–10 (Wells); Exeter II, 20.
[69] *C&S* II, 1062–69, 1076.   [70] Exeter II, 8.
[71] Exeter II, 8, 36.   [72] Exeter II, 29; cf. *C&S* II, 174, 309, 606, 713.

could be checked at the synod) but also 'should soundly understand the same and use it' before the next Michaelmas under the heavy penalty of one mark paid to his archdeacon.[73] This indicates examination by diocesan officials, which would discover not only ignorance but also misinterpretation. Whether the treatise was used in practice could not be so readily ascertained, though it might be asked after at visitations.[74] The archdeacons had a strong incentive to be thorough in their inquiries: they pocketed the fines.[75]

Quinel also included provisions regarding liturgy in the parish church. He provided a detailed list of the vessels, vestments and books that each church was required to have, again including the statutes and *summula*, before the next Michaelmas.[76] He listed forty-three feasts that he ordered to be celebrated, including that of the patronal saint of the church and the anniversary of its dedication.[77] Further endorsing patronal cults, he directed that each parish church should have a statute of the Virgin and one of the patron saint.[78] Quinel exhorted his clergy to diligence in saying and singing the offices by night and day and ordered that they 'diligently admonish and effectively induce their parishioners' to frequent the church on Sundays and feast days.[79] The injunction of Salisbury I (and apparently Exeter I) to teach about transubstantiation was repeated.[80] Quinel encouraged parishioners to donate alms for candles to burn on the altar by granting an indulgence of fifteen days' enjoined penance.[81] He noted that people bowed at the elevation, and ordered priests to instruct them to kneel as well while bells were rung to excite devotion.[82] Despite Pecham's injunction in the recent Council of Lambeth that the chalice must not be given to the laity, Quinel retained the language of Richard Poore, probably copied by Exeter I, indicating that the laity were still to be given the chalice.[83] Although the liturgical use of Exeter is not mentioned as such in the statutes, our earliest glimpse of it comes from Quinel's register. In a paragraph among entries dating to 1285, an insertion between the *Pax* and the *Agnus Dei* at high mass is given; this would extend the time between transubstantiation and fraction.[84] The priest and clerk were to prostrate themselves and recite Psalm 122 (123) with the *Gloria Patri*, followed by the *Kyrie* and *Pater noster*; then come responses from the petitions of the *Te Deum laudamus*

---

[73] Exeter II, 20.   [74] E.g. Whitley, 'Visitations', 451.   [75] *C&S* II, 1077.   [76] Exeter II, 12.
[77] Exeter II, 23.   [78] Exeter II, 12.   [79] Exeter II, 21–22; cf. *C&S* II, 77–78.
[80] Exeter II, 4.   [81] Exeter II, 4.
[82] Sanctus bells were found at some of the churches visited in 1281: Exeter Cathedral, Dean and Chapter MS. 3672 (a).
[83] *C&S* II, 894–95; cp. Exeter II, 4 *in fine*; *C&S* II, 78.
[84] *Reg. Quivil*, 326. See also pp. 124–25 above.

and finally a prayer for the king. Whether this was an innovation or a codification of existing practice cannot be known.[85]

Quinel's register shows him enforcing the provision of Pecham's Council of Lambeth of 1281 that rectors or vicars licensed for temporary non-residence must make extra monetary provision for the poor of their parishes.[86] Quinel interpreted the poor to include the Franciscans and Dominicans, each of whom received a third of the required provision.[87] His register includes an *inspeximus* of a 1281 letter sent to him by Pecham, itself an *inspeximus* of a 1265 bull of Clement IV confirming the privileges of the Friars Minor to preach, hear confessions and assign penances with episcopal or papal licence, notwithstanding any objections from lower clergy.[88] Quinel gave such authorisation coequally to Preachers and Minors in his statutes, ordering that they be admitted for pastoral purposes and treated well throughout the diocese.[89] Although the bull *Ad fructus uberes* (1281) rendered such episcopal licence unnecessary in theory, its enforcement often depended on the bishop in practice.

These are only some of the more salient points of Quinel's statutes and administration. While Quinel did affirm previous trends in pastoral care in the diocese, the sheer volume of pastoral material he put into the hands of parish clergy, and the forceful way that he did so, surely constituted a major departure by itself in the quantity and manner of textual clerical education for the care of Devonian and Cornish souls. The extant administrative records of the bishopric in the rest of the century are meagre, making it difficult to know how effectively Quinel's precepts were enforced after his death. Not only have Quinel's later records perished: the register of his successor, Thomas de Bitton, bishop 1291–1307, is also lost.[90]

THE LANDSCAPE OF PASTORAL CARE

Exeter Diocese, nearly coterminous with the counties of Devon and Cornwall, had some 583 parishes in four archdeaconries: Devon comprised those of Exeter, Totnes and Barnstaple, while that of Cornwall covered its eponymous county. Barlow suggests that the distribution of rural deaneries, 'nine in Exeter, six in Barnstaple, nine in Totnes, and seven in Cornwall ... probably fairly represent the density of settlement in the

[85] On Exeter liturgy, see Graves, *Form and Fabric*, 113–50.   [86] *C&S* II, 907–8.
[87] *Reg. Quivil*, 313, 321 (*bis*): presumably the Exeter convents.
[88] *Reg. Quivil*, 328.   [89] Exeter II, 5 *in fine*.
[90] Some collected material is in *Reg. Quivil*, 390–437 and G. Oliver, *Lives of the Bishops of Exeter* (Exeter, 1861), 52–54.

several areas.[91] Cornwall thus had 22.6 per cent of the deaneries; with 174 parishes it had 30 per cent of those in the diocese;[92] and Cornwall covered 34.25 per cent of the land in diocese.[93] Cornish parishes were thus, on average, 22.4 per cent larger than those in Devon, a fact that suggests that the statistically average Cornishman found his parish church slightly less accessible.

In practice, however, disparities in rural parish size and convenience of access are less a matter of counties and statistics and more a result of history and topography. History had its hand in the endurance of great minster parishes, particularly Hartland, Tiverton, Crediton and Plympton.[94] The largest of these four was Hartland, covering 17,900 acres, or thirty square miles.[95] The secular collegiate church that had once been its minster was re-founded under the Rule of St Augustine as an Arroasian house in the 1160s, leaving the territory to a parish church.[96] Tiverton, also known as Twyford, was nearly as large, at 16,790 acres.[97] Crediton, just north of Exeter, exceeded twelve thousand acres, supporting a collegiate church with twelve (usually absent) canons and their respective dozen vicars choral, one of whom acted as parochial vicar. As the former cathedral of the diocese, it remained an episcopal peculiar.[98] Plympton, just east of Plymouth, covered over ten thousand acres. Its major church, once a secular collegiate minster, was re-founded as a priory of Augustinian Canons in 1121. The parish church of St Mary was appropriated to the canons, who also appointed the vicar. The fact that it was the priory's most profitable church by far suggests a large population. Plympton Priory also had the advowson of the parish of Plymouth and appointed the dean of the rural deanery.[99] Though the taxation of 1291 records no chapels-of-ease for any of these four, Crediton had at least two by 1254; Hartland had several by 1261 and would have eleven by the sixteenth century.[100] Those attending the minster churches found 'a large church building and a more elaborate worship, [and] it brought to the town some learned and literate clerics'.[101] It is difficult to know whether laypeople

[91] *EEA* 11, xxx. [92] Orme, *Saints of Cornwall*, 46–49.
[93] According to Bartholomew, *Atlas*, 13, Cornwall was 868,220 statute acres, and Devon 1,667,154 statute acres. This comparison discounts Thorncombe (Dorset), a detached parish of Exeter Diocese, and Stockland (Devon), a detached parish of Salisbury Diocese, on the premise that they are of similar size.
[94] C. Holdsworth, 'From 1050 to 1307', in N. I. Orme, ed., *Unity and Variety: A History of the Church in Devon and Cornwall* (Exeter, 1991), 23–52, at 29.
[95] Hoskins, *Devon*, 405. [96] Hoskins, *Devon*, 406; *MRH*, 426, 158; *Reg. Quivil*, 463.
[97] W. White, *History, Gazetteer and Directory of Devonshire* (Sheffield, 1850), 305.
[98] Hoskins, *Devon*, 378; *MRH*, 424; Orme, 'Crediton'.
[99] *EEA* 11, 168; Hoskins, *Devon*, 462; Kemp, *Acta*, 44; Fizzard, *Plympton*, 249.
[100] *Reg. Quivil*, 454, 457, 463, 466; Orme, 'Crediton', 119; *Reg. Bronescombe*, 335.
[101] Orme, 'Crediton', 126.

living in distant parts of these parishes found that allure sufficient to walk or ride to church regularly: except for its eastern edge, Devon tended to have dispersed or partially nucleated rather than highly nucleated settlements, meaning that getting to the parish church was more onerous for some parishioners than for others.[102]

Physical geography influenced ecclesiastical life in multiple ways. The wealthier parts of England were generally south-east of a diagonal line running from the head of the Humber estuary to that of the Severn, or running from the Tees to the Exe, excluding the West Country peninsula. Even where farmland was highly productive, the cost of transportation to major markets discouraged intensive grain production in favour of wool.[103] The average value of land in Lincoln Diocese, and thus the tithes gathered per square mile, was three times as high as the average in Exeter.[104] Exeter's rural parishes were therefore bound to be larger, or poorer, or both. There were also topographical disparities within the diocese, particularly between moorland and heath on the one hand and fertile arable on the other. Some of the largest parishes were situated on the moors, where a larger area would be needed to support a parish church. Hartland, in addition to its past as a minster parish, comprised much of the moor and heath of the north-western peninsula of Devon.[105] Hartland and its neighbouring parishes on the Hartland Moors were characterised by watercourses cutting deep valleys that ended in waterfalls down coastal cliffs.[106] If there were no church or chapel in one's valley, travel to the nearest church would require climbing up over the ridge separating the valleys and down the other side. Dartmoor was sparsely inhabited, though it was not untouched by assarting; at least six settlements are first recorded in the early fourteenth century.[107] The diocese's only recorded complaint of geographical inaccessibility in the thirteenth century comes from Dartmoor, an area not well served by roads.[108] The inhabitants of the Dartmoor hamlets of Babeny and Pizwell had to travel eight miles in good weather and fifteen in bad, as an enquiry confirmed, to reach

---

[102] Ryder, *Devon*, 6–13; Hoskins, 'Agrarian Landscape'.   [103] Bailey, *Marginal Economy*, 21.
[104] Campbell and Bartley, *Eve of the Black Death*, maps 18.5, 18.6; C. Daniell, *Atlas of Medieval Britain* (London, 2008), 91; L. Cantor, ed., *The English Medieval Landscape* (Philadelphia, 1982), 21–22; B. M. S. Campbell, 'North-South Dichotomies, 1066–1550', in A. Baker and M. Billinge, eds, *Geographies of England: The North-South Divide, Real and Imagined* (Cambridge, 2004), 145–74; R. A. Donkin, 'Changes in the Early Middle Ages', in H. C. Darby, ed., *A New Historical Geography of England* (Cambridge, 1973), 75–135, at 78–79.
[105] Hoskins, 'Agrarian Landscape', 326.
[106] Ryder, *Devon*, 124; Bartholomew, *Atlas*, plate 68. Similar topography, implying similar challenges to mobility, may be found across the diocese: H. P. R. Finberg, *Tavistock Abbey* (New York, 1969), 29.
[107] Hoskins, 'Agrarian Landscape', 318–19; Newman, 'Tinworking', 124–25; Ryder, *Devon*, 14–15.
[108] Grundy, 'Ancient Highways'.

their parish church of Lydford, nor could they afford to build a chapel-of-ease.[109] Bishop Bronescombe therefore granted them permission in 1260 to attend the closer parish church at Widdecombe instead, except for an annual visit and oblation to Lydford on the feast of St Petrock, a Cornish saint popular throughout the diocese, to whom Lydford's church was dedicated.[110] For people making their living in remote locales without chapels-of-ease – in this case, probably by animal husbandry and tin extraction – those aspects of pastoral care that required ready access to the parish church, or parish priest, were not as adequately provided.[111] As Lydford parish was by far the largest in the diocese, covering some 56,000 acres (87.5 square miles), much of it rough moorland, the inhabitants of other new hamlets probably faced similar problems.[112] We learn something of Bronescombe's priorities from this compromise, in which he favoured pastoral necessity while respecting parochial rights. The terms of his decision also remind us of the importance of the saints' cults of parish churches in the geography of devotion.[113]

The city of Exeter exhibited marked pastoral contrasts not only with the countryside, as might be expected, but also with other cathedral cities. Although the *Breve Chronicon Exoniense* records that 'the boundaries of the parishes of the city of Exeter were fixed' in 1222, the city's churches remained, technically, mere chapels, for none had its own cemetery: the first funeral mass was obligatorily celebrated in the cathedral and all burials went to the cathedral graveyard, except occasional burials in religious houses.[114] This is doubtless why thirteenth-century records refer to them as *capellae* rather than *ecclesiae*.[115] The cathedral's burial monopoly affected lay relationships with the cathedral, including pastoral care in the form of prayers for the dead. Though Adam de Collecote simply bequeathed 'his body to holy burial' in 1269, his son Henry, who died in 1294, more specifically bequeathed 'my body to be buried in the cemetery of the Blessed Peter of Exeter, in the place where my father and mother rest'. Walter Gervas, a layman who died around 1258, similarly wished to be buried next to his father in the cathedral cemetery, 'wherever it shall

---

[109] *Reg. Bronescombe*, 292.   [110] Orme, *Saints of Cornwall*, 55.

[111] Newman, 'Tinworking'; M. Kowaleski, *Local Markets and Regional Trade in Medieval Exeter* (Cambridge, 1995), 17–18.

[112] Hoskins, *Devon*, 427; Hoskins, 'Agrarian Landscape', 294–95.

[113] Cornwall, in particular, had churches dedicated to many saints not commemorated elsewhere. The fact that the parish dedication so often became the common name for a place suggests that these local loyalties mattered but exactly what they meant to thirteenth-century laypeople is difficult to know. Orme, *Saints of Cornwall*; Orme, *Dedications*.

[114] *Ordinale Exon.*, xxi. Perhaps because they received no burial fees, some were barely solvent (*Reg. Quivil*, 451). See also Graves, *Form and Fabric*, 67.

[115] *EEA 12*, 190; *Reg. Bronescombe*, 818; *Reg. Quivil*, 451.

happen for me to die, and with my body I bequeath my horse by the name of "Proved Friend"'.[116] Exeter's urban churches, having no church-yards, had little room for expansion and rebuilding, so they tended to be cramped into odd shapes not always ideal for liturgical celebration.[117]

The profile of the cathedral liturgy was raised by contrast. Even by the end of the thirteenth century, as Sekules has noted, the cathedral had 'no relic so important and unique as to make Exeter a place of particu-lar pilgrimage'.[118] She suggests that the bishops from the late thirteenth century onwards, possibly beginning with Quinel, moved to invest the office of the bishop itself with the status of a saint's shrine and the liturgy of the canons and choir as a centre of liturgical devotion comparable to a saint's cultus.[119] The liturgy was partly visible from the north and south choir aisles, to which the laity were admitted.[120] Moreover, according to the *Ordinale Exon.*, the earliest extant revision of the Exeter Cathedral liturgy, the laity were to be asperged with holy water and given a ser-mon before high mass from Advent to Septuagesima, which would imply that they attended in some numbers.[121] While the *Ordinale* dates to 1337, Bishop Grandisson, who compiled it, was collating existing Exeter cus-toms with Sarum use. Earlier Exeter distinctives include the raising of the feast of the Archangel Gabriel to a level on par with Christmas and Easter and an unusually sophisticated use of music in liturgy, both aris-ing from Bronescombe's initiatives.[122] Similarly, although little is known about the earlier thirteenth-century art and architecture of the choir, the programme that culminated in the early fourteenth century was appar-ently conceived and begun before 1300. The building processes may have made the choir liturgy temporarily more visible during the rebuilding of the screens and, perhaps, temporary relocation of the canons and choir when scaffolding and building processes rendered the east wing of the church unusable.

The liturgy of Exeter Cathedral may have been effectively exported around the diocese through an export of personnel. The dean and chapter held the advowsons of many parish churches in the diocese; the cathedral also had a large body of literate clergy consisting of the vicars choral and various chaplains. Lists of these lower cathedral clergy

[116] Lepine and Orme, *Death and Memory*, 140, 143, 147; *Reg. Quivil*, 435–36.
[117] Graves, *Form and Fabric*, 67.
[118] Sekules, 'Furnishings', 174. There were other sites of pilgrimage in the diocese: N. I. Orme, 'Indulgences in the Diocese of Exeter, 1100–1536', *RTDA* 120 (1988), 15–32; N. I. Orme, 'Indul-gences in Medieval Cornwall', *Journal of the Royal Institution of Cornwall* n.s. 2 (1992), 149–70.
[119] Sekules, 'Furnishings'.   [120] Graves, *Form and Fabric*, 49–55.
[121] Graves, *Form and Fabric*, 71; *Ordinale Exon.*, 293–94.
[122] Sekules, 'Furnishings', 178. Also related was Bronescombe's 1277 injunction that a vicar choral must be replaced within thirty days of his death or resignation: Orme, 'Medieval Clergy I', 83.

survive from the fourteenth and fifteenth centuries, and they show them serving as a drawing-pool for presentation to cathedral benefices.[123] This was doubtless the case in the thirteenth century as well, especially given Bronescombe's injunction of 1270 that the dean and chapter must present him with a suitable candidate within one month of the vacancy of any church in their gift.[124] Subtracting the time for news to reach them and for them to contact the bishop, they would need qualified men ready at all times; few would be handier or more thoroughly vetted than their own minor clergy. Bishop Quinel attempted in 1281 to end the practice of vicars choral serving churches, yet in 1284 we find a vicar choral still doubling as vicar of Heavitree, a parish just east of Exeter and under capitular jurisdiction; he repeated his injunction in 1291, explicitly referring to city churches.[125] Presumably this indicates that some of the relatively poor city churches would only be served by a priest with another source of income. While some aspects of the Use of Exeter could not reasonably be imitated in parochial churches, others could, such as the inserted prayers from Quinel's register or the promotion of certain feasts such as that of Gabriel. The diffusion of minor cathedral clergy around the diocese would result in greater liturgical standardisation, skill and complexity.

Education in the cathedral city may have had a similar effect. The cathedral's song school is first mentioned in 1175, when it was taught by Master Raymund, a cathedral clerk.[126] Through most of the thirteenth century, the precentor had nominal oversight but in 1276 Elias de Cyrencestre, a vicar choral, was made the first formal succentor (precentor's deputy), with charge of the choristers' musical education.[127] This is the time when we see increasing complexity in the liturgical music.[128] Though some of the choristers became secondaries (minor clerks with changed voices but too young to become priests) and lifelong vicars choral, others may have taken their education and liturgical familiarity in other directions, leading them ultimately to parish altars. Grammar and theology seem also to have been taught at Exeter by 1200.[129] We have already met Laurence, vicar of South Tawton, licensed to come to Exeter to study scripture in 1283; a less detailed licence was given in the same year to the rector of Sydenham Damarel, just on the Devon side of the Cornish border, to study *in sacra pagina* (in Holy Writ) at Exeter for a year.[130] These coincide with Quinel's arrangement in that same year

---

[123] Orme, *Minor Clergy*, xix.   [124] *Reg. Bronescombe*, 819.
[125] Orme, 'Medieval Clergy I', 83–84.   [126] Orme, *West of England*, 45.
[127] Ibid., 43; Orme, *Minor Clergy*, 11, 13; *Reg. Bronescombe*, 1154.   [128] Sekules, 'Furnishings', 178.
[129] Orme, *West of England*, 52.   [130] *Reg. Quivil*, 375.

which established that henceforth all chancellors should teach theology or canon law in Exeter.[131] Moreover, clerical students may have been still more welcome than the laity to view and even participate in the cathedral liturgies, though there are no explicit arrangements for this. Clergy who lived close to or in the town could have resorted to the schools there much more readily without licences of non-residence and thus gone unrecorded. Nor was Exeter the only place of study. A school is mentioned in Plympton in 1263, and ca. 1276 the collegiate church of Penryn in Cornwall had choirboys and clerks (probably akin to secondaries) in addition to its canons and vicars choral.[132] Other schools or liturgical training centres doubtless existed but mention of them has not survived.

The Dominicans had settled in the cathedral city by 1232, the Franciscans by 1240.[133] There were thirty-four Franciscans and thirty-six Dominicans in 1297.[134] Seven surviving thirteenth-century Exeter wills record bequests to the friars of Exeter. Two gave unevenly: in 1263 the archdeacon of Totnes left more to the Franciscans than to the Dominicans and in 1290 a layman left his mortal remains and a substantial sum to the Franciscans, but nothing to the Dominicans. The other five, including a cathedral canon in 1244; laymen in 1258, 1267 and 1294; and a cathedral vicar choral in 1296, all left equal amounts to both convents.[135] In 1266, Roger de Thoriz, archdeacon of Exeter, bequeathed fourteen biblical and theological volumes – including part of the Sentences commentary of Alexander of Hales OFM, the Dominican biblical concordance and Hugh of St-Cher OP's postills on the Psalms – to the shared use of the Franciscans and Dominicans of Exeter.[136] When Bishop Quinel allowed non-residence for study and required payments to friars along with the parish poor, in each case the money was to be shared equally by the two orders, which implies that Quinel too esteemed them equally.[137] These bequests and payments suggest some sort of parity, whether in numbers, the local population's respect, or both.

Exeter was at the nexus of a network of roads that reached within twenty miles of every part of the diocese and within ten miles of most of it, allowing for easy travel for the friars. In 1301, parishioners of Colyton testified that

[131] Orme, *West of England*, 52–53.   [132] Ibid., 103, 167.   [133] *EEFP*, 106–7; *MRH*, 216, 225.
[134] Little and Easterling, *Franciscans and Dominicans*, 22; *MRH*, 216.
[135] Lepine and Orme, *Death and Memory*, 139–54.
[136] *Reg. Bronescombe* III, 58–59; Little and Easterling, *Franciscans and Dominicans*, 59; Humphreys, *Friars' Libraries*, 210–12.
[137] *Reg. Quivil*, 313, 321 (*bis*).

their vicar is an honest man, and he preaches to them so far as he knows, but not sufficiently in their eyes. They also say that his predecessors were accustomed to call friars to instruct them on the salvation of [their] souls; but he does not trouble to do so, and if they happen to come by he does not receive them … whence they request that he be corrected.[138]

Colyton is twenty miles east of Exeter along the road to Dorchester.[139] The friars' more advanced preaching techniques seem to have raised the parishioners' homiletic expectations: perhaps this vicar's sermons and catechesis would have been acceptable decades before. Their vicar, William, might not be blamed too harshly if he considered friars a disruptive and undermining influence.

Friars of both major orders could thus easily reach most locales, though some of the more remote moors and headlands may have been less frequently visited. A greater barrier would be language. There is no *a priori* reason to doubt a high degree of multilingualism along a linguistic frontier such as central Cornwall but focused recruitment and careful deployment would be required to reach Cornishmen more effectively. This may be why the Dominicans settled at Truro by 1259 and the Franciscans at Bodmin by 1260.[140] The port-town of Plymouth was settled by Carmelites between 1289 and 1296, the fifth and final friary established in the diocese before 1300.[141] By the century's end, only north Devon was particularly remote from mendicants, yet an Exeter Dominican 'was accused of openly disregarding an interdict which had been laid on the parish of Tawstock before 1302, and encouraging the secular priests to do likewise'.[142] Tawstock is just south of Barnstaple, over forty miles northwest of Exeter by a main road; one could scarcely go further from a thirteenth-century friary in the diocese.[143] This Friar Hamelyn OP may have been disruptive to ecclesiastical discipline but he could hardly have been guilty of disregarding an interdict without exercising pastoral office.

CONDITION OF THE DIOCESE, 1281–1301

Visitation records made by cathedral canons towards the end of the century give us a glimpse of parochial life in churches under the chapter's jurisdiction. While they represent a small minority of the diocese's parishes, these visitation records are the only ones to survive. They must be used with caution: the over-representation of cathedral jurisdictions among surviving visitation records is a problem across England before the

---

[138] *Reg. Stapledon*, 111.   [139] Hoskins, 'Agrarian Landscape', 298; Grundy, 'Ancient Highways', 158.
[140] *MRH*, 219, 223.   [141] *MRH*, 236.   [142] Little and Easterling, *Franciscans and Dominicans*, 40.
[143] The road running north-west from Exeter on Map 4 (now the A377).

fifteenth century. Archdeacons, responsible for visiting most parishes, did not normally preserve their records over the long term, and few survive today from this period.[144] This might signify little if there were no difference between cathedral peculiars and archdeaconry churches but this is not the case. Archdeacons received a significant part of their income from procurations and fines, which they could only collect when they visited the churches in their jurisdiction. Cathedral chapters were established corporations that were better at preserving records but also had many other concerns and there is reason to suspect that their appropriated churches often suffered from the tragedy of the commons. Both as a general principle and in the particular case of these visitations, we should expect that the average archdeaconry parish was visited and corrected more often and that these parishes, which were visited by cathedral clergy, represent worse-than-average levels of discipline.

The question of jurisdiction over some of these parishes had apparently been unsettled until 1270, when Bronescombe determined that the cathedral dean was to have archidiaconal jurisdiction in those churches in the diocese appropriated to the cathedral and that he would have the same jurisdiction over parishes in the cathedral city except when the archdeacon of Exeter was also a canon of the cathedral.[145] Two canons went on a visitation tour in 1281, covering seventeen parishes in Devon and eight in Cornwall. None of these was a prebendal church, with a particular cathedral canon as *ex officio* rector, as was the case in other secular cathedrals. Exeter's chapter gave equal stipends of £4 to all prebendaries from the common fund, to which these churches and other sources of revenue contributed.[146] Individual canons were thus not responsible for individual churches. Most of these parishes were peculiars of the Dean and Chapter, but three were under the authority of the archdeacons while either appropriated to the cathedral or owing it an annual pension.[147]

At some parishes, the visitors discovered problems that had been going on for years. At Colebrook, the jurors informed them that the vicar had taken a layman's wife, had kept her in remote places over the past four years and had sired four offspring by her. The vicar, they further complained, did not do the work of the church well or visit the sick of the parish: one imagines that he was visiting his illicit household instead.[148] At Ashburton, the vicar, two chaplains and a deacon were all commonly

[144] R. N. Swanson, '*Universis Christi Fidelibus*: The Church and Its Records', in R. Britnell, ed., *Pragmatic Literacy, East and West, 1200–1330* (Woodbridge, 1997), 147–64.
[145] *EEA 12*, 320; *Reg. Bronescombe*, 818–19.   [146] *Fasti* Exeter, xvii.
[147] Winkleigh, Harberton and Upottery, all in Devon: *Reg. Bronescombe*, 798 (cf. *EEA 12*, 257); *Reg. Bronescombe*, 841; *EEA 12*, 258, 298n.
[148] Exeter, Dean and Chapter MS. 3672(a), f. 6v.

suspected of unchastity – here the clergy and women are all named – and at least one of these unions had resulted in several children.[149] Clerical concubinage should not surprise us, but carrying on so boldly for so long suggests that oversight had been lax. Similarly, at Staverton, one Master John de Esse had carried off the good psalter five years before and had not returned it, while the lessee of the manor there had unlawfully alienated some of its property six years before.[150] Most of the churches had structural defects as well. At five churches, the chancel roof needed repair; at five, the chancel windows were variously inadequate; at five more, both roof and windows were faulty; at one, the tower was almost completely unroofed, exposing the bell frame to the weather. At Littleham-cum-Exmouth, in addition to its faulty chancel roof, one chancel wall was said to be nearly ruinous.[151] So much dilapidation and indiscipline could not have sprung up overnight, so this implies widespread neglect of visitation in these churches for a long time, apparently six years or more. Nonetheless, the liturgical books, ornaments and vestments catalogued at each parish were sufficient for performance of the liturgy in nearly every case.[152]

The chapter archives preserve another visitation record from 1301, comprising the visitations of fifteen parish churches and three dependent chapels, all in Devon, and mostly overlapping with the churches visited in 1281.[153] It is unclear whether there had been visitations since 1281. Clyst Honiton, which was perhaps the worst supplied of the churches in 1281 – it seems to have been missing most of the liturgical books, vestments and furnishings, and its church bells were hung in a live tree – was no better off in 1301, with the chancel now noted as dilapidated as well.[154] At St Mary Church, the vicar frequently absented himself for a week or two at a time to Moreton Hampstead, for reasons not recorded; in his absence the archdeacon's chaplain sometimes officiated. There were still leaky roofs and unglazed or broken windows. The vicar of Colebrook, who was suspected of incontinence, only said mass every other day and, while he expounded the Gospel each Sunday in his own way, he neglected to teach the articles of faith, Decalogue and seven sins.[155]

Whatever the chapter's frequency of visitations, however, not all was neglect and decay. At Harberton and Dawlish, the chancels had recently

---

[149] Ibid., f. 7r.   [150] Ibid., f. 7r–v.   [151] Ibid., f. 5r.

[152] This is Orme's observation of the lists for Cornish parishes: N. Orme, 'Visitations of Cornish Churches, 1281–1331', *Cornish Studies* 21 (2013), 76–103. The observation generally holds true for the Devon parishes in this manuscript as well.

[153] Exeter, Dean and Chapter MS. 3673; parts printed in *Reg. Stapledon*, 107–409, *passim*, and Whitley, 'Visitations'.

[154] Exeter, Dean and Chapter MS. 3672(a), f. 1r; *Reg. Stapledon*, 107; Whitley, 'Visitations', 461.

[155] *Reg. Stapledon*, 109–10; Whitley, 'Visitations', 451.

been rebuilt handsomely by the chapter, while St Mary Church and Salcombe Regis had liturgical books given by the chapter.[156] The record of 1301 also gives more details concerning the parochial clergy than the 1281 visitations. Despite the few complaints, what is most striking is the laity's high rate of reported approval. The only recorded fault of William, vicar of Culmstock, was delaying too long between matins and mass on feast days; otherwise, he was described as diligent in his pastoral duties and upright in his life.[157] At Colyton, the vicar kept a holy-water bearer in minor orders instead of the deacon his predecessors had supplied and he refused to admit friars to preach regardless of the laity's requests, but the other chaplains and clergy were said to live honestly and chastely.[158] If these clergy were typical of those in the diocese in 1301, decades of diligent diocesan oversight had provided parish clergy who, by and large, satisfied their parishioners' expectations, if not always their bishop's.

Exeter was thus quite a different diocese from Lincoln. Situated in the south-west, it had less fertile land with a much lower average value and its rural population lived in thinly dispersed rather than nucleated settlements.[159] Its cathedral nave did not host a parochial congregation, as Lincoln's and some others did, and it had no saint's tomb to draw pilgrims but it did exercise a burial monopoly over the city, positioning it unequivocally as the mother church. There is also evidence that its liturgy was more musically advanced than most, and that laypeople continued to receive the chalice in their parishes when it was ceasing to be the norm elsewhere. The chapter's apparent inattention to its appropriated churches would be hard to imagine under a Grosseteste or a Sutton, though Quinel's statutes and tract on confession gave his clergy extensive and detailed instruction in the care of souls. Friars, and presumably secular clergy as well, had to contend with a linguistic frontier and each friary was responsible for a much larger district than would be the case in Lincoln. However, we do find friars active many miles from their convents and their settlement in Cornwall indicates that they were active evangelisers there as well. The Carmelites only appeared near the end of the century, and the Austins did not arrive before 1330, so, whatever was distinctive about their pastoral impact, they had little effect here. As we turn to Carlisle Diocese, we shall see the church in another western and less wealthy region of the country but adapting in quite different ways, including a more prominent role for canons regular.

---

[156] *Reg. Stapledon*, 132–33, 337–38, 345; Whitley, 'Visitations', 452, 455, 457, 459; W. R. Brownlow, 'A Visitation of St Mary Church in AD 1301', *RTDA* 25 (1893), 431–48.

[157] *Reg. Stapledon*, 130–31; Whitley, 'Visitations', 462.   [158] *Reg. Stapledon*, 111.

[159] S. Turner and R. Wilson-North, 'South-West England', in N. Christie and P. Stamper, eds, *Medieval Rural Settlement: Britain and Ireland, AD 800–1600* (Oxford, 2012), 135–50.

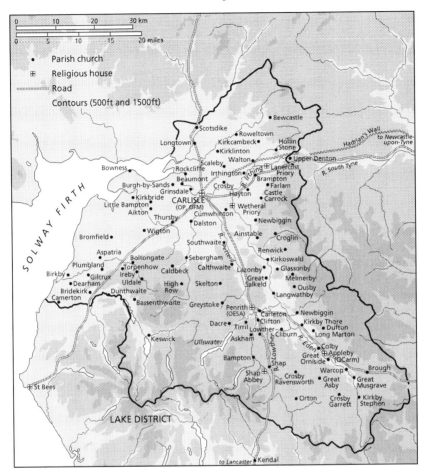

Map 5   The Diocese of Carlisle. *Sources:* Nicholson and Burn, *Westmorland and Cumberland* (map of Westmorland facing title page in vol. I, map of Cumberland facing title page in vol. II); *Survey Atlas*, Plates 13, 16–19; B. P. Hindle, 'Medieval Roads in the Diocese of Carlisle', *TCWAAS* n.s. 77 (1977, 83–95).

Chapter 12

THE DIOCESE OF CARLISLE

DIOCESAN ADMINISTRATION AND THE CARE OF SOULS

In the thirteenth century, Carlisle was the youngest dioceses in England, the last to be established before the Reformation. Created amid shifting political and ecclesiastical borders from land contested among the dioceses of York, Durham and Glasgow, it received in 1133 its first bishop, Aethelwulf, who died in 1156 or 1157. The diocese was also under the Scottish crown's control from 1136 to 1157.[1] When Aethelwulf died, no successor was chosen and the see was vacant until nearly the end of the century. Attempts to fill it were stymied by the extreme poverty of the see. Between them, the diocese's sole archdeacon and the prior of the Augustinian chapter of the cathedral managed ecclesiastical affairs. Strictly episcopal functions, such as ordination, confirmation and consecration of churches, could be carried out by a bishop granted authority to do so in the diocese; the Scottish bishop of Whithorn is known to have served on occasion.[2] Even when the diocese did have a bishop, few *magistri* wore its mitre; many of its bishops were royal administrators, chosen above all for their loyalty to the crown and effectiveness in defending the Scottish border.[3] By the end of the century, it only had four friaries, one of each order, and those of the two smaller orders did not appear before 1280. From a pastoral standpoint, it might appear that Carlisle was a dismal backwater, not so much ministered to as administered, with little to propel it from twelfth-century rural parochial conservatism to the new scholastic ideas making headway elsewhere in England. Nonetheless, the pastoral reforms of the thirteenth century took root here as they did elsewhere, even if they grew in different ways.

[1] *Fasti* Monastic, 19; N. McGuigan, 'Neither Scotland nor England: Middle Britain, c. 850–1100' (unpubl. PhD thesis, St Andrews, 2015), 195–202.
[2] Summerson, *Carlisle*, 70–72; Cheney, *Innocent III*, 74; Kemp, *Acta*, 8–10; L. A. S. Butler, 'Suffragan Bishops in the Medieval Diocese of York', *Northern History* 37 (2000), 49–60.
[3] Gibbs and Lang, *Bishops and Reform*, 185–99, and below.

At the opening of the thirteenth century, the diocese once again had a bishop, though he is an enigmatic figure whose contributions are uncertain. From 1198 to 1214, some episcopal functions were provided by Bernard, archbishop of Ragusa (modern Dubrovnik); the reasons for his exile are unknown.[4] Bernard remained in Carlisle during the interdict, making it the only diocese in England that consistently had a bishop present during the period, though he could not perform most religious rites and Cheney supposed that Bernard 'counted for nothing'.[5] Carlisle's proximity and historic ties to Scotland would have made it easy to issue letters dimissory, permitting new rectors and vicars to cross the border to be ordained by Scottish bishops.[6] Carlisle Diocese thus may have come out of the interdict somewhat ahead of others. Bernard's *acta* include the ordinations of several perpetual vicarages.[7] Whatever gains may have been made, however, were probably offset by four years of ecclesiastical chaos following Bernard's death. When Carlisle was taken by the Scots in the invasion of 1216–17, the chapter welcomed the conquerors and elected a Scottish bishop, a fact which testifies to the strength of cross-border sympathies. The legate Guala quashed the election, expelled the chapter and directed the new chapter he installed to elect the Cistercian Hugh of Beaulieu in 1218, a worldly monk who had been deposed as an abbot but was loyal to John.[8] Like Bernard, Hugh ordained vicarages, though few were specified as perpetual.[9] Another of Hugh's actions was to confirm the position of underage sons of clergy who had inherited their fathers' benefices, contrary to the decree of the Fourth Lateran Council.[10] The original *actum* is lost and is only known because of a papal letter censuring the policy. This may reveal less about the bishop's wishes than about the entrenched conservatism he found in his diocese, which has some contemporary parallels elsewhere.[11] Adam, rector of Crosthwaite, who became bishop Hugh's official in 1220, left behind a wife and three children when he died around 1250; another son, who predeceased him and was probably the eldest, was old enough to witness a charter with his father before 1214.[12] In Carlisle the offspring of such liaisons seemingly

[4] Cheney, *Innocent III*, 73–74; *EEA 30*, xxxvii–xxxviii; *Fasti* Monastic, 19.

[5] Cheney, *Innocent III*, 315.

[6] *C&S* II, 147 suggests that crossing borders for ordination was common.

[7] *EEA 30*, 14, 15, 18, 20; cf. 23, 33.

[8] *Fasti* Monastic, 20; *EEA 30*, xxxvii–xxxix; Summerson, *Carlisle*, 97–101; J. Sayers, *Papal Government and England during the Pontificate of Honorius III* (Cambridge, 1984), 60; Harvey, *Episcopal Appointments*, 109, 277.

[9] *EEA 30*, 45, perpetual; and e.g. 43, 48, 62, not perpetual.   [10] *EEA 30*, 42; *CPL*, 91.

[11] Summerson, *Carlisle*, 99; Cheney, *Innocent III*, 407; Cheney, *Becket to Langton*, 14–15, 137–38; Bartlett, *Gerald*, 34–35; *CPL*, 85; Thibodeaux, *Manly Priest*.

[12] W. G. Collingwood, 'Thirteenth-Century Keswick', *TCWAAS* n.s. 21 (1921), 159–73, at 161–63; *EEA 30*, 18, 19.

formed an interest group powerful enough to persuade the bishop to flout recent canon law. The situation also reflects the weakness of Hugh's position as only the second bishop in a diocese that had learned to live without one, elected moreover by a chapter specially imported for the purpose. Given these limitations, perhaps it was best for the strength of episcopacy in Carlisle that he held the see for less than five years, dying in June 1223.

Walter Mauclerc, like Hugh, was a man with strong royal connections. He was consecrated bishop of Carlisle less than a year later.[13] He continued to participate heavily in government and was often out of his diocese, a problem doubtless compounded by its remoteness. He can have had little to do with the foundation of the Franciscan and Dominican houses in his cathedral city in 1233, for he was far from his see in that year and dealing with complex political problems but the fact that he resigned his mitre in 1246 to become an Oxford Dominican testifies to a degree of piety and zeal that may have affected his episcopal governance in the preceding years, although his extant *acta* are not of the sort that could show it.[14] His successor, Silvester of Everton, bishop from 1246 to 1254, was likewise a royal clerk and had been *de facto* chancellor; little can be said of his episcopate except that in three cases he re-ordained vicarages because the original emoluments had been too small.[15] He also encouraged pilgrimage to Durham by granting an indulgence of forty days' enjoined penance to those who visited the shrine of St Cuthbert and gave offerings.[16]

Silvester was succeeded by Robert de Chaury in 1257.[17] Though he was yet another bishop of Carlisle with royal connections, he was also attentive to pastoral care.[18] Because of the survival of his statutes, the only ones known to have been issued in thirteenth-century Carlisle, more can be learned about his direction of pastoral care than about all the other thirteenth-century bishops of Carlisle combined. Robert's statutes date from 1258 or 1259.[19] They were a reissue with a few amendments of the statutes of Bishop William Bitton of Bath and Wells, probably originally issued in 1258.[20] Bitton, along with the bishop of Salisbury, consecrated de

---

[13] *EEA 30*, xxxix–xl; Summerson, *Carlisle*, 101; Harvey, *Episcopal Appointments*, 277.

[14] Stevenson, ed., *Chronicon de Lanercost*, 42–43; N. Vincent, 'Mauclerk, Walter (d. 1248)', *ODNB*; *EEFP*, 104–5.

[15] *EEA 30*, xli; 113, 114, 119.   [16] *EEA 30*, 78.   [17] *Fasti Monastic*, 20.   [18] *EEA 30*, xli–xlii.

[19] *C&S* II, 626–30; C. R. Cheney, 'The Medieval Statutes of the Diocese of Carlisle', *EHR* 62 (1947), 52–57.

[20] Because they are so close to the Wells statutes, Powicke and Cheney did not print them *in extenso* in *C&S* II, but only the variations from Wells (pp. 586–626, cited below as 'Wells' with chapter numbers as in *C&S* II). D. M. Smith has provided a fresh edition of the Carlisle statutes in *EEA 30*, 169–201. These are cited below as 'Carlisle' with the chapter numbers as in Smith, which differ from the Wells sequence.

Chaury in 1258[21] and the new bishop of Carlisle may have sought Bitton's statutes at this time to give him a framework for diocesan governance. Because they originated in the Province of Canterbury, the statutes were shaped by provincial legislation (including Langton's Council of Oxford of 1222) that had not previously applied in the Northern Province; with the adoption of the same Bath and Wells statutes at York in 1259, half of the Northern Province had incorporated legislation originally issued by archbishops of Canterbury.[22]

These statutes were extensive, covering much of the same ground as other sets of statutes of the period; most of their important provisions came from earlier statutes, and many would later be adopted in Exeter II.[23] Each sacrament was given a homiletic chapter; that on confirmation was the longest to date.[24] In the chapter on the mass, the ringing of a bell was enjoined at the consecration, and at the Lord's Prayer two clerics, or laymen in the absence of clerics, were to bring extra candles to the top step of the altar. To ensure a supply of candles for this purpose, ten days' enjoined penance was relaxed for each donor. While other diocesan statutes had also ordered that the host being borne to the sick should be accompanied by a lantern and bell and that the laity should reverence its passing in the road, the bishop additionally relaxed seven days' penance to those who knelt when the procession passed by.[25] The necessary ornaments and books for the liturgy were enumerated; for Carlisle, the books were to be of the use of Carlisle, York or Salisbury, and the practice of using cast-off service books from monasteries, which the statute suggests was common, was forbidden.[26]

Confessors were to be appointed to shrive parish clergy, and episcopal penitentiaries, who may also have dealt with lay cases, were mentioned.[27] We have seen above that some bishops considered Canon 21 of Lateran IV, requiring annual confession, to be inadequate, recommending thrice per year instead; the Wells/York/Carlisle statutes stand alone in commending four times per year, though it is not clear when the fourth season was supposed to be.[28] The statutes also stipulated

that Friars Preachers and Minors going about parishes, in and out of Lent, shall be permitted to hear the confessions of the faithful and to enjoin penances on those who wish to confess to them, first seeking licence from their own [parish] priests and paying the accustomed and owed oblations to their parish churches.

[21] *C&S* II, 586. [22] *C&S* II, 658–59; Carlisle, 1, 6, 15.
[23] *C&S* II, 984–1059, and see above, pp. 230–33. [24] Carlisle, 3; Wells, 3.
[25] Carlisle, 4; Wells, 5. [26] Carlisle, 9. [27] Carlisle, 6; Wells, 7.
[28] Carlisle, 5; Wells, 6; and see above, pp. 140–41.

And since their preaching and holiness of life are known to produce considerable fruit in the church of God, we command that they should be admitted with honour and reverence wherever they should go in our diocese.[29]

The parish clergy were also given direction in hearing confessions. Adding to the text's main sources (Salisbury I and Exeter I), they were here told that, when hearing the confession of a sick person unlikely to recover, he should be commended to divine mercy; he should be told what his owed penance would be if he recovered, so that if he should escape hell, his penance could be served in purgatory.[30] The statutes also gave unprecedented weight to extreme unction, threatening any priest with suspension if through his negligence one of his flock should die without its benefit.[31] Because of the difficulties of transporting the deceased, all chapels-of-ease more than two or three miles distant from the mother church were to have their own graveyards, though the right of the parish church to customary oblations was safeguarded.[32] The bishop explained that he would be circulating through the diocese to dedicate the new cemeteries; he also required all churches to be properly dedicated and the anniversaries of their dedications to be observed by all parishioners making offerings, just as at Christmas.[33]

Oversight of the parish clergy included directions to the archdeacon of Carlisle regarding visitations, not only in forbidding abuses but also in ensuring that the liturgy was performed properly. The latter implies that the archdeacon would observe the parish priest performing the liturgy and would perhaps follow up with a corrective discussion.[34] As at Exeter, the archdeacon and bishop's official were ordered to examine incumbent vicars and rectors on their literacy, knowledge and ability to preach catechetically, especially regarding the Decalogue, seven sins, seven sacraments and Athanasian, Nicene and Apostles' Creeds. Those badly ignorant were to be denounced to the bishop.[35] To support learning, churches near schools were to maintain a clerk as holy-water bearer, enabling him to study when his services were not required (presumably every day apart from Sundays and feast days).[36] Rural chapters were to be called only in convenient places four times a year, lasting only one day and supervised by the archdeacon or official, not the rural dean; priests from remoter areas were not to be detained afterwards, in case emergency pastoral care

[29] Carlisle, 6; cf. Wells, 6. [30] Carlisle, 5; Wells, 6. [31] Carlisle, 7; Wells, 8.
[32] Carlisle, 13; Wells, 21. [33] Carlisle, 1, 10; Wells, prologue, 17, 18. [34] Carlisle, 38.
[35] Carlisle, 27; Wells, 43; and see above, p. 232.
[36] Carlisle, 19; Wells, 33. Cf. Exeter II, 29 (*C&S* II, 1026–27), which replaced the vague 'vicine' with a radius of ten miles.

was required in their parishes.[37] Vicars and serving rectors were required under penalty of deprivation to reside and be sufficiently ordained.[38] As in Exeter Diocese, no priest was to undertake care of souls in the first year of his priesthood, unless the holding of a vicarage or rectory required it.[39] An addition to the Wells statutes mandated observing the two feasts of St Cuthbert.[40] It is not certain that this was part of the original Carlisle series but Cuthbert was certainly a popular saint in thirteenth-century Carlisle.[41] A list of church dedications in the diocese shows Saints Michael and Cuthbert tied for most popular church dedicatee in the Middle Ages, with eleven parish churches apiece. The addition of a number of chapels and a well dedicated to Cuthbert tip the balance towards him as the diocese's most popular saint.[42] Bishop Silvester's indulgence for pilgrims to Durham merely confirmed a long association with Cuthbert.[43]

With the election of Ralph de Ireton, prior of Guisborough (North Yorkshire) as bishop in December 1278, the cathedral priory chose a fellow northerner and Augustinian Canon; most of Carlisle's bishops were Augustinians over the next hundred years.[44] He paid at least two visits to Guisborough during his episcopate, on one occasion granting its canons the right to institute one of their number as vicar of their appropriated parish church of Bridekirk, at the western end of his diocese.[45] As the following pages will show, this practice was a common one in Carlisle Diocese. That Ireton was criticised for his frequent visitations by one of the authors of the Lanercost Chronicle shows his energy in this regard, though it is unclear whether his visitations included parish churches. It certainly included Lanercost Priory itself, which he visited in 1281.[46] He held at least one diocesan synod, in 1283, and is known to have kept a register which disappeared around 1600. He was pressed into service in 1291 as the collector of the crusading tenth in Scotland, which reflects both his perceived abilities and his familiarity with northern Britain.[47]

---

[37] Carlisle, 40, where 'official' seems to mean the bishop's official; cf. Wells, 57, which clearly indicates the archdeacons' officials.

[38] Carlisle, 29–30; Wells, 44–45.   [39] Carlisle, 31; Wells, 46.

[40] Carlisle, 58; *C&S* II, 627–28.   [41] *EEA 30*, 169.

[42] T. H. B. Graham and W. G. Collingwood, 'Patron Saints of the Diocese of Carlisle', *TCWAAS* n.s. 25 (1925), 1–27; Orme, *Dedications*, 41; V. Tudor, 'St Cuthbert and Cumbria', *TCWAAS* n.s. 84 (1984), 67–77.

[43] *EEA 30*, 78.

[44] *Fasti Monastic*, 21; *John le Neve, Fasti Ecclesiae Anglicanae 1300–1541 VI: Northern Province*, ed. B. Jones (London, 1963), 97–98; *EEA 30*, xlii–xliii.

[45] *EEA 30*, 191, 203. In 1307, a secular vicar resigned, mentioning another secular as his predecessor, and was replaced by one of the canons of Guisborough, but it is conceivable that a canon served before them. *Reg. Halton* I, 284.

[46] Stevenson, ed., *Chronicon de Lanercost*, 102, 106.

[47] *EEA 30*, 201; H. Summerson, 'Irton [Ireton], Ralph of (d. 1292)', *ODNB*.

Ireton died in 1292 and was succeeded by another northern Augustinian Canon, John de Halton, cellarer of Carlisle. He was also an Oxford alumnus and his administrative abilities and local knowledge may be judged by Edward I's immediately appointing him Ireton's successor as collector of the papal tenths in Scotland, many records of which are in his episcopal register, the earliest to survive from Carlisle. Although he was often engaged in Anglo-Scottish business, much of it did not take him far from his diocese.[48] An episcopal visitation of the deanery of Westmorland in 1302 is mentioned in passing in his register.[49] His register includes Boniface VIII's bull *Super cathedram*[50] and shows that he ordained seculars, friars and religious with some frequency.

Thus, while details of the administrations of all of the thirteenth-century bishops are much more limited than what we can learn about their colleagues in other dioceses, it is clear enough that the bishops at least from 1257 were capable men who attended to the needs of their small diocese and governed it effectively. Brentano judged that, by the 1280s, the diocese had been transformed into 'an extraordinarily well-disciplined administrative unit', though 'ordinarily' well-disciplined might be more accurate.[51] Seldom can the effects of pastoral care be quantified, but Summerson described the rate of violent crimes reported at the eyres of 1278/9 and 1292/3 as 'low figures, though no lower than those found elsewhere', and suggested, not implausibly, that despite its remoteness, relative poverty and human shortcomings, the church in Carlisle was neither negligent nor ineffective in its duties.[52]

THE LANDSCAPE OF PASTORAL CARE

Carlisle Diocese, covering the northern parts of Cumberland and Westmorland counties, was more thinly populated than many other English dioceses, perhaps more closely resembling Wales and Scotland. Cumberland was described in the 1840s as 'A maritime county of England ... All but the north part of this country is very hilly, or even mountainous ... [with] some heights exceeding 3000 feet ... There is good pasturage even among the hills, and the arable land is fertile.' Westmorland 'is a mountainous country; two ridges cross the county, with peaks about 3000 feet high, and run towards the sea to the south west ... There are some vales fruitful in corn and pastures, and the hills serve to feed a great

[48] *Fasti* Monastic, 21; *Reg. Halton* I, i–xliii; M. J. Kennedy, 'John Halton, Bishop of Carlisle, 1292–1324', *TCWAAS* n.s. 73 (1973), 94–110; H. Summerson, 'Halton [Halghton], John (d. 1324)', *ODNB*.
[49] *Reg. Halton* I, 197. [50] Ibid. I, 124–28.
[51] Brentano, *York Jurisdiction*, 85. [52] Summerson, *Carlisle*, 168–70.

number of sheep.'[53] Such terrain led to a thinly distributed population: even in 1801, much of the area covered by the medieval diocese had on average fewer than one hundred persons per one thousand acres,[54] and the *Survey Atlas* of 1903 showed scattered farmsteads, but few villages of any size, on land over six hundred feet.[55] In the clerical taxation record of 1291, only ninety-four parishes are recorded in the diocese, just over 1 per cent of those it recorded in England.[56] Many of these parishes were of considerable size. Away from the cathedral town, the parishes tended to coincide with secular lordships that included smaller areas of lowland arable and large areas of upland used as summer pasture for the estate's cattle.[57] For example, the parish of Addingham, whose church sat on the east bank of the Eden, is not in one of the more remote locales, yet it covered some ten thousand acres.[58] Most churches were close to streams or rivers, the lowland part of the parish where most people doubtless chose to live if they could.[59] This situation meant that herders would have found access to their churches difficult during the summer, requiring as it would a climb down into the dale and back again. Gradual assarting and settlement of upland areas continued across the thirteenth century, reaching its maximum extent around 1300.[60] For those living year-round in upland settlements, getting to church at all, especially in wintry weather, would have tested their devotion. Their challenges are suggested by the 'corpse roads' that developed to enable parishioners from isolated villages to bring their dead to the church for burial.[61]

Given these constraints, it is not perhaps surprising that Carlisle was England's poorest bishopric, its episcopal income ranking among the Welsh sees and half that of Rochester, the second-poorest English see.[62] The diocese's small population, relative youth and contested status between England and Scotland had given its bishops little opportunity

[53] P. Park and J. Arnison, ed., *National Index of Parish Registers, Vol. 10 Part 3: Cumberland and Westmorland* (London, 1999), 1, quoting *Barclay's Complete and Universal English Dictionary*.
[54] J. W. Watson and J. B. Sissons, *The British Isles: A Systematic Geography* (London, 1964), 228.
[55] Bartholomew, *Atlas*, plates 13, 16 and 17.
[56] Astle et al., ed., *Taxatio*, 318–20. The number should be at least 96. Lanercost Priory also served as a parish church (see below) and the survey omitted Holy Trinity, Carlisle: D. R. Perriam, 'An Unrecorded Carlisle Church: The Church of Holy Trinity, Caldewgate', *TCWAAS* n.s. 79 (1979), 51–55.
[57] Winchester, *Cumbria*, 6, 26, 92–99.
[58] C. J. Gordon, 'A Submerged Church in the River Eden', *TCWAAS* n.s. 14 (1914), 328–36 plus plates.
[59] Nicholson and Burn, *Westmorland and Cumberland*; map of Westmorland facing title page in vol. I, map of Cumberland facing title page in vol. II; A. Winchester and A. Crosby, *England's Landscape: The North West* (London, 2006), 88–91.
[60] Ibid., 39–40, 76–80; Winchester, *Cumbria*, 39–40.
[61] Hindle, 'Medieval Roads', 85.   [62] Astle et al., ed., *Taxatio*, 320.

to amass endowment. These determinants of its low episcopal income did not necessarily indicate that the average parish church, or the average parishioner, was very poor. Mineral wealth, including silver, lead, coal and iron, was being exploited in the north-west in the twelfth and thirteenth centuries and this contributed, according to some estimates, to a slightly greater degree of average wealth per square mile than Exeter Diocese had, though still approximately one-third of the average land value in Lincoln. Like Exeter, it was part of the northern and western 'highland' pastoral zone. It also lacked eastward-facing ports for trade with the Continent and was a good deal farther from London than Exeter was, depressing the market value of agricultural exports.[63]

The cathedral town sat in the most fertile and densely settled area of the diocese, a fertile lowland crescent of Cumberland along the shores of the Solway Firth and extending south-east from Carlisle up the Eden Valley.[64] Uniquely in England, Carlisle's cathedral chapter consisted of Augustinian Canons. The town was not subject to the canons as an ecclesiastical borough and so was perhaps exempt from the frictions between townspeople and religious that prevailed in some monastic towns.[65] But the church in general, and the cathedral in particular, was still a dominant force in the city and the region. The canons were active in diocesan administration. The cathedral and castle formed the focal points of the small city, occasionally jostling for power, as in the Scottish invasion of 1216, when the castle garrison formed the only part of the city that did not side with the Scots against King John, while the chapter elected a Scottish bishop.[66] The city proper, as defined by the walls, was only half a mile long (including the castle) and a quarter mile broad. The fact that the Franciscans and Dominicans were able to secure sites within the walls in the 1230s suggests that even this small area was not yet densely settled. The intramural area also included the cathedral precinct, St Cuthbert's parish church and churchyard, and St Alban's church and churchyard. Taken together, ecclesiastical land occupied just under a quarter of the intramural territory, almost half of that total being the cathedral precinct. The cathedral nave also served as the church of St Mary's parish, which covered the northern part of the city and an extramural district, while St Cuthbert's church served the southern part (which included both friaries) and an extramural district of its own.[67] St Alban's, an ancient church near the cathedral precinct, did not have full parochial status; Summerson supposed that the

---

[63] See above, p. 236.
[64] A. Winchester and A. Crosby, *England's Landscape: The North West* (London, 2006), 20–21; Winchester, *Cumbria*, 8–9.
[65] Summerson, 'Cathedral and City', 31.   [66] Summerson, *Carlisle*, 97.
[67] The castle being excluded. Ibid., 160.

cathedral canons were unable to close it down entirely but kept its status low to avoid liturgical competition within their parish.[68] This is an interesting counter-example to other instances of shared churches that we have seen. At Lincoln Cathedral and at Oseney and St Frideswide's churches in Oxford, the canons found parochial liturgies in their naves to be troublesome enough that they paid to build new parish churches to move them out.[69] Had the canons of Carlisle wished to oust their parishioners, there was another church already waiting to receive them but there is no sign of any attempt to do so. Perhaps St Alban's was too small; perhaps the canons preferred keeping the parish under their direct supervision, for reasons of power and status; perhaps the parishioners had been made responsible for a share of the costs of building and maintaining the cathedral nave, and the canons could ill afford the loss of that part of their revenues.

For the cathedral was also a construction site for much of the thirteenth century. Only two bays and one transept of the twelfth-century nave remain, one transept having been partially rebuilt with the thirteenth-century choir and the remaining bays of the nave pulled down in the seventeenth century. The parochial part of the church, therefore, was left largely intact while the choir was being rebuilt between the 1220s and the early 1280s. Moving the axis of the new choir to the north may have allowed construction to begin before the old choir was demolished but it is difficult to judge how liturgical practice continued when the canons' choir was unusable.[70] The most likely explanation is that they moved into the nave and parochial services were scheduled around theirs. However the services were arranged, in 1282 the bishop allowed the cathedral priory to appropriate the parish of Addingham on the grounds that many clergy and people regularly assembled at the cathedral and this imposed extraordinary burdens.[71] The number of visitors could only have grown in 1291, when the pope granted an indulgence of one year and forty days' worth of penance to visitors to Carlisle's cathedral, which must have been particularly convenient for those who were already its parishioners.[72] The cathedral was badly damaged in a city-wide fire the next year, which doubtless made the offerings of pilgrims that much more welcome. As the cathedral priory received funds from tithes, offerings and rents, it also spent them, and their direct and indirect economic footprint – such as

[68] Ibid., 32.   [69] See above, pp. 209, 211–12.
[70] Summerson, 'Cathedral and City', 31–32; R. Plant, 'The Romanesque Fabric of Carlisle Cathedral', in M. McCarthy and D. Weston, eds, *Carlisle and Cumbria: Roman and Medieval Architecture, Art and Archaeology* (London, 2004), 89–105; J. Alexander, 'The Construction of the Gothic Choir of Carlisle Cathedral', in ibid., 106–26.
[71] Raine, ed., *Northern Registers*, 251.   [72] Summerson, *Carlisle*, 158.

food purchased by builders employed on the cathedral fabric – must have been a significant part of the town's economic life.

Carlisle was also home to a school, which had been founded by bishop Aethelwulf in the twelfth century, with one of the cathedral canons its first schoolmaster. It was still operating in the later 1180s, despite the episcopal vacancy. Given the general paucity of sources, the fact that it is next documented in the 1280s need not indicate any significant break in its operations. Bishop Ireton attempted to endow support for twelve poor scholars in 1285, though his arrangements were overturned in 1291. The size, curriculum and clientele of the school are unknown but it is most likely that it catered both to aspiring clerics and to the children of gentry and merchants who sought the benefits of literacy.[73]

The Franciscans and Dominicans who settled in the cathedral city in 1233 were the only resident friars in the diocese for some fifty years. The Carmelite Friars settled at Appleby, along the Eden River, between 1281 and 1293.[74] The Eden Valley, along which many parish churches were situated, was part of the main route between Carlisle and York, where the Carmelites had settled in mid-century.[75] Appleby was the only town in the diocese to have two parish churches (except Carlisle, which had four), and only these two towns in the diocese sent members to Parliament in the thirteenth century.[76] We have seen that, outside their towns, the friars were most often found along well-travelled roads.[77] Not only could Carmelites travel up towards Carlisle or down towards York, but also the Franciscans and Dominicans from the cathedral city could readily visit Appleby. In 1300, there were twelve Carmelites at Appleby.[78] Their names suggest that they succeeded success in recruiting locally. John of Kirkoswald (a parish about twenty miles downstream) was ordained priest in 1305.[79] While Walter of Newbiggin, ordained acolyte and subdeacon in 1307, may have come from any of the seven northern English places of that name, six of those are within twenty miles of Appleby, one of them just seven miles down the Eden.[80] The other Carmelite ordinands in these years were mostly of northern origin, such as Richard and Alexander of Alnwick (Northumberland), John of Selby (Yorkshire) and Robert of York, while John of Aylesbury (Buckinghamshire) forms a connection to the order's first English house.[81] Success in local recruitment suggests that the Carmelites were having some impact. This is a striking contrast to the Franciscans and Dominicans of Carlisle, who included among their

---

[73] Ibid., 88, 166–68.   [74] Egan, 'Carmelite Houses', 2–4.   [75] Summerson, *Carlisle*, 73.
[76] Hindle, 'Medieval Roads', 85.   [77] See above, pp. 178, 207, 240–41, 244.   [78] *MRH*, 234.
[79] *Reg. Halton* I, 244.   [80] *Reg. Halton* I, 279; *Survey Atlas*, plates 16–17.
[81] *Reg. Halton* I, 272, 280, 187, 281, 279.

number very few men with local names.[82] Men from the diocese may have joined those orders and been sent to other houses, where they are harder to trace; but, even if this was the case, Carlisle's native population would have seen familiar faces and heard familiar accents predominantly among the Carmelites.

The Austin Friars arrived around 1291, settling at Penrith, situated in another well-settled riverside area.[83] There were nine parish churches within a five-mile radius of the friary, including one in the town itself. Penrith was a market town before 1300 and, since Roman times, a crossroads: the main Roman road from Carlisle, still used in the Middle Ages and now approximately the A6, followed not the more populous Eden Valley but the more direct Petteril Valley, dividing just south of Penrith to go south by Shap towards Lancaster or southeast up the Eden by Appleby towards York.[84] There were only eight Austins here in 1300.[85] Recruitment seems to have been problematic in this corridor between the Carmelites at Appleby on one hand and the Franciscans and Dominicans at Carlisle on the other. Only three Austins occur in ordination lists between 1292 and 1324 and none of them has an identifiably local name.[86] Perhaps the Austins had to import friars from areas with higher recruitment rates to maintain their presence here. With a smaller convent in a smaller town, no visible local recruitment and better-established competition, the Austins' impact was probably felt only in the neighbouring parishes to the west of the Eden.

Whatever the role of the friars, they were in a diocese whose canons regular, perhaps following the lead of the cathedral priory, were more directly active in pastoral care than those of other parts of the country. The Augustinian priory of St Mary Magdalene at Lanercost, on the north bank of the River Irthing, was never the centre of a nucleated settlement but it was along the main route to Newcastle-upon-Tyne, approximately following Hadrian's Wall.[87] Lanercost has left us not only its famous chronicle but also its cartulary.[88] When the priory was founded, around 1169, it was in Walton parish, the church of which was two miles east of the priory.[89] Walton had a dependent chapel at Triermain, three miles north-east of the priory, and the new foundation was on land in Triermain's chapelry district. Walton and Triermain, along with the nearby churches of Irthington, Brampton, Carlatton and Farlam, were part of Lanercost's original endowment.[90] By 1180, Lanercost also held the more

[82] Summerson, *Carlisle*, 162.   [83] Roth, *Austin Friars* I, 324.   [84] Hindle, 'Medieval Roads', 85.
[85] Roth, *Austin Friars* I, 325.   [86] *Reg. Halton* I, 38, 263; II, 27.
[87] Summerson and Harrison, *Lanercost*, 21; Summerson, *Carlisle*, 73; Hindle, 'Medieval Roads'.
[88] Stevenson, ed., *Chronicon de Lanercost*; *Lan. Cart.*
[89] Summerson and Harrison, *Lanercost*, 3–5.   [90] *Lan. Cart.*, I, 170–71.

distant churches of Lazonby and Grinsdale.[91] In the late twelfth and early thirteenth centuries, Pope Lucius III, Bishop Bernard and the archdeacon of Carlisle all granted the canons of Lanercost permission to serve their parish churches either themselves or through their own chaplains rather than through instituted secular vicars; if canons served, three or four were to reside together, one of whom would be presented to the bishop and instituted as vicar.[92] The question remains, however: did the canons ever serve these churches themselves?

Lanercost Priory's community was never very numerous; Summerson suggests that only in the thirteenth century did it exceed thirteen canons.[93] The foundation could hardly have served more than one parish church at a time under these conditions unless canons could be sent out to nearby churches by day but remain resident at the priory. Secular vicars are mentioned at Walton in 1252 and 1287[94] and at Irthington in 1224–25 and 1275,[95] while the advowson of the vicarage of Lazonby was surrendered to the bishop in 1272.[96] Lazonby and Grinsdale were also rather distant for maintaining due supervision of regular clergy. Carlatton was not firmly in the priory's possession until the fourteenth century, and neither the archdeacon nor the bishop had included it the list of parishes they allowed the canons to serve personally.[97] Neither was Triermain; yet it is the one church in which we know they did. By 1252, Triermain's chapelry district was called a *parochia* and the canons were to have the chapel served at their expense, though mortuary dues still went to the vicar of Walton.[98] In 1237, an inquisition heard the depositions 'of elders' (*antiquorum*) that

the Prior and canons had caused that chapel [Triermain] to be served sometimes by their canons and sometimes by seculars, and all the men of Triermain received all their ecclesiastical sacraments [*omnia sacramenta sua ecclesiastica*] at Lanercost, giving all kinds of oblations and tithes there, and doing all other such things that pertain to be done by parishioners to their mother church [*ecclesie sue matrici*].[99]

Omnia sacramenta sua ecclesiastica implies that full pastoral service was sometimes offered by canons, including baptism, confession and Easter communion. This inquisition by papal judges-delegate was concerned with Lanercost's obligation to have the chapel served in divine service two days a week to pray for the soul of Roland de Vaux, who had given

[91] Ibid., 36–39, 93–95.
[92] Ibid., 173 (= Kemp, *Acta*, 12), 174 (= *EEA 30*, 25), 190. Triermain is not mentioned.
[93] Summerson and Harrison, *Lanercost*, 20.   [94] *Lan. Cart.*, 184, 238.
[95] Ibid., 226, 225.   [96] Ibid., 211 (= *EEA 30*, 152).
[97] Summerson and Harrison, *Lanercost*, 5; *Lan. Cart.*, 173–74; *Reg. Halton* I, 299–300; II, 33–35.
[98] *Lan. Cart.*, 183.   [99] Ibid., 346.

Walton, Triermain and other churches to the priory: the canons were derelict in this duty, perhaps hoping that the chapel would be abandoned and that all the people of its *parochia* would come to Lanercost for service, as eventually happened. For the time being, however, the priory agreed to have divine service celebrated twice a week at Triermain;[100] it was not stipulated by whom, and it was probably easier and cheaper to send a canon than to find a secular priest. Only liturgical provision is mentioned but, when canons served the chapel and no secular priest was around, a designated canon presumably performed other pastoral duties. In 1287 the vicar of Walton renounced any rights in the chapel and Bishop Ralph referred to it as the chapel of the church of Lanercost.[101] By 1314 the nave of the priory church had become the place of worship for the Lanercost/ Triermain parish and had a secular vicar.[102] Summerson argues that the choir screen was not solid 'so that people in the nave could observe the performance of divine service in the choir'.[103] Even with a small community of canons, this would have provided a more dramatic liturgical backdrop than most parish churches could aspire to.

The Premonstratensian abbey of Shap in Westmorland, twenty miles south of Penrith along the river Lowther, used its privilege to serve parish churches through canons. Shap parish church, one mile east, was given to the priory as part of the foundation and confirmed by Bishop Bernard.[104] Bampton parish church, six miles north down the Lowther valley, was also acquired early.[105] In 1263, Bishop Robert de Chaury confirmed these appropriations, and noted,

having respect for their poverty … we grant to them, for ourselves and our successors, that they may serve in the foresaid churches through two or three of their canons, *just as they have always been accustomed to do*, of whom one shall be presented to us and to our successors as vicar … on the condition, however, that they shall have in each parish church one secular chaplain who may hear confessions and do other things that cannot be done properly by the canons.[106]

This privilege was confirmed in similar terms in 1287 and 1295; in the latter year a canon was presented to Shap and instituted as vicar, and in 1300 Bampton received a canon as vicar.[107] When the parish church of Warcop (thirty miles east) was appropriated to Shap in 1307, the same arrangement was made and the former prior instituted as vicar the next

---

[100] Ibid., 352–54.   [101] Ibid., 238, 240.   [102] Summerson and Harrison, *Lanercost*, 12–13.

[103] Summerson and Harrison, *Lanercost*, 13.   [104] *EEA 30*, 28, 29; Colvin, *White Canons*, 168–70.

[105] *EEA 30*, 117, 123; Colvin, *White Canons*, 169–70; Nicholson and Burn, *Westmorland and Cumberland* I, 461. According to Nicholson and Burn, Shap and Bampton parishes adjoined.

[106] *EEA 30*, 161; italics mine.

[107] *EEA 30*, 201; *Reg. Halton* I, 39–41, 122–23. The vicar of Bampton resigned due to age in 1309 and was replaced by another canon: ibid., 319–20.

year.[108] Shap, unlike Lanercost, could afford to export personnel, though one suspects that the vicars of Bampton, and especially of Shap, returned to the priory at nightfall or at some other point each day.

The people of Shap had one further feature in their ecclesiastical landscape: a Carmelite hermitage. On 18 December 1293, the bishop ordained two Carmelites, Thomas of Coldal and Gilbert of Sleagill, each described as 'de ordine Carmelitorum de Hepp' (as Shap was then spelt).[109] The latter was doubtless another Carmelite of local origin, since Sleagill is four miles north of Shap, while 'Coldal' might refer to Keld, one mile southwest of Shap, or Keldhead six miles north-west.[110] No further mention of these men or their settlement appears in Halton's register, or indeed anywhere else, but nothing on the manuscript suggests an error by the registrar.[111] Some of the land around Shap exceeded one thousand feet in elevation and cannot have been densely populated: a marginal area just ten miles from Appleby would have been ideal for a Carmelite hermitage, and hermits did not necessarily cut themselves off from visitors. Since Gilbert features at his ordination as priest he could have heard confessions. However, if he was at Shap because even the small town of Appleby was not remote enough for him, we may guess that did not leave his hermitage much and his sphere of influence would be limited to those who came to see him. Since the road from Carlisle to Kendal passed through Shap, the Carmelite hermitage was reasonably accessible from the populous area around Penrith, through which the same road passed, resulting in still more competition for the Austins.

At least one chapel and two other parish churches in the diocese were served by regular clergy in the thirteenth century.[112] Little Salkeld was a chapel of Addingham parish on the east bank of the Eden; the parish with both churches was appropriated to Carlisle Cathedral Priory and Bishop Mauclerc had given an endowment to support 'two canons regular as chaplains to celebrate divine service in [Salkeld chapel] for ever'.[113] At Askham, five miles south of Penrith, an Augustinian Canon of Warter Priory (East Yorkshire) resigned the vicarage in 1295; the priory presented another of its canons, who was instituted by the bishop provided that he keep a fellow canon with him.[114] At Orton, six miles southeast of Shap, one Augustinian Canon of Conishead Priory (Lancashire)

[108] Ibid. I, 292–94; II, 33.   [109] Ibid. I, 24–25.   [110] Bartholomew, *Atlas*, plate 17.
[111] Cumbria Record Office, MS. DRC/1/1, 11–12.
[112] Guisborough Priory (OSA, York Diocese) was permitted in 1287 to serve their parish church of Bridekirk, at the western extremity of Carlisle Diocese, through a canon with *socius* and chaplain: *EEA 30*, 191. However, when a canon was instituted vicar in 1307, two previous vicars were mentioned, both secular: *Reg. Halton* I, 284–85.
[113] Summerson, *Carlisle*, 154, his translation; see also *EEA 30*, 169.   [114] *Reg. Halton* I, 54–55.

replaced another as vicar in 1280 or 1281; both predecessor and successor were required to have a fellow canon and a secular chaplain, but the parishioners were to receive the sacraments from the canons while the chaplain would take on duties which could not be done decently by an Augustinian Canon.[115] The Rule prohibited travelling alone, so pastoral visitation would have fallen to the chaplain. Bishop Ralph noted at this presentation that living under the discipline of a rule gave knowledge and good morals that would enrich the canons' care of souls: this is striking but perhaps unsurprising given that he too was an Augustinian Canon.

Such was not always the case. In 1258, Robert, the cathedral prior, resigned in order to forestall his removal by the bishop; the bishop instituted Robert as rector of Corbridge (Durham Diocese) and sent him and a fellow canon to live there. Robert's *socius* left and within months the former prior was living in such scandalous dissolution that Carlisle Cathedral Priory petitioned the pope to order him back to the cloister.[116] Robert was apparently a bad egg before he arrived at Corbridge and the situation smacks of the bishop exiling a problematic member for the sake of the priory rather than presenting responsibly to the care of souls. But sending canons to act as vicars was clearly well established in the north-west,[117] probably because the less fertile terrain made it all the more important for religious houses there to make the most of their endowments: the vicarages of these large parishes were often generously endowed and by this means most vicarial revenues could be diverted to support members of the convent. In exchange for his poverty, the chaplain might at least receive good instruction in liturgical practice, which he might take to a better-paid cure elsewhere, while the parishioners benefited from more elaborate liturgical service. Perhaps canons in this region also had enough of remoteness to satisfy their desire for solitude and thus were considerably more willing than their brethren elsewhere to embrace the active side of their tradition, following the example of the cathedral priory which had become accustomed to external cares during the long years in which the diocese was *sede vacante*.[118] The visible participation of canons regular in pastoral care and ecclesiastical administration presumably represents a great deal of further but unrecorded activity that enabled

---

[115] *EEA* 30, 172. The vicarage fell vacant in 1294, and another canon was given custody of it for about three months, until a secular vicar was instituted: *Reg. Halton* I, 6, 8.

[116] *EEA* 30, 129; *CPL*, 361–62; *Fasti* Monastic, 22.

[117] The trend continued in the fourteenth century; e.g. *Reg. Halton* I, 277, 325.

[118] In addition to the service of parishes and a background for several of its bishops, we find R., subprior of the cathedral, assisting in diocesan administration in 1267–68 (*Lan. Cart.*, 314, 208). Cf. Postles, 'Austin Canons'.

the diocese to operate more effectively than we might have guessed from the relative weakness of secular church structures there.

By 1300, the diocese stood on the verge of the Anglo-Scottish wars, which would reinforce the lower productivity of land and low population density that had been among the defining factors of its peculiar ecclesiastical evolution. Lanercost Priory was damaged by the Scots in 1296.[119] Carlisle too suffered that year, though as it had been consumed by fire in 1292, including severe damage to the cathedral and the Franciscan convent buildings, much of what was lost in 1296 may have been temporary structures.[120] Regional recovery was choked not only by intermittent Scottish raids but also by the presence of the English king, nobility and armies draining the resources of church and countryside, as for example when the royal household spent the winter of 1306–7 at Lanercost Priory. The Lanercost Chronicle records that, in July 1315, King Robert Bruce led his full host to Carlisle, besieged the city for ten days, 'trampling all the crops underfoot, devastating the suburbs and everything around, burning the whole land and gathering as booty a great herd of cattle from Allerdale, Copeland and Westmorland', while a siege engine hurled stones at the cathedral; once the town walls were breached, citizens fell back to defend the precincts of the Franciscans and Dominicans.[121] Since cattle were such an important part of the region's economy, their loss must have been economically crippling.[122] The resulting damage to the church in the region is visible in a revised parochial taxation table of 1318 showing, in some cases, a massive diminution of ecclesiastical revenues.[123] And yet, while crisis loomed and revenues dwindled, the need for pastoral care by a damaged church in a damaged society could only grow: the dead would be buried, the widowed remarried; masses needed to said for peace, prosperity and the repose of the dead, while preaching and confession would aim to prevent the degeneration into lawlessness that social upheaval could bring.

The thirteenth-century Diocese of Carlisle appears very different from Lincoln and Exeter. Its ecclesiastical organisation, shaped by geography and history, led to large parishes, a weaker bishop and a greater role for canons regular. The diocese's situation in the Province of York precluded direct impetus for reform from Canterbury, though Robert de Chaury's replication of the statutes of Wells in his diocese incidentally imported some Canterbury legislation. Given the lack of bishops' registers before 1292, the statutes are where we can most clearly see the

---

[119] Stevenson, ed., *Chronicon de Lanercost*, 174; Summerson and Harrison, *Lanercost*, 12–15.
[120] Summerson, *Carlisle*, 177–79, 193–94.   [121] Stevenson, ed., *Chronicon de Lanercost*, 205–6.
[122] Winchester, *Cumbria*, 6.
[123] Astle et al., eds, *Taxatio*, 318–20; *Reg. Halton* I, xviii, 195–97; II, 183–89.

bishop directly informing the clergy about developing expectations for clerical life and pastoral care. The presence of a school in Carlisle doubtless improved the level of literacy and capability among the clergy. The Franciscans and Dominicans arrived surprisingly early, given the remoteness of Carlisle. However, if, as Brentano argued, Carlisle was a 'well-disciplined administrative unit' by 1280, this does not indicate that pastoral care there was indistinguishable from what parishioners experienced elsewhere.[124] Much of the ecclesiastical landscape, especially further from Carlisle or the main overland routes, may have borne closer comparison with other English dioceses fifty or more years earlier. The peculiar blend of what might be called old and new made pastoral care in the Diocese of Carlisle very different from the other parts of England we have examined. The topographical, economic and ecclesiastical features of this under-studied diocese, paralleled in the neighbouring counties of Lancashire and Cheshire, should act as a strong corrective to universal descriptions of English church life.[125]

Exeter and Carlisle dioceses lacked not only Lincoln's absolute number of parishes and mendicant houses but also their density. This corresponded to economic necessity: while Lincoln Diocese had some of the highest land values in England, Exeter and Carlisle had some of the lowest.[126] Travel within these dioceses could also be challenging: Cumbria and the West Country were the two parts of England where settled areas were the most 'fragmented and limited in extent by vast tracts of barren and empty moorland and mountainside'.[127] The schools in Exeter and Carlisle were probably smaller affairs than Lincoln's and certainly could not compete with Oxford. Lincoln Diocese benefited from an abundance of university-educated clerics whom its bishops put into service as archdeacons, administrators and even parish priests. While some Exeter and a few Carlisle clergy had Oxford educations, the relative poverty of their land, benefices and bishoprics compared to Lincoln reduced the number of clergy they could afford to support there as well as the number of graduates either diocese could recruit. These features may have led to a slower transition to the Parisian view of the care of souls there, as these were some of the most obvious channels for transmitting those ideas and practices, though it is also true that both Exeter and Carlisle had much more extensive diocesan statutes than Lincoln had. However, as with other historical narratives of development or reform, it would be an

---

[124] Brentano, *York Jurisdiction*, 85.
[125] N. J. Higham, *A Frontier Landscape: The North West in the Middle Ages* (Macclesfield, 2004).
[126] Campbell and Bartley, *Eve of the Black Death*, maps 18.5, 18.6; C. Daniell, *Atlas of Medieval Britain* (London, 2008), 91.
[127] Winchester, *Cumbria*, 2.

error to assume a uniform goal and to measure all regions by their progress towards it. The social and economic contexts of the north-west and the south-west differed not only from Lincolnshire and Oxfordshire but also from one another, while none of these regions was uniform within itself. As the preceding chapters have demonstrated, this resulted in a great deal of variety in the care of English souls.

CONCLUSION

HOW PASTORAL CARE CHANGED

If a reform-minded bishop paused in 1300 to reflect on the changes of the past century, he might have found reason for cautious optimism. The evidence presented above suggests that pastoral care in England had seen significant change from the days when Peter the Chanter, William de Montibus, Stephen Langton, Richard Poore and the future Innocent III rubbed elbows in Paris, and that it increasingly reflected their agenda. The development of parish ministry was impeded by the interdict of 1208–14, but the hierarchy of the English Church and the position of the parish in local life re-emerged with renewed vigour in the following years. The disruption of the interdict may even have provided leading churchmen with an opportunity to press for more far-reaching reforms thereafter, such as increasing episcopal control over the institution of parish clergy.[1] Investigations of parochial life at official visitations became increasingly searching, allowing standards of education and behaviour, already on the rise in the twelfth century, to be enforced more effectively.[2] The uses to which this authority was put expanded from basic literacy and sobriety at the beginning of the century, to Poore's and Grosseteste's directives to learn some moral theology, to Pecham's mandatory preaching syllabus and Quinel's enforced use of a substantial tract on confession. There was also an inverse bell curve of literary complexity in pastoral literature for parish priests: late twelfth-century works were often well-intentioned but relatively inaccessible; in the early thirteenth century there was the simple Latin and pedagogical genius of de Montibus and Poore; and, as the century progressed, the more challenging Wells/York/Carlisle statutes were surpassed by the demanding legislation of Quinel and Pecham. This suggests that higher clergy first became better at presenting their ideas in a comprehensible form to parish clergy, whose capacity to read and understand pastoral manuals then rose in turn. While we cannot ascertain

---

[1] Major, *Acta*, xxxv–xxxvii; Cheney, *Becket to Langton*, 136–39. [2] Forrest, 'Visitation'.

quantitative changes in preaching or confession, the content of new *pastoralia* was intended to effect substantial qualitative change in both.

In 1220, England did not yet have a single friar; by 1300, they may have exceeded five thousand, about one for every two parishes.[3] Each new friar represented both a man who had been attracted to a life of holy asceticism – himself the product of successful pastoral care – and a potential pastor to others. Not every friar was pastorally active but itineration allowed each one who was so active to preach to and shrive far more people in a year than a parish priest, giving mendicant pastoral care an influence out of proportion to the relative numbers of friars and parish priests. The mendicants combined higher standards of education and behaviour with a flexibility to pastoral demand that parishes could not always provide. Only in liturgy could the parish clergy effectively compete, though indications of laypeople choosing to attend mendicant rather than parish liturgies demonstrate that some urban and suburban parish clergy struggled here too. If Moorman was correct to suggest that competition from the friars goaded parish clergy into action, he underestimated how successfully the latter rose to the challenge.[4]

WHAT PASTORAL CARE CHANGED

Was thirteenth-century pastoral care effective? This question could mean many things – effective therapeutically, or theologically or behaviourally – not all of which are answerable. Pastoral care was the closest medieval analogue to counselling psychology but we have no empirical data to determine whether it made people more emotionally whole. Whether pastoral care made atonement for sins is a question for theologians, not for historians. How it affected people's beliefs and behaviour *is* a historical question but a difficult one: it hovers just out of sight in our sources, in the 'layperson-shaped hole in the middle of the evidence', in oblique references such as bequests to friars, genuflection to the host and what preachers thought their audiences already knew.[5] It is not a question to be avoided but it is one best addressed now that all the evidence and arguments of this book have been set forth. To approach it, let us take an example from the end of the century.

On Friday, 13 May, 1300 – fifty years to the day after Grosseteste delivered his denunciation of abuses at the papal curia – a humbler ecclesiastical gathering took place in Worcester Diocese, where clergy and laity of the rural deanery of Wych met in the parish church of Dodderhill.[6]

[3] Moorman, *Church Life*, 412.   [4] Ibid., 79–80.
[5] Arnold, *Belief and Unbelief*, 22.   [6] See above, p. 1.

Twenty couples from eight parishes stood accused of fornication or adultery and one man of beating his wife. One fornicator was a chaplain. Several were recidivists. A few were cleared but most confessed, renounced their sin and were flogged. Subsequent monthly meetings told much the same tale.[7] Although flogging may not appear very pastoral to modern eyes, such a court was part of the machinery of public penance, falling within Pecham's definition of the *cura animarum*. The Worcester diocesan statutes of 1229 had forbidden priests to allow manifest fornicators to remain in their parishes without sending word to the rural dean's officers.[8] The statutes of 1240 ordered that engaged couples be warned not to copulate before marriage, for those who had done so would have to receive public penance.[9] On this Friday, we are seeing those statutes enacted. Was the church, then, succeeding in persuading and transforming? Perhaps not. Stricter views of sex and marriage had gained widespread acceptance in principle, yet adultery, fornication and clerical incontinence remained common in practice.[10] While the Exeter visitation records of 1301 seem to reflect satisfactory clergy, Canterbury visitation records from the 1290s show us that not all was decent and orderly.[11] Such records suggest that preaching, confession and even corporal punishment were no match for glandular impulses.

Yet, paradoxically, the medieval church's imperfections were one of its strengths. Its reformers, even those we think of as idealists, were realistic about the gradual and limited changes that they could achieve. Grosseteste may have commiserated with Adam Marsh over the state of the parish clergy, yet he still instituted over two thousand men to benefices in Lincoln Diocese and sought to make the best of it. Theologians might hope for extensive knowledge of the faith among the laity but they were prepared to accept a bare minimum, and they found practical ways to establish more extensive programmes of catechesis such as Grosseteste's proposal to teach the lectionary, Pecham's *Ignorantia sacerdotum* and the support of friars.[12] Clergy had to offer carrots as well as sticks. Their success depended on force at times, as at the rural dean's court, but more often required tactful persuasion.[13] To read documents such as these deans'

---

7 F. S. Pearson, ed., 'Records of a Ruridecanal Court of 1300', in S. G. Hamilton, *Collectanea Edited for the Worcestershire Historical Society* (London, 1912), 69–80; P. Hyams, 'Deans and Their Doings: The Norwich Inquiry of 1286', *Proceedings of the Sixth International Conference on Canon Law, Berkeley, California, 28 July–2 August 1980* (Vatican City, 1985), 619–46.
8 *C&S* II, 179.   9 *C&S* II, 302.
10 d'Avray, *Marriage Sermons*; d'Avray, *Symbolism and Society*.
11 Whitley, 'Visitations'; Woodruff, 'Visitation Rolls'.   12 See Chapter 5 above.
13 Biller, 'Intellectuals'; Tanner and Watson, 'Least of the Laity'.

court records only as evidence of failed social control because people kept sinning, and thereby to declare pastoral care unsuccessful, is to miss the point. For all their moralising, medieval churchmen fully expected that people would continue to sin. Pastors offered a two-pronged response, offering forgiveness to the penitent and persuasion and castigation to the disobedient with the hope that they should repent.[14]

The most powerful evidence for the effectiveness of pastoral care is a category that has been studiously avoided above: the English religious world after 1300. Pastoral care in thirteenth-century England was deeply formative of the later medieval English culture so richly described by Eamon Duffy, Robert Swanson and countless others.[15] The sermons and homilies discussed in Chapter 5 must have been the sort of preaching that Richard Rolle of Hampole and the *Pearl* poet grew up hearing. The golden age of post-Plague preaching consisted largely of the elaboration and intensification of themes and methods already developed before 1300.[16] While Chaucer's *Canterbury Tales* show the Friar, the Summoner and the Pardoner as rascals, it is to his honest, godly Parson – whose 'tale' is indebted to a thirteenth-century text on the seven virtues – that Chaucer gave the final word.[17] Even Langland's *Piers Plowman* and the writings of the Lollards, which question and reject the pastoral activities of the friars in particular, are ultimately indebted to their nemeses, for the friars helped to create a cultural world in which significant numbers of devout laymen would read and write such works.[18]

HOW PASTORAL CARE VARIED

The rise of the friars provided laypeople across the social spectrum with an unprecedented degree of choice. Parishioners were rarely under compulsion to attend friars' sermons or liturgies, to resort to them as confessors, or to give them alms: rather, they voted with their feet and their purses, and even fought for the right to do so. While the aristocracy had long been able to choose chaplains and confessors, now even the rustic labourer and urban apprentice could do the same. This created what we should now call a marketplace of religion, in which laypeople made choices based at least in part on what benefit they believed their souls

---

[14] M. G. Muzzarelli, ed., *From Words to Deeds: The Effectiveness of Preaching in the Late Middle Ages* (Turnhout, 2014).

[15] Duffy, *Stripping of the Altars*; Swanson, *Church and Society*.   [16] Wenzel, *Sermon Collections*.

[17] S. Wenzel, ed., *Summa Virtutum de Remediis Anime* (Athens, GA, 1984), 2–12; L. D. Benson, ed., *The Riverside Chaucer* (3rd edn, Boston, MA, 1987), 287–327.

[18] W. Scase, *Piers Plowman and the New Anticlericalism* (Cambridge, 1989).

would receive. In other words, in this marketplace, they were discerning consumers of pastoral care. If we want to understand medieval lived religion, we must look to the variety and options that laypeople had and the ways in which they interacted rather than studying either the secular church or the friars in splendid isolation. The criteria according to which people made their choices are not always clear now (was confessing to a Carmelite noticeably different from confessing to a Franciscan?); but the bald fact of people's exercise of choice is not in doubt.

Geographical case studies remind us, however, that choice was never evenly distributed. By 1300, a wealthy town such as King's Lynn had one friary of each of the main mendicant orders, the same number of friaries that served the whole Diocese of Carlisle. Cornish speakers probably had to wait longer than neighbouring Anglophones for ready access to friars speaking their language. While some people travelled to distant saints' shrines to be healed, they generally tried local ones first. A monk or canon serving as a vicar added variety to the ecclesiastical landscape but not necessarily choice. Village dwellers could attend mass much more readily than shepherds grazing their flocks in summer hill pastures. Our limited evidence of friars active far from their convents shows them near major roadways. While Innocent III hoped for his Lateran canons to be promulgated in every diocese and obeyed in every parish, they were not.[19] Each bishop implemented them in his diocese in the ways and to the extent that he saw fit and even then enforcement was difficult. The divergences in diocesan statutes clearly demonstrate intentional adaptation to local circumstances. Through these statutes and other *pastoralia*, bishops in almost all dioceses gave their parish clergy detailed written instruction in the care of souls but this happened decades earlier in some dioceses than in others. Statutes differed on such important issues as the minimum frequency of confession, the pastoral privileges of friars, whether to give the chalice to the laity and what articles of faith and morals the laity were to be taught. Varying levels of episcopal and archidiaconal diligence disciplined parish clergy unevenly. The coming of the friars, disagreement about the frequency of confession and the appropriate times for baptism, lingering minsters and parochial monasteries, new optimism about religious life outside the cloister, rapidly developing styles of preaching, developments in eucharistic devotion, increasing scrutiny in confession and many other elements made for an increasingly complex ecclesiastical world.

Our evidence, therefore, is consistent with the thesis that pastoral care 'worked' in transforming society and culture but, as it also demonstrates

---

[19] Gibbs and Lang, *Bishops and Reform*, 174.

that pastoral care was diverse and occurred in diverse contexts, we should not expect that its effects were uniform. If pastoral care 'worked' in that it changed religious expectations, aspirations, devotions and reactions, then it follows that variations in pastoral care created different environments of lay religion and bequeathed them to the later Middle Ages. Perhaps thirteenth-century church reforms reinforced the evolution of 'cultural provinces', or determined the later geographical extent of mysticism or Lollardy or even the Reformation; perhaps the upheavals of the Black Death, or the further reforming activity of fourteenth-century churchmen such as Bishop Grandisson of Exeter and Archbishop Thoresby of York, or the circulation of vernacular devotional texts, erased much of the thirteenth-century map and re-drew it over a barely detectable palimpsest.[20] Future research, it is to be hoped, will take up the question.

Just as invoking the Reformation is not necessary to justify the study of late medieval English religion, however, whether the landscape of pastoral care in thirteenth-century England can be shown to correlate to any of these other geographies may be beside the point. The history of any period is worth studying not only as a precursor to later ages but as an example of particular modes of human existence. Even if fourteenth-century developments changed the map beyond recognition, the fact remains that locally determined diversity was a very real feature of the lived religion of thirteenth-century England and people at the time probably knew it. The overall successes and failures of the English church now discussed by historians were visible then only to elites who were able to take a broad view. We now have access to every surviving set of diocesan statutes, every extant thirteenth-century episcopal register and thousands of ecclesiastical charters and *acta* in print. Despite vast losses of material, our view can be much more holistic. The knowledge of each bishop, archdeacon, parish priest, monk, friar or layperson was much more limited, geographically and temporally. Yet in some ways this made their individual impressions more true than a homogenised historical composition could ever be. Only a few parishes were so remote that they never saw a friar and not many had Augustinian Canons as vicars; but, for the people who lived in them, this was the reality of their religious experience. If laypeople in a given parish perceived pastoral care as becoming less rather

---

[20] Pantin, *Fourteenth Century*, 252. Gregory argues that the church in northern England in the late fourteenth and fifteenth centuries was more successful at satisfying the laity's spiritual aspirations than its counterpart in the south; there were few Lollards in the North, therefore, because an alternative to the institutional church had less appeal: C. Gregory, 'The Geography of Dissent: Lollardy, Popular Religion, and Church Reform in Late Medieval York' (unpubl. PhD thesis, Yale, 2003).

than more responsive to their spiritual needs – as a result of the disruption of warfare, for example, or in a parish whose rector was a negligent absentee or an indifferent monastery – then this was just as important to them, and should be just as important to us, as that of twenty other parishes in which parishioners had the opposite experience. As Christopher Brooke observed, it is in this variety, in the range of possibilities open to people, that one finds a truer key for understanding.[21]

---

[21] Brooke, *Collected Essays*, 172.

SELECT BIBLIOGRAPHY

Excludes sources already listed in the abbreviations

I SOURCES IN MANUSCRIPT

Aberdeen, University Library, MS. 24
Baltimore, MD, Walters Museum, MS. W. 15
Cambridge, Peterhouse College, MS. 255 Part III
Cambridge, St John's College, MS. 255/S19
Cambridge, University Library, MS. Ee.3.59
Carlisle, Cumbria Record Office, MS. DRC/1/1
Edinburgh, National Library of Scotland, MS. Advocates 18.7.21
Exeter, Exeter Cathedral Archive, Dean and Chapter MSS. 3672 (a), 3673
Hereford, Herefordshire Record Office, MS. series AL 19/ and CA 19/
Lincoln, Lincolnshire Archive Office, Dean and Chapter MS. Dij/64/2, no. 7
Lincoln, Lincolnshire Archive Office, Episcopal Register I, f. 149r–v.
London, British Library, Add. Ch. 21888
London, British Library, Add. MSS. 35296, 47677
London, British Library, Cotton Charter V.33
London, British Library, Harley MS. 632
London, British Library, Royal MSS. 7.D.i, 10.A.ix
Oxford, Bodleian Library, Bodley MS. 655 (consulted in typescript of Joseph Goering)
Oxford, Bodleian Library, Laud Misc. MS. 2
Oxford, Bodleian Library, Laud Misc. MS. 471
Oxford, Bodleian Library, Lat. MS. th.e.24
Paris, Bibliothèque Nationale, MS. 14947
Worcester, Worcester Cathedral Library, MS. Q.46

II PUBLISHED PRIMARY SOURCES

Adam of Eynsham, *Magna Vita S. Hugonis*, ed. and trans. D. L. Douie and D. H. Farmer (Oxford, 1985).
Anthony of Padua, *Sermones for the Easter Cycle*, ed. and trans. G. Marcil and H. Eller (St Bonaventure, NY, 1994).
Astle, T., S. Ayscough and J. Caley, eds, *Taxatio Ecclesiastica Angliae et Walliae, Auctoritate P. Nicholai IV, circa AD 1291* (London, 1802).

Select Bibliography

Bacon, Roger, *Opera Quaedam Hactenus Inedita*, ed. J. S. Brewer (Rolls Series, 1859).

Bailey, M., ed. and trans., *The English Manor c. 1200–c. 1500* (Manchester, 2002).

Bihl, M., ed., 'Statuta Generalia Ordinis Edita in Capitulis Generalibus Celebratis Narbonae an. 1260, Assisii an. 1279 atque Parisiis an. 1292', *Archivum Franciscanum Historicum* 34 (1941), 13–94.

Bonaventure of Bagnoreggio, *Doctoris Seraphici S. Bonaventurae S. R. E. Episcopi Cardinalis Opera Omnia*, iussu et auctoritate R. P. Aloysii a Parma [et al.]; edito studio et cura PP. Collegii a S. Bonaventura (Ad Claras Aquas (Quaracchi), 1889–1902).

Brooke, Christopher, and M. M. Postan, eds, *Carte Nativorum: A Peterborough Abbey Cartulary of the Fourteenth Century* (Northamptonshire Record Society, 1960).

Butler, H. E., ed. and trans., *The Chronicle of Jocelin of Brakelond* (London, 1949).

Carlin, M., and D. Crouch, ed., *Lost Letters of Medieval Life: English Society, 1200–1250* (Philadelphia, 2013).

Cheney, Christopher, and Mary G. Cheney, eds, *The Letters of Pope Innocent III (1198–1216) Concerning England and Wales* (Oxford, 1967).

Cheyney, E. P., trans., 'English Manorial Documents', *Translations and Reprints from the Original Sources of European History* III (Philadelphia, 1907), no. 5.

Dalton, J. N., ed., *Ordinale Exon* I (London, 1909).

Denifle, H., ed., 'Constitutiones antique ordinis fratrum predicatorum', *Archiv für Litteratur- und Kirchengeschichte des Mittelalters* I (1885), 193–227.

Ehrle, F., ed., 'Die ältesten Redactionen der Generalconstitutionen des Franziskanerordens', *Archiv für Literatur- und Kirchengeschichte des Mittelalters* VI (1892), 1–138.

Farmer, David H., ed., 'The Canonization of St Hugh of Lincoln', *Lincolnshire Architectural and Archaeological Reports and Papers* 6.2 (1956), 86–117.

Feltoe, C. L., and E. H. Minns, eds, *Vetus Liber Archidiaconi Eliensis* (Cambridge, 1917).

Gerald of Wales, *Giraldi Cambrensis Opera*, ed. J. S. Brewer, J. F. Dimock and G. F. Warner (Rolls Series 21, in 8 vols, 1861–91).

Gieben, Servus, 'Robert Grosseteste at the Papal Curia, Lyons 1250: Edition of the Documents', *Collectanea Franciscana* 41 (1971), 340–93.

   'Robert Grosseteste on Preaching, with the Edition of the Sermon *Ex Rerum Initiatarum*', *Collectanea Franciscana* 37 (1967), 101–41.

Goering, Joseph, ed., *William de Montibus: The Schools and the Literature of Pastoral Care* (Toronto, 1992).

Goering, Joseph, and P. Payer, eds, 'The "Summa penitentie Fratrum Predicatorum": A Thirteenth-Century Confessional Formulary', *Mediaeval Studies* 55 (1993), 1–50.

Grosseteste, Robert, *Templum Dei*, ed. Joseph Goering and F. A. C. Mantello (Toronto, 1984).

Harper-Bill, Christopher, ed., *The Cartulary of the Augustinian Friars of Clare* (Woodbridge, 1991).

Harvey, P. D. A., ed., *Manorial Records of Cuxham, Oxfordshire ca. 1200–1359* (London, 1976).

Herbert, J. A., ed., *Catalogue of Romances in the Department of Manuscripts in the British Museum* III (London, 1910).

Hinnebusch, J. F., ed., *The Historia Occidentalis of Jacques de Vitry* (Fribourg, 1972).

Hoskin, Philippa, *Robert Grosseteste as Bishop of Lincoln: The Episcopal Rolls, 1235–1253* (Woodbridge, 2015).

Humbert of Romans, *Opera de Vita Regulari*, ed. Joachim Joseph Berthier (Torino: in 2 vols, 1956).

Jones, David, trans., *Friars' Tales: Thirteenth-Century Exempla from the British Isles* (Manchester, 2011).

Kemp, Brian, ed., *Twelfth-Century English Archidiaconal and Vice-Archidiaconal Acta* (C&YS, 2001).

Lawrence, Clifford Hugh, ed. and trans., *The Life of Saint Edmund by Matthew Paris* (London, 1999).

Legg, J. Wickham, ed., *The Sarum Missal, Edited from Three Early Manuscripts* (Oxford, 1916).

Little, A. G., ed., *Liber Exemplorum ad Usum Praedicantium Saeculo xiii Compositus a quodam Fratre Minore Anglico de Provincia Hiberniae* (Aberdeen, 1908).

Little, A. G., and D. Douie, eds, 'Three Sermons of Friar Jordan of Saxony, the Successor of St Dominic, Preached in England, A.D. 1229', *English Historical Review* 54 (1939), 1–19.

Lombard, Peter, *The Sentences, Book 4: On the Doctrine of Signs*, trans. G. Silano (Toronto, 2010).

London, V., ed., *The Cartulary of Canonsleigh Abbey* (Torquay, 1965).

Luard, H. R., ed., *Roberti Grosseteste Episcopi Quondam Lincolniensis Epistolae* (Rolls Series 25, 1861).

Maitland, F. W., ed., *Select Pleas in Manorial and other Seignorial Courts, vol. I: Reigns of Henry III and Edward I* (London, 1889).

Major, Kathleen, ed., *Acta Stephani Langton Cantuariensis Archiepiscopi A.D. 1207–1228* (C&YS 50, 1950).

Millet, Bella, trans., *Ancrene Wisse: Guide for Anchoresses* (Exeter, 2009).

Monti, D., ed. and trans., *St Bonaventure's Works Concerning the Franciscan Order* (St Bonaventure, NY, 1994).

Pecham, John, *Fratris Johannis Pecham quondam Archiepiscopi Cantuariensis Tractatus Tres de Paupertate*, ed. C. L. Kingsford et al. (Aberdeen, 1910).

Raimundus de Pennaforte, *Summa de Paenitentia* [= Summa de Casibus Penitentiae], ed. X. Ochoa and A. Diez (Rome, 1976).

Raine, J., ed., *Historical Papers and Letters from the Northern Registers* (Rolls Series 61, 1873).

Rider, Catherine, ed., '*Sciendum est autem sacerdotibus (Penitens accedens ad confessionem)*: A Short Thirteenth-Century Treatise on Hearing Confessions', *Mediaeval Studies* 73 (2011), 147–82.

Robert of Flamborough, *Liber Poenitentialis*, ed. J. J. F. Firth (Toronto, 1971).

Roth, F., *The English Austin Friars, 1249–1538, vol. II: Sources* (New York, 1961).

Saggi, Ludovico, ed., 'Constitutiones Capituli Burdigalensis Anni 1294', *Analecta Ordinis Carmelitanum* New Series XVIII (1953), 123–85.

    ed., 'Constitutiones Capituli Londoniensis Anni 1281', *Analecta Ordinis Carmelitanum* New Series XV (1950), 203–45.

Saint-Amour, William of, *De periculis novissimorum temporum*, ed. and trans. G. Geltner (Leuven, 2008).

Salter, H. E., ed., *The Cartulary of Oseney Abbey* III (Oxford, 1931).

Select Bibliography

Samuel Presbiter, *Notes from the School of William de Montibus*, ed. A. N. J. Dunning (Toronto, 2016).

Sandon, Nick, ed., *The Use of Salisbury, I: The Ordinary of the Mass* (Newton Abbot, 1984).

Sbaralea, J. H., ed., *Bullarium Franciscanum Romanorum Pontificum: constitutiones, epistolas, ac diplomata continens* ... (Rome, in 5 vols, 1759–1804; reprinted Assisi, 1983).

Smith, D. M., ed., *The Acta of Hugh of Wells, Bishop of Lincoln, 1209–1235* (Lincoln Record Society 88, 2000).

Sparrow-Simpson, W., ed., 'Visitations of Churches in the Patronage of St Paul's Cathedral, 1249–1252', in *The Camden Miscellany IX* (Camden Society New Series 53, 1895), iii–xix, 1–38.

    ed., *Visitations of Churches Belonging to St Paul's Cathedral in 1297 and in 1458* (Camden Society New Series 55, 1895).

Stevenson, Joseph, ed., *Chronicon de Lanercost MCCI-MCCCXLVI, e Codice Cottoniano Nunc Primum Typis Mandatum* (Maitland Club, 1839).

Thomas of Chobham, *Summa de Arte Praedicandi*, ed. F. Morenzoni (Turnholt, 1988).

    Thomae de Chobham Summa Confessorum, ed. F. Broomfield (Louvain, 1968).

Trivet, Nicholas, *Annales Sex Regum Angliae*, ed. Thomas Hog (London, 1845).

Tugwell, Simon, *Early Dominicans: Selected Writings* (Mahwah, NJ, 1982).

    'The Evolution of Dominican Structures of Government III: The Early Development of the Second Distinction of the Constitutions', *Archivum Fratrum Praedicatorum* 71 (2001), 1–182.

van Luijk, Benignus, *Bullarium Ordinis Eremitarum S. Augustini: Periodus Formationis, 1187–1256* (Wuerzburg, 1964).

Welter, J.-Th., ed., *Le Speculum Laicorum* (Paris, 1914).

Wenzel, S., ed., 'Robert Grosseteste's Treatise on Confession, "Deus Est"', *Franciscan Studies* 30 (1970), 218–93.

Whitley, H. M., trans., 'Visitations of Devonshire Churches', *RTDA* 42 (1910), 446–74.

Wilmart, D. A., ed., 'Un Opuscule sur la Confession composé par Guy de Southwick vers la Fin du XIIe siècle', *Recherches de Théologie Ancienne et Médiévale* 7 (1935), 337–52.

Woodruff, C. E., ed., 'Some Early Visitation Rolls Preserved at Canterbury', *Archaeologia Cantiana* 32 (1917), 143–80, continued in vol. 33 (1918), 71–90.

III PUBLISHED SECONDARY SOURCES

Akae, Yuichi, *A Mendicant Sermon Collection from Composition to Reception: The Novum opus dominicale of John Waldeby, OESA* (Turnhout, 2015).

Anciaux, Paul, *La Théologie du Sacrement de Pénitence au XIIe siècle* (Louvain, 1949).

Andrews, Frances, *The Other Friars: The Carmelite, Augustinian, Sack, and Pied Friars in the Middle Ages* (Woodbridge, 2006).

Arnold, John, *Belief and Unbelief in Medieval Europe* (London, 2005).

    ed., *The Oxford Handbook of Medieval Christianity* (Oxford, 2014).

Ault, Warren, 'The Village Church and the Village Community in Mediæval England', *Speculum* XXXIV (1970), 197–215.

Select Bibliography

Bailey, Mark, *A Marginal Economy? East Anglian Breckland in the Later Middle Ages* (Cambridge, 1989).

Baldwin, John, *Masters, Princes and Merchants: The Social Views of Peter the Chanter and His Circle* (Princeton, 1970).

Bannister, H. M., 'A Short Notice of some Manuscripts of the Cambridge Friars, Now in the Vatican Library.' In *Collectanea Franciscana I*, ed. A. G. Little et al. (Aberdeen, 1914), 124–40.

Barr, Beth Alison, *The Pastoral Care of Women in Late Medieval England* (Woodbridge, 2008).

Barrow, Julia, *The Clergy in the Medieval World: Secular Clerics, Their Families and Careers in North-Western Europe, c.800–c.1200* (Cambridge, 2015).

Bartholomew, J. G., *The Survey Atlas of England and Wales* (Edinburgh, 1903).

Bartlett, Robert, *England under the Norman and Angevin Kings, 1075–1225* (Oxford, 2000).

Gerald of Wales, 1146–1223 (Oxford, 1982).

Bériou, Nicole, *L'Avènement des Maîtres de la Parole: La Prédication á Paris au XIIIe siècle* (Paris, 1998).

Biller, Peter, 'Intellectuals and the Masses: Oxen and She-asses in the Medieval Church', in John Arnold, ed., *The Oxford Handbook of Medieval Christianity* (Oxford, 2014), 323–39.

Biller, Peter, and A. J. Minnis, eds, *Handling Sin: Confession in the Middle Ages* (Woodbridge, 1998).

Binski, Paul, *Becket's Crown: Art and Imagination in Gothic England* (New Haven, CT, 2004).

Blair, John, 'St. Frideswide's Monastery: Problems and Possibilities', in *Saint Frideswide's Monastery at Oxford: Archaeological and Architectural Studies*, ed. John Blair (Gloucester, 1990), 221–58.

Bossy, John, 'The Mass as a Social Institution, 1200–1700', *Past and Present* 100 (1983), 29–61.

Boyle, Leonard, 'The Inter-Conciliar Period and the Beginnings of Pastoral Manuals', in *Miscellanea Rolando Bandinelli, Papa Alessandro III*, ed. F. Liotta and R. Tofanini (Siena, 1986), 45–56.

'The *Oculus Sacerdotis* and Some Other Works of William of Pagula', *Transactions of the Royal Historical Society* 5th s. 5 (1955): 82–110.

Pastoral Care, Clerical Education and Canon Law, 1200–1400 (London, 1981).

Brentano, Robert, *Two Churches: England and Italy in the Thirteenth Century* (Princeton, 1968; 2nd edn, Berkeley, 1988).

York Metropolitan Jurisdiction and Papal Judges-Delegate (1279–1296) (Berkeley, CA, 1959).

Brooke, Christopher, *Medieval Church and Society: Collected Essays* (London, 1971).

Brooke, Rosalind, *The Coming of the Friars* (London, 1975).

Brooke, Zachary, *The English Church and the Papacy from the Conquest to the Reign of John* (Cambridge, 1931).

Brown, Andrew, *Popular Piety in Late Medieval England: The Diocese of Salisbury 1250–1550* (Oxford, 1995).

Burger, Michael, *Bishops, Clerks and Diocesan Governance in Thirteenth-Century England* (Cambridge, 2012).

Select Bibliography

Burgess, Clive, '"A Fond Thing Vainly Invented": An Essay on Purgatory and Pious Motive in Later Medieval England', in *Parish, Church and People: Local Studies in Lay Religion 1350–1750*, ed. Susan Wright (London, 1988), 56–79.

Burgess, Clive, and Eamon Duffy, eds, *The Parish in Late Medieval England* (Donington, 2006).

Byng, Gabriel, *Church Building and Society in the Later Middle Ages* (Cambridge, forthcoming).

Campbell, B. M. S., and K. Bartley, *England on the Eve of the Black Death: An Atlas of Lay Lordship, Land and Wealth 1300–49* (Manchester, 2006).

Catto, J. I., ed., *The Early Oxford Schools* (Oxford, 1984).

Cels, Marc, 'Interrogating Anger in the New Penitential Literature of the Thirteenth Century', *Viator* 45.1 (2014), 203–20.

Cheney, Christopher, *English Synodalia of the Thirteenth Century* (2nd edn, Oxford, 1968).

From Becket to Langton: English Church Government 1170–1213 (Manchester, 1956).

'King John and the Papal Interdict', *Bulletin of the John Rylands Library* XXXI (1948), 295–317.

Pope Innocent III and England (Stuttgart, 1976).

Churchill, Irene, *Canterbury Administration: The Administrative Machinery of the Archbishopric of Canterbury, Illustrated from Original Records* I (London, 1933).

Clanchy, Michael, *From Memory to Written Record: England 1066–1307* (3rd edn, Oxford, 2013).

Cole, P., *The Preaching of the Crusades to the Holy Land, 1095–1270* (Cambridge, MA, 1991).

Colvin, H. M., *The White Canons in England* (Oxford, 1951).

Constable, Giles, *Monastic Tithes from Their Origin to the Twelfth Century* (Cambridge, 1964).

Cragoe, Carol Davidson, 'The Custom of the English Church: Parish Church Maintenance before 1300', *Journal of Medieval History* 30 (2010), 1–19.

d'Avray, David, *Medieval Marriage Sermons: Mass Communication in a Culture without Print* (Oxford, 2001).

Medieval Marriage: Symbolism and Society (Oxford, 2005).

The Preaching of the Friars: Sermons Diffused from Paris before 1300 (Oxford, 1985).

Denton, Jeffrey, 'Quinil [Quivil], Peter (c. 1230–1291)', *ODNB*.

Derolez, A., *The Palaeography of Gothic Manuscript Books from the Twelfth to the Early Sixteenth Century* (Cambridge, 2003).

Dickinson, J. C., *The Origins of the Austin Canons and Their Introduction into England* (London, 1950).

Dodd, Anne, 'Churches and Religious Houses in Norman Oxford', in Anne Dodd, ed., *Oxford before the University: The Late Saxon and Norman Archaeology of the Thames Crossing, the Defences and the Town* (Oxford, 2003), 56–59.

Dohar, W. J., *The Black Death and Pastoral Leadership: The Diocese of Hereford in the Fourteenth Century* (Philadelphia, PA, 1995).

'Sufficienter litteratus: Clerical Examination and Instruction for the Cure of Souls', in *A Distinct Voice*, ed. W. Brown and J. Stoneman (Notre Dame, IN, 1997), 305–21.

Douie, Decima, *Archbishop Pecham* (Oxford, 1952).

Duffy, Eamon, *The Stripping of the Altars: Traditional Religion in England, 1400–1580* (New Haven, CT, 1992).

Dyer, Christopher, *Everyday Life in Medieval England* (London, 1994).

Edwards, Kathleen, *The English Secular Cathedrals in the Middle Ages* (2nd edn, Manchester, 1967).

Egan, K. J., 'Medieval Carmelite Houses: England and Wales', in *Carmel in Britain, Volume I: Essays on the Medieval English Carmelite Province*, ed. P. Fitzgerald-Lombard (Rome, 1992), 1–85.

Firey, Abigail, ed., *A New History of Penance* (Leiden, 2008).

'Blushing before the Judge and Physician', in *A New History of Penance*, ed. Abigail Firey (Leiden, 2008), 173–200.

Fizzard, A., *Plympton Priory* (Leiden, 2008).

Forrest, Ian, 'The Transformation of Visitation in Thirteenth-Century England', *Past and Present* 221 (2013), 3–38.

French, Katherine, *The People of the Parish: Community Life in a Late Medieval English Diocese* (Philadelphia, PA, 2001).

Frere, Walter Howard, *Visitation Articles and Injunctions of the Period of the Reformation* I (London, 1910).

Gemmill, Elizabeth, *The Nobility and Ecclesiastical Patronage in Thirteenth-Century England* (Woodbridge, 2013).

Gibbs, Marion, and Jane Lang, *Bishops and Reform: 1215–1272: with Special Reference to the Lateran Council of 1215* (London, 1934).

Goering, Joseph, 'Robert Grosseteste at the Papal Curia', in *A Distinct Voice*, ed. W. Brown and J. Stoneman (Notre Dame, IN, 1997), 253–76.

'The Summa "Qui bene presunt" and Its Author', in *Literature and Religion in the Later Middle Ages*, ed. R. Newhauser and J. Alford (Binghamton, NY, 1995), 143–59.

'When and Where Did Grosseteste Study Theology?', in *Robert Grosseteste: New Perspectives on His Life and Scholarship*, ed. James McEvoy (Turnhout, 1995), 17–51.

Gratien de Paris, *Histoire de la Fondation et l'Évolution de l'Ordre des Frères Mineurs au XIIIe siècle* (Rome, 1982).

Graves, C. Pamela, *The Form and Fabric of Belief: An Archaeology of the Lay Experience of Religion in Medieval Norwich and Devon* (Oxford, 2000).

Grundy, G. B., 'Ancient Highways of Devon', *The Archaeological Journal* 98 (1941), 131–64.

Gunn, C., and C. Innes-Parker, eds, *Texts and Traditions of Medieval Pastoral Care: Essays in Honor of Bella Millet* (York, 2009).

Hackett, Benedict, 'The Spiritual Life of the English Austin Friars of the Fourteenth Century', in *Sanctus Augustinus, Vitae Spiritualis Magister* II (Rome, 1956), 421–92.

Haines, Roy, *Ecclesia Anglicana: Studies in the English Church of the Later Middle Ages* (Toronto, 1989).

Hallam, H. E., et al., *The Agrarian History of England and Wales, vol. II: 1042–1350* (Cambridge, 1988).

Haren, Michael, 'Confession, Social Ethics and Social Discipline in the *Memoriale presbiterorum*', in *Handling Sin: Confession in the Middle Ages*, ed. Peter Biller and A. J. Minnis (Woodbridge, 1998), 109–22.

Sin and Society in Fourteenth-Century England: A Study of the Memoriale Presbiterorum (Oxford, 2000).

Harper, John, *The Forms and Orders of Western Liturgy from the Tenth to the Eighteenth Century* (Oxford, 1991).

Hartridge, R. A. R., *A History of Vicarages in the Middle Ages* (Cambridge, 1930).

Harvey, K., *Episcopal Appointments in England, c. 1214–1344* (Farnham, 2014).

Heath, Peter, 'Between Reform and Reformation: The English Church in the Four-teenth and Fifteenth Centuries', *Journal of Ecclesiastical History* 41 (1990), 647–78.

Hindle, Brian, 'Medieval Roads in the Diocese of Carlisle', *TCWAAS* 77 (1977), 83–95.

Hoskins, W. G., *Devon* (London, 1954).

'The Making of the Agrarian Landscape', in *Devonshire Studies*, ed. W. G. Hoskins (London, 1952), 289–333.

Humphreys, K. W., ed., *The Friars' Libraries* (London, 1990).

Hyams, Paul, *Rancor and Reconciliation in Medieval England* (Ithaca, NY, 2013).

Jones, W. R., 'Franciscan Education and Monastic Libraries', *Traditio* 30 (1974), 435–45.

Kennedy, V. L., 'The Moment of Consecration and the Elevation of the Host', *Mediaeval Studies* 6 (1944), 121–50.

Kingsford, C., *The Grey Friars of London* (Aberdeen, 1915).

Larson, Atria, *Master of Penance: Gratian and the Development of Penitential Thought and Law in the Twelfth Century* (Washington, DC, 2014).

Lawrence, C. H., *The Friars: The Impact of the Early Mendicant Movement on Western Society* (London, 1994).

Lepine, David, and Nicholas Orme, *Death and Memory in Medieval Exeter* (Exeter, 2003).

License, Tom, *Hermits and Recluses in English Society, 950–1200* (Oxford, 2011).

Little, A. G., *Franciscan Papers, Lists and Documents* (Manchester, 1943).

The Grey Friars in Oxford (Oxford, 1891).

Studies in English Franciscan History (Manchester, 1917).

Little, A. G., and R. C. Easterling, *The Franciscans and Dominicans of Exeter* (Exeter, 1927).

Little, Lester, *Religious Poverty and the Profit Economy in Medieval Europe* (London, 1978).

Logan, F. Donald, *University Education of the Parochial Clergy in Medieval England: The Lincoln Diocese, c. 1300–c. 1350* (Toronto, 2014).

MacKinnon, Hugh, 'William de Montibus, a Medieval Teacher', in *Essays in Medieval History Presented to Bertie Wilkinson*, ed. T. Sandquist and M. R. Powicke (Toronto, 1969), 32–45.

Macy, Gary, *The Theologies of the Eucharist in the Early Scholastic Period: A Study of the Salvific Function of the Sacrament According to the Theologians, c. 1080–c. 1220* (Oxford, 1984).

Maier, Christoph, *Preaching the Crusades: Mendicant Friars and the Cross in the Thirteenth Century* (Cambridge, 1994).

Mansfield, Mary, *The Humiliation of Sinners: Public Penance in Thirteenth-Century France* (Ithaca, NY, 1995).

Mason, Emma, 'A Truth Universally Acknowledged', *SCH* 16 (1979), 171–86.

Mayr-Harting, Henry, *Religion, Politics and Society in Britain 1066–1272* (Harlow, 2011).

Meens, Robert, *Penance in Medieval Europe, 600–1200* (Cambridge, 2014).

Millet, Bella, 'The Discontinuity of English Prose: Structural Innovation in the Trinity and Lambeth Homilies', in A. Oizumi et al., eds, *Text and Language in Medieval English Prose* (Frankfurt, 2005), 129–50.

'The Pastoral Context of the Trinity and Lambeth Homilies', in W. Scase, ed., *Essays in Manuscript Geography* (Turnhout, 2007), 43–63.

Moorman, J. R. H., *A History of the Franciscan Order from Its Origins to the Year 1517* (Oxford, 1968).

Church Life in England in the Thirteenth Century (Cambridge, 1945).

Morris, Richard, *Churches in the Landscape* (London, 1989).

Mulchahey, Marian Michèle, *'First the Bow Is Bent in Study': Dominican Education before 1350* (Toronto, 1998).

Murray, Alexander, 'Confession as a Historical Source in the Thirteenth Century', in *The Writing of History in the Middle Ages*, ed. R. H. C. Davis and J. M. Wallace-Hadrill (Oxford, 1981), 275–322.

'Counselling in Medieval Confession', in *Handling Sin: Confession in the Middle Ages*, ed. Peter Biller and A. J. Minnis (Woodbridge, 1998), 63–77.

Newman, P., 'Tinworking and the Landscape of Medieval Devon', in *Medieval Devon and Cornwall: Shaping an Ancient Countryside*, ed. S. Turner (Macclesfield, 2006), 123–43.

Nicholson, J., and R. Burn, *The History and Antiquities of the Counties of Westmorland and Cumberland* (London, 1777).

O'Carroll, Mary E. [= Maura O'Carroll], *A Thirteenth-Century Preacher's Handbook: Studies in MS Laud Misc. 511* (Toronto, 1997).

ed., *Robert Grosseteste and the Beginnings of a British Theological Tradition* (Rome, 2003).

Olson, Sherri, *A Mute Gospel: The People and Culture of the Medieval English Common Fields* (Toronto, 2009).

Orme, Nicholas, 'The Church in Crediton from St. Boniface to the Reformation', in *The Greatest Englishman: Essays on St. Boniface and the Church at Crediton*, ed. Timothy Reuter (Exeter, 1980), 95–131.

Education in the West of England, 1066–1548 (Exeter, 1976).

English Church Dedications, with a Survey of Cornwall and Devon (Exeter, 1996).

English Schools in the Middle Ages (London, 1973).

'The Medieval Clergy of Exeter Cathedral, I: The Vicars and Annuellars', *RTDA* 113 (1981), 79–102.

The Minor Clergy of Exeter Cathedral, 1300–1548 (Exeter, 1980).

The Saints of Cornwall (Oxford, 2000).

Owen, Dorothy, *Church and Society in Medieval Lincolnshire* (Lincoln, 1971).

Pantin, William, *The English Church in the Fourteenth Century* (Cambridge, 1955).

Payer, Pierre, *Sex and the New Medieval Literature of Confession, 1150–1300* (Toronto, 2009).

Select Bibliography

Postles, David, 'The Austin Canons in English Towns, c.1100–1350', *BIHR* 66 (1993), 1–20.

Pounds, Norman, *A History of the English Parish: The Culture of Religion from Augustine to Victoria* (Cambridge, 2000).

Powicke, Sir F. Maurice, *Modern Historians and the Study of History* (London, 1955).
  Stephen Langton (Oxford, 1928).

Raftis, J. Ambrose, *Peasant Economic Development within the English Manorial System* (Montreal and Kingston, 1996).

Raitt, Jill, ed., *Christian Spirituality: High Middle Ages and Renaissance* (New York, NY, 1988).

Reeves, Andrew, 'English Secular Clergy in the Early Dominican Schools: Evidence from Three Manuscripts', *Church History and Religious Culture* 92 (2012), 35–55.
  Religious Education in Thirteenth-Century England: The Creed and Articles of Faith (Leiden, 2015).

Richardson, H. G., 'The Parish Clergy of the Thirteenth and Fourteenth Centuries', *TRHS* 3rd s. 6 (1912), 88–128.

Rider, Catherine, 'Lay Religion and Pastoral Care in Thirteenth-Century England: The Evidence of a Group of Short Confession Manuals', *Journal of Medieval History* 36 (2010), 327–40.

Rivi, Prospero, 'Francis of Assisi and the Laity of His Time', *Greyfriars Review* 15 (Supplement, 2001).

Robinson, David, *Beneficed Clergy in Cleveland and the East Riding, 1306–1340* (York, 1969).
  The Geography of Augustinian Settlement in Medieval England and Wales I (Oxford, 1980).

Rodes, R. E., Jr., *Ecclesiastical Administration in Medieval England* (Notre Dame, 1977).

Roest, Bert, *A History of Franciscan Education* (Leiden, 2000).
  Franciscan Learning, Teaching and Mission, c. 1220–1650 (Leiden, 2015).

Ross, Ellen, *The Grief of God: Images of the Suffering Jesus in Late Medieval England* (Oxford, 1997).

Roth, F., *The English Austin Friars, 1249–1538, vol. I: History* (New York, NY, 1966).

Rouse, Richard H., and Mary A. Rouse, *Preachers, Florilegia and Sermons: Studies on the Manipulus Florum of Thomas of Ireland* (Toronto, 1979).

Rubin, Miri, *Corpus Christi: The Eucharist in Late-Medieval Culture* (Cambridge, 1991).

Ryder, L., *The Historic Landscape of Devon* (Oxford, 2013).

Sayers, Jane, *Papal Judges Delegate in the Province of Canterbury 1198–1254* (Oxford, 1971).

Sekules, V., 'The Liturgical Furnishings of the Choir of Exeter Cathedral', in *Medieval Art and Architecture at Exeter Cathedral*, ed. F. Kelly (Oxford, 1991), 172–79.

Şenocak, Neslihan, *The Poor and the Perfect: The Rise of Learning in the Franciscan Order* (Ithaca, NY, 2012).

Sharpe, Richard, ed., *A Handlist of the Latin Writers of Great Britain and Ireland before 1540* (Turnhout, 1997; reissued with additions and corrections, 2001).

Shaw, David, *The Creation of a Community: The City of Wells in the Middle Ages* (Oxford, 1993).
  Necessary Conjunctions: The Social Self in Medieval England (New York, NY, 2005).

Select Bibliography

Shinners, John, 'Parish Libraries in Medieval England', in *A Distinct Voice*, ed. W. Brown and J. Stoneman (Notre Dame, IN, 1997), 207–30.

Smith, David M., ed., *Guide to Bishops' Registers of England and Wales* (London, 1981).

Southern, Sir Richard, *Robert Grosseteste: The Growth of an English Mind in Medieval Europe* (2nd edn, Oxford, 1992).

Stansbury, R. J., ed., *A Companion to Pastoral Care in the Late Middle Ages* (Leiden, 2010).

Summerson, Henry, 'Medieval Carlisle: Cathedral and City from Foundation to Dissolution', in *Carlisle and Cumbria: Roman and Medieval Architecture, Art and Archaeology*, ed. M. McCarthy and D. Weston (Leeds, 2004), 29–38.

    Medieval Carlisle: The City and the Borders from the Late Eleventh to the Mid-Sixteenth Century I (Kendal, 1993).

Summerson, Henry, and S. Harrison, *Lanercost Priory, Cumbria* (Kendal, 2000).

Swanson, Jenny, *John of Wales: A Study of the Works and Ideas of a Thirteenth-Century Friar* (Cambridge, 1989).

Swanson, Robert, *Church and Society in Late Medieval England* (Oxford, 1989).

    Indulgences in Late Medieval England: Passports to Paradise (Cambridge, 2008).

    Religion and Devotion in Europe, c.1215–c.1515 (Cambridge, 1995).

Tanner, Norman, and Sethina Watson, 'Least of the Laity: The Minimum Requirements of a Medieval Christian', *Journal of Medieval History* 32 (2006), 395–423.

Teetaert, Amédée, *La confession aux laïques dans l'Église Latine* (Louvain, 1926).

Tentler, T., 'The Summa for Confessors as an Instrument of Social Control', in *The Pursuit of Holiness in Late Medieval and Renaissance Religion*, ed. C. Trinkhaus and H. Oberman (Leiden, 1974), 103–22.

Thibodeaux, Jennifer, *The Manly Priest: Clerical Celibacy, Masculinity, and Reform in England and Normandy, 1066–1300* (Philadelphia, PA, 2015).

Thomas, Hugh, *The Secular Clergy in England, 1066–1216* (Oxford, 2014).

Thompson, A. Hamilton, *The English Clergy and Their Organization in the Later Middle Ages* (Oxford, 1947).

    'Pluralism in the Medieval Church', *Associated Architectural Societies Reports and Papers* 33 (1915–16), 35–73.

Vicaire, M.-H., *Saint Dominic and His Times*, trans. Kathleen Pond (London, 1964; trans. from French edn, Paris, 1957).

Vincent, Nicholas, *Peter des Roches: An Alien in English Politics, 1205–1238* (Cambridge, 1996).

Wagner, K., '*Cum aliquis venerit ad sacerdotem*: Penitential Experience in the Central Middle Ages', in *A New History of Penance*, ed. Abigail Firey (Leiden, 2008) 201–18.

Walsh, K., *A Fourteenth-Century Scholar and Primate: Richard FitzRalph in Oxford, Avignon and Armagh* (Oxford, 1981).

Wenzel, Siegfried, *Latin Sermon Collections from Later Medieval England* (Cambridge, 2005).

    Medieval Artes Praedicandi: A Synthesis of Scholastic Sermon Structure (Toronto, 2015).

    Verses in Sermons: 'Fasciculus Morum' and Its Middle English Poems (Cambridge, MA, 1978).

Winchester, Angus, *Landscape and Society in Medieval Cumbria* (Edinburgh, 1987).

IV UNPUBLISHED THESES

Black, Winston E., 'The Medieval Archdeacon in Canon Law' (PhD thesis, University of Toronto, 2008).

Campbell, William H., 'Franciscan Preaching in Thirteenth-Century England: Sources, Problems, Possibilities' (Licentiate in Mediaeval Studies thesis, Pontifical Institute of Mediaeval Studies, 2012).

Carroll-Clark, Susan M., 'The Practical Summa *Ad Instructionem Iuniorum* of Simon of Hinton, OP: Text and Context' (PhD thesis, University of Toronto, 1999).

Cornett, Michael E., 'The Form of Confession: A Later Medieval Genre for Examining Conscience' (PhD thesis, University of North Carolina–Chapel Hill, 2011).

Cragoe, Carol Davidson (as Davidson, Carol Foote), 'Written in Stone: Architecture, Liturgy and the Laity in English Parish Churches, c.1125–c.1250' (PhD thesis, University of London, 1998).

Geddes, Ann M., 'The Priory of Lanthony by Gloucester' (PhD thesis, Johns Hopkins University, 1997).

Goering, Joseph W., 'The Popularization of Scholastic Ideas in Thirteenth-Century England and an Anonymous Speculum Iuniorum' (PhD thesis, University of Toronto, 1977).

Mokry, Robert, 'An Edition and Study of Henry Wodestone's *Summa de Sacramentis*' (PhD thesis, Heythrop College, University of London, 1997).

Pelle, Stephen A., 'Continuity and Renewal in English Homiletic Eschatology, *ca.* 1150–1200' (PhD thesis, University of Toronto, 2012).

Williams, Daniel T., 'Aspects of the Career of Boniface of Savoy, Archbishop of Canterbury 1241–70' (PhD thesis, University of Wales, 1970).

INDEX

284

Index

Index

Index

liturgy, 103, 119–39, 164, 182, 184, 201
  cathedral, 224, 238, 239–40
  liturgical year, 103, 108, 111, 154, 186, 196,
    202, 203
  mendicant, 135–39, 218
  monastic, 86, 87, 91, 259, 261
  parish, 122–35, 233, 243, 250
  social and emotional implications, 127–34
  use of Exeter, 233
Llanfaes, 66
Lollards, 119, 137, 268, 270
Lombard, Peter, 75, 97, 149, 163, 205
London, 59, 64, 65, 66, 67, 70, 71, 106, 254
  bishops of, 146
  diocese of, 53, 120, 138
  legatine council of (1237), 7, 183
  legatine council of (1268), 7, 185
  St Paul's Cathedral, 33, 42, 183, 210
Lossenham, 69
Lowther River Valley, 259
Lucius III, pope, 258
Ludham, Godfrey, archbishop of York, 209
Lydford, 237
Lyons, First Council of (1245), 184
Lyons, Second Council of (1274), 79, 214,
  229

Maldon, 146
Manchester, University of, 13, 14
manor, 37–41, 44, 45, 86, 131, 171–72, 198, 205,
  210, 216, 227, 228, 243
marriage, 33, 44, 49, 103, 116–17, 121, 183, 195,
  198, 267
Marsh, Adam, 4, 6, 8, 20, 51, 53, 56, 57, 74, 185,
  202–04, 207, 214, 215, 217, 267
Marsh, Robert, 202, 214
Marshall, Henry, bishop of Exeter, 224
Martin IV, pope, 144, 156
Mary, mother of Jesus, 6, 63, 233
mass, 4, 6, 7, 19, 30, 31, 32, 33, 43, 50, 54, 57,
  84, 89, 100, 122–39, 155, 162, 182, 183, 184,
  187, 209, 233, 237, 238, 243, 244, 249, 262,
  269
Matilda, empress, 25
Mauclerc, Walter, bishop of Carlisle, 248,
  260
Memoriale presbiterorum, 158, 165
mendicants. *See* friars
Merevale Abbey, 85
Merton College, 45, 48, 216
Merton Priory, 48
Minorites. *See* Franciscan Order
minsters, 27, 82, 120, 211, 235–36, 269
miracles, 85, 90, 112, 127, 137, 207, 208
missals, 103, 120, 122–24, 125

monasteries, 2–3, 10, 19, 21, 32, 39, 42, 43,
  81–93, 151, 172, 179, 188, 189–90, 194, 209,
  249, 269, 271. *See also* cathedrals, monastic
Montibus, William de, 30, 46, 48, 52, 100, 102,
  113, 149, 153, 159, 205–07, 265
Moorman, J. R. H., 15, 17, 62, 67, 99, 266
moral teaching, 6, 48, 54, 62, 77, 98, 104, 105,
  107, 112, 113, 153, 155, 218, 265, 268,
  269
mortuary dues, 38, 92, 258
music, 47, 48, 50, 123, 125, 238, 239, 244. *See also*
  choirs, choristers; singing

Nequam or Neckham, Alexander, 213
Neuilly, Fulk de, 52
Nicene Creed, 101, 123, 232, 250
Nicholas III, pope, 186
Nicholas IV, pope, 255
non-residence. *See* absentee clergy; pluralism
Norman Conquest, 9, 25
Northampton, 52, 66, 68, 193, 195, 197, 198, 203,
  212
Northern Homily Cycle, 91, 101
Northumberland, 176
Norwich, 64, 66, 67, 68
  bishop of, 146
  diocese of, 33, 87
  statutes of, 101
novices, novitiates, 48, 71–72, 80, 92
nuns, 18, 26, 58, 91, 92

office of the dead. *See* prayers, for the dead
officials
  of archdeacons, 51, 197, 198, 210–11, 213, 229,
    251
  of bishops, 34, 56, 146, 185, 189, 199, 202, 203,
    216, 227, 230, 233, 247, 250
Omnis utriusque sexus fidelis, 35, 140–41, 142, 144,
  154
ordination, 6, 34, 39, 44, 49, 50, 51, 57, 86, 121,
  182, 184, 186, 196, 197, 202, 203, 212, 228,
  229, 230, 232, 246, 251, 252
  by Irish, Scottish or Welsh bishops, 34, 56,
    246, 247
  examination before, 27, 46, 47, 56, 57, 184,
    195–96, 203, 232
  of friars, 203, 204, 252, 256, 257, 260
Ormulum, 29, 101
Orton, 260
Oseney Abbey, 42, 82, 211–12, 215, 255
Otto, cardinal and papal legate, 7, 43, 53, 183–84,
  185, 188, 189
Ottobuono, cardinal and papal legate, 7, 185–86,
  188, 189
Owst, Gerald Robert, 11

Index

Oxford, 4, 29, 42, 55, 59, 64, 65, 66, 68, 80, 82, 97, 147, 192, 197, 198, 203, 211–18, 248, 255. *See also* Oseney Abbey, St Frideswide's Priory
  archdeaconry of, 196, 219
  archdeacons of, 147. *See also* Marsh, Richard
  Council of (1222), 36, 41, 57, 103, 182, 190, 195, 226, 249
Oxford University
  in Middle Ages, 43, 56, 73–76, 78–79, 187, 192, 198, 203, 205, 207, 212–18, 252, 263
  in twentieth century, 13–15
Oxford, Master Philip of, 30

Pagula, William of, 6, 18, 152
Palm Sunday, 110
Pandulf, papal legate, 182
Pantin, William, 14, 15, 16
papal bulls. *See* bulls, papal
papal judges-delegate, 33, 213, 258
Paris, 26, 61, 124, 173, 217, 263
  and preaching, 30, 83, 99, 107, 213, 214, 217
  circle of Peter the Chanter at, 4, 28–30, 35, 52, 54, 124, 149, 205, 265
  university of, 52, 73, 75, 79, 143, 187, 194, 206, 214
Paris, Matthew, 134, 137, 142, 145, 149, 198, 208, 225, 227
parish, 171
  boundaries of, 71
  church building, 9, 25, 84, 134–35, 210, 212
  clergy, 1, 28, 37–59, 137
  liturgy, 32, 50, 80, 85, 119–35, 187, 233
  rural, 37, 176, 202, 262, 270
  social dynamics, 46, 127–35, 157, 165, 166, 172
  urban, 37, 176, 209, 211–19, 224, 237, 254–55
Parma, John of, 49
Paston Letters, 18
pastoral care, definition of, 3–7, 89
pastoralia, 15, 16, 29, 53, 54, 55, 63, 81, 90, 91, 103, 151, 179, 200, 266, 269
Paternoster, 31, 79, 98, 100–01, 115, 123, 124, 125, 129, 152, 159, 208, 249
patron saints, 6, 91, 233
patronage, 17, 34, 39–40, 44, 45, 46, 57, 89, 131, 135, 172, 174, 201, 211, 218
peace
  gesture in mass, 125, 126, 127, 133–34, 233
  making or keeping of, 7, 35, 46, 104, 132–34, 155, 156, 165, 185, 225
  prayer for, 125, 262
Pecham, John, archbishop of Canterbury, 3, 4, 5–6, 7, 16, 18, 20, 57, 74–75, 77, 84, 101, 105, 115, 142, 143, 147, 164, 186–87, 200, 232, 233–34, 265, 267

Peñaforte, Raymond of, 75, 77, 90, 92, 145, 152, 163
penance
  of clergy, 55–56
  public, 30, 143–44, 162, 164–65, 167, 187, 266–67
  sacrament of, 5, 6, 28, 30, 31, 54, 75, 109, 140–67, 183, 205, 226, 230
  satisfaction, 4, 32, 111, 114, 147–51, 157–60, 162–67, 199, 200, 204, 208, 209, 211, 226, 233, 234, 248, 249–50, 255
penitentials, 54, 148, 152, 158, 162, 163, 224
penitentiary, 54, 55, 56, 164, 193, 226, 230–31, 249
  friar as, 143, 204
  monk or canon as, 211
Penrith, 257, 259, 260
Pentecost, 35, 83, 141, 154, 183, 186, 193, 226
Peraldus, William. *See* Peyraut, Guillaume
Pershore Abbey, 84
Peter the Chanter. *See* Chanter, Peter the
Peterborough Abbey, 40, 84
Peyraut, Guillaume, 77
Pied Friars, 79
Piers Plowman, 268
pilgrims, pilgrimage, 89–90, 162, 164, 189, 207–09, 212, 238, 244, 248, 251, 255
Pisa, Agnellus of, 64, 74
pluralism, pluralists, 27, 42, 186, 227, 228. *See also* absentee clergy
Plymouth, 88, 235, 241
Plympton, 235, 240
Plympton Priory, 88, 235
poor, alms for the, 3, 5, 41, 42–43, 44, 73, 84, 88, 89, 109, 111, 157, 162, 165, 178, 234, 240
Poore, Richard, bishop of Salisbury and Durham, 7, 28, 36, 56, 124, 126, 190, 197, 199–200, 225–26, 233, 265
pope, 1, 2, 3, 4, 11, 12, 14, 18, 25, 32, 34, 35, 36, 49, 53, 62, 69, 79, 82, 87, 89, 105, 138, 139, 142, 143, 144, 145, 150, 155, 156, 181, 183, 184, 185, 186, 204, 227, 247, 252, 255, 258, 261, 265, 269. *See also* bulls, papal; curia
Portsmouth, 71
poverty, of friars, 58, 61, 63, 72, 136, 178, 234, 240, 268
Powicke, Sir F. Maurice, 13–15, 225
prayer, 5, 26, 55, 69, 84, 91, 104, 110, 159, 201, 234, 239. *See also* Ave Maria; devotions; liturgy; Paternoster
  as penance, 32, 162
  at confession, 152
  for peace, 125, 262
  for the dead, 32, 43, 88, 92, 121, 125, 127, 138–39, 237, 258, 262

Index

Sempringham, St Gilbert of, 19, 48, 85
serfs, sons of, becoming clergy, 39
Serlo, Master, 166
sermo modernus, 18, 83, 106–11, 114–15
sermon books. *See* homilaries; preaching handbooks
sermons, 4, 5–6, 7, 9, 15, 21, 26, 29, 33, 46, 51, 52, 53, 56, 58, 64, 70, 72, 73–74, 75, 76–77, 83–84, 91, 99, 101–02, 118, 123, 129, 136, 145, 152, 173, 209, 213, 215, 217
service books. *See* liturgical books
seven deadly or capital sins, 30, 54, 55, 57, 62, 99, 100, 101, 103, 115, 153, 155, 156, 158, 159, 201, 232, 243, 250, 268
shame, 55, 148–50, 162, 165. *See also* contrition; tears
Shap, 257, 259–60
   Abbey, 259–60
shrines, 6, 19, 32, 85, 89–90, 93, 162, 207–09, 212, 238, 248, 269
singing, 50, 82, 84, 135, 136, 196, 212, 233. *See also* choirs, choristers; music
Solet annuere. See Regula Bullata
South English Legendary, 101, 112
South Tawton, 229–30
Southern, Sir Richard, 14, 198
Southwick, Guy of, 29, 91
Speculum iuniorum, vii, 16, 148, 150, 152, 157, 159, 162
Speculum Laicorum, 112, 113, 117
St Davids, diocese of, 33, 229
St Frideswide's Priory, Oxford, 29, 82, 211–13, 218, 255
St Mary Church (Devon), 103, 243–44
St Paul's Cathedral. *See* London, St Paul's Cathedral
Stamford, 66, 197, 203, 215
Stavensby, Alexander, bishop of Coventry and Lichfield, 101, 104, 158, 197, 200
Staverton, 103, 243
St-Cher, Hugh of, 75, 240
Stephen, king of England, 25
Stow, archdeaconry of, 205, 209–11
St-Victor, Paris, canons of, 26, 72, 151
subdeacons, 49–50, 57, 123, 131, 196–97, 256
Sudbury, 68
Sully, Maurice de, bishop of Paris, 29, 30, 101
Sully, Odo de, bishop of Paris, 28
Summa de vitiis et virtutibus, 77
Summa iuniorum, 78, 115
Super cathedram, 144, 147, 204, 252
Sutton, Oliver, bishop of Lincoln, 56, 57, 82, 84, 138, 164, 203–04, 209, 210–11, 213, 215, 216, 217, 244
Swanson, Robert, 10, 173, 268

Swinfield, Richard, bishop of Hereford, 146
synods, diocesan, 29, 36, 53, 179, 186, 188, 233, 251

Tawstock, 241
tears, 26, 109, 111, 134, 148, 149. *See also* affective devotion; contrition; shame
Templum Dei, 78, 100, 153, 158, 159, 200
Ten Commandments, 30, 57, 100, 101, 115, 153, 158, 200, 201, 232, 243, 250
thema, 107, 109–10, 116
Third Lateran Council, 27, 28, 30–31, 49, 52, 87
Thurgarton, 87
tithes, 3, 10, 33, 38, 40–42, 43, 45, 73, 177, 218, 226, 236, 255, 258
titles for ordination, 49, 232
Tiverton, 235
Totnes, archdeacon or archdeaconry of, 234, 240
towns, 9, 18, 37–38, 59, 65, 66, 68, 69, 70–71, 82, 93, 106, 131, 136, 143, 178, 203, 211, 212, 218, 254, 269
township, 37–38, 45
Triermain, 257–59
Trinity and Lambeth Homilies, 29, 101
Trinity, doctrine of, 35, 97, 103, 152
Trivet, Nicholas, 63, 65
Truro, 68, 241
twelfth-century renaissance, 7, 25
Twyford, 235

Urban IV, pope, 146, 185

Verbum Abbreviatum, 29
vernacular texts, 15, 29, 53, 55, 91, 98, 101–02, 270
vicarages, 27, 51, 93, 199, 214, 215, 232
   ordination of, 182, 189–90, 194, 195, 211, 227, 228, 230, 247, 248
   value of, 40–43, 48, 140, 182, 195, 216, 248, 261
vicars, 43–45
vicars choral, 224, 235, 238–40
Victorines. *See* St-Victor, Paris, canons of
vill, 37
Virgin Mary. *See* Mary, mother of Jesus
visitation, 17, 179, 233, 265
   by archdeacons, 43, 57, 101, 182, 184, 186, 195, 210, 228, 242, 250
   by bishops, 2, 46, 87, 89, 98, 106, 146, 147, 182, 183, 184–85, 186, 187, 189, 190, 195, 198, 199, 201, 202, 209, 227–28, 230, 251, 252

Printed in the United States
By Bookmasters